T0347375

The American Experience in World War II

Edited with introductions by

Walter L. Hixson
University of Akron, Ohio

A ROUTLEDGE SERIES

Contents of the Collection

Volume 1
The United States and the Road to War in Europe

Volume 2
Isolationists and Internationalists:
The Battle over Intervention

Volume 3
The United States and the Road to War in the Pacific

Volume 4
Pearl Harbor in History and Memory

Volume 5
The United States in the European Theater

Volume 6
The United States in the Pacific War

Volume 7
The Atomic Bomb in History and Memory

Volume 8
American Diplomacy in the Second World War

Volume 9
American Culture at War: The Homefront

Volume 10
The American People at War:
Minorities and Women in the Second World War

Volume 11
Remembering and Representing the Second World War

Volume 12
The United States Transformed:
The Lessons and Legacies of the Second World War

The American Experience in World War II

Volume 8
American Diplomacy in the Second World War

Edited with introductions by

Walter L. Hixson
University of Akron, Ohio

Routledge
New York and London

Published in 2003 by
Routledge
29 West 35th Street
New York, NY 10001
www.routledge-ny.com

Published in Great Britain by
Routledge
11 New Fetter Lane
London EC4P 4EE
www.routledge.co.uk

Routledge is an imprint of the Taylor & Francis Group.

10 9 8 7 6 5 4 3 2 1

Library of Congress Cataloging-in-Publication Data

The American experience in World War II / edited with introductions by Walter Hixson.
    p. cm.
    Contents: v. 1. The United States and the road to war in Europe—v. 2. Isolationists and
internationalists : the battle over intervention—v. 3. The United States and the road to war
in the Pacific—v. 4. Pearl Harbor in history and memory—v. 5. The United States in the
European theater—v. 6. The United States in the Pacific war—v. 7. The atomic bomb in history and memory—v. 8. American diplomacy in the Second World War—v. 9. American culture at war : the homefront—v. 10. The American people at war : minorities and women in
the Second World War—v. 11. Remembering and representing the Second World War—
v. 12. The United States transformed : the lessons and legacies of the Second World War.
    ISBN 0-415-94028-1 (set)—ISBN 0-415-94029-X (v. 1: alk. paper)—ISBN 0-415-94030-
3 (v. 2: alk. paper)—ISBN 0-415-94031-1 (v. 3: alk. paper)—ISBN 0-415-94032-X (v. 4:
alk. paper)—ISBN 0-415-94033-8 (v. 5: alk. paper)—ISBN 0-415-94034-6 (v. 6: alk.
paper)—ISBN 0-415-94035-4 (v. 7: alk. paper)—ISBN 0-415-94036-2 (v. 8: alk. paper)—
ISBN 0-415-94037-0 (v. 9: alk. paper)—ISBN 0-415-94038-9 (v. 10: alk. paper)—ISBN 0-
415-94039-7 (v. 11: alk. paper)—ISBN 0-415-94040-0 (v. 12: alk. paper).
    1. World War, 1939–1945—United States. 2. United States—History—1933–1945.
I. Title: American experience in World War Two. II. Title: American experience in World
War 2. III. Hixson, Walter L.
B769.(title entry)
940.53'73—dc21   2002031849

Contents

vii   Series Introduction

xi   Volume Introduction

1   A Half Century of Conflict: Interpretations of U.S. World War II Diplomacy
Mark A. Stoler

30   The Imperialism of Decolonization
William Roger Louis and Ronald Robinson

80   Determination Versus Drift: The Anglo-American Debate over the Trusteeship Issue, 1941–1945
John J. Sbrega

105   The Anglo-American Alliance, 1941–45
G. D. Sheffield

121   Mission to America: Maksim M. Litvinov in the United States, 1941-43
Hugh Phillips

137   Joseph E. Davies and Soviet-American Relations, 1941–1943
Elizabeth Kimball Maclean

159   Spheres of Influence in Soviet Wartime Diplomacy
Albert Resis

183   Death and Politics: The Katyn Forest Massacre and American Foreign Policy
Crister S. Garrett and Stephen A. Garrett

201   The Sino-American Alliance during World War II and the Lifting of the Chinese Exclusion Acts
Xiaohua Ma

225   America, Britain, and Palestine: The Anglo-American Committee of Inquiry and the Displaced Persons, 1945–46
Leonard Dinnerstein

245   A Peripheral View of the Origins of the Cold War: The Crises in Iran, 1941–47
Stephen L. McFarland

265 Indochina and Anglo-American Relations, 1942–1945
Christopher Thorne

289 The Other China Hands: U.S. Army Officers and America's
Failure in China, 1941–1950
Marc Gallicchio

314 The U.S. Army, Unconditional Surrender, and
the Potsdam Declaration
Brian L. Villa

341 Acknowledgments

Series Introduction

World War II overshadows the twentieth century. The conflict, truly global in scope, transformed the world. While less *directly* affected than most nations, the United States underwent fundamental change as a result of its participation in the Second World War. The volumes in this collection reflect the profound changes in American military history, foreign policy, domestic politics, social relations, and its memory and representation of the war over succeeding generations.

World War II evolved in Europe primarily as a result of the aggression built into the national socialist German regime under the dictatorship of Adolf Hitler. The Nazi leader's brutal racialist expansionism made war virtually inevitable. After a series of aggressive acts in central Europe, Britain, France, and allied nations declared war on Germany. In the United States, President Franklin D. Roosevelt monitored these events with increasing concern but neither he nor the vast majority of the American public, imbued with bitter memories of World War I, wished to get involved in the early stages of the war. By the summer of 1940, however, with Germany in the course of bombing Britain and having sacked the Low Countries and France, the United States began to move toward intervention. The articles in volume 1, "The United States and the Road to War in Europe," analyze these developments.

The path toward intervention precipitated a bitter battle between so-called "isolationists"—really non-interventionists—and proponents of U.S. involvement in the European war. The two sides waged a political struggle over the direction and character of U.S. foreign policy between 1939 and December 7, 1941. By that date the Roosevelt administration had orchestrated a series of steps that found the United States directly aiding the Allies and determined to play a key role in preventing German domination of Europe. The articles in volume 2, "Isolationists and Internationalists: The Battle over Intervention," address the history and the historical debate over the struggle for the soul of the nation's foreign policy on the eve of World War II.

The United States ultimately became a belligerent as a result of events in Asia. Japanese intervention in China, Indochina, and other regions clashed with European imperialism and the rising American empire in Asia. The articles in volume 3, "The United States and the Road to War in the

Pacific," chronicle the coming of the Pacific War between the United States and Japan. War came with the Japanese assault on Pearl Harbor on December 7, followed by Hitler's declaration of war on the United States. The world thus became embroiled in a deadly struggle, with monumental implications, between the Axis powers led by Germany and Japan, and the United Nations under the stewardship of the United States, Great Britain, and the Soviet Union.

In the more than sixty years that have passed since the outbreak of the war, Americans have been drawn back to its origins at Pearl Harbor. Articles in volume 4, "Pearl Harbor in History and Memory," analyze the origins of the Japanese surprise attack, the American response, the groundless conspiracy theories focusing on the Roosevelt administration, the lasting imprint of Pearl Harbor on American memories, and its influence on U.S.-Japanese relations throughout the postwar era.

Well before the outbreak of war, the Roosevelt administration and military planners had already agreed on a "Europe-first" strategy. The articles in volume 5, "The United States in the European Theater," examine U.S. military strategy and engagements from the outbreak of war, through the D-Day invasion, the Battle of the Bulge, and the ultimate defeat of the Nazi regime in May 1945. Volume 6, "The United States in the Pacific War" analyzes American strategy to defeat Japan, "island hopping," key battles such as Midway, and the ultimate defeat of Japan in August 1945.

In volume 7, "The Atomic Bomb in History and Memory," scholars probe the origins and evolution of the American decision to drop atomic bombs on Hiroshima and Nagasaki on August 6 and 9, 1945. No shortage of controversy prevails over issues such as Japan's readiness to surrender, American non-nuclear options, and other paths not taken at the end of the Pacific war. Debate, implications, lessons, memories, and cultural resonances all receive attention from the contributors to the volume, a chronicle on the fiery birth of the nuclear age.

The American victory on both fronts in World War II would have been impossible without the careful cultivation of allies. The articles in volume 8 focus on American diplomacy in the Second World War. Despite the close affinity between the United States and Great Britain, tension over strategy and war aims surfaced throughout the war. Similarly, the United States and the Soviet Union, while able to cooperate militarily, held the other's ideology in contempt and distrusted the rival state's political aims. Volume 8 analyzes these and other diplomatic relationships throughout the war.

While statesmen conducted diplomacy and soldiers waged war, the American people found their lives dramatically affected on the homefront. The articles in volume 9, "American Culture at War: The Homefront," reflect the transformations wrought by the war effort, including rationing, unprecedented mobility, attitudes about war, and the experiences of individual communities and regions of the country. The lives of women, African-Americans, and other minorities were so dramatically affected by the war as to merit separate treatment, which they receive in volume 10, "The American People at War: Women and Minorities in the Second World War." These articles explore issues such as the new role of women as industrial workers, as frontline nurses, and in combat. Other essays analyze the "Double V" campaign of African-Americans and the impetus the war gave to the modern civil rights movement. The internment of Japanese-Americans and the effects of the war on other ethnic groups are also addressed in this volume.

As a result of the war's pervasive impact on American life and its obvious significance to history, it is no surprise that the conflict has been the subject of countless memoirs, novels, films, and other representations in the popular culture. Volume 11 explores "Remembering and Representing the Second World War," with particular emphasis on filmic representations. Articles in the volume range from analyses of wartime propaganda to popular films of the postwar era, including two Steven Spielberg epics, "Schindler's List" and "Saving Private Ryan."

The final volume of the twelve-part series addresses "The United States Transformed: Lessons and Legacies of the Second World War." Having emerged relatively unscathed and as the most powerful nation in the world, the United States faced a host of issues ranging from economic adjustments at home to foreign policy challenges—notably decolonization and the Cold War—abroad. The nation's ability to respond to these and other challenges would characterize the postwar years, an era forever changed by World War II and its many legacies.

Walter L. Hixson

The editor would like to extend special appreciation
to Brian Himebaugh.

Volume Introduction

World War II brought together coalitions of unlikely allies and remade the map of the world. The demands of managing the war and planning for the postwar era taxed the allied statesmen Winston Churchill, Franklin D. Roosevelt, and Joseph Stalin. In the first entry in this volume, diplomatic historian Mark A. Stoler offers readers a guide to fifty years of historical writing on the controversial and multi-faceted diplomacy of World War II.

Although the war concluded with the defeat of Germany and Japan, the European colonial powers came to grief in efforts to reassert their control over dependent peoples in Asia and Africa. However, in an oft-cited article, William Roger Louis and Ronald Robinson explain how indigenous elites and former British colonizers accommodated themselves to rising American power, which brought a continuation of a system of informal imperial control of the former British empire in the wake of World War II. John J. Sbrega argues that, by failing to maintain an aggressive posture of decolonization, the United States caved in to allied efforts to attempt to reassert their control over dependent peoples. Similarly, G. D. Sheffield probes beneath the surface to underscore profound tensions within the wartime Anglo-American alliance.

The Anglo-American relationship mattered, but it was the Soviet-American relationship that determined the postwar balance of power. Hugh Phillips analyzes the ultimately futile efforts of Soviet ambassador Maxsim M. Litvinov to promote a climate favorable to postwar cooperation between the United States and the Soviet Union. Along the same lines, Elizabeth Kimball Maclean explores the pivotal role played by former U.S. ambassador to Moscow, Joseph Davies, in encouraging a softened image of Soviet generalissimo Joseph Stalin as a means of promoting the wartime Grand Alliance between the United States, the USSR, and Great Britain. As Albert Resis makes clear, none of the major powers sought the division of Europe between East and West—one of the most significant outcomes of World War II—yet they proved powerless to stop this development. In "Death and Politics," Crister S. Garrett and Stephen A. Garrett reconstruct the painful history of the Katyn Forest massacre of Polish army officers, an atrocity blamed on the Nazis but actually perpetrated by the Soviet Union.

Turning to Asian diplomacy, Xiaohua Ma argues that the "imaginations and experiences" that Americans developed pertaining to China during World War II plagued the Sino-American relationship for the rest of the century. Two articles in this volume explore Middle East diplomacy. Leonard Dinnerstein analyzes the Anglo-American Committee of Inquiry into the thorny issues of the Palestinian mandate and the quest for a Jewish homeland. Stephen L. McFarland argues that Soviet-American conflict over Iran, which spurred the evolution of the Cold War in 1946, actually found its roots in the World War II policies of the two great powers toward Iran.

In "Indochina and Anglo-American Relations 1942–1945," Christopher Thorne examines the diplomacy that led to the abandonment of a commitment to decolonization of the region that became the site of a series of bitter postwar conflicts. In "The Other China Hands," Marc Gallicchio argues that American army officers exaggerated their wartime effectiveness in preparing the Chinese nationalist forces, thus contributing to a postwar backlash when the communists triumphed in China. Brian L. Villa argues that a tenacious State Department defense of the wartime policy of "unconditional surrender" undermined efforts to negotiate with Japan on the status of the emperor in the postwar era.

HISTORIOGRAPHY

A Half Century of Conflict: Interpretations of U.S. World War II Diplomacy

MARK A. STOLER[*]

No event in U.S. history save the Civil War has assumed the mythic proportions of World War II, or resulted in such a deluge of scholarly as well as popular studies. Historiographical analyses of those scholarly studies, however, are in much shorter supply, especially in regard to U.S. wartime diplomacy. The fiftieth anniversary commemorations of the war now in progress, along with the enormous number of publications that have preceded and accompanied those commemorations, make this a particularly appropriate time to provide such an analysis.[1]

In an earlier, 1981 assessment, I noted that the historiography of U.S. diplomacy during World War II possessed characteristics both similar to and different from other areas of intense historical dispute. Major similarities included the large volume of writings, the impact of contemporary concerns on evolving interpretations, and the effect of new schools of thought regarding U.S. foreign relations in general. World War II diplomacy was a unique field, however, in at least two important respects. First, the combination of massive documentary evidence and continued popular interest in the war had already resulted by 1981 in a volume of literature so enormous and so rapidly growing as to merit special mention. Second, although the resulting schools of

---

[*]The author wishes to thank Warren F. Kimball, David Reynolds, and Theodore A. Wilson for their invaluable criticism and advice regarding earlier drafts of this article, as well as Michael J. Hogan for his encouragement and patience.

[1]In light of both my own 1981 analysis of the literature and the volume of works to appear since then, much of this essay will focus on interpretations published between 1981 and 1993. For greater detail on earlier interpretations see my "World War II Diplomacy in Historical Writing: Prelude to Cold War," in *American Foreign Relations: A Historiographical Review*, ed. Gerald K. Haines and J. Samuel Walker (Westport, 1981), 187–206.

The first part of this essay essentially summarizes what I said in 1981 about those early interpretations. I have revised my assessments of works published during the 1970s, however, as well as focused on works of the 1980s and early 1990s; approximately two thirds of this essay is devoted to such works. Both the 1981 analysis and this one focus exclusively on U.S. wartime diplomacy after official U.S. entry into the conflict in December 1941.

interpretation reflected to an extent those of U.S. diplomacy in general, they possessed a distinctive quality because of the enormous influence of the Cold War on the interpreters. That influence, I emphasized, had led most historians to analyze World War II diplomacy primarily in terms of its role in the postwar Soviet-American conflict.[2]

Interpretations of World War II diplomacy published since 1981 continued these trends. Of special noteworthiness is the ongoing and apparently insatiable public as well as scholarly interest in the war, fanned since 1989 by fiftieth anniversary commemorations, and the ensuing enormous volume of works being published. One historian has recently predicted that in the next two decades, World War II will replace the Civil War as "the most popular war in the public imagination."[3] Equally noteworthy is the continued impact of the Cold War on World War II interpretations. Highly illustrative of this impact is the fact that in numerous historiographical and bibliographical studies published during the 1980s, World War II diplomacy was combined with the origins of the Cold War rather than receiving separate treatment.[4]

The early 1980s witnessed a sharp deterioration in Soviet-American relations, however, as well as dramatic, related changes in the domestic American environment. In the wake of these developments, what had appeared in 1981 to be a promising interpretive synthesis was replaced by renewed interpretive controversy. Neither the ensuing return of détente nor the unexpected conclusion of the Cold War in 1989–1991 ended these controversies. But they no longer monopolize the historiographical agenda. The simultaneous development during the 1980s of new schools of interpretation regarding U.S. foreign relations in general led to important new approaches to the years 1941–1945, some of which have clearly begun to shift the focus away from the Cold War.

Early interpretations viewed U.S. diplomacy during World War II as the first round in the Cold War and thus did not follow the standard historiographical pattern of official version, revisionism, response, and synthesis.[5] Instead, scholarship highly critical of U.S. policy surfaced first and practically became the official version. Although defenses of U.S. World War II diplomacy did appear during the first twenty years after the war, most of them accepted revisionist arguments to an extraordinary extent.

The focal points of this early criticism were the supposed blunders and naïveté of President Franklin D. Roosevelt and other U.S. policymakers in their wartime relations with the Soviet Union, which had resulted in a massive

---

[2] Ibid.

[3] Ronald Spector comments in "The Scholarship on World War II: Its Present Condition and Future Possibilities," ed. Richard H. Kohn, *Journal of Military History* 55 (July 1991): 382.

[4] See, for example, Robert L. Messer, "World War II and the Coming of the Cold War," in *Modern American Diplomacy*, ed. John M. Carroll and George C. Herring (Wilmington, DE, 1986), 107–25; Joseph A. Fry, "United States Diplomacy: A Bibliography of Historiographical Works," Society for Historians of American Foreign Relations *Newsletter* 20 (September 1989): 26–29; and Donald Cameron Watt, "Britain and the Historiography of the Yalta Conference and the Cold War," *Diplomatic History* 13 (Winter 1989): 67–98.

[5] See Warren F. Kimball, "The Cold War Warmed Over," *American Historical Review* 79 (October 1974): 1119. See also Watt, "Yalta and the Cold War," 70–73, for an alternative, six-stage historiographical pattern.

and unnecessary extension of Soviet power. Early proponents of this interpretation included Roosevelt's prewar domestic as well as foreign policy opponents and former advisers, such as Ambassador William C. Bullitt and General John R. Deane, who had disagreed with the president's cooperative wartime policies toward the Soviets. The group also included British and American journalists, such as Chester Wilmot and Hanson W. Baldwin, who saw British Prime Minister Winston S. Churchill's rejected wartime proposals and policies as the ones the United States should have followed vis-à-vis the Soviets.[6] Although Churchill himself consciously downplayed Anglo-American wartime differences in his memoirs so as not to damage postwar relations between the two countries, those memoirs nevertheless provided substantial ammunition for such attacks on U.S. policies and exercised an extraordinary influence over historians because of their high quality and early publication before the release of many documents. This impact was far from accidental. "History will bear me out," Churchill had boasted, "particularly as I shall write that history myself." He did indeed, albeit with an attitude, as paraphrased by Sir William Deakin, that "this is not history; this is my case."[7]

International and domestic events in the decade following World War II made this assault on U.S. wartime diplomacy not only popular but also an extremely powerful and emotional political issue. Indeed, the frustrations of perceived Cold War defeats in China and Korea, combined with loss of the U.S. nuclear monopoly and revelations regarding wartime Soviet spies, led Republican politicians such as Joseph R. McCarthy to fame and power by accusing Roosevelt and his associates of treason rather than mere naïveté. By the early 1950s the wartime Yalta Conference in the Crimea had become virtually synonymous with such charges and had acquired, as Donald Cameron Watt has noted, "a connotation of shameful failure, if not outright treason, matching that attached to the Munich Conference of September 1938."[8]

Roosevelt's supporters and numerous historians within the emerging realist school criticized the ahistorical framework upon which such assaults were based. The framework of 1941–1945 had not been the Cold War, they pointedly noted, but military necessity and the need to maintain the Grand Alliance in order to defeat the Axis. That defeat and military realities, most notably those created by the advancing Red Army, rather than blunders,

---

[6]See William Henry Chamberlin, *America's Second Crusade* (Chicago, 1950); Harry Elmer Barnes, ed., *Perpetual War for Perpetual Peace* (Caldwell, ID, 1953); William C. Bullitt, "How We Won the War and Lost the Peace," *Life* 25 (30 August 1948): 82–97; John R. Deane, *The Strange Alliance: The Story of Our Efforts at Wartime Co-operation with Russia* (New York, 1947); Hanson W. Baldwin, *Great Mistakes of the War* (New York, 1949); and Chester Wilmot, *The Struggle for Europe* (New York, 1952). See also Stoler, "World War II Diplomacy," 188–90.

[7]Quoted in Warren F. Kimball, "Wheel Within a Wheel: Churchill, Roosevelt and the Special Relationship," in *Churchill*, ed. Robert Blake and William Roger Louis (New York, 1993), 294. See also Winston S. Churchill, *The Second World War*, 6 vols. (Boston, 1948–53). For Churchill's downplaying of Anglo-American differences see John Colville, *The Fringes of Power: Downing Street Diaries, 1939–1955* (New York, 1985), 658; and David Reynolds, "Roosevelt, Churchill, and the Wartime Anglo-American Alliance: Towards a New Synthesis," in *The "Special Relationship": Anglo-American Relations since 1945*, ed. William Roger Louis and Hedley Bull (Oxford, 1986), 17–18.

[8]Watt, "Yalta and the Cold War," 79. See also Athan G. Theoharis, *The Yalta Myths: An Issue in U.S. Politics, 1945–1955* (Columbia, MO, 1970).

naïveté, or treason, had led inevitably to an enormous increase in Soviet power. Joseph Stalin's supposed territorial gains at Yalta, historians John L. Snell, Forrest C. Pogue, Charles F. Delzell, and George A. Lensen emphasized in this regard in their 1956 *The Meaning of Yalta*, preceded and resulted from these realities rather than from Roosevelt's policies.[9]

Other defenses of U.S. wartime diplomacy published from 1945–1965 exhibited a fascinating duality, however, for most of the writers agreed with the charges of naïveté being leveled against Roosevelt and his advisers if not with the more extreme partisan charges of treason being leveled by the McCarthyites. Naïveté was one of the basic characteristics of all U.S. foreign policy, according to the realist critique then being expounded.[10] It was also a key component of traditional American self-perception. Furthermore, most of Roosevelt's defenders had by this time become Cold Warriors themselves and were thus neither willing nor able to defend his cooperative approach toward the Soviets during the war. Hence, in the process of defending U.S. wartime diplomacy against its extreme critics, most of these individuals wound up attacking it on grounds similar to those the critics had used.

This duality clearly affected the comprehensive and excellent "first generation" histories of the wartime alliance by William H. McNeill and Herbert Feis,[11] as well as the numerous interpretive assessments of U.S. foreign and military policies in general written between 1945 and 1965. During these two decades, most scholars modified their general support of U.S. policy during the war by criticizing the policymakers' separation of military from political issues, their single-minded devotion to military victory, and their naive Wilsonianism regarding the postwar world. Roosevelt was further criticized for placing too much faith in Stalin's goodwill and in his own powers of persuasion. All of these criticisms had originally been made by Roosevelt's detractors, and by the early 1960s this view thus constituted the dominant consensus. Indeed, by that time scholars such as Anne Armstrong, Tang Tsou, and Gaddis Smith appeared to be agreeing with Roosevelt's severest critics in the process of supposedly attacking them.[12]

This historical consensus was clearly related to the Cold War consensus that had come to dominate American politics. And just as that latter consensus was shattered by the events of the 1960s, most importantly the war in

---

[9] John L. Snell, ed., *The Meaning of Yalta: Big Three Diplomacy and the New Balance of Power* (Baton Rouge, 1956).

[10] See, for example, George F. Kennan, *American Diplomacy, 1900–1950* (Chicago, 1951).

[11] William Hardy McNeill, *America, Britain, & Russia: Their Cooperation and Conflict, 1941–1946*, a volume in *Survey of International Affairs, 1939–1946*, ed. Arnold Toynbee (London, 1953); Herbert Feis, *Churchill, Roosevelt, Stalin: The War They Waged and the Peace They Sought* (Princeton, 1957). McNeill did see the breakup of the Grand Alliance as a natural result of victory rather than anyone's fault, but he still criticized FDR along the lines discussed above.

[12] Anne Armstrong, *Unconditional Surrender: The Impact of the Casablanca Policy in World War II* (New Brunswick, 1961); Tang Tsou, *America's Failure in China, 1941–50* (Chicago, 1963); Gaddis Smith, *American Diplomacy during the Second World War, 1941–1945*, 1st ed. (New York, 1965). See also Samuel P. Huntington, *The Soldier and the State: The Theory and Politics of Civil-Military Relationships* (Cambridge, MA, 1957), 315–44, for a similar critique of Roosevelt's military advisers.

Vietnam, so too was the historical one as two new schools of interpretation emerged in that decade to challenge the prevailing wisdom.

The first of these, which included historians preparing the U.S. Army's massive official military history of the war as well as others who made use of these volumes and/or the enormous documentary record then becoming available, argued that U.S. wartime policies and strategies had been highly realistic rather than naive and that the president had clearly controlled his military advisers rather than vice versa.[13] John L. Snell went even further in 1963, arguing in a brief, comparative history of wartime diplomacy that Axis leaders, rather than Roosevelt, had based their policies on illusions and thereby lost the war. The president's policies, on the other hand, had been highly realistic and resulted in total military victory. Because cooperation with the Soviets was essential to that victory and expanded postwar Soviet power was an inevitable outcome of it, Roosevelt's cooperative approach was "virtually imposed by necessity." Snell further defended Roosevelt's much-maligned unconditional surrender policy and his postponement of all territorial settlements as highly realistic and pragmatic attempts to promote U.S. interests while simultaneously reconciling Allied differences and maintaining domestic support. In pursuing these policies, the president had concurrently established the key prerequisites for both wartime victory and postwar cooperation with the Soviets and placed limits on their expansion should cooperation not occur—limits clearly illustrated by the fact that Stalin's territorial gains did not exceed those Czar Nicholas II would have obtained at the end of World War I had he remained in power.[14]

This thesis received reinforcement in the late 1960s from two directions. In major reassessments of Roosevelt, Robert A. Divine and James M. Burns argued that the president had been highly pragmatic and realistic. Rather than FDR being duped by Stalin, Divine argued, historians and the public had been duped by the president's Wilsonian public statements, which were delivered to protect his domestic flank but which were contradicted by his pragmatic private comments and actions. Such pragmatism, both historians argued, had helped the Grand Alliance maintain itself during the war but ironically doomed Roosevelt's hopes for postwar cooperation—because it led him to misunderstand Stalin, according to Divine; and/or because it increased Soviet suspicions, according to Burns.[15] Simultaneously, British as well as U.S.

---

[13]See, for example, William Emerson, "Franklin Roosevelt as Commander-in-Chief in World War II," *Military Affairs* 22 (Winter 1958–59): 181–207; Maurice Matloff, "Franklin Delano Roosevelt as War Leader," in *Total War and Cold War: Problems in Civilian Control of the Military,* ed. Harry L. Coles (Columbus, OH, 1962), 42–65; and Kent Roberts Greenfield, *American Strategy in World War II: A Reconsideration* (Baltimore, 1963), 49–84. See also Willard Range, *Franklin D. Roosevelt's World Order* (Athens, OH, 1959); and directly below. Entitled *United States Army in World War II,* the official army history eventually included some eighty volumes and a special collection of essays, *Command Decisions,* ed. Kent Roberts Greenfield (Washington, 1960).

[14]John L. Snell, *Illusion and Necessity: The Diplomacy of Global War, 1939–1945* (Boston, 1963), 116, 137–43, 209–16. See also Raymond G. O'Connor, *Diplomacy for Victory: FDR and Unconditional Surrender* (New York, 1971).

[15]Robert A. Divine, *Roosevelt and World War II* (Baltimore, 1969); James MacGregor Burns, *Roosevelt: The Soldier of Freedom, 1940–1945* (New York, 1970). See also Geoffrey Warner, "From Teheran to Yalta: Reflections on F.D.R.'s Foreign Policy," *International Affairs* 43 (July 1967): 530–36.

historians began to reexamine the supposedly realistic alternative strategies and policies that Churchill had provided. Many of them concluded that fear of postwar Soviet power was a much less important motivation than the British prime minister had led his readers to believe, and that irrational as well as narrowly nationalistic motivations lay behind his proposals.[16]

The second school of interpretation to challenge the prevailing consensus on U.S. wartime diplomacy during the 1960s was the so-called New Left. It, too, made extensive use of the massive documentation then becoming available to attack the notion of American blunders and naïveté during the war, but in such a way as to sharply condemn rather than defend U.S. policy and to assert that aggressive U.S. behavior during the war had been a, if not the, primary cause of the ensuing Cold War.

This New Left assault was far from monolithic, however. Basing their work on the Open Door thesis that William Appleman Williams (and Charles Beard before him) had developed to critique U.S. foreign policy in general, historians such as Lloyd C. Gardner published broad and highly critical economic interpretations of all of Roosevelt's foreign policies. Gabriel Kolko provided the most extensive and extreme socioeconomic criticism of U.S. wartime diplomacy, maintaining that Washington had realistically and aggressively attempted to promote its own postwar capitalist expansion at the expense of the British Empire, the Soviet Union, and the indigenous Left throughout the world.[17] In more specialized revisionist works, however, other scholars, such as Gar Alperovitz and Diane Shaver Clemens, harkened back to D. F. Fleming's earlier and more specific Cold War revisionism, rather than to Williams's general economic approach, to defend Roosevelt's cooperative policy with the Soviet Union and to blame his successor, Harry S. Truman, for reversing it. Alperovitz saw such a reversal in Truman's decision to drop the atomic bomb on Hiroshima, a decision motivated primarily by a desire to blackmail the Soviets rather than to end the war quickly, as Herbert Feis had earlier claimed. Clemens concluded her detailed revisionist analysis of Yalta by maintaining that Truman, rather than Stalin, had broken the accords, even though Stalin, rather than Roosevelt, had made the bulk of the concessions at the conference.[18]

Consensus historians sharply attacked this New Left assault on prevailing interpretations of World War II diplomacy and the origins of the Cold War,

---

[16]See Michael Howard, *The Mediterranean Strategy in the Second World War* (London, 1968); Stephen E. Ambrose, *Eisenhower and Berlin, 1945: The Decision to Halt at the Elbe* (New York, 1967); O'Connor, *Diplomacy for Victory*; and Trumbull Higgins, *Soft Underbelly: The Anglo-American Controversy over the Italian Campaign, 1943-1945* (New York, 1968).

[17]William Appleman Williams, *The Tragedy of American Diplomacy*, enlarged rev. ed. (New York, 1962); Lloyd C. Gardner, *Economic Aspects of New Deal Diplomacy* (Madison, WI, 1964); idem, *Architects of Illusion: Men and Ideas in American Foreign Policy, 1941-1949* (Chicago, 1970); Gabriel Kolko, *The Politics of War: The World and United States Foreign Policy, 1943-1945* (New York, 1968).

[18]Gar Alperovitz, *Atomic Diplomacy: Hiroshima and Potsdam: The Use of the Atomic Bomb and the American Confrontation with Soviet Power*, 1st ed. (New York, 1965); D. F. Fleming, *The Cold War and Its Origins, 1917-1960* (New York, 1961); Herbert Feis, *Japan Subdued: The Atomic Bomb and the End of the War in the Far East* (Princeton, 1961); Diane Shaver Clemens, *Yalta* (New York, 1970). Secretary of State Edward R. Stettinius had first argued that Stalin made most of the concessions in *Roosevelt and the Russians: The Yalta Conference* (Garden City, 1949). See also Stoler, "World War II Diplomacy," 196–98.

with the debate often as heated as the larger political one on the Vietnam War. By 1973, it included name calling and accusations of gross distortion and misuse of historical evidence that spilled beyond the confines of the profession and onto the pages of the *New York Times*.[19] Ironically, however, new works on U.S. diplomacy during World War II as well as during the Cold War were by that time moving far beyond such polarized confrontations and into an era of detailed monographs, attempted synthesis, and entirely new approaches.

Numerous factors accounted for this shift. The early debate had clearly reached a stalemate by the mid-1970s, while many historians had begun to realize that the divergent schools did share some important conclusions—such as the universalistic nature of U.S. policies during the war as compared with those of the other Allied powers. As the years passed, such shared conclusions became more visible, partially as a result of the calmer political environment that followed Watergate and the end of the Vietnam War, and partially as a result of the emergence of a new generation of historians not personally linked to the older battles—or to the personal experience of World War II for that matter.[20]

This new generation in turn possessed new documentary evidence not available to its predecessors. The works of the 1960s had been based primarily on documentary information in the numerous volumes published during those years within the State Department's *Foreign Relations* series and the British and American official history series, as well as memoirs and recently opened manuscript collections.[21] The bulk of the official World War II documentary

---

[19]See Robert James Maddox, *The New Left and the Origins of the Cold War* (Princeton, 1973); and *New York Times Book Review*, 17 June 1973.

[20]See, for example, Lloyd C. Gardner, Arthur Schlesinger, Jr., and Hans Morgenthau, *Origins of the Cold War* (Waltham, MA, 1970). For early attempted syntheses from the revisionist and traditionalist perspectives, respectively, see Gardner, *Architects of Illusion*; and John Lewis Gaddis, *The United States and the Origins of the Cold War, 1941–1947* (New York, 1972). For the continuing enormous impact of the war on historians who lived through it see Richard Wrightman Fox et al., "A Round Table: The Living and Reliving of World War II," *Journal of American History* 77 (September 1990): 553–93.

[21]As a result of the domestic political uproar over Yalta, a special *Foreign Relations* volume on that conference was published in 1955. Not until the 1960s, however, did the regular chronological series reach the war years and companion volumes begin to appear for the other wartime conferences; more than thirty volumes covering the period 1941–1945 would be published during the decade. The key British collections were the *Grand Strategy* military series of six volumes edited by J. R. M. Butler (London, 1956–76); and Sir Llewellyn Woodward's *British Foreign Policy in the Second World War*, published in an abridged single volume in 1962 and then in five volumes between 1970 and 1976. See also Wesley F. Craven and James L. Cate, eds., *The Army Air Forces in World War II*, 7 vols. (Chicago, 1948–49); Samuel Eliot Morison, *History of United States Naval Operations in World War II*, 15 vols. (Boston, 1947–62); and the previously cited eighty-volume *U.S. Army in World War II*. Most of Roosevelt's key advisers published memoirs in the three decades after the war. The last major one to appear was W. Averell Harriman's *Special Envoy to Churchill and Stalin, 1941–1946* (New York, 1975).

Roosevelt died before he could write any memoirs himself, but selections from his wartime diplomatic correspondence with Churchill and Stalin appeared in numerous volumes of the *Foreign Relations* series. Churchill's memoirs also contained extensive Big Three correspondence. In 1957 the Soviet Ministry for Foreign Affairs published Stalin's complete correspondence with Churchill and Roosevelt as *Russia: Correspondence between the Chairman of the Council of Ministers of the U.S.S.R. and the Presidents of the U.S.A. and the Prime Ministers of Great Britain during the Great Patriotic War of 1941–1945*, 2 vols. (Moscow, 1957). The Churchill-Roosevelt correspondence received separate, full-scale treatment only in the 1970s and 1980s. See Francis L. Lowenheim, Harold Langley, and Manfred Jonas, eds., *Roosevelt and*

record remained classified until the early 1970s, however, when most of it was opened in both England and the United States. The result was quantitatively and qualitatively staggering. U.S. Army files alone weighed 17,120 tons, enough to fill 188 miles of filing cases end to end.[22] And within those files lay not only enormously detailed evidence to revise previous analyses but also revelations that opened entirely new areas of inquiry. Most publicized was the so-called Ultra Secret, the Anglo-American breaking of the highest German military code, which had remained unrevealed until 1974 and which after that date precipitated the creation of virtually a new subfield in World War II scholarship: cryptography and deception. The ramifications for the diplomatic history of the war of these and other aspects of intelligence, which one British diplomat labeled "the missing dimension of most diplomatic history," are still being explored.[23]

Two additional and related factors also deserve mention, although their full impact would not be felt until the 1980s. Historical study in general was being altered by the use of new social science models and the computer as well as by a new emphasis on social, cultural, and comparative history. Furthermore, diplomatic historians came under sharp attack for not participating in these changes and for limiting both their research and their focus to the United States. According to Alexander DeConde, diplomatic history underwent "perhaps . . . more criticism than any other comparable field of historical investigation." Although this criticism was overstated and ignored numerous pioneering efforts in the new areas and methods of inquiry, it clearly affected numerous scholars who attempted to incorporate such approaches into their work.[24]

Churchill: Their Secret Wartime Correspondence (New York, 1975); and Warren F. Kimball, ed., *Churchill & Roosevelt: The Complete Correspondence*, 3 vols. (Princeton, 1984).

[22] Kent Roberts Greenfield, *The Historian and the Army* (New Brunswick, 1954), 6.

[23] See David Dilks, ed., *The Diaries of Sir Alexander Cadogan, 1938–1945* (New York, 1972), 21; and Christopher Andrew and David Dilks, ed., *The Missing Dimension: Governments and Intelligence Communities in the Twentieth Century* (Urbana, 1984).
The first work to reveal Ultra was F. W. Winterbotham's memoir, *The Ultra Secret* (New York, 1974). A complete note on all the related material published since would run many pages, and the interested reader is advised to consult both the *International Journal of Intelligence and Counterintelligence* and John Lewis Gaddis's "Intelligence, Espionage, and Cold War Origins," *Diplomatic History* 13 (Spring 1989): 191–212. Although primarily concerned with the impact of intelligence on the Cold War, Gaddis's article contains much information on the World War II years and a good summary of key works in the field. The most recent is Bradley F. Smith's *The Ultra-Magic Deals and the Most Secret Special Relationship, 1940–1946* (Novato, CA, 1993).

[24] The most famous and cited of these attacks is Charles S. Maier's "Marking Time: The Historiography of International Relations," in *The Past before Us: Contemporary Historical Writing in the United States*, ed. Michael Kammen (Ithaca, 1980), 355–87. See also Sally Marks, "The World According to Washington," *Diplomatic History* 11 (Summer 1987): 281–82; and Christopher Thorne, "After the Europeans: American Designs for the Remaking of Southeast Asia," ibid. 12 (Spring 1988): 206–8. Excellent summaries of new approaches in the field can be found in Michael J. Hogan and Thomas G. Paterson, eds., *Explaining the History of American Foreign Relations* (Cambridge and New York, 1991), a compilation based upon earlier symposia in *Journal of American History* 77 (June 1990): 93–182, and *Diplomatic History* 14 (Fall 1990): 553–605. Other attacks, as well as the DeConde quote, are in Stephen G. Rabe's review of *Explaining the History*, "Reports of Our Demise Are Greatly Exaggerated," *Diplomatic History* 16 (Summer 1992): 481–82. A summary of the attacks can also be found in Edward P. Crapol's recent historiographical essay, "Coming to Terms with Empire: The Historiography of Late-Nineteenth-Century American Foreign Relations," ibid. (Fall 1992): 573–76.

The resultant outpouring during the 1970s of scholarship on World War II diplomacy cut in many directions. The new availability of military as well as diplomatic and British as well as U.S. documents led to numerous reexaminations of Anglo-American as well as Soviet-American wartime relations in general and of such highly controversial alliance issues as aid to Russia, the second front dispute, the Darlan affair, postwar decolonization and economic organization, Middle Eastern oil, the atomic bomb decision, and the treatment of postwar Germany.[25] Contradicting the image Churchill had sought to project in his memoirs, many of these studies emphasized intense Anglo-American as well as Soviet-American differences and tensions throughout the war. In his 1978 *Imperialism at Bay*, William Roger Louis took such analyses a step further by using multiarchival research to examine intragovernmental as well as Anglo-American conflicts over postwar decolonization and trusteeships during the war.[26] Simultaneously, other scholars used the newly available material to shift the focus away from Anglo-American as well as Soviet-American relations and onto U.S. wartime policies vis-à-vis other nations during the war, as well as colonial areas. Once again, however, this shift reflected the consistent search for World War II roots to contemporary concerns. As the publication during the 1960s of studies on wartime Franco-American relations had coincided with Charles de Gaulle's return to power and removal of his country from the unified NATO military command,[27] so in the 1970s did the large number of studies on U.S. wartime policies regarding China, Indochina, and the Middle East parallel three areas of critical concern for U.S. foreign policy during that time period.[28] But the

---

[25]See, for example, Robert Beitzell, *The Uneasy Alliance: America, Britain, and Russia, 1941–1943* (New York, 1972); Gaddis, *The United States and the Origins of the Cold War*; Richard W. Steele, *The First Offensive, 1942: Roosevelt, Marshall and the Making of American Strategy* (Bloomington, IN, 1973); Richard C. Lukas, *Eagles East: The Army Air Forces and the Soviet Union, 1941–1945* (Tallahassee, 1970); Arthur L. Funk, *The Politics of TORCH: The Allied Landings and the Algiers Putsch, 1942* (Lawrence, KS, 1974); Mark A. Stoler, *The Politics of the Second Front: American Military Planning and Diplomacy in Coalition Warfare, 1941–1943* (Westport, 1977); Brian J. Villa, "The U.S. Army, Unconditional Surrender, and the Potsdam Declaration," *Journal of American History* 63 (June 1976): 66–92; idem, "The Atomic Bomb and the Normandy Invasion," *Perspectives in American History* 11 (1977–78): 463–502; Walter S. Dunn, Jr., *Second Front Now 1943* (University, AL, 1980); John Grigg, *1943: The Victory That Never Was* (New York, 1980); George C. Herring, *Aid to Russia, 1941–1946: Strategy, Diplomacy, and the Origins of the Cold War* (Baltimore, 1973); Thomas G. Paterson, *Soviet-American Confrontation: Postwar Reconstruction and the Origins of the Cold War* (Baltimore, 1973); Leon Martel, *Lend-Lease, Loans and the Coming of the Cold War: A Study of the Implementation of Foreign Policy* (Boulder, 1979); Alfred E. Eckes, Jr., *A Search for Solvency: Bretton Woods and the International Monetary System, 1941–1971* (Austin, 1975); Armand Van Dormeal, *Bretton Woods: Birth of a Monetary System* (London, 1978); Warren F. Kimball, *Swords or Plowshares? The Morgenthau Plan for Defeated Nazi Germany, 1943–1946* (Philadelphia, 1976); and Bruce Kuklick, *American Policy and the Division of Germany: The Clash with Russia over Reparations* (Ithaca, 1972). See also directly below, footnotes 26–32.

[26]William Roger Louis, *Imperialism at Bay, 1941–1945: The United States and the Decolonization of the British Empire* (New York, 1978). See below, footnotes 37 and 65, for additional works that focus on Anglo-American and/or intragovernmental conflicts during the war.

[27]See Dorothy S. White, *Seeds of Discord: de Gaulle, Free France and the Allies* (Syracuse, 1964); and Milton Viorst, *Hostile Allies: FDR and Charles de Gaulle* (New York, 1965).

[28]See Barbara W. Tuchman, *Stilwell and the American Experience in China, 1911–1945* (New York, 1970); Michael Schaller, *The U.S. Crusade in China, 1938–1945* (New York, 1979); Edward R. Drachman, *United States Policy toward Vietnam, 1940–1945* (Rutherford, NJ, 1970); Gary R. Hess, "Franklin Roosevelt and Indochina," *Journal of American History* 59 (September

9

sheer volume of new documentation, combined with the rise of polycentrism and Third World issues in general during the 1970s, also led to a flood of specialized studies on wartime relations with a host of other countries.[29]

On some issues the result was the creation of a new consensus. Most notable in this regard were works on the atomic bomb by Barton J. Bernstein and Martin J. Sherwin. Working with newly declassified material as well as with the existing and conflicting interpretations, each concluded independently that the United States had indeed practiced "atomic diplomacy" against the Soviets as Alperovitz had argued, but that this had been a secondary motive to ending the war quickly, as Feis had earlier maintained. They also emphasized that such atomic diplomacy had been a key component of Roosevelt's policy and that Truman had thus not reversed his predecessor's attitudes on the weapon vis-à-vis the Soviets.[30] A new consensus also began to emerge on wartime policy toward China, although here the result was more a reversal than a synthesis of previous interpretations. Those interpretations, written at the height of Sino-American conflict in the 1950s and 1960s, had criticized U.S. wartime policymakers for insufficient support of Jiang Jieshi (Chiang Kai-shek) and nonrecognition of the menace posed by the Communist Mao Zedong (Mao Tse-tung).[31] Writing in the 1970s, a decade of intense Sino-Soviet conflict and tremendously improved Sino-American relations, Barbara Tuchman and Michael Schaller criticized policymakers for not having dropped the hopeless Jiang in favor of Mao during the war.[32]

The decade ended with two major works that attempted both to synthesize the numerous recent monographs into a new consensus and to point the way

---

1972): 353–68; Walter LaFeber, "Roosevelt, Churchill, and Indochina, 1942–1945," *American Historical Review* 80 (December 1975): 1277–95; Christopher Thorne, "Indochina and Anglo-American Relations, 1942–1945," *Pacific Historical Review* 45 (February 1976): 73–96; Phillip J. Baram, *The Department of State in the Middle East, 1919–1945* (Philadelphia, 1978); and John A. DeNovo, "The Culbertson Economic Mission and Anglo-American Tensions in the Middle East, 1944–1945," *Journal of American History* 63 (March 1977): 913–36.

[29]See, for example, Walter R. Roberts, *Tito, Mihailovic and the Allies, 1941–1945* (New Brunswick, 1973); Roger J. Bell, *Unequal Allies: Australian-American Relations and the Pacific War* (Melbourne, 1977); Richard C. Lukas, *The Strange Allies: The United States and Poland, 1941–1945* (Knoxville, 1978); James J. Dougherty, *The Politics of Wartime Aid: American Economic Assistance to France and French West Africa, 1940–1946* (Westport, 1978); Gary R. Hess, *America Encounters India, 1941–1947* (Baltimore, 1971); Frank D. McCann, Jr., *The Brazilian-American Alliance, 1937–1945* (Princeton, 1973); Randall B. Woods, *The Roosevelt Foreign-Policy Establishment and the Good Neighbor: The United States and Argentina, 1941–1945* (Lawrence, 1979); Irwin F. Gellman, *Good Neighbor Diplomacy: United States Policies in Latin America, 1933–1945* (Baltimore, 1979); and Gerald K. Haines, "Under the Eagle's Wing: The Franklin Roosevelt Administration Forges an American Hemisphere," *Diplomatic History* 1 (Fall 1977): 373–88. This list is far from complete. For additional works see Richard Dean Burns, ed., *A Guide to American Foreign Relations since 1700* (Santa Barbara, 1982).

[30]Barton J. Bernstein, "Roosevelt, Truman and the Atomic Bomb, 1941–1945: A Reinterpretation," *Political Science Quarterly* 90 (Spring 1975): 23–69; idem, "The Uneasy Alliance: Roosevelt, Churchill, and the Atomic Bomb, 1940–1945," *Western Political Quarterly* 29 (June 1976): 202–30; Martin J. Sherwin, *A World Destroyed: The Atomic Bomb and the Grand Alliance* (New York, 1975).

[31]See Anthony Kubek, *How the Far East Was Lost: American Policy and the Creation of Communist China, 1941–1949* (Chicago, 1963); and Tsou, *America's Failure in China*. For an early defense of U.S. policies see Herbert Feis, *The China Tangle: The American Effort in China from Pearl Harbor to the Marshall Mission* (Princeton, 1953).

[32]Tuchman, *Stilwell and the American Experience in China;* and Schaller, *The U.S. Crusade in China*.

for new lines of inquiry. In a detailed and exhaustive analysis of all of Franklin Roosevelt's foreign policies from 1932 to 1945, Robert Dallek sided with a decade of FDR defenders by dismissing all the supposed "blunders" listed by previous critics and by emphasizing both FDR's realism and the severe domestic as well as international constraints under which he had operated. Dallek's assessment was not uniformly positive, however. Echoing a series of recent studies, he criticized the president sharply for his "unnecessary and destructive compromises of legal and moral principles," most notably his sanctioning of illegal wiretaps and mail openings as well as the internment of Japanese-Americans, and his overly cautious response (or lack of response) to the Nazi destruction of European Jewry.[33] Simultaneously, British historian Christopher Thorne broke new ground by publishing the first diplomatic history of the Pacific war and by emphasizing within that pathbreaking work of multiarchival research racism, anticolonialism, Anglo-American friction, and relations with other Pacific nations as key themes.[34]

Additional studies soon appeared that both supported and filled in gaps within these two key works. Although his 1982 *Strategies of Containment* focused on the postwar years, John Lewis Gaddis began the work by crediting Roosevelt with a highly realistic though flawed wartime strategy of "containment by integration" of the Soviet Union into his proposed postwar order and by arguing, as had Dallek and a few others, that had Roosevelt lived longer he probably would have shifted to a tougher strategy after obtaining victory over the Axis.[35] Simultaneously, Martin Gilbert, David S. Wyman, and numerous other scholars expanded upon previous criticisms of U.S. and Allied refugee policy during the Holocaust in comprehensive, multiarchival works,[36] while Terry H. Anderson, Alan P. Dobson, Fraser J. Harbutt, Robert M. Hathaway, and John J. Sbrega explored Anglo-American wartime conflicts within their multiarchival analyses of U.S.-British relations during and immediately after World War II. So did David Reynolds and others,

---

[33]Robert Dallek, *Franklin D. Roosevelt and American Foreign Policy, 1932–1945* (New York, 1979). Early works on the United States and the Holocaust include Arthur D. Morse, *While Six Million Died: A Chronicle of American Apathy* (New York, 1968); Henry L. Feingold, *The Politics of Rescue: The Roosevelt Administration and the Holocaust, 1938–1945* (New Brunswick, 1970); Saul S. Friedman, *No Haven for the Oppressed: United States Policy toward Jewish Refugees, 1938–1945* (Detroit, 1973); and David S. Wyman, *Paper Walls: America and the Refugee Crisis, 1938–1941* (Amherst, MA, 1968). See below, footnote 36, for more recent studies.

[34]Christopher Thorne, *Allies of a Kind: The United States, Britain and the War against Japan, 1941–1945* (New York, 1978).

[35]John Lewis Gaddis, *Strategies of Containment: A Critical Appraisal of Postwar American National Security Policy* (New York, 1982), 3–16. See also Terry H. Anderson, *The United States, Great Britain, and the Cold War, 1944–1947* (Columbia, MO, 1981), 41–51, 199–200 n. 49. Interestingly, Gaddis in 1983 noted a parallel emerging consensus on the origins of the Cold War. See his "The Emerging Post-Revisionist Synthesis on the Origins of the Cold War," with responses by Lloyd C. Gardner, Lawrence S. Kaplan, Warren F. Kimball, and Bruce R. Kuniholm in *Diplomatic History* 7 (Summer 1983): 171–204.

[36]See Martin Gilbert, *Auschwitz and the Allies* (New York, 1981); Walter Laqueur, *The Terrible Secret: Suppression of the Truth about Hitler's "Final Solution"* (Boston, 1980); David S. Wyman, *The Abandonment of the Jews: America and the Holocaust, 1941–1945* (New York, 1984); Monty Noam Penkower, *The Jews Were Expendable: Free World Diplomacy and the Holocaust* (Urbana, 1983); Richard Breitman and Alan M. Kraut, *American Refugee Policy and European Jewry, 1933–1945* (Bloomington, 1987); and Deborah Lipstadt, *Beyond Belief: The American Press and the Coming of the Holocaust, 1933–1945* (New York, 1985).

thereby completing the demolition of Churchill's one-sided interpretation and exposing a relationship that, although indeed "remarkable," had been marked by severe disagreements and became "special" only gradually, fitfully, and incompletely.[37]

In regard to other issues raised by Thorne in *Allies of a Kind*, Akira Iriye's 1981 *Power and Culture* offered an original and provocative comparative analysis of U.S. and Japanese societies and their values throughout the Pacific conflict, one that emphasized their similarities even in war. In his 1986 *War without Mercy*, John W. Dower made extensive use of evidence within popular culture to analyze in detail the racist views each nation held of the other and their consequences during the war. Thorne himself produced a comparative follow-up study in 1985, *The Issue of War*, a thematic analysis that attempted to remove the boundaries between Western and non-Western history and to fuse diplomatic with economic and intellectual history as well as sociology and social psychology into a new "international history." Frank A. Ninkovich and Michael S. Sherry also made extensive use of cultural and intellectual history in their respective studies of U.S. foreign policy regarding cultural relations from 1938–1950 and the rise of American air power before and during World War II.[38]

Many of these themes and approaches were also evident in the continuing flood of studies on U.S. wartime relations with other nations and parts of the world. As in the 1970s, such studies continued to focus (although not exclusively) on areas of recent and contemporary concern, most notably Indochina and the Middle East. With the opening of Korean War documentation came an additional focus on the wartime origins of that conflict. Many of these new bilateral studies extended into the late 1940s or early 1950s rather than stopping in 1945, thereby continuing the tendency to

[37]Reynolds, "Roosevelt, Churchill, and the Wartime Anglo-American Alliance, 1939–1945," 17–41. See also Anderson, *The United States, Great Britain, and the Cold War*; Alan P. Dobson, *U.S. Wartime Aid to Britain, 1940–1946* (London, 1986); Fraser J. Harbutt, *The Iron Curtain: Churchill, America and the Origins of the Cold War* (New York, 1986); Robert M. Hathaway, *Ambiguous Partnership: Britain and America, 1944–1947* (New York, 1981); John J. Sbrega, *Anglo-American Relations and Colonialism in East Asia, 1941–1945* (New York, 1983); as well as other works cited in Reynolds, 17–41; Reynolds, *The Creation of the Anglo-American Alliance, 1937–1941: A Study in Competitive Co-operation* (Chapel Hill, 1981); and idem, with David Dimbleby, *An Ocean Apart: The Relationship Between Britain and America in the Twentieth Century* (New York, 1988), chap. 8.

[38]Akira Iriye, *Power and Culture: The Japanese-American War, 1941–1945* (Cambridge, MA, 1981); John W. Dower, *War without Mercy: Race and Power in the Pacific War* (New York, 1986); Christopher Thorne, *The Issue of War: States, Societies, and the Far Eastern Conflict of 1941–1945* (New York, 1985); Frank A. Ninkovich, *The Diplomacy of Ideas: U.S. Foreign Policy and Cultural Relations, 1938–1950* (New York, 1981); Michael S. Sherry, *The Rise of American Air Power: The Creation of Armageddon* (New Haven, 1987). See also Ronald Schaffer, *Wings of Judgment: American Bombing in World War II* (New York, 1985). On the new international/cultural history see Akira Iriye, "The Internationalization of History," *American Historical Review* 94 (February 1989): 1–10; idem, "Culture and Power: International Relations as Intercultural Relations," *Diplomatic History* 3 (Spring 1979): 115–28; Christopher Thorne, *Border Crossings: Studies in International History* (Oxford, 1988), a collection of previously published essays; and idem, "After The Europeans," a critique of traditional U.S. diplomatic history.

focus on the diplomacy of the World War II years as a prelude to Cold War-era policies.[39]

The 1980s also witnessed a major outpouring of biographical studies of key Roosevelt advisers, most notably Harry Hopkins and the much-maligned members of the wartime Joint Chiefs of Staff. These both represented and fueled a growing interest in the interaction between military and diplomatic issues during the war while providing substantial additional evidence of political astuteness by the president and his advisers.[40]

The tremendous impact of all of these studies, from the late 1960s through the mid-1980s, and the differences between the old consensus and the newly emerging one, could be most clearly seen in a comparison of the first

[39]The number of pages in each work devoted to World War II rather than the early Cold War years varied enormously, with the 1941-1945 period providing merely an introduction to some and nearly all the content of others. See Lloyd C. Gardner, *Approaching Vietnam: From World War II through Dienbienphu* (New York, 1988); Gary R. Hess, *The United States' Emergence as a Southeast Asian Power, 1940-1950* (New York, 1987); Bruce Cumings, ed., *Child of Conflict: The Korean-American Relationship, 1943-1953* (Seattle, 1983); James I. Matray, *The Reluctant Crusade: American Foreign Policy in Korea, 1941-1950* (Honolulu, 1985); Marc S. Gallicchio, *The Cold War Begins in Asia: American East Asian Policy and the Fall of the Japanese Empire* (New York, 1988); Wesley M. Bagby, *The Eagle-Dragon Alliance: America's Relations with China in World War II* (Newark, DE, 1992); Irvine H. Anderson, *Aramco, the United States, and Saudi Arabia: A Study in the Dynamics of Foreign Oil Policy, 1933-1950* (Princeton, 1981); Michael B. Stoff, *Oil, War, and American Security: The Search for a National Policy on Foreign Oil, 1941-1947* (New Haven, 1980); Aaron D. Miller, *Search for Security: Saudi Arabian Oil and American Foreign Policy, 1939-1949* (Chapel Hill, 1980); Bruce Robellet Kuniholm, *The Origins of the Cold War in the Near East: Great Power Conflict and Diplomacy in Iran, Turkey, and Greece* (Princeton, 1980); David S. Painter, *Oil and the American Century: The Political Economy of U.S. Foreign Oil Policy, 1941-1954* (Baltimore, 1986); Mark H. Lytle, *The Origins of the Iranian-American Alliance, 1941-1953* (New York, 1987); and Barry Rubin, *The Great Powers in the Middle East, 1941-1947: The Road to the Cold War* (London, 1980). For U.S. relations with European countries see Julian G. Hurstfield, *America and the French Nation, 1939-1945* (Chapel Hill, 1986); and James Edward Miller, *The United States and Italy, 1940-1950* (Chapel Hill, 1986).

[40]An interesting set of articles that focuses on this interaction can be found in Walter Laqueur, ed., *The Second World War: Essays in Military and Political History* (London, 1982). On Hopkins see George T. McJimsey, *Harry Hopkins: Ally of the Poor and Defender of Democracy* (Cambridge, MA, 1987); Dwight William Tuttle, *Harry L. Hopkins and Anglo-American Soviet Relations, 1941-1945* (New York, 1983); and the earlier Henry H. Adams, *Harry Hopkins* (New York, 1977).

Biographies of each of the four members of the wartime Joint Chiefs of Staff were published during the 1980s. Most notable was the fourth and final volume of Forrest C. Pogue's official biography of the army chief and later secretary of state, *George C. Marshall: Statesman, 1945-1959* (New York, 1987). Briefer works on Marshall include Ed Cray, *General of the Army: George C. Marshall, Soldier and Statesman* (New York, 1990); Thomas Parrish, *Roosevelt and Marshall: Partners in Politics and War* (New York, 1989); and Mark A. Stoler, *George C. Marshall: Soldier-Statesman of the American Century* (Boston, 1989). For the other Joint Chiefs see Thomas B. Buell, *Master of Sea Power: A Biography of Fleet Admiral Ernest J. King* (Boston, 1980); Thomas M. Coffey, *HAP: The Story of the U.S. Air Force and the Man Who Built It, General Henry "Hap" Arnold* (New York, 1982); and Henry H. Adams, *Witness to Power: The Life of Fleet Admiral William D. Leahy* (Annapolis, 1985). See also Eric Larrabee, *Commander in Chief: Franklin Delano Roosevelt, His Lieutenants, and Their War* (New York, 1987); D. Clayton James, *A Time for Giants: The Politics of the American High Command in World War II* (New York, 1987); B. Mitchell Simpson III, *Admiral Harold R. Stark: Architect of Victory, 1939-1945* (Columbia, SC, 1989); and David Eisenhower, *Eisenhower: At War, 1943-1945* (New York, 1986). More critical were three works on Douglas MacArthur published in the 1980s: D. Clayton James's third volume, *The Years of MacArthur: Triumph and Disaster, 1945-1964* (Boston, 1985); Carol M. Petillo's *Douglas MacArthur: The Philippine Years* (Bloomington, 1981); and Michael Schaller's *Douglas MacArthur: The Far Eastern General* (New York, 1989). For Roosevelt's secretary of war see Godfrey Hodgson's *The Colonel: The Life and Wars of Henry Stimson, 1867-1950* (New York, 1990).

and second editions of one of the major syntheses and undergraduate texts in the field, Gaddis Smith's *American Diplomacy during World War II*. When first published in 1965, that volume had clearly illustrated the extent to which Roosevelt's supposed defenders had accepted the critics' assault on his diplomacy. Although Smith had claimed he would analyze the issues in the context of the period 1941–1945 rather than the ensuing Cold War, he did the exact opposite by sharply attacking Roosevelt for placing military considerations before political ones, for having too much faith in a Wilsonian postwar collective security organization, and for efforts to "charm" Stalin that had been based on naive "hopes and illusions" instead of reality. In the preface to the second edition, published in 1985, however, Smith openly admitted that the environment of the early 1960s had led him to be "too harsh" in his judgments and "insufficiently appreciative of the limits of American power and of the intractable obstacles facing even the most conscientious, competent, and well-intentioned leader." Although he did not alter his overall assessment of Roosevelt's postwar policies as a failure, he did conclude that the president had been less naive than he originally thought. He also altered his tone so that there was "less stridency in condemnation" and "a greater effort to understand what Roosevelt sought and why he failed." While continuing to condemn Roosevelt for glossing over deep differences with Stalin and for equating international with domestic disputes (and thus conflicts over ends with conflicts over means), for example, Smith now openly questioned whether American interests, which focused first and foremost on Axis defeat, would have been better served by the open arguments within the tenuous alliance that would have flowed from different policies. He concluded in this regard that the president's approach might have been based on a "deeper realism." Equally noteworthy was the much greater emphasis in the second edition on decolonization as a major wartime issue and on U.S. policies regarding Latin America, the Middle East, and the Far East—especially Korea, China, and Indochina.[41]

Smith's work and others notwithstanding, the promising new synthesis did not continue far into the 1980s. Instead, the second half of that decade witnessed both extensive fragmentation and another massive interpretive debate over World War II diplomacy, one that in many ways repeated with equal intensity and heat those that had taken place in the early 1950s and late 1960s. The focus of the renewed debate was, once again, Franklin Roosevelt's policies toward the Soviet Union. Dallek's 1979 synthesis was essentially the capstone of the defense of Roosevelt-as-realist that had become more and more pronounced throughout the 1960s and 1970s. As such, it was able to subsume the earlier interpretations within this school and, to an extent, those of the New Left critics as well. The schools that had combined in the 1950s and early 1960s to form the original, negative assessment of Roosevelt remained only partially convinced at best, however, and in the mid 1980s they replied. So did some New Left historians from the late 1960s, such as Gar Alperovitz, who, in a second, 1985 edition to his 1965 *Atomic Diplomacy*,

---

[41]Gaddis Smith, *American Diplomacy during the Second World War, 1941–1945*, 2d ed. (New York, 1985), vii–viii, 12–13.

essentially reiterated and defended an updated version of his original interpretation against numerous critics.[42]

For the most part, however, the 1980s critique of U.S. wartime diplomacy echoed earlier criticisms from the right rather than the left and focused on Roosevelt's supposed blunders, naïveté, and failures vis-à-vis the Soviet Union. Smith, as previously noted, retained his 1965 critique of Roosevelt in this regard, albeit in milder form. Attacks also emerged in two 1985 studies of the previously neglected 1943 Cairo and Tehran summit conferences, Keith Eubank's *Summit at Teheran* and Keith Sainsbury's *The Turning Point*. Both historians saw Tehran as the pivotal wartime summit, one that in many ways determined both the agenda for and the results of the later Yalta meeting, and both in effect projected the old criticism of American and Rooseveltian naïveté at Yalta back to this earlier meeting—although for the British Sainsbury, as for Smith, with clear recognition of the numerous limits within which FDR had to work and the dangers posed by an alternative policy of confrontation. Russell D. Buhite revealed a similar depth of understanding in his 1988 *Decisions at Yalta*, while echoing similar criticisms of the president's poor diplomacy. He also criticized FDR for being too concerned with the domestic consequences of failure at Yalta and for even desiring the conference in the first place; summit conferences in general, Buhite concluded, were counterproductive and invited the sorts of misunderstandings and defeats that had taken place in the Crimea.[43]

Nineteen eighty-eight also witnessed the publication of two works more critical of Rooseveltian diplomacy than any published since the 1950s: Robert Nisbet's *Roosevelt and Stalin: The Failed Courtship*, and Frederick W. Marks III's *Wind over Sand*. Nisbet's brief volume essentially updated and reiterated the old assault on Roosevelt for extraordinary naïveté regarding Stalin, with the Tehran Conference replacing Yalta as the place where FDR "played essentially the role Chamberlain had at Munich" and where the Cold War had begun.[44] Marks went even further, arguing that Roosevelt's diplomacy from 1933–1945 had been marked by ambivalence, indecisiveness, narrow domestic motivation, parochialism, and failure. Although most of the volume concerned diplomacy before Pearl Harbor, one chapter extended this attack to the years 1941–1945. "Never was he the absolute prisoner of events," Marks insisted in countering Roosevelt's defenders on relations with Stalin during the war; rather, he "gave away much of his hand in a game whose rules he did not comprehend." Beyond that he "accumulated the largest overseas

---

[42]Gar Alperovitz, *Atomic Diplomacy: Hiroshima and Potsdam*, expanded and updated ed. (New York, 1985). More recently, Diane S. Clemens has provided additional evidence of a policy reversal regarding the Soviets at the time of Roosevelt's death and Truman's ascension to the presidency in her "Averell Harriman, John Deane, the Joint Chiefs of Staff, and the 'Reversal of Co-Operation' with the Soviet Union in April 1945," *International History Review* 14 (May 1992): 277–306.

[43]Keith Eubank, *Summit at Teheran* (New York, 1985); Keith Sainsbury, *The Turning Point: Roosevelt, Stalin, Churchill, and Chiang Kai-shek, 1943: The Moscow, Cairo, and Teheran Conferences* (New York, 1985); Russell D. Buhite, *Decisions at Yalta: An Appraisal of Summit Diplomacy* (Wilmington, DE, 1986). See also Paul D. Mayle, *Eureka Summit: Agreement in Principle and the Big Three at Tehran, 1943* (Newark, DE, 1987).

[44]Robert Nisbet, *Roosevelt and Stalin: The Failed Courtship* (Washington, 1988), 12. See also directly below.

credibility gap of any president on record," was contemptuously disliked by his overseas contemporaries, and was the "fitting symbol" for an American "age of delayed adolescence in international affairs."[45]

This renewed assault on Roosevelt was clearly linked to the domestic and international environments of the 1980s, which differed substantially from those of the 1970s. Most important in this regard was the rise of the neoconservative movement and the revival of the Cold War that accompanied Ronald Reagan's election to the presidency in 1980 and the ensuing revival of a Manichaean worldview that labeled the Soviet Union the "evil empire." The late 1980s will probably be remembered in history as the time of the great "thaw" and the end of the Cold War, but the first half of the decade witnessed, as one popular college text in U.S. diplomatic history aptly noted in 1988, "some of the gloomiest and scariest times in the Cold War."[46] Along with this came a revival of the view that cooperation with the Soviet Union was and always had been impossible given its ideology, and that Roosevelt had thus been a fool to try it.

In 1985, the fortieth anniversary of the war's end, the neoconservative journal *Commentary* published a series of articles from Roosevelt's British and American critics that hammered away at these points. The British criticism came from Sir John Colville, Churchill's personal secretary, whose extensive and revealing diaries had just been published.[47] Although Colville carefully noted the impact of the decision-making vacuum created by Roosevelt's death in 1945, he also blasted the president's naïveté and blunders regarding the Soviets in terms that seemed to repeat *verbatim* the criticisms Bullitt, Wilmot, Baldwin, and others had uttered more than three decades earlier. The three Allies had won the war, Colville began in a virtual paraphrase of Bullitt's 1948 contention, but "it was the Soviets who won the peace" due to the president's naïveté, his "complete sellout to Stalin" at Yalta regarding Poland, the narrowly military and apolitical perspective of the admirals and generals who took over as his health declined, and the anti-British bias of most U.S. policymakers due to their negative view of colonialism. In a *Commentary* symposium a few months later on U.S. foreign policy since 1945, four of the respondents directly or indirectly supported Colville. The indirect support came from neoconservative writer Irving Kristol, who ranked Yalta as one of the nation's three "major and costly mistakes" since 1945 (Suez and Vietnam were the other two), and former UN ambassador Jeane Kirkpatrick, who noted that the international organization so central to Roosevelt's position at Yalta had been based on a wartime American "falsification" regarding the nature of the Soviet Union. The direct support came from Lionel Abel and Robert Nisbet. Abel attacked the liberal view of foreign policy in general and held Roosevelt personally responsible for the "terrible" decisions Colville had described. Nisbet blasted Roosevelt for "credulity" regarding Stalin, "pathetic ignorance of political history and

---

[45]Frederick W. Marks III, *Wind over Sand: The Diplomacy of Franklin Roosevelt* (Athens, GA, 1988), 172, 260, 287.

[46]Thomas G. Paterson, J. Garry Clifford, and Kenneth J. Hagan, *American Foreign Policy: A History*, vol. 2, *Since 1900*, 3d ed. (Lexington, MA, 1988), 658.

[47]Colville, *The Fringes of Power*.

geopolitics," and "colossal naivete," while maintaining that his more realistic successors had been tremendously hampered in the Cold War by the "pro- or at least anti-anti-Soviet" view of "substantial parts" of the American public, that is, the liberals.[48]

In an early 1986 issue of the *New York Review of Books*, an aroused Theodore Draper launched a massive counterattack against this "neoconservative history," which he bluntly labeled, in a thinly veiled reference to McCarthyism, another effort to make history "serve current political extremism." Making extensive use of the previous decade's defenses of Roosevelt and attacks on Churchill as well as of Warren F. Kimball's recently published complete Roosevelt-Churchill correspondence,[49] Draper maintained that the Red Army, rather than Roosevelt, had given Stalin control of Eastern Europe, that conservatives such as John Foster Dulles had supported the same "illusions and compromises" as FDR, and that "the Western allies did not give away anything at Yalta that they actually had; they did get some promissory notes which they could not cash in once Stalin decided to stop payments." The "defamatory fury" of the neoconservative assault on Roosevelt, he bluntly concluded, an assault guilty of "ignorance and effrontery," had "less to do with the past than with the present"—that is, the neoconservative ideology and its hatred of "liberal internationalism." Despite the rhetorical similarity to earlier conservatism, this ideology was actually a new and extreme fusion of isolationism and interventionism whose real enemy and target were domestic liberals, a group the neoconservatives had once belonged to and one they were thus now attacking via historical character assassination as a means of displacing their own guilt for previous actions.[50]

The ensuing rejoinders made such language appear mild in comparison. Nisbet accused Draper of misreading and misrepresenting the Churchill-Roosevelt correspondence, while Abel labeled Roosevelt "the accomplice of Stalin—as is Mr. Draper by defending him—in the enslavement of Eastern Europe." Draper in turn labeled Abel's comments a McCarthyite "political obscenity," and Nisbet's a "largely fraudulent" misuse of documents that he doubted would be tolerated from an undergraduate.[51] In an only somewhat milder retrospective on this battle of words in *Commentary* a few months later, political scientist Paul Seabury attacked Draper's "near hysterical defamation" as well as his "tortured attempt" to paint Churchill as unrealistic and insisted that Roosevelt had "abandoned politics" and concerned himself

---

[48]John Colville, "How the West Lost the Peace in 1945," *Commentary* 80 (September 1985): 41–47; "How Has the United States Met Its Major Challenges since 1945: A Symposium," ibid. (November 1985): 25–28, 50–52, 56–60, 73–76.

[49]Kimball, ed., *Churchill & Roosevelt*.

[50]Theodore Draper, "Neoconservative History," *New York Review of Books*, 16 January 1986. Melvyn P. Leffler went even further than Draper in "Adherents to Agreements: Yalta and the Experiences of the Early Cold War," *International Security* 11 (Summer 1986): 88–123, by questioning whether Stalin was the only one who decided to "stop payments" on the Yalta accords. In a balanced and detailed assessment clearly influenced by recent Soviet-American tensions and charges, he concluded that each power had complied with some components of the accords while disregarding others and that Washington had used supposed Soviet violations as a "convenient lever" to excuse its own.

[51]*New York Review of Books*, 24 April 1986.

solely with military victory.[52] These were far from the final words in the debate. Nisbet followed with a two-part article in *Modern Age*, which he expanded into his previously mentioned 1988 book, and Draper with a three-part review of David Eisenhower's wartime biography of his grandfather that emphasized his politico-military realism and the centrality of the Soviet war effort to all U.S. strategy and diplomacy; in 1988 he republished all these essays in *A Present of Things Past.*[53] Interestingly, although many of the participants in this debate were scholars, not one was a U.S. diplomatic historian. Clearly, World War II diplomacy remained a heated issue of concern to many beyond the profession and specialization, with this particular confrontation boldly revealing its continued link to both the state of the Cold War and domestic politics.

Draper, of course, was far from the only defender of Roosevelt and U.S. World War II diplomacy during the 1980s. Most of the previously cited works published during the decade provided at least partial defenses. They tended to echo Draper and Dallek, however, in emphasizing the domestic and international constraints under which the president had to work and thus his lack of viable alternatives regarding the Soviet Union. Warren F. Kimball, who in 1984 had published with detailed commentary the entire Churchill-Roosevelt correspondence, challenged this conclusion in his 1991 *The Juggler*, a series of essays seeking to comprehend Roosevelt's assumptions and worldview as well as his specific actions. Such an analysis was more an exploration and explanation than a defense of Roosevelt's ideas and policies, but in the environment of the 1980s simply to argue that FDR possessed an overall vision and made logical choices was to defend him from severe critics like Marks. Similarly, Kimball's use of "liberal" as a key descriptive term for the president's vision rather than as an epithet, and his equation of liberalism with "Americanism," constituted a powerful if indirect defense of Roosevelt against the neoconservative assault.[54]

Reinforcement for both sides in this renewed debate came from scholars working with the thin but growing trickle of available Soviet sources. Many of them emphasized Stalin's caution, pragmatism, and lack of any overall "master plan" during the war years, as well as his desire to obtain limited gains within a framework of continued collaboration with his wartime allies. They disagreed, however, on how extensive his aims actually were and on whether a clear definition of acceptable limits by FDR and Churchill during the war would have made any difference. Vojtech Mastny and William Taubman saw those aims as quite extensive and were highly critical of

---

[52]Paul Seabury, "Yalta and the Neoconservatives," *Commentary* 82 (August 1986): 47–49.

[53]Nisbet, *Roosevelt and Stalin*; Theodore Draper, "Eisenhower's War," *New York Review of Books*, 25 September and 9 and 23 October 1986, reproduced along with his "Neoconservative History" in *A Present of Things Past: Selected Essays* (New York, 1990), 3–66, 247–65.

[54]Warren F. Kimball, *The Juggler: Franklin Roosevelt as Wartime Statesman* (Princeton, 1991); idem, *Churchill & Roosevelt*. See also Kimball's "Franklin D. Roosevelt: Dr. Win-the-War," in *Commanders in Chief: Presidential Leadership in Modern Wars*, ed. Joseph G. Dawson III (Lawrence, 1993), 87–105; and Gary R. Hess's defense of Roosevelt as a "practical idealist" in his brief survey, *The United States at War, 1941–1945* (Arlington Heights, IL, 1986). Roosevelt biographer Frank Freidel's final volume, *Franklin D. Roosevelt: A Rendezvous with Destiny* (Boston, 1990), offers a more traditional analysis and defense of Roosevelt's wartime diplomacy. See also directly below.

Roosevelt's refusal to provide such a definition, although they held that postwar Soviet suspicion, hostility, and aggression would have resulted from any U.S. policy.[55] Similar criticisms and conclusions appeared in Edward M. Bennett's 1990 study of Roosevelt's wartime policy toward the Soviet Union, but alongside a strong defense of FDR's overall approach and record. Although he joined Mastny and others in criticizing Roosevelt for numerous errors in his dealings with Stalin, most notably his procrastination on territorial settlements that could have limited postwar Soviet influence in Eastern Europe and the excessive faith he placed in the ability of a postwar United Nations to settle great-power disputes, Bennett concluded that FDR's pragmatic approach to Soviet-American relations did secure his primary objectives of Axis defeat and "far more than the twenty-five years of peace he once said he hoped to ensure."[56]

Debate during the 1980s was by no means limited to assessments of Soviet-American diplomacy. The decade also witnessed an outpouring of scholarship on major British figures during the war, most notably Martin Gilbert's completion of the multivolume official biography of Churchill,[57] and on Anglo-Soviet as well as Anglo-American relations during the conflict. These also provided ammunition for both sides in the debate over U.S. policies. Although the biographical studies tended to defend the British position in Anglo-American wartime disputes, the studies of Anglo-Soviet relations were marked by detailed analyses of disagreements within the British government over Soviet policy and conclusions just as polarized as those to be found in the decade's studies of U.S.-Soviet diplomacy. Examining those relations during the early years of the war, for example, Gabriel Gorodetsky and Steven Merritt Miner reached diametrically opposed conclusions. Gorodetsky sharply criticized Churchill and some of his advisers for a virtual nonpolicy, if not an anti-Soviet one, and implied that the more cooperative approach supported by Ambassador Sir Stafford Cripps as well as by Roosevelt might have avoided the Cold War if implemented. Miner, on the other hand, sharply criticized the British for trying to appease Stalin and pointed to the hard-line American opposition to territorial settlements in 1942 as the policy London should have followed.[58] Ironically, the procooperation

---

[55]Vojtech Mastny, *Russia's Road to the Cold War: Diplomacy, Warfare, and the Politics of Communism, 1941–1945* (New York, 1979); William Taubman, *Stalin's American Policy: From Entente to Detente to Cold War* (New York, 1982). For different conclusions see William O. McCagg, *Stalin Embattled, 1943–1948* (Detroit, 1978); Martin McCauley, *The Origins of the Cold War* (London, 1983); Albert Resis, "The Churchill-Stalin Secret 'Percentages' Agreement on the Balkans, Moscow, October 1944," *American Historical Review* 83 (April 1978): 368–87; and idem, "Spheres of Influence in Soviet Wartime Diplomacy," *Journal of Modern History* 53 (September 1981): 417–39.

[56]Edward M. Bennett, *Franklin D. Roosevelt and the Search for Victory: American-Soviet Relations, 1939–1945* (Wilmington, DE, 1990), 183–88.

[57]See in particular Martin Gilbert, *Winston S. Churchill*, vol. 7, *Road to Victory, 1941–1945* (Boston, 1986). See also Elisabeth Barker, *Churchill and Eden at War* (London, 1978); David Fraser, *Alanbrooke* (New York, 1982); Raymond A. Callahan, *Churchill: Retreat from Empire* (Wilmington, DE, 1984); and Alex Danchev, *Very Special Relationship: Field-Marshal Sir John Dill and the Anglo-American Alliance, 1941–1944* (London, 1986).

[58]Gabriel Gorodetsky, *Stafford Cripps' Mission to Moscow, 1940–1942* (Cambridge, England, 1984); Steven Merritt Miner, *Between Churchill and Stalin: The Soviet Union, Great Britain, and the Origins of the Grand Alliance* (Chapel Hill, 1988). See also Arnold A. Offner, "Uncommon Ground: Anglo-American-Soviet Diplomacy, 1941–1942," *Soviet Union/Union*

Gorodetsky thereby indirectly provided Roosevelt's anticooperation critics with additional ammunition, while the anticooperation Miner did the same for Roosevelt's defenders.

As this irony clearly reveals, by the late 1980s the earlier conflicting schools of interpretation had become hopelessly confused as a result of this complex outpouring of scholarship and polemics. Indeed, by decade's end at least five separate positions on Roosevelt and U.S. wartime diplomacy, distinct from yet related to the earlier positions of the 1950s and 1960s, were clearly visible. At one extreme stood Roosevelt-as-ultimate-realist, a position supported by both FDR defenders, who praised this realism while emphasizing the domestic and international limits under which he had to work, and some New Left critics, who attacked it as aggressive. At the other extreme was Roosevelt the naive and idealistic blunderer who had never understood the Soviet Union or international relations, a reiteration by neoconservatives and revisionists of the charges originally leveled during the late 1940s and 1950s. In between were at least three composites: Roosevelt the realist who actually had more maneuverability than he thought and who therefore could have done better than he did to check the Soviets; Roosevelt the skillful pragmatist who unfortunately worked under a series of mistaken conceptions regarding the Soviet Union; and Roosevelt the combined "idealist/realist" who possessed a clear and defensible vision of a reformed international order and who chose to compromise that vision because of wartime exigencies and dilemmas.

Where one stood on this spectrum seemed to depend not only on one's politics in the 1980s and reading of the documents but also on whether one was a believer in the "Yalta"or the "Riga" axioms regarding the USSR that Daniel Yergin had posited in 1977.[59] Although artificial and overstated, this dichotomy remains as useful for understanding contemporary World War II historiographical disputes as the origins of the Cold War—if not more so. For one's opinion of Roosevelt's policies vis-à-vis the Soviet Union does depend to a large extent upon whether one views that nation as simply a traditional Great Power with whom compromise was possible or as an ideological monstrosity incapable of cooperation or normal diplomatic behavior.

Soviétique 18 (1991): 237–57; Roy Douglas, *From War to Cold War, 1942–1948* (New York, 1981); Martin Kitchen, *British Policy towards the Soviet Union during the Second World War* (New York, 1986); Graham Ross, ed., *The Foreign Office and the Kremlin: British Documents on Anglo-Soviet Relations, 1941–1945* (Cambridge, England, 1984); Victor Rothwell, *Britain and the Cold War, 1941–1947* (London, 1982); Julian Lewis, *Changing Direction: British Military Planning for Post-war Strategic Defence, 1942–1947* (London, 1988); Ann Deighton, ed., *Britain and the First Cold War* (New York, 1990); P. M. H. Bell, *John Bull and the Bear: British Public Opinion, Foreign Policy and the Soviet Union, 1941–1945* (London, 1990); David Reynolds, "The 'Big Three' and the Division of Europe, 1945–48: An Overview," *Diplomacy & Statecraft* 1 (July 1990): 111–36; and Watt, "Yalta and the Cold War," 85–98. Watt argues that British scholarship, unimpressed by New Left revisionism but deeply affected by events in Europe, moved in very different directions during the 1970s and 1980s and should continue to do so. "Failing the release of new evidence, which only the Soviet authorities can authorize," he concluded in 1989, "further debate will be only for the obsessed, not for the most active and able of British historians today." The recent release of such evidence, discussed below, as well as the debate described above, obviously call into question such a conclusion.

[59]Daniel Yergin, *Shattered Peace: The Origins of the Cold War and the National Security State* (Boston, 1977), rev. ed. (New York, 1990).

Reinforcing the importance of one's politics and preconceived notions regarding the USSR in assessing U.S. diplomacy during World War II was Roosevelt's notorious secrecy and deviousness, which, despite the enormous volume of his papers, resulted in a paucity of meaningful and clear statements of what he truly believed. In 1942 he revealingly told his military chiefs to alter strategic memorandums that he feared future historians would interpret as a proposal to abandon England. He also informed Secretary of State Cordell Hull that publication of notes taken at the 1919 Paris Peace Conference should be postponed and that such notes never should have been taken in the first place. And when the secretary of the Joint Chiefs of Staff tried to take notes at a wartime presidential meeting, Roosevelt, according to General George C. Marshall, "blew up."[60]

Even when FDR did break down and say something meaningful for the record, one was often unsure if it was what he really thought, or even of what it meant. One of the most notable examples in this regard was the president's comment to Churchill in March 1942 that he personally knew how to "handle" Stalin in regard to the demand for recognition of Soviet territorial conquests in Eastern Europe in 1939–40. In their 1986 debate, Nisbet and Draper both used this document, Nisbet to illustrate the president's naïveté vis-à-vis Stalin and Draper to illustrate his hard-headed realism in opposing recognition and in taking the initiative from Churchill, who was ready to grant recognition.[61] One could almost hear the ghost of the Hyde Park squire laughing as scholars argued over what in the world he had meant by this and similar comments, as well as empathize with Henry Stimson's 1940 lament that speaking with FDR was "like chasing a vagrant beam of sunshine around a vacant room."[62] One of Roosevelt's recent biographers, relating a "recurrent and maddening dream" about card games with his subject during which FDR would from time to time "wink, take a card from his hand, and slip it inside his jacket," has aptly concluded that "it's safe to say . . . all of Franklin Roosevelt's cards were never on the table."[63]

While scholars of Roosevelt and the Grand Alliance continued to argue throughout the 1980s, other diplomatic historians proceeded during this time to explore the new areas and approaches being illuminated by social scientists and social/cultural historians as they applied to World War II. In doing so they began to alter the terms of the debate over wartime diplomacy by redefining the major issues, questions, and themes to be addressed. The pathbreaking

---

[60]Mark A. Stoler, "The 'Pacific First' Alternative in American World War II Strategy," *International History Review* 2 (July 1980): 442; Burns, *Roosevelt*, 427–28; Larry I. Bland, ed., *George C. Marshall Interviews and Reminiscences* (Lexington, VA, 1991), 623. The very volume of Roosevelt's papers, according to adviser Rexford Tugwell, was "a gigantic trap for historians," who would be kept too busy "to ask embarrassing questions." Citing this quotation as well as FDR's tampering with the documentary record, one recent biographer has concluded that "Roosevelt was confident that he would enjoy a favorable historical reputation, to be sure; but just to be on the safe side, he took certain precautions." See Patrick J. Maney, *The Roosevelt Presence: A Biography of Franklin Delano Roosevelt* (New York, 1992), 194.

[61]Kimball, *Churchill & Roosevelt* 1:421, and footnotes 49–51 above.

[62]Stimson Diary, 18–19 December 1940, as quoted in Warren F. Kimball, *The Most Unsordid Act: Lend-Lease, 1939–1941* (Baltimore, 1969), 4.

[63]Geoffrey Ward, "On Writing about FDR," *American Heritage* 23 (Summer 1991): 119.

works of Christopher Thorne, Akira Iriye, John Dower, and others in the realms of multiarchival research and the comparative cultural approach of the new international history have already been noted in this regard.[64] Equally notable was an increasing emphasis on bureaucratic politics as an explanation for U.S. wartime policies. While historians such as J. Garry Clifford, Theodore Wilson, Irvine Anderson, and Jonathan Utley focused on this mode of analysis to explain those policies prior to Pearl Harbor, others, such as William Roger Louis, Philip J. Baram, Randall B. Woods, Leon Martel, and this author, used it as one of their major tools for analyzing wartime policies and disputes regarding decolonization, global strategy, postwar allied relations, and relations with Latin America and the Middle East.[65]

In one sense, this was nothing new; analysis of disagreements within Roosevelt's notoriously chaotic bureaucracy had always been part of World War II diplomatic histories, and the archival openings of the 1970s enabled historians to trace in detail internal disagreements and their resolution within the policymaking process. Some scholars began to argue, however, that social science theories of bureaucratic behavior were central to understanding why as well as how specific policies had been initiated and implemented. This argument held profound consequences for the debate over Roosevelt and U.S. diplomacy in that it implicitly rejected FDR's centrality by denying his ability, or that of any other single individual, to dictate or implement policy. U.S. diplomacy, these scholars maintained, often emerged from a welter of bureaucratic desires and conflicts that bore little if any relationship to U.S. interests or to what Roosevelt had desired—or ordered.[66]

Political scientist Leon Sigal's 1988 *Fighting to a Finish* boldly illustrated the revolutionary consequences of such an analysis. Making use of the bureaucratic and "non-rational actor" models that Graham Allison had earlier developed to analyze the 1962 Cuban missile crisis, Sigal dismissed all previous interpretations of the atomic bomb/Japanese surrender controversy by arguing that neither the United States nor Japan had followed any rational plan for ending the war. Rather, different segments of the bureaucracy in each country had proposed policies geared to their own worldviews and self-aggrandizement. Although Japanese army and navy leaders planned for a

---

[64]See above, footnotes 34 and 38. See also Iriye's chapter on "Culture and International History," in Hogan and Paterson, eds., *Explaining the History of American Foreign Relations*, 214–25.

[65]For a discussion of bureaucratic politics as a model and the relevant literature see J. Garry Clifford, "Bureaucratic Politics," in Hogan and Paterson, eds., *Explaining the History of American Foreign Relations*, 141–50. See also Irvine H. Anderson, Jr., *The Standard-Vacuum Oil Company and United States East Asian Policy* (Princeton, 1975); J. Garry Clifford and Samuel R. Spencer, *The First Peacetime Draft* (Lawrence, 1986); Jonathan G. Utley, *Going to War with Japan, 1937–1941* (Knoxville, 1985); Theodore A. Wilson, *The First Summit: Roosevelt and Churchill at Placentia Bay, 1941*, rev. ed. (Lawrence, 1991); Louis, *Imperialism at Bay*; Baram, *The Department of State and the Middle East*; Woods, *The Roosevelt Foreign Policy*; idem, *A Changing of the Guard: Anglo-American Relations, 1941–1946* (Chapel Hill, 1990); Martel, *Lend-Lease*; Stoler, *Politics of the Second Front*; idem, "The 'Pacific-First' Alternative," 432–52; and idem, "From Continentalism to Globalism: General Stanley D. Embick, the Joint Strategic Survey Committee, and the Military View of American National Policy during the Second World War," *Diplomatic History* 6 (Summer 1982): 303–21.

[66]Gabriel Kolko had been one of the first scholars to reject Roosevelt's centrality in his 1968 *The Politics of War*, but hardly on the basis of bureaucratic politics or a split between U.S. policies and U.S. interests.

massive "final battle" to impress the Americans, they did so with different times and different locations in mind. Similarly, each segment of the U.S. defense establishment supported the dropping of atomic bombs for different bureaucratic reasons, none of which constituted a rational strategy to bring about Japan's surrender.[67]

Culture and bureaucratic politics were by no means the only new areas to be explored in the 1970s and 1980s. Major analyses focusing on gender, ideology, psychology, corporatism, "mental maps," public opinion, world systems, national security, balance of power, and international organization as explanations of U.S. foreign relations in general also emerged during these decades.[68] Although only a few of the new studies focused exclusively on World War II, that conflict played an important role in many of them. Numerous gender studies, for example, emphasized the complex impact of the war on American women as well as the relationship among gender, ideology, and war in general. In a fascinating 1975 article, Alan Henrikson explored the dramatic shift that had occurred in the American mental map of the globe during World War II and its impact on the origins of the Cold War.[69] Thomas G. Paterson, Les Adler, and Edward Mark similarly analyzed the impact of World War II on American ideological perceptions of Stalin and the Soviet Union, while Melvin Small, Ralph Levering, and others focused on wartime public opinion of the Soviet Union. Scholars also examined numerous other aspects of public opinion, with more than one asking if this might not be the key motivating factor in FDR's postwar planning.[70] Thomas Campbell and, more recently, Robert Hilderbrand explored the triumph of purely national over truly international definitions of security in the wartime formulation of the postwar international security organization, and Melvyn P. Leffler carefully noted the importance of the World War II experience in the

---

[67]Leon V. Sigal, *Fighting to a Finish: The Politics of War Termination in the United States and Japan, 1945* (Ithaca, 1988). See also J. Samuel Walker, "The Decision to Use the Bomb: A Historiographical Update," *Diplomatic History* 14 (Winter 1990): 97–114; Graham T. Allison, *Essence of Decision: Explaining the Cuban Missile Crisis* (Boston, 1971); Martel, *Lend-Lease*; and Sherry, *The Rise of American Air Power.*

[68]All of these approaches are summarized in Hogan and Paterson, eds., *Explaining the History of American Foreign Relations.* See also directly below.

[69]Ibid., 33–35, 177–92; Alan Henrikson, "The Map as an 'Idea': The Role of Cartographic Imagery during the Second World War," *The American Cartographer* 2 (April 1975): 19–53.

[70]William C. Widenor, "American Planning for the United Nations: Have We Been Asking the Right Questions?" *Diplomatic History* 6 (Summer 1982): 245–65. On ideology see Les K. Adler and Thomas G. Paterson, "Red Fascism: The Merger of Nazi Germany and Soviet Russia in the American Image of Totalitarianism, 1930's–1950's," *American Historical Review* 75 (April 1970): 1046–64, revised and reprinted in Thomas G. Paterson, *Meeting the Communist Threat: Truman to Reagan* (New York, 1988), 3–17; and Edward Mark, "October or Thermidor? Interpretations of Stalinism and the Perception of Soviet Foreign Policy in the United States, 1927–1947," *American Historical Review* 94 (October 1989): 937–62. On public opinion see Ralph B. Levering, *American Opinion and the Russian Alliance, 1939–1945* (Chapel Hill, 1976); and Melvin Small, "How We Learned to Love the Russians: American Media and the Soviet Union during World War II," *The Historian* 36 (May 1974): 455–78. See also Allan M. Winkler, *The Politics of Propaganda: The Office of War Information, 1942–1945* (New Haven, 1978); Holly Cowan Shulman, *The Voice of America: Propaganda and Democracy, 1941–1945* (Madison, 1990); Michael Leigh, *Mobilizing Consent: Public Opinion and American Foreign Policy, 1937–1947* (Westport, 1976); and Richard W. Steele, "American Popular Opinion and the War against Germany: The Issue of a Negotiated Peace, 1942," *Journal of American History* 65 (December 1978): 704–23.

new, global definition of American national security, which he viewed as central to the origins and development of the Cold War. Of related interest and focus were works by Lynn Davis, Geir Lundestad, Edward Mark, and, more recently, Lloyd Gardner that reassessed U.S. wartime attitudes toward spheres of influence.[71]

That these new approaches became increasingly voluminous as the decade of the 1980s came to an end and the 1990s began was far from accidental. Indeed, their rise coincided to an extent with the dramatic changes taking place within Eastern Europe, capped in the years 1989–1991 by the end not only of the Soviet empire but also of the Cold War and even of the Soviet Union itself. These extraordinary events, it appeared, were helping to break the virtual stranglehold the Cold War had held over interpretations of World War II diplomacy for the preceding forty to forty-five years.

Although this may have been true to an extent, it is important to note that all of these new approaches had first appeared while the Cold War was still in progress and that in many ways they reflected changes within America more than changes in its foreign relations. Furthermore, numerous scholars made use of many of these approaches to reassess and reargue the traditional questions about Roosevelt and the origins of the Cold War rather than to explore different themes. And although the dramatic events in Eastern Europe may have indirectly added to the popularity within the profession of different themes, those events were simultaneously laying the groundwork for another generation of Soviet-American World War II studies by accelerating both scholarly contact between the two countries and the long-desired opening of Soviet World War II archives. Without those archives all diplomatic histories of the Grand Alliance had been woefully incomplete; with them, scholars began to glimpse the possibility of researching and writing definitive histories of the coalition from all three national archives, rather than one or two. Consequently, the late 1980s and early 1990s witnessed a continued deluge of scholarship on the Grand Alliance that paralleled and often intersected with the deluge of new approaches to the World War II years.

It is still far too soon to ascertain the results. The past few years have witnessed the publication and translation of some key Soviet documents and reminiscences, as well as revelations regarding both Stalin and a few specific wartime episodes—most notably the Katyn Forest massacre of Polish

---

[71]Thomas M. Campbell, *Masquerade Peace: America's UN Policy, 1944–1945* (Tallahassee, 1973); Robert C. Hilderbrand, *Dumbarton Oaks: The Origins of the United Nations and the Search for Postwar Security* (Chapel Hill, 1990); Melvyn P. Leffler, *A Preponderance of Power: National Security, the Truman Administration, and the Cold War* (Stanford, 1992); Lynn Ethridge Davis, *The Cold War Begins: Soviet-American Conflict over Eastern Europe* (Princeton, 1974); Geir Lundestad, *The American Non-Policy towards Eastern Europe, 1943–1947: Universalism in an Area Not of Essential Interest to the United States* (New York, 1978); Edward Mark, "American Policy toward Eastern Europe and the Origins of the Cold War, 1941–1946: An Alternative Interpretation," *Journal of American History* 68 (September 1981): 313–36; and Lloyd C. Gardner, *Spheres of Influence: The Great Powers Partition Europe, from Munich to Yalta* (Chicago, 1993). On these issues see also Robert A. Divine, *Second Chance: The Triumph of Internationalism in America during World War II* (New York, 1971); Michael S. Sherry, *Preparing for the Next War: American Plans for Postwar Defense, 1941–1945* (New Haven, 1977); Charles F. Brower IV, "Sophisticated Strategist: General George A. Lincoln and the Defeat of Japan, 1944–1945," *Diplomatic History* 15 (Summer 1991): 317–37; and Stoler, "From Continentalism to Globalism," 303–21.

officers.[72] Furthermore, a small group of Soviet, American, and British World War II scholars has been meeting on a regular basis since 1986 to reanalyze the Grand Alliance, and the results of these meetings are in the process of being published in all three countries. The meetings have also influenced recent book-length studies by some of the participants.[73] Release of Soviet documents, however, remains highly erratic, incomplete, and unpredictable.[74] Furthermore, neither the documents released to date nor the post-Cold War international environment has resulted in any resolution of the existing historiographical disputes over U.S. wartime diplomacy. Indeed, two studies of Allied wartime diplomacy in general published in the early 1990s clearly illustrate that, far from resolving the debate, recent events and new Russian documents are merely providing additional ammunition to continue it. In his 1990 *Stalin, Churchill, and Roosevelt Divide Europe*, Remi Nadeau argued that recent revelations of Stalin's atrocities and the speed with which his Eastern European empire was dismantled serve only to reemphasize William Bullitt's 1948 charge that Roosevelt won the war but lost the peace because his innocence and misplaced idealism allowed Europe to be divided in the first place. In his 1991 biographical study of the Big Three, however, Robin Edmonds cited recently published Russian documents as well as U.S. and British sources and recent events to argue that a consistently pragmatic Roosevelt had been largely successful—as had his Big Three colleagues. Although the Grand Alliance had admittedly failed to resolve the contemporary issues of nuclear weapons and the future of Central Europe, he concluded, it had succeeded in totally destroying Nazism and establishing a

---

[72]For a useful but already dated summary see Walter Laqueur, *Stalin: The Glasnost Revelations* (New York, 1990). Recent translated Soviet works include Dmitrii Volkogonov, *Stalin: Triumph and Tragedy* (New York, 1991); Andrei Gromyko, *Memoirs* (New York, 1989); Albert Resis, ed., *Molotov Remembers: Inside Kremlin Politics; Conversations with Felix Chuev* (Chicago, 1993); Nataliya Lebedeva, "The Katyn Tragedy," *International Affairs* 6 (June 1990): 98–115, 144; and Vladimir Abarinov, *The Murderers of Katyn* (New York, 1993). I am grateful to Steven Miner for his assistance and advice regarding this material.

Also noteworthy are five still untranslated, pre-*glasnost* collections of wartime documents from the Soviet Ministry of Foreign Affairs. The most relevant one for U.S. diplomatic historians is *Sovetsko-amerikanskie otnosheniia vo vremia Velikoi Otechestvennoi voiny, 1941–1945: dokumenty i materialy* [Soviet-American relations during the Great Patriotic War, 1941–1945: Documents and materials], 2 vols. (Moscow, 1984). The others consist of parallel two-volume collections on Anglo-Soviet and Franco-Soviet relations, Soviet foreign policy in general during the war, and Soviet policy at the wartime conferences. See Watt, "Yalta and the Cold War," 74 n16, for these works and pre-*glasnost* Soviet diplomatic histories of the war that make use of them.

[73]Selected and revised papers from the first, 1986 Soviet-American conference were published in Russian and English as *Soviet-U.S. Relations, 1933–1942*, ed. W. F. Kimball and G. N. Sevost'ianov (Moscow, 1989). A trilateral volume edited by David Reynolds, Warren F. Kimball, and A. O. Chubarian, *Allies at War: The Soviet, American and British Experience, 1939–1945*, has just been published by St. Martin's Press. Recent diplomatic works by U.S. conference participants include Kimball, *The Juggler*; Gardner, *Spheres of Influence*; Wilson, *The First Summit*; Stoler, *Marshall*; Resis, ed., *Molotov Remembers*; Bennett, *Roosevelt and the Search for Victory*; Miner, *Between Churchill and Stalin*; Woods, *A Changing of the Guard*; Elizabeth Kimball MacLean, *Joseph E. Davies: Envoy to the Soviets* (Westport, 1992); and Hugh D. Philipps, *Between the Revolution and the West: A Political Biography of Maxim M. Litvinov* (Boulder, 1992).

[74]The Cold War International History Project of the Woodrow Wilson Center in Washington, DC, has been making a vigorous, though perhaps vain, effort to keep abreast of these documents insofar as they relate to the Cold War.

sound UN structure—one that was now finally capable of fulfilling its potential.[75]

   As of 1993, recent interpretations of U.S. diplomacy during World War II can thus be divided into two major and separate if overlapping categories: those that make use of the new documentation, approaches, and international environment to reargue the original debate over U.S. and Rooseveltian näiveté; and those that use the new documentation, approaches, and environment to redefine the questions being asked. Although historians have anything but a good track record in the realm of prophecy, it seems safe to conclude that both groups of studies will continue throughout the remainder of the 1990s and beyond. Furthermore, both sets of approaches will probably continue to be visible within a continuing flood of specialized studies that fill in the remaining gaps in the literature, as well as those that perceive new subjects to explore.[76]

   Despite the deluge of studies in the 1970s and 1980s, those gaps are far more numerous than one might imagine. No recent biographies exist, for example, on such pivotal figures as Secretary of State Cordell Hull or Undersecretary of State Sumner Welles, although scholarly works are in progress on both. Similar gaps exist in the study of U.S. wartime relations with individual countries and parts of the world—especially within Africa. The Anglo-Soviet-American wartime conferences have each received multiple book-length treatments, but most of the Anglo-American summit conferences remain neglected.[77]

   Within future works, one should expect continued debates over both Roosevelt's importance vis-à-vis the bureaucracy and his responsibility for the Cold War—despite the demise of that conflict and the Soviet Union. Indeed, although the opening of Soviet archives will enable scholars finally to analyze the alliance from a trilateral perspective, it will probably continue to reinforce

---

[75]Remi Nadeau, *Stalin, Churchill, and Roosevelt Divide Europe* (New York, 1990); Robin Edmonds, *The Big Three: Churchill, Roosevelt, and Stalin in Peace & War* (New York, 1991). See also the conflicting interpretations in the works cited in footnote 73.

[76]The author is well aware of the pitfalls of prophecy and presents these conclusions and projections with great trepidation. That trepidation is only increased by his recognition of how different these pages would have been had they been written in mid-1991, when they were originally due, rather than in 1993! The extraordinary and thoroughly unexpected events of the last two years have clearly influenced the analyses and conclusions expressed here while making clear to the author just how uncertain and subject to change they are.

[77]Jonathan Utley is working on Cordell Hull and Irwin Gellman on the personal interaction among Sumner Welles, Hull, and FDR. For studies of Tehran and Yalta see above, footnotes 4, 8, 9, 18, and 43. See also Richard F. Fenno, Jr., ed., *The Yalta Conference*, 2d ed. (Lexington, MA, 1972); Jean Laloy, *Yalta: Yesterday, Today, Tomorrow*, trans. William R. Tyler (New York, 1988); and Floyd H. Rodine, *Yalta—Responsibility and Response, January–March 1945* (Lawrence, 1974). On Potsdam see Herbert Feis, *Between War and Peace: The Potsdam Conference* (Princeton, 1960); and Charles L. Mee, Jr., *Meeting at Potsdam* (New York, 1975). On Anglo-American meetings, Theodore A. Wilson has completed a major revision of his 1969 study on the 1941 Atlantic Conference, *The First Summit*; and Keith Sainsbury covers the two 1943 Cairo Conferences in *The Turning Point*. The other Anglo-American summits have received no book-length treatment based on archival research. An analysis of some of them based on published documents can be found in Beitzell, *The Uneasy Alliance*, while books on specific issues associated with individual conferences (the atomic bomb and Potsdam; unconditional surrender and Casablanca; the Morgenthau Plan and the second Quebec Conference) often provide important if incomplete material on those meetings.

rather than resolve the old debate. The present direction of Russian scholarship is toward sharper and sharper condemnation of Stalin's policies, condemnation that has already provided additional ammunition for Roosevelt's critics.[78] As previously noted, however, it has also provided ammunition for Roosevelt's defenders. Furthermore, to assume that this anti-Stalin trend will continue indefinitely, or that all of the Soviet documents will support this approach, would be extraordinarily naive. As Russian scholarship develops and as additional archives are opened (assumptions that are in themselves questionable in light of the present uncertainty regarding Russia's political future), sharp disagreements should be expected to take place. Because Stalin was at least as secretive and confusing as Roosevelt, those documents will also in all likelihood be inconclusive. Thus, no final and definitive conclusions may be possible on numerous issues, and the debate over Soviet-American relations during World War II is far from over. A new synthesis does appear to be emerging on Anglo-American wartime relations,[79] but debates continue on Anglo-Soviet relations and Anglo-American wartime conflicts regarding the Soviets.

Along with the continuing debates over Roosevelt and the Cold War, one should expect to see new studies addressing areas of contemporary international concern. These would include, but by no means be limited to, U.S. wartime policies toward the different groups within the former Yugoslavia, Italy's African colonies, Palestine, the Islamic world, Japan, Germany, and international organization. Within these studies a myriad of the new approaches will be used, often in combination. These will tend to further blur the distinctions between diplomatic and other histories in terms of topics and research.

The limits of the new approaches for World War II diplomacy are as unclear as the results of the end of the Cold War. They raise important new questions and provide fresh perspectives, but presently they are not sufficiently numerous or complete to allow substantial conclusions as to their overall impact. Furthermore, the previously mentioned works notwithstanding, many if not most of the diplomatic studies that emphasize these new approaches are strangely silent on the years 1941–1945, even though these years are pivotal for their approach. Corporatist scholars, for example, have so far focused on the years between the two world wars and the years after the second conflict, thereby creating a major gap in their efforts to achieve an

---

[78]It also led to criticism of the view of Stalin as cautious and defensive in foreign affairs. See R. C. Raack, "Stalin's Plans for World War II," *Journal of Contemporary History* 26 (April 1991): 215–27.

Most of the archival revelations and condemnations have focused on Stalin's domestic policies, however, a fact that has led some Roosevelt critics and supporters to debate the relationship between Soviet domestic and foreign policies during the war. It has also led some writers to sweeping conclusions based upon very limited and insufficient evidence. Amos Perlmutter's *FDR & Stalin: A Not So Grand Alliance, 1943–1945* (Columbia, MO, 1993), is the most recent example of such overgeneralization and misuse of very limited archival documentation.

[79]See Reynolds, "Roosevelt, Churchill, and the Wartime Anglo-American Alliance," 17–41, for a detailed analysis.

overall synthesis in U.S. diplomatic history.[80] Specialists in other new areas have devoted greater attention to the years 1941–1945, as already noted. For most of them, however, as for their predecessors in the field, World War II seems to constitute merely a precursor or "seed time" to the really important years that followed.

Such a tendency is completely understandable—and perhaps inevitable. It also has positive consequences in that it links ideas and events in the war years to their full development and results after the achievement of victory in 1945. It is regrettable, however, in that it fails to deal with World War II on its own terms. Indeed, it often distorts U.S. policies during the war by ignoring wartime as opposed to postwar priorities and by sharply separating U.S. diplomacy into pre- and post-Pearl Harbor eras that seem to bear little if any relationship to each other. It also risks a continuation of the Cold War era tendency to project later conflicts, issues, and perspectives onto an earlier time period, as more than one scholar has warned.[81] Rather than more studies that try to cover wartime diplomacy as a precursor to what followed, one would hope to see more studies analyzing that diplomacy on its own, and/or as the result of what preceded it. Such a reconnection of the pre- with the post-Pearl Harbor years may well enable historians not only to better understand World War II diplomacy but also to obtain a truly comprehensive perspective on what Warren Kimball has recently and aptly labeled the nation's wartime transition from "a major power to a superpower," as well as on the global expansion of American interests that took place throughout the 1930s and 1940s.[82]

The present lack of synthesis on U.S. diplomacy during World War II, or even a hint of future synthesis, is far from surprising. The multiple and often conflicting approaches, as well as conclusions, clearly reflect the fragmentation within both the discipline of history and U.S. society as a whole. Nor is this necessarily a sign of weakness. Thomas Paterson recently noted in this regard that the history of U.S. foreign relations in general possesses "a good number" of syntheses, but that diplomatic historians find them "contending or unsatisfying" and that "few subfields of history have produced syntheses that have remained dominant."[83] Clearly this is the case

---

[80]See Michael J. Hogan's "Corporatism" chapter in Hogan and Paterson, eds., *Explaining the History of American Foreign Relations*, 226–36. A recent symposium in the pages of this journal revealed a similar gap among scholars focusing on the roles of culture and gender in foreign relations; the two essays dealt with the pre-Pearl Harbor and the Cold War years, as did much of the ensuing commentary. The years 1942–1945 were thus neatly sandwiched—and either ignored or subordinated to what followed or preceded them. See "Culture, Gender, and Foreign Policy: A Symposium," *Diplomatic History* 18 (Winter 1994): 47–124.

[81]See, for example, D'Ann Campbell, *Women at War with America: Private Lives in a Patriotic Era* (Cambridge, MA, 1984), 213–38. Martin Kitchen provides the most recent scholarly warning against this tendency as applied to the Cold War in *British Policy towards the Soviet Union*.

[82]Warren F. Kimball, ed., *America Unbound: World War II and the Making of A Superpower* (New York, 1992), 1. Other recent notable efforts in this regard include Akira Iriye and Warren Cohen, eds., *American, Chinese, and Japanese Perspectives on Wartime Asia, 1931– 1949* (Wilmington, DE, 1990); Hess, *The United States' Emergence as a Southeast Asian Power, 1940–1950*; Miller, *The United States and Italy, 1940–1950*; and Hurstfield, *The United States and the French Nation, 1939–1945*.

[83]Hogan and Paterson, eds., *Explaining the History of American Foreign Relations*, 43–45.

with U.S. diplomacy during World War II, and clearly, as with the history of U.S. foreign relations in general, the field is flourishing rather than floundering. Within the old framework, continued disagreements will remain linked to the state of Russian-American relations, domestic politics, and one's ideology as well as to the release of new documentation. Similarly, the new frameworks will in all likelihood be heavily influenced by these factors as we pass through the last decade of the century. One hopes that such influences will enlighten more than they distort the 1941–1945 record as we continue to try to come to terms with the enormous impact of World War II on our lives.

The Imperialism of Decolonization

WM. ROGER LOUIS and RONALD ROBINSON

It ought to be a commonplace that the post-war British Empire was
more than British and less than an *imperium*. As it survived, so it was
transformed as part of the Anglo-American coalition. Neglecting the
American role, imperial historians often single out British enfeeblement
as prime cause of an imperial demise.[1] The presumption is that an
imperial state caved in at the centre like Gibbon's Rome, with infirmity
in the metropole and insurgency in the provinces. For the 'Gibbonians',
the Empire therefore ends with political independence. Dependent
though they remained in other ways, the new states are said to be
decolonized.[2] Historians of the cold war necessarily take more account
of invisible empires, but the imperial effects of the trans-Atlantic
alliance are not their concern, except for some writers who suspect that
the expansion of American capitalist imperialism swallowed up the
Empire.[3] Far from being decolonized, in this view, the British system
was neo-colonized more intensively under new management. Each of
these interpretations may be true in some instances, given a particular
definition of empire. The overall picture is none the less confusing. To
see the transformation of an imperial coalition as if it were the collapse
of an imperial state is like mistaking the melting tip for the iceberg.
Without defining the relativities of imperial power, it is hard to tell how
much metropolitan infirmity, nationalist insurgency, and American or
Soviet expansion contributed to whatever happened to the post-war
Empire.

The difficulty of attributing the fall to British decline is that it leads us
into paradox. Colonial emancipation is not necessarily a sign of metropolitan weakness. Virtual independence was conceded to Canadian,
Australasian, and South African nationalists before 1914, when Britain
was at her strongest. Conversely, when she was much weaker during the
inter-war years, the Empire reached its greatest extent, with the
addition of much of the Middle East and more of Africa. By 1940, when
there was scarcely strength to defend the home islands, the British were
able to crack down on nationalists in India, Egypt, and Iran and
mobilize the Empire for war. When peace came, a bankrupt metropole
somehow reconstructed the imperial system in the familiar Victorian
style of trade without rule where possible, rule for trade where

The Journal of Imperial and Commonwealth History, Vol. 22, No. 3, pp.462–511
PUBLISHED BY FRANK CASS, LONDON

necessary. The 'Imperialism of free trade', or rather, of the sterling area continued. Weak or strong, the metropole was clearly not the only source of imperial strength. Gibbon will not help us with these difficulties. How is the survival of the Empire to be explained? Was it in fact decolonized by the 1960s, or informalized as part of the older story of free trade imperialism with a new American twist? It is with the answers given by British and American officials at the time that this article is concerned.

A more refined notion of the ingredients of imperial power is required to explain the Empire's capacity for regenerating on alternative sources of strength and for exchanging informal and formal guises. In peace time the United Kingdom government invested relatively few resources in the imperial upkeep. The British state provided military forces in emergency, a string of bases from Gibraltar to Singapore, and not least the necessary prestige. Whitehall monitored what was in effect a self-generating and self-financing system. It could not have been otherwise. Had ministers tried to project so vast an empire with metropolitan resources, they would have been driven from office before they ruined the country. At the centre of an imperial economy, the international financial and commodity markets of London held the system's bread and butter together, whether the branches were politically dependent or not. Most of Britain's chief trading partners belonged to the sterling area.[4] Imperial preferences encouraged their exchanges. Tight state controls over capital and commodity movements persisted from wartime into the mid-1950s. No longer the hub of a global economy, London remained the central banker and market for the world's largest trading area.[5]

Our hypothesis suggests that, more than a project of the British state, imperial sway by 1939 derived mainly from profit-sharing business and power-sharing with indigenous elites overseas. At the country level, the system relied on unequal accommodations with client rulers or proto-nationalists who multiplied British power locally with their own authority for their own advantage.[6] Contracts could not be too unequal or collaborators would lose their constituents and the system would break down. As local sub-contractors became better organized the terms for co-operation turned progressively in their favour. The final settlement would be with national successors who would secure British economic and strategic assets under informal tutelage. Local bargains could not be struck to imperial advantage if other great powers competed in the bidding. International alliances – at least 'hands-off' arrangements – were essential if the Empire were to be defended and the imperial balance sheets kept out of the red. The object was not that Britain should sustain the Empire, but that the Empire should sustain Britain. From Canning to Churchill, British geo-strategists looked to 'the continuous creation of new sources of power overseas to redress the balance of the Old World'.[7] They once sought those sources of power in Latin America. They found ample reward in India. In the 1900s they looked to the Japanese alliance and the Anglo-French and Anglo-Russian Ententes. They were to turn to the United States. The various local coalitions depended on international alignments to tilt internal and global balances in their favour.

Finally, the system required the tolerance of the British voter. Terms for the metropolitan contract were those of 'empire on the cheap' – that tax payers should not be asked to meet the cost at the expense of their home comforts; that a benign imperial image assuage the latent forces of anti-imperial opinion; that British industry remain strong enough to drive the imperial economy; and that the economic prizes to be won were worth more than the imperial cost of winning them. The state of imperial power at different places and times may therefore be measured in the contracts required to win collaboration and head off resistance at international, metropolitan, and local levels. Bargains were interdependent.[8] As we have argued in an earlier essay,[9] an alteration of terms at one level implied corresponding changes on the others. The Second World War overthrew the balance of pre-war terms. A different Britain re-formed the post-war Empire in another world.

I

Clement Attlee's government faced devastating problems of economic recovery in 1945–46. When American Lend-Lease ended, he protested that the very living conditions of people in the British Isles depended on the continued flow 'both of food and . . . raw materials' from the United States.[10] There were no dollars to pay for them.[11] The cumulative shortfall on current account stood at £10 billions. Even if the economy could be re-jigged to export 75 per cent above pre-war levels, the estimated balance of payments deficit would still be running at over a billion pounds in 1951. Fifteen billion dollars was owing to Washington. Three billion pounds was due to sterling countries, especially to India and Egypt for defence costs. The British were no longer the creditors, but the debtors of the Empire. John Maynard Keynes, the Treasury's most influential adviser, concluded: 'We cannot police half the world at our own expense when we have already gone into pawn to the other half.'[12]

There was no recourse but to go cap in hand for a dollar grant or loan.

With or without the American loan, ministers had to choose between financing their domestic recovery and their imperial commitments. To reduce food rations further was not practical politics. In 1945–46, as in every budget thereafter, the promised welfare state competed with the Empire for scarce resources.[13] The Treasury warned: 'a straight issue would be reached with the Middle East and India. Either they would have to lend us the money for our troops there, or we should have to move our troops out.'[14] Keynes emphasized that, 'the American loan is primarily required to meet the political and military expenditure overseas.' Without it 'a large-scale withdrawal . . . [from our] international responsibilities' was inevitable.[15]

On what terms would Washington with its plans for global free trade agree to underwrite Britain and the Empire?[16] During the eighteen months between the end of the hot war and the beginning of the cold, most Americans regarded empires as obsolete. British claims to world power seemed pathetic. To save their wartime ally from 'starvation corner', Congress wrote off the Lend-Lease debt, but saw no reason to rescue the Empire. In return for a dollar loan of £3.75 billion, which the Canadians topped up to £5 billion, the British were forced to make the pound convertible into the dollar within twelve months. The imperial economy, in effect, was to be dismantled.[17] Meanwhile, nationalist protests against stringent economic controls erupted throughout the dependent Empire. Imperial contracts were falling apart at all levels in 1945–47, as Attlee recognized. 'It may be,' he foresaw in March 1946, 'we shall have to consider the British Isles as an easterly extension of a strategic [arc] the centre of which is the American continent rather than as a Power looking eastwards through the Mediterranean to India and the East.' In Attlee's forthright estimate, 'we cannot afford . . . the great sums of money for the large forces involved.'[18] His acidic foreboding of Britain reduced to a small Empire in Africa seems, in retrospect at least, more realistic than his Foreign Secretary Ernest Bevin's case for holding the Middle East.[19] Much depended on 'what the Americans are prepared to do.'[20]

The Cabinet debate echoed in the Colonial Office where J.S. Bennett argued that 'the United States cannot be expected to underwrite the British Empire either *in toto* or unconditionally. In consequence, the system and objectives of [pre-war] colonial administration . . . no longer correspond to the realities of the situation.' Either the British could 'hang on' until international and related internal pressures became overwhelming, as in India, or they could wind up colonial commitments in the Middle East and South-East Asia in return for 'maximum practical' support from the United States. 'The Colonial

Empire . . . would thus be reduced to Africa, the Pacific and the Caribbean.'[21] But British recovery depended largely on the imperial cohesion of the sterling area. From the economic standpoint, Hilton Poynton commented: 'The point surely is that USA must help the British Empire to underwrite the world.'[22] The issue remained in doubt up to the end of 1947.[23] By that time the Americans were doing a great deal to prop up the Empire, especially in the eastern Mediterranean and the Middle East.[24] Meanwhile the Cabinet withdrew the troops fighting the communists in Greece and gave up the Turkish commitment. They were determined to leave India, Burma, and Ceylon, and they were soon to abdicate in Palestine.

Attlee felt morally obliged to concede Indian independence. For all that, the British were being driven out. The National Congress had gained the momentum of a popular movement in the 1930s, but the outbreak of war put an end to provincial power-sharing with Indian ministers.[25] After crushing the 'Quit India' rising of the Congress in 1942, the Raj relied on Muslim collaborators for the war effort, and alienated its remaining indigenous support. By 1945, the Viceroy, Lord Wavell, could no longer rely on Indian loyalty in the army and public services. The pre-war contracts for local co-operation had run out of time. In John Gallagher's irreverent metaphor, nationalists and imperialists were propping each other up like punch-drunk boxers lest they both fall into chaos. One question only remained – how to find a viable and amenable successor. At the Indian elections of 1946 the avowed British intention to leave in 1948 evoked not one possible successor but two. Fearing entrapment in a terrible communal war, Attlee and Lord Mountbatten, the last Viceroy, brought the departure date forward to 1947. The emergency enabled Mountbatten to settle with Congress for a strong central government over most of the subcontinent. In exchange, Congress yielded to Jinnah's claims to Pakistan.[26] Both new states unexpectedly joined the Commonwealth, which now began its uncomfortable mutation from an English-speaking club to a multi-racial association.[27]

There had been no significant superpower intervention in India, as there was to be in Palestine. Since the Indian empire had always drawn its strength from local allies more than from the metropole, the idea that the British 'transferred power' is a half truth. The other half is that the divided communities once articulated by the Raj had become national-ized. It was the emergence of two national fronts of non-cooperation that drove the bitter transition to a relatively stable and scarcely revolutionary succession. A partition that left the Indian Army[28] divided between two hostile states was the solution that the British had tried above all to avoid.[29] Informal affiliations none the less continued to serve imperial objectives in unforeseen ways.

In Palestine,[30] there were no effective power-sharing contracts to expire.[31] Separate administrative arrangements with the Arab and Jewish communities had been incompatible, especially after the Arab revolt in 1936. As Bevin complained, President Truman's intervention on behalf of Jewish refugees and Zionist aspirations exacerbated the conflict. When the plan for partition gained momentum in 1947, Attlee and Bevin were ready to throw in their hand. Even Churchill insisted on withdrawal: 'there is the manpower of at least 100,000 men in Palestine who might be at home strengthening our depleted industry. . . . What good are we getting out of it?'[32] After the attempt at convertible sterling in July 1947 turned into a disastrous run on the pound and exhausted almost all of the American loan, the imperative to leave Palestine became overwhelming. On 15 May 1948, the British withdrew from an imbroglio in another communal war that was disrupting their Arab alliances throughout the Middle East.[33] Against the advice of the Secretary of State, George C. Marshall, Truman immediately recognized the state of Israel. An American-sponsored government had taken over much of the British Mandate. Zionist contracts with the White House had prevailed. Two can make viable imperial contracts. Three is a crowd. Four is an impossibility. Palestine showed how an intrusive superpower allied with a nationalist revolt could upset the collaborative equations of Empire.

The ensuing Arab–Israeli war eventually forced the Americans to resume their partnership with the British. Washington felt morally obliged to defend Israel while the British were treaty-bound to defend Transjordan.[34] Washington and London could easily be drawn into the war by proxy on opposite sides. 'This must not be allowed to happen,' Truman vowed after his election in November 1948.[35] He compelled the Israelis to withdraw from Egyptian territory by ultimatum,[36] though they acquired the territory of the Negev. At Bevin's request Truman appeased the Arabs by agreeing to incorporate Arab Palestine into British-allied Jordan.[37] The Anglo-American schism over Palestine had to be repaired to bring about an armistice and a *de facto* territorial settlement.

II

As the cold war intensified from 1947 to 1951, competition between the two superpowers came to the rescue of the Empire. Faced with the Czech crisis and the Berlin blockade, the United States hastened to strengthen Britain and France in defence of Western Europe. As Senator Henry Cabot Lodge, Jr., told the Senate Hearings on the North Atlantic Treaty, 'we need . . . these countries to be strong, and they cannot be strong without their colonies'.[38] After the fiasco of convertibility, the dollar underwrote the sterling area up to 1951, and at need thereafter.[39] Under the Truman Doctrine, American power reinforced the traditional imperial 'Great Game' of checking Russian advances into the eastern Mediterranean and the Middle East.[40] By the end of 1947, the American Chiefs of Staff had recommended 'all feasible political, economic, and if necessary military support . . . to the United Kingdom and the communications of the British Commonwealth'.[41] With the Maoist triumph in China and the Korean War, Washington relied on the British and French empires to block Sino-Soviet expansion into the lands on the rim of southern and western Asia. Much as some American officials disliked it, the State Department and the Pentagon found their 'most important collaborators' in the British and their Empire-Commonwealth.[42]

After 1947 the Americans subsidized the imperial system generously in one way or another to defend the United States. Robert Hall of the Cabinet Office summed up the tally in 1951: 'We have had . . . an average of over a billion dollars a year . . . since 1946 and of course under Lend/Lease we had a great deal more. In fact our whole economic life has been propped up in this way.'[43] Keynes had earlier underlined the imperial effect: 'America . . . was underwriting British policy in other parts of the world.'[44] Marshall Plan aid and the Mutual Security programme[45] met the otherwise prohibitive charge on the balance of payments of sustaining British power overseas. The British voter could have his imperial cake and eat at the same time. In return, Bevin undertook to assume the lead in saving Europe for social democracy and 'primary responsibility' for defending the Middle East.[46] With joint policies in Europe and mutual support in Asia,[47] the Empire could rely on the American shield against Sino-Soviet intervention. Aligned with Washington's cold war strategy, the keystone of the reconstituted imperial system was thus the Middle East, a region honeycombed with British air bases and military installations. The oil fields there were as vital to European defence as they were to British prosperity. So too were the tin and rubber of Malaya. Whitehall relied largely on the sterling countries between Suez and Singapore for the dollar earnings required to make up the British trade deficit.[48] The potential of Africa's minerals and vegetable oil was also linked more and more to British recovery. With India and Pakistan hived off and Palestine shrugged aside, the Empire reasserted itself in the Middle East and Africa.

Much of the pre-war Empire survived locally to be slotted into the post-war design. Even so, local continuities masked the basic discontinuity. At metropolitan and international levels British imperial power was substantially an Anglo-American revival. Neither side cared to publish the fact, the one to avoid the taint of imperialism, the other to keep the prestige of Empire untarnished. An imperial coalition was as unnatural for the Americans as it was demeaning for the British. Whether or not the Congress needed a Communist devil to assure the American people of the innocence of their global expansion,[49] Washington's Cold War approach often departed from London's Great Game of Empire. Endless talks were devoted to straddling the divergence to permit concerted action. A consensual if not a common official mind worked to achieve the 'overlap' of inter-dependence in the cold war. It was not merely a question of 'he who pays the piper'.[50] As Bevin analysed the situation in October 1949:

> Western Europe, including its dependent overseas territories, is now patently dependent on American aid . . . The United States recognises that the United Kingdom and the Commonwealth . . . are essential to her defence and safety. Already it is, apart from the economic field, a case of partial inter-dependence rather than of complete dependence. As time goes by [in the next ten to twenty years] the elements of dependence ought to diminish and those of inter-dependence to increase. The United Kingdom in particular, by virtue of her leading position both in Western Europe and in the Commonwealth, ought to play a larger and larger part in a Western system.[51]

Bevin accepted that, 'In all fields in which the United States makes the major contribution, whether financial, military or otherwise, it is inevitable that proportionate (although not always determining) weight must be given to her views.'[52] Dependence could weaken imperial ties. Interdependence could strengthen them. A study of some regional crises will show how much and how little the Anglo-American alliance disturbed the balance of imperial contracts locally.

So long as the cold war left tropical Africa aside, the Americans had few interests and exerted little influence in the colonial management. In 1948 Attlee's ministers faced a crisis in British West Africa when riots in Ghana[53] and strikes in Nigeria threatened colonial control. Dissatisfied with low prices from colonial marketing boards and inflated charges for British imports, the dollar-earning cocoa farmers and palm oil collectors were turning for economic relief to national leaders. Drs Nkrumah and

Azikiwe campaigned for immediate independence. The British took account of American and international anti-colonial opinion.[54] But the balance of payments deficit, together with the Labour Party's expectations of a better deal for African workers, convinced the Cabinet that the iron hand of economic control required the velvet glove of power-sharing.[55] The quasi-democratic reforms of 1951–52 in Ghana and Nigeria aimed at bringing conservative chiefs and their moderate nationalist spokesmen into executive government. The popularity of the traditional allies of colonial administration would thus be strengthened against their radical critics.[56] By this route, the two dependencies were expected to achieve self-government 'within a generation'.[57] Their connection with the imperial economy eventually would be politically informalized within the Commonwealth.

In British central Africa it was white rather than black nationalists who brought about a crisis from 1949 onwards. Roy Welensky, the European leader in the dependency of Northern Rhodesia, could halt the copper mines on which the British economy and large American stock-piling contracts depended. Sir Godfrey Huggins, the premier of self-governing Southern Rhodesia, controlled the railways required for mineral export. To expand the dollar-earning capacity of the region, the agitation of the European miners and tobacco farmers against colonial control had to be appeased. By 1953, under a Tory government, the velvet glove of power-sharing took the shape of a white Rhodesian federation imposed on the black majority.[58]

Under the impact of the Far Eastern crisis in 1949–51, imperial Anglo-Americanism solidified, though with many a crack, from Europe and the Middle East to eastern and southern Asia. Once the People's Republic had driven the Kuomintang regime out of mainland China, Soviet-allied power seemingly dominated the Euro-Asian land mass. As the global balance shifted in July 1949, Dean Acheson, the Secretary of State, accepted Bevin's invitation to make 'a trip around the world . . . in a matey sort of way' to see whether Britain and the United States might pursue a common policy against the spread of communism in the Far East.[59] In a series of private talks they reached a workable consensus in every area but one. To save the Hong Kong trade and to accommodate the Indian championing of the principle of pan-Asian self-determination, the British insisted on recognizing Communist China. The Americans by contrast still recognized and protected Chiang Kai-shek's Nationalist government on Taiwan. With the unexpected outbreak of the Korean War in June 1950, the two policies undercut each other. Taiwan now acquired strategic significance in the American defence of Japan and the Pacific. Acheson told Bevin that if the British wanted their global common front, they had better not keep asking the Americans to abandon Taiwan.[60]

The rift widened in the vicissitudes of late 1950 in the Korean War, despite the common UN cause. A token British force belatedly joined the Americans in repelling the North Korean invasion. But 'it was almost universally felt in England that MacArthur had provoked the [subsequent] Chinese attack in N. Korea' by advancing to the Yalu River and bombing North Korea.[61] Consequently the left wing of virtually all of Attlee's government feared that General MacArthur, if not President Truman (who had admitted the possible use of atomic weapons), was bent on reconquering China for Chiang Kai-shek. Much more important, the allies in NATO bristled at the prospect of the United States becoming absorbed in a major Asian war that could leave Europe undefended.[62]

It was usually the Americans who warned the Europeans of the penalties for aggressive imperialism in the cold war, but when Attlee flew to Washington in December 1950, the imperial boot was on the other foot. The Prime Minister in effect admonished the President against allowing MacArthur any more scope for what most European socialists and Asian nationalists regarded as American imperialist intervention in China.[63] If the American people could not rely on their allies in the East, Truman remarked, they would no longer subscribe to a common front in the West.[64] None the less, the two leaders agreed to put real teeth into NATO. Attlee undertook the trebling of British defence expenditure over the next three years.[65] The Americans promised to 'pick up the tab' on the balance of payments costs.[66] Much of the Anglo-American wartime apparatus for allocating strategic supplies globally was reactivated in the Korean emergency. The reuniting of priorities was symbolized by the recall of MacArthur from Korea four months later and the advent of Eisenhower as Supreme Commander, Europe.[67] The Prime Minister and the President agreed to differ over China for the sake of their 'identity of interests generally throughout the world'. In view of 'Korean aggression', their subordinate officials laid the ground for dealing with other Soviet-inspired Koreas anticipated in Greece, Germany, Iran, and South-East Asia.[68]

The ambivalence of Washington as a centre of Western imperial power[69] emerged sharply in 1949 when Secretary Acheson and Ernest Bevin discussed the domino effect of a Communist China on South-East Asia. In 'a turmoil of revolutionary nationalism' left by the Japanese retreat, the French in Indo-China as well as the Dutch in Indonesia were fighting to regain colonial control. Their intransigence, the State Department believed, was 'doomed to ultimate failure'. They were driving nationalists into the arms of the communists at the cost of draining men and money away from 'the revitalization of Western Europe'. On the other hand, it was feared, 'the only alternative to imperial rule is chaos in Indonesia and communism in Indochina'. European 'self-support' depended on the 'economic attachment' of these areas to their respective metropoles. To ride 'rough-shod' over European pride would strain vital NATO alliances.[70] This was to be the American dilemma wherever colonial empires became involved in the cold war.[71]

Bevin agreed with Acheson on the only way to square the circles of local and international collaboration in this region. They fruitlessly pressed the French and Dutch to follow the American example in the Philippines and to do what the British had done in India and were doing in Malaya.[72] The French and Dutch colonial presence would have to take on the mantle of informal association. Anything that looked like imperialism or Western dictation, Bevin warned, would alienate the newly independent countries of southern Asia. But the Western Allies, with their strategic priorities in Europe and in the Far East, had few resources left for the area. South-East Asia must be persuaded to defend itself, with Indian support.[73] Given political independence, the nationalists would stand on their own feet against the communists. A relatively small amount of economic and military aid from the West would win their alliance and secure Europe's economic assets. Then, as British and American officials agreed, the Western powers could 'keep out of the limelight' and 'pull the strings whenever necessary'.[74]

American anti-colonialism evidently did not extend to informal sway; nor after the outbreak of the Korean War in June 1950 did it run to handing over colonies to communists or to chaos. American subsidies for the defence of Indo-China against the communist Viet-Minh by 1954 fell little short of the French investment. Washington blessed the British colonial campaign against Chinese communists in Malaya. Yet, in January 1949, the Americans had vetoed a Dutch re-conquest of an anti-communist nationalist regime in Indonesia by threatening to end Marshall aid to the Netherlands.[75] Ideally, the United States preferred 'independence' and covert influence to colonialism. In practice the Americans gave priority to anti-communism over anti-colonialism. It was admittedly for the Europeans to decide. Determined not to commit American ground troops to mainland Asia after the Korean truce, Washington necessarily pursued the cold war through imperial proxies. At the local level, the Americans, under protest, acted as sleeping partners in the British and French empires wherever the latter could cope with local communist subversion.

In South Asia the Americans relied chiefly on Britain and the Commonwealth to take the major responsibility. 'We are becoming engaged in a competition with the USSR for the favor and resources of South Asia,' the State Department and the Joint Chiefs of Staff reported in 1949. 'Bearing in mind our commitments elsewhere, it would appear to be in our interest for the British to bear as great a share of this burden as they possibly can.'[76] The demise of the imperial raj served the purpose in unforeseen ways. Despite Jawaharlal Nehru's 'non-alignment', a powerful Indian buffer state stood in the way of Sino-Soviet expansion.[77] A successful Indian democracy would show the rest of Asia that Mao's path was not the only road to modernization. To support Nehru in his involuntary roles, Washington first supplemented and soon surpassed the inadequate supply of British and Common-wealth aid in competition with Moscow.[78] From 1953 to 1961 the foreign exchange costs of Delhi's five-year plans were subsidized by the United States to the extent of two and a half billion dollars.[79] Meanwhile, the British retained a strong market for their exports.[80] India remained an important member of the Commonwealth. From 1949 onward the Pentagon joined the War Office in the traditional imperial great game of securing the Indian subcontinent's frontiers from Kabul and Herat to Rangoon and Singapore. As F.P. Bartlett, Director of South Asian Affairs in the State Department, observed, Curzon's strategy in 1889 for containing Russian expansion in central Asia 'applied very much today'.[81]

Unlike the Indians, the Pakistanis joined the Baghdad and SEATO defence pacts under direct and indirect Anglo-American auspices, and provided strategic air bases.[82] In return they received two billion dollars of military and economic aid in the 1950s.[83] They were soon affiliated more closely with the United States than with the Commonwealth. Under the shadow of cold war, a once British Empire modulated strategically into an Anglo-American field of influence, and thence into a predominantly American commitment. Similarly, in the ANZUS pact of 1951, the American 'off-shore island' chain around Communist China took in the Australasian Commonwealth.[84] Australia and New Zealand, none the less, continued to be bound up with Britain financially and commercially in the sterling area up to 1960.[85]

III

At the centre of the post-war Empire, paramountcy in the Middle East worked through a network of client dynasties that were in the political, military, and financial grip of British diplomatic missions, military bases, and oil companies.[86] Americans in the tradition of the open door objected to these discriminatory satrapies. In 1945 the State Department regarded them as 'outmoded' and 'dangerous to peace'.[87] The Kings and Emirs asked for American help to escape the imperial thrall. By the end of 1947 Marshall had undertaken with Bevin to restrain the oil rivalry, and to abstain from intervening competitively in British relations with Egypt, Iraq, Jordan, and the Gulf states.[88] Communist encroachment threatened the security of the Middle East, especially the oil fields of the two allies. By July 1950, British and American officials agreed that a Soviet attack on Iran would 'raise the question of a general war'. The northern Iranian frontier was the 'stop line' equivalent to the 38th parallel in Korea. No less important, the Middle East had become an area of Anglo-American interdependence in oil. Any conflict between Middle Eastern client governments and the oil companies could open the way to Soviet influence. Early in 1951 Washington as a precaution urged on the British the wisdom of conceding a fifty-fifty share in the Anglo-Iranian Oil Company's profits to the Shah's government. The American oil company in Saudi Arabia (Aramco) had already yielded as much.[89] The British company, however, was slow in following the American example until it was too late.[90] In May 1951 the Iranian premier, Mohammed Musaddiq, put Anglo-American solidarity to the test by nationalizing the Anglo-Iranian concession.[91]

A legacy of the British Great Game in south-western Asia, the Pahlavi dynasty in Teheran had been in every sense a creation of the British. Under the Shah, Mohammad Reza, Iran produced more oil than all the Arab states combined and figured largely in the sterling balance of payments. If Musaddiq were 'allowed to get away with it', Emanuel Shinwell, the Defence Minister, warned Attlee's Cabinet that other clients would nationalize their way to financial freedom. 'The next thing might be an attempt to nationalise the Suez Canal.'[92] But to re-occupy the Abadan oil fields would be costly and militarily precarious.[93] Washington warned that use of force could provoke a communist rising with Soviet backing in northern Iran.[94] With American co-operation, the British resorted to blockading Iran's oil exports. When Musaddiq refused to talk to the British any longer in October 1952, the Americans attempted to broker a settlement.

The Americans now feared that strangling Iran's main revenue would prove a double-edged weapon. If rising economic discontent destroyed Musaddiq's popularity, he could only turn to the pro-communist faction for support. Moscow in that case might bail out his regime. On several occasions American officials, such as Defense Secretary Robert Lovett, argued for going it alone and lifting the oil embargo to save Musaddiq as the only non-communist leader in sight; but, as a British official put it to Acheson, 'the choice before you is whether Iran goes Commie, or Brit[ain] goes bankrupt'.[95] Acheson decided that 'only by correlating our efforts with the British' could the Middle East be stabilized.[96] The Anglo-American blockade continued. In March 1953 President Eisenhower's National Security Council, like Truman's before it, first considered settling with Musaddiq without the British. Charles Wilson, the Defense Secretary, asked 'whether [the United States] were not in fact in partnership with the British in Iran'. John Foster Dulles, now Secretary of State, acknowledged that 'this had been the case until fairly lately, but that the British had now been thrown out'. The President stated that he 'certainly [did not] . . . want a break with the British'.[97] Dulles eventually decided that selling out to Musaddiq might have grave effects on United States oil concessions in other parts of the world. 'We cannot force the British hand,' he concluded.[98]

In August 1953 the critical problem of saving Iran from communism without damaging the British required a desperate gambit. A coup promoted by British and American intelligence services restored the Shah to power on the shoulders of the army of General Fazlollah Zahedi.[99] American military aid consolidated the regime and strengthened the Iranian buffer in the northern tier of Middle Eastern defence. Washington willy nilly had taken over the senior part of partnership in Iran. The consequent oil settlement in 1954 registered the shift in local collaborative terms. The percentages of the consortium were: Anglo-Iranian Oil Company, 40 per cent; Royal Dutch-Shell, 14 per cent; Standard Oil of New Jersey, 7 per cent; Socony Vacuum Oil Company, 7 per cent; Standard Oil of California, 7 per cent; Gulf Oil Corporation, 7 per cent; Texas Company, 7 per cent; Compagnie Française des Pétroles, 6 per cent; and a 5 per cent interest by a group of nine American independents. Much of the British oil stake had been saved, but the Americans now held 33 per cent of the Iranian market. Even though the percentage of the American independents was minor, the reason for their inclusion was significant. If they were left out, warned a former Ambassador to Britain who had oil contacts, Lewis Douglas, there would be an explosion in the United States Senate that would blow the new consortium into 'little bits as effectively as a hydrogen bomb'.[100]

There was complaint in some British circles that the Americans had taken over a British monopoly. But it was not the case that the Americans had ousted the British in Iran. They had taken over when the British could no longer cope. Lord Salisbury, the influential Tory minister, warned against recrimination: 'If we give the impression in

Washington that we are only concerned with our oil to the exclusion of
. . . keeping Persia in the anti-communist camp, we may lose all control
over American actions. That would be disastrous.'[101] The Americans
were highly sceptical of the ability of the Anglo-Iranian Oil Company to
adjust to twentieth-century conditions, but Eisenhower, like Truman
before him, was certain that 'US-UK agreement is necessary for any
settlement of Middle Eastern problems'.[102] Vulnerable to Soviet pressure
in the Middle East, the British had to keep in line with American cold
war strategy, just as American strategy had to align on the strong points
of the British Empire. If Washington forced the British to change their
unrealistic imperial policies in Iran, Egypt, and elsewhere, Dulles
admitted in April 1954, it would 'have the effect of tearing the free
world coalition to pieces'. Nevertheless, he continued, the Americans
could not 'go on forever' avoiding these great issues. 'The peoples of the
colonial states would never agree to fight Communism unless they were
assured of their freedom.'[103] For the British, the Iranian crisis had
demonstrated another, equally compelling, principle. If Musaddiq's
view had prevailed, then nationalists throughout the world might
abrogate British concessions. Intervention could be effective. But as a
precedent for Suez, the British lesson from the Persian oil crisis was
disastrous.

IV

In the Tory governments 1951–57, first Churchill and then Eden fell
increasingly out of step with their wartime comrade Eisenhower. In the
Far East the allies divided bitterly over Communist China, Taiwan, and
Quemoy. To Washington's dismay, London and Paris took advantage of
the advent of 'peaceful co-existence' to initiate dealings with Moscow.
They went to Geneva in 1954 and partitioned Indo-China with Chairman Mao. Dulles lamented, 'We can no longer run the free world.'[104]
For the Americans, the British appeared far too ready to insure their
eastern Empire at the expense of 'free world' territory. Tory ministers in
Whitehall did indeed resolve to rebuild imperial strength, which they
regarded as the main opportunity for national solvency. American
financial aid dwindled from 1952 to 1956. Despite recovery, British
exports could not balance overseas payments under the overload of
debt, social welfare, and massive rearmament. Two solutions were
discussed in 1952. One was to expand exports to hard currency markets
by £600 million a year at the expense of austerity at home and power
abroad.[105] The other was through tighter imperial control to develop
dollar-earnings and savings in the sterling system.[106] Washington prodded

London towards convertibility and the General Agreement on Tariffs and Trade. As Harold Macmillan put it, 'This is the choice – the slide into a shoddy and slushy Socialism [as a second-rate power], or the march to the third British Empire.'[107] In the continual fear of a run on the pound, the Churchillians marched to the imperial drum up to 1956. International confidence in sterling seemed to depend on Britain acting as a great imperial power. 'Our economic survival in the next year or two will largely depend upon world confidence in sterling.'[108] This might be muddled economics, but it was good Tory politics.

At the same time, the British relied on Washington not to retaliate against their discriminatory imperial economy.[109] They hoped that American capital would share in developing sterling area assets.[110] They needed the backing of economic and military aid from Washington to sterling countries in order to stabilize them against Soviet influence.[111] In the last resort, the Cabinet relied on American strategic cover in Europe and the world at large.[112] Yet the British aspired to a sterner, less dependent imperialism. By their own reckoning, they were caught between their vision of the Britishness of the Third British Empire and their actual dependence on the Americans.

Friction was most acute in the Middle East. Anxious to keep up international confidence in sterling, especially after losing Abadan, London meant to confront 'nationalists sapping at our position as a world power'.[113] On the other side of the Atlantic, influential officials were bending policy in favour of substituting direct American alliances for British influence in the Arab states. For a time in 1953, Dulles pressed the British to evacuate the Suez base unconditionally in the hope of winning the good will of General Neguib and Colonel Nasser.[114] The Americans expected the British to concede the Buraimi oasis to please the new King of Saudi Arabia, Saud Ibn Abdul Aziz al-Feisal, thereby to protect Aramco and the connection between that country and the United States. To Churchill and Eden, the Americans seemed far too eager to woo Arab nationalists away from Soviet blandishments at imperial expense. Washington certainly looked forward to some such outcome in the long run. But the Pentagon and the Treasury wanted the British to bear the burden in the Middle East. The State Department did not want to weaken NATO. Given the heavy demand on American resources, and in view of Eisenhower's conservative fiscal policies, it seemed wiser for the time being to rely on the existing imperial positions in Libya, Jordan, Iraq, and the Gulf states.[115]

Despite the deviations, the Americans generally returned to supporting British positions in the Arab states. With the French, the British and Americans doled out arms supplies to the region and so regulated the balance of power. Aided by the Americans, the British in 1954 at last achieved a Suez base treaty with a right of re-entry in case of war.[116] Together, the two allies had tried and failed to entice Egypt into the western alliance and peace with Israel. Despite misgivings, Washington backed the military association of Iraq with Iran and Turkey under British auspices in the Baghdad Pact.[117] It was not the Americans but the British who finally tried to go it alone when the rivalry between the American cold war and the imperial Great Game came to a head in 1956. The Suez Crisis thus becomes a touchstone of the inquiry into the nature of post-war imperial power.

Once the evacuation of some 80,000 troops at Suez had been scheduled, the British had few cards to play in Cairo, except remote control of the White Nile in Uganda.[118] Throughout the Arab Middle East, anti-British feeling combined with resentment against American sponsorship of Israel. The Egyptians united behind Gamal Abdel Nasser. Like Musaddiq, Nasser skilfully played the American and Soviet ends against the British middle. Unlike the Iranian leader, he had no oil to embargo, and the Russians agreed to buy his cotton. By November 1955 the Egyptian premier had clinched the Czech arms deal with Moscow and upset the regional power balance. The Soviets were dangling economic aid for his Aswan dam project as well as arming his Syrian allies, and offering munitions to Saudi Arabia and Yemen. As the Americans admitted, the communists had executed 'a brilliant series of economic forward passes', and mounted a 'new and monumental threat' to the Middle East.[119] Eisenhower saw the beginning of a great struggle between communist and free world economies for control over the development of the Third World.[120] Dulles averred that no cleavage between British and American policy could be allowed, if the Middle East and Africa were not to become another Communist China.[121]

It had long been evident, according to Sir Humphrey Trevelyan (the British Ambassador in Cairo) that the British retained their position in the Middle East only because of the relatively low level of Russian intervention.[122] Anthony Eden commented: 'We are [now] compelled to outbid them, or lose the main source of [oil] on which our economy depends.' Only by enlisting the Americans and their money could the British stave off Russian influence in Cairo and over the Canal. 'On our joint success in excluding the Russians from this [Aswan] contract,' Eden wrote to Eisenhower in November 1955, 'may depend the future of Africa.'[123] A joint bid was entered with 330 million American dollars and 80 million British pounds.

London and Washington saw eye to eye on the danger that the Egyptian ruler represented. By June 1956 he was viewed as an involuntary pawn of the Russians. He was inciting the Arab states to rise against Western domination. Eisenhower and Dulles feared not only for 'the jugular vein' of Western Europe's oil; they also believed that Nasser was rallying the Arabs for a final assault on Israel.[124] To Eden, the Egyptian 'Mussolini' with his pan-Arab ambitions threatened to become 'a Caesar from the Atlantic to the Gulf. . . . It is either him or us.'[125] From March 1956 the British Cabinet set in train plans to re-invade Egypt.[126] Three months later, the Anglo-American offer for the Aswan dam was cancelled. It was no longer possible to get Congressional aid for so menacing a regime. In riposte on 26 July after the last British troops had left the Suez base, Nasser nationalized the Suez Canal Company. British and French control of the Canal was the final emblem of his country's bondage. The result was explosive. The Canal carried two-thirds of Europe's oil supply.

The Americans also wished for Nasser's downfall, but, as Eden was repeatedly told from April 1956 onwards, they were unalterably opposed to military intervention. Dulles suspected a British attempt to manoeuvre Washington into reasserting British imperial supremacy in the Middle East.[127] If Egypt were invaded, the President predicted, every Arab state would swing towards Moscow. Revenge would be taken on American as well as British oil companies, and the British thus would lose the assets and the prestige they hoped to secure.[128] Washington preferred covert methods of a kind familiar in Latin America. They had succeeded in Teheran, and the CIA was already plotting a coup against the pro-Nasser regime in Damascus. The Americans had every reason to dissociate themselves publicly from British military action.

The Great Game was now being played for the highest stakes in the cold war. Eden's ministers agreed with the Bank of England that Egyptian 'piracy' on the Canal 'imperils the survival of the U.K. and the Commonwealth, and represents a very great danger to sterling'.[129] An expedition was prepared 'to bring about the fall of Nasser and create a government in Egypt which will work satisfactorily with ourselves and other powers'.[130] Harold Macmillan, Chancellor of the Exchequer, pointed out that Nasser, like Arabi Pasha in 1882, would block the Canal in self-defence. In that case, American finance would be needed to meet the dollar cost of alternative oil supplies from Venezuela and the Mexican Gulf.[131] The British presumably took it for granted that their ally would gladly accept and pay for a *fait accompli*. There is only circumstantial evidence that they meant to stage a 'Boston Tea Party' in reverse on the Nile. At Eisenhower's request, the British waited to see if Dulles could persuade Nasser to 'disgorge the canal' to international management. The indefatigable Dulles failed on this occasion. Keeping Washington in the dark, the British decided to go it alone, or rather, with the French and the Israelis. On 5 November 1956 an Anglo-French expedition landed on the Canal in the guise of peace-keepers come to stop a second Israeli–Egyptian war.

In the event, forebodings were realized. The Canal was blocked, pipe lines were sabotaged, and the oil ceased to flow. Far from saving sterling, the intervention set off a disastrous run on the pound. As the reserves ran out, Macmillan presented his colleagues with two alternatives: either to float the pound – a 'catastrophe affecting not merely the [British] cost of living but also . . . all our external economic relations'; or to ask for massive American aid.[132] Only after Eden had agreed to leave Egypt unconditionally did Eisenhower rescue the pound, with a billion dollars from the International Monetary Fund and the Export-Import Bank.[133] As the expedition took to its boats, Nikita Khrushchev rattled the nuclear sabre over London and Paris. Eisenhower shielded his errant allies with a similar threat against Moscow.[134]

It was the Americans, not the Russians, who had vetoed the Anglo-French effort at imperial reassertion in the Middle East and North Africa. At the peak of the crisis, Dulles told the National Security Council, in a now famous comment, that for many years the United States had been 'walking a tight rope' between backing Europe's empires and trying to win the friendship of countries escaping from colonialism. Unless the United States now asserted leadership, all those countries would turn to the Soviet Union.[135] Eisenhower asked: 'How can we possibly support Britain and France if in doing so we lose the whole Arab world?'[136] The Americans insisted that their major European allies give priority to the cold war over their empires. Yet the prize of Arab friendship eluded the righteous. The Arabs gave the credit for defeating imperialism mostly to the Egyptians and the Russians. Nasser and Nasserism were exalted. It was Eden who was toppled. American anti-imperialism in the Middle East provoked anti-Americanism in Europe and threw NATO into disarray. It was difficult not to fall off Dulles's tight rope.

A triumph for the non-aligned nations, the Suez fiasco was a disaster for the Empire. It ended British aspirations to imperial dominance in the Middle East. It showed that international confidence in the sterling empire still rested on the alignment of Anglo-American aims. Once and for all, it was established that Britain had to work in concert with the United States in the 'peripheral regions' no less than in Europe or suffer humiliating consequences. What Dulles called the 'violent family quarrel' over Suez had exposed the American essentials underlying British imperial power for all to see. The colonial periphery of the First Empire had become the centre of the Third.

V

In 1957, at Bermuda and later in Washington, Macmillan, now Prime Minister, and Eisenhower hastily revised and renewed the Anglo-American contract. Once more, as in 1947, the British were cutting their European and imperial commitment to save their payments balance.[137] Once again, the Americans repaired British power as the 'core of the [revitalized] NATO alliance and . . . an important element in SEATO and the Baghdad Pact'.[138] Like Attlee and Truman before them, the two leaders pledged 'joint policies' over the whole range of world affairs.[139] Bevin had looked forward to equality. But this time the Prime Minister spoke of British 'junior partnership' and declared 'interdependence'. With the Soviet Sputnik signalling nuclear parity with the United States, 'no country can do the job alone'.[140] The extreme danger of the Allies acting at cross-purposes in Suez fashion had become undeniable.

The understandings reached at Washington in 1957 initiated a concerted Anglo-American strategy in Asia and Africa to match the closer relationship in Europe. Eisenhower equipped the British with ballistic missiles and agreed to covert joint leadership in NATO. In return, Macmillan undertook not to negotiate with Moscow over disarmament or Germany without the Americans. He also agreed to keep his troops on the Rhine. As an American official put it, 'They can't ask for a 50 per cent interest in the political profits and then draw down their share in the firm's assets from 30 to 10 per cent. . . . if . . . sterling is really heading to disaster, we will have to bail them out in our own interests.'[141] There would be no more British talk of seating Communist China at the United Nations. It was understood that independence for co-operative nationalists was the best chance of saving Africa from communist subversion. Under the Eisenhower doctrine, which carried with it an allocation of up to 200 million dollars a year for the Middle East, the Americans were taking over the lead there as elsewhere.[142] Nevertheless, the British position in Iraq and the Gulf states was to be respected and supported. The oil there was vital to British prosperity, Washington noted, and the British would fight for it.[143] Along those lines, the President and the Prime Minister subscribed to 'coordinated effort and combined planning in the field of production, defense and economic warfare' towards a global common front.[144] In 1958 they faced the sequel of the Suez Crisis together.

Eisenhower found the root of the trouble in 'Nasser's capture of Arab loyalty and enthusiasm throughout the region'.[145] A Nasserite coup had ejected Soviet influence from Damascus and had merged Syria with Egypt in the United Arab Republic. Pan-Arab disturbances, seemingly directed from Cairo and Damascus, were undermining every ally of the West from Beirut to Kuwait and Aden. In the spring of 1958 the Americans prepared for military action with British participation in support of President Chamoun in Lebanon. To strengthen their clients, the British in turn had supported the proposal of their most loyal collaborator in the Middle East, Nuri al-Said of Iraq, to form a union of Iraq and Jordan. On 14 July, however, another 'pro-Nasser, anti-Western coup' swept away the pro-British regime and the Hashemite dynasty in Baghdad.[146] Would Brigadier Abdul Qasim's revolutionary junta join forces with Nasser's United Arab Republic, or would he oppose Nasserite aggrandizement with communist support?[147] The question had wide ramifications. The British had lost their Iraqi air bases, they might lose their Iraqi oil fields,[148] and worse still, Qasim might invade Kuwait, which was now the chief supplier of oil to the sterling area.[149] The Americans feared that if the King of Jordan fell the Israelis would move into the West Bank and start a general war in the Middle East.[150]

Now it was Eisenhower's turn to fulminate against 'the struggle of Nasser to get control of these [petroleum] supplies – to get the income and power to destroy the Western world'.[151] Like Eden in 1956, he felt that 'the most strategic move would be to attack Cairo'[152] and 'turn Israel loose on . . . the head of the snake'.[153] Unlike Eden, the President knew 'of course [that] this can not be done'. Critics in Congress and the world at large, Foster Dulles added, would say 'we are simply doing what we stopped the British and French from doing'.[154] But pro-Western rulers from Turkey and Israel to Saudi Arabia and Pakistan had requested immediate American or Anglo-American military support. Either the United States and Britain would have to respond, according to Eisenhower, or they would have to 'get out of the Middle East entirely'.[155] On the day of the Baghdad coup, brushing aside the Prime Minister's idea of a joint expedition to clear up the whole situation in the Middle East, the President ordered the Marines into the Lebanon.[156] By agreement, the British sent a contingent to Jordan as an insurance for the King and a warning to Qasim.

Most of Asia and much of Africa condemned the military inter-vention. 'If we stay on,' Eisenhower was advised, '. . . the USSR will beat us to death in public opinion. We must adjust to the tide of Arab nationalism . . . before the hot heads get control in every country. The oil companies should be able to roll with the punches.'[157] Such were the guidelines of American and Anglo-American policy thereafter. In October 1958 Eisenhower's Marines left the Lebanon. Macmillan in turn withdrew the troops from Jordan and Washington provided most of the money needed to support the King with a credible army.

It was recognized after 1958 that friendly regimes, if only to survive, had to temper their pro-Western stance and share power with the more moderate pan-Arabs.[158] As Macmillan put it, the cold war in the Middle East and elsewhere had become a question of winning the battle against 'so-called neutralism'.[159] The British accordingly dismantled their formal controls over Kuwait.[160] They trod warily in Iraq, where Anglo-American co-operation aimed at encouraging Qasim 'to resist pro-communist and pro-Nasserite forces equally'.[161] Qasim denounced his British defence treaty, left the Baghdad Pact, and took military aid from Moscow. But the Iraqis resisted Soviet pressure to nationalize the British and American oil concessions through the 1960s. Qasim's army had to be paid. Forewarned by Musaddiq's fate, even revolutionary nationalists could not afford to lose three-quarters of their revenue.[162] In Iraq and Iran the politics might be nationalized, but the invisible empire of oil remained.

Throughout the 1950s Anglo-American strategy rested on an oil cartel that allegedly fixed prices and divided 'producing and marketing territories' for 85 per cent of the world's supply outside the United States.[163] The five American and two British multinationals involved represented the substance of empire in the Middle East. Their interests were so enmeshed with Western economic and strategic security that American anti-trust proceedings against them hung fire throughout the decade.[164] The American companies with more capital expanded their areas of production in the region more than the British. Through the opening of new oil fields, American influence was eroding British sway in much of the Middle East and North Africa.[165] Most of the 'British' Middle East became an Anglo-American concern after 1958. Only in the Gulf states and the Red Sea could British power cope single-handed. It was not a matter of simple metropolitan enfeeblement. All the combined influence of the United States and Britain proved insufficient to shape the turmoil of pan-Arabism into stable informal sway.

VI

The new Tory government of 1957 under Harold Macmillan set sights on an empire in the post-colonial world. A system of influence was to be won by converting discontented subjects into loyal allies. The strategy was nothing if not Anglo-American. Imperial defence was realigned on joint plans for by-passing the Canal and re-routing Europe's oil supplies around Africa. As the 'air barrier' over the eastern Mediterranean 'thickened', the only sure way for reinforcing the security of the Gulf states and the Indian ocean seemed to be a string of airfields connecting Kano (in Northern Nigeria) to Nairobi and Aden.[166] Control in the Red Sea became the pivot of the scheme. The Middle East Command moved its headquarters to Aden – the only major base left in the Arabian peninsula. The Colony also housed the regional oil refinery of the Anglo-Iranian Oil Company (now British Petroleum). But the local nationalists listened to the 'Voice of the Arabs' broadcasts from Cairo and could no longer be kept at bay with colonial gradualism. In 1958 the Colonial Secretary, Alan Lennox-Boyd, set about saddling the trade-unionized port with the clutter of tribal sheikdoms inland in a federation weighted in favour of collaboration with the British after independence.[167] It was an unlikely scheme. In Aden the British were gambling against the odds for high strategic stakes.[168]

During the scramble into Africa in the 1890s Lord Salisbury had worked at keeping hostile powers away from the upper Nile region and the Horn of Africa.[169] Five decades later the British were pursuing a similar plan in the colonial scramble out of Africa. Only the method and the enemies had changed. In 1957 the members of Macmillan's government were bent on erecting buffer states against 'the southward drive of Nasser and the Russians' towards the projected trans-African life line to Aden and Singapore. For that purpose it was essential for the British and Americans to persuade the peoples of Somalia and Ethiopia 'to live together as good neighbours'. Ethiopian co-operation depended largely on American subsidies to Emperor Haile Selassie. 'Inevitably, American money would have to finance the greater part of this policy.'[170]

At first, the Nile Valley had been sealed off in the Sudan, where the British had advanced the anti-Egyptian party to independence by 1956 in the course of outbidding Cairo and the pro-Egyptian party for Sudanese loyalty. Two years later, General Ibrahim Abboud's coup in Khartoum re-opened the way for Nasserite influence. For 'a counter-poise' the British turned to the Somalis.[171] In the familiar style, Macmillan's government bought nationalist co-operation with imperial strategy at the price of independence. After the United Nations had decreed independence for Italian Somalia in 1960, the Cabinet with American support united the British Somali clans with their neighbours in a greater Somali state. Given their national aspirations, Lennox-Boyd judged, 'the moderate political parties and the mass of the people would cooperate fully' with the Western powers.[172]

British officials concentrated on independence for tropical Africa after 1957 – independence in the north-east, independence in the west – above all independence to prolong imperial sway and secure British economic and strategic assets. It was increasingly urgent to exchange colonial control for informal empire.[173] To turn this trick, the last aces in the African colonial hand would have to be played before they were forced. In West Africa the game had already been played out with some success despite errors. The constitution that Attlee's government had introduced into the Gold Cost (Ghana) in 1951 had been designed for the British to share power with conservative chiefs and nationalists.[174] It was a British initiative. However, the psephology proved mistaken, and Kwame Nkrumah's young 'Independence Now' party won an unexpected majority in the Legislative Assembly; he had to be let out of jail and endowed with the executive power intended for his 'elders and betters'.[175] First as 'Leader of government business', and soon as Prime Minister, Nkrumah won prestige as the next ruler of Ghana. His Convention People's Party undermined the chiefs' hold over their local communities and won more elections. The British Governor had 'only one dog in [his] kennel'. As the only effective collaborator with the colonial administration in sight,[176] the Ghanaian leader was able to bargain his country's way to political, if not economic, independence by 1957.[177] Whitehall was consoled that Ghana had been stabilized under British influence.[178] But, as Lord Home, the Commonwealth Secretary, observed, Nkrumah 'sees himself as a Messiah sent to deliver Africa from bondage.'[179] He was becoming the Nasser of black Africa.

According to the French, Nkrumah's progress spawned nationalists and discouraged the friends of colonial gradualism throughout West Africa and beyond.[180] Concessions yielded in Accra were immediately demanded in Lagos and Dakar. Colonial governors warned that if the claims to power of 'responsible' national leaders were denied they would lose their followers to revolutionaries.[181] Step by step behind the Ghanaians, the Nigerians, followed by the Sierra Leonians, advanced to political independence in 1960 and 1961 respectively. A Nigerian federation was negotiated to yoke the radical Yoruba and Ibo leaders of the southern provinces with the conservative pro-British emirs in the Muslim north. With 'our very good friend'[182] Abubaker Balewa, the northern leader, as federal prime minister, the British had done their best to construct a reliable and congenial succession. Partly as a result of the domino effect, but chiefly because of the writing on the wall in Algeria, the French followed the British example in West Africa in 1960.[183] The acceleration to independence had made sport of imperial time tables. In the 1930s the Colonial Office expected the tropical

African empire to last into the twenty-first century, and in 1945, for another sixty years. By 1950 the end of colonial rule in Nigeria and Ghana was predicted for the 1970s. In façt the span of imperial longevity in West Africa was cut off within a decade.

The pace of events in this region owed little to direct pressure from the superpowers. Until 1960 Soviet intervention remained prospective rather than actual. With little leverage in tropical Africa, Eisenhower and Dulles found that 'we must tailor our policies . . . to . . . our over-all relations with the metropolitan powers' in NATO. 'Premature independence would be as harmful to our interests . . . as . . . a continuation of nineteenth century colonialism.'[184] Paris was thus enabled to ignore American advice and continue the Algerian war with American financial support.[185] London proceeded single-handed with its own collaborative arrangements in tropical Africa. From 1956 onwards, none the less, Washington, fearing a build-up to another Suez, pressed the colonial powers to consult and coordinate their African policies with the Americans in the councils of NATO.[186] Anglo-American diplomacy narrowly placated the Graeco-Turkish struggle over Cyprus that imperilled a vital Western base and the integrity of NATO and CENTO.[187] Salvation in 1960 took the form of rule of the once-exiled Archbishop Makarios over an independent Cyprus.[188] To coordinate the African policies of the NATO powers proved even harder.

At Dulles's request in June 1959, Macmillan instructed his officials to survey the African endgame in a comprehensive inter-departmental report under the auspices of the Africa Committee of the Cabinet chaired by Burke Trend of the Cabinet Office and composed of representatives of the Colonial Office, Foreign Office, Commonwealth Relations Office, the Treasury, and the Ministry of Defence.[189] Written as a possible basis for Anglo-American consensus, the document testified to the shared belief that Africa's future would be shaped by the relationship between Britain and America.[190] British officials approached the crisis of African independence with no solid belief in the potentiality of black nationalism among so many divided ethnic communities. They regarded the freedom movements as essentially anti-European, not to say racist. What impressed them was the speed with which handfuls of urban nationalists were stirring up popular black resentment against white rule.[191] 'Africanism', as some preferred to call it,[192] was spreading from the Niger to the Zambesi and the Nile. The agitation could be contained at local levels, but the use of force would defeat the object. As the Colonial Office noted, 'It would be difficult for us to create some new authoritarian force artificially, and if we tried to do so . . . to the exclusion of people like Nkrumah or [Obafemi] Awolowo [in Nigeria] or [Julius] Nyerere [in Tanganyika] – it would probably lead to the creation of a revolutionary force against the set-up that we had created.'[193] The good will of amenable national leaders had to be won before independence, if they were to be allied after independence.

Anticipations of Soviet intervention and fears of an alliance between Nkrumah's pan-Africanism and Nasser's pan-Arabism multiplied the significance of local nationalist agitation. In the Cabinet Office's analysis, Moscow was alert to every chance of promoting African freedom movements. The Russians would be competing with the West for the sponsorship of every ex-colonial state. They were already making overtures in Ghana and Guinée as well as Ethiopia. The well-worn phrases of Anglo-American discourse ran through the Cabinet Office report: 'If the Western Governments appear to be reluctant to concede independence . . . they may turn [African opinion] towards the Soviet Union; if . . . they move too fast, they run the risk of leaving large areas . . . ripe for Communist exploitation.'[194] Only nationalists with independence could form a 'strong, indigenous barrier to the penetration of Africa by the Soviet Union and the United Arab Republic'.[195] The American analysis of African prospects followed similar lines.[196] Washington was as sure as London that tropical Africa was far from ready for independence. Every other consideration pointed to the necessity of keeping in step with African national aspirations.

By the late 1950s British hopes for the economic future were veering away from the Empire towards Europe. Sterling was on the verge of full convertibility. The preferences and financial controls of the imperial economy had given way to freer world trade. In 1957 Macmillan had requested a 'profit and loss account'[197] for the colonies that had found, ambiguously, that British trade might be better served if independence came sooner rather than later. Two years later colonial controls were clearly no longer indispensable for metropolitan prosperity. The inevitable political informalization of the Empire in its final stages went hand in hand with the desirable economic informalization of the sterling area.[198]

The economics of dependence after political independence was the key to the Cabinet Office's plan for African informal empire. Since 1957, British and American officials had agreed that the African dependencies must evolve 'towards stable self-government or independence' as rapidly as possible 'in such a way that these [successor] governments are willing and able to preserve their economic and political ties with the West.'[199] Economic and military aid with technical advisers would bind the new states to their former rulers. An ambitious plan for Africa would be underwritten by the Americans.[200] It was all to the good that they had few economic interests and large cold war stakes in the continent. The British would share the profits of American investment. They were relying a great deal on the Americans financially and strategically for the imperial future in Africa.[201] Although some of his officials were talking about an African Marshall plan, Eisenhower and the Treasury wanted the British and French to carry the burden of assistance 'with the Americans picking up the slack'.[202] Whatever the source, the influence to be won from aid would go to the donor. If there were to be an African informal empire, the British Cabinet Office report implied, it would be increasingly Anglo-American rather than British.

Everything now depended on winning and keeping African goodwill. It would all be lost, the Colonial Office feared in 1959, unless the struggle for independence between black majorities and white minorities in Kenya and the Central African Federation could be resolved.[203] 'If we fail to . . . demonstrate that we are not seeking an unqualified white supremacy [there], we may lose West Africa as well.'[204] African goodwill rested on the outcome of the racial struggle in East and Central Africa. In Kenya since 1921, a few thousand European settlers, with the racial sympathy of British voters, had vetoed African advancement by threatening revolt.[205] After British troops had put down the Mau Mau rising in the early 1950s, Whitehall had more control over the situation. Even so, Downing Street was reluctant to impose black majority rule on British kith and kin. It might lose the next British election. It would certainly alienate white Southern Rhodesia and the Union of South Africa from the Commonwealth. Yet the Africa Committee report of 1959 argued that unless the British could build 'a viable non-racial state' in Kenya, the entire African position would be jeopardized.[206]

Until late 1959, none the less, Macmillan and Lennox-Boyd were determined that British authority in East Africa would prevail for at least another decade. It seemed vital to secure the air bases at Nairobi and Entebbe and the sea base at Mombasa. Peter Ramsbotham, the Foreign Office liaison with the Chiefs of Staff objected: 'Are we to adopt a political policy in East Africa which is almost certain to poison our future relations with Africa as a whole because of a possible strategic need outside Africa?'[207] By May 1960 it was not practical politics for the Nigerians to give the British base rights in Kano. According to Iain Macleod, who had become Colonial Secretary in October 1959: 'They would be very glad to see their airfields used to help us in a struggle in which we supported Blacks against Whites but might not like them used if we supported Whites against Blacks.'[208]

With the collapse of Belgian rule and Soviet intervention in the Congo, the trans-African reinforcement route to the Red Sea and the Gulf proved to be an illusion.[209] Amphibious forces on a scale that Britain could not afford would be needed when the East African bases were lost. The projected informal empire in the Red Sea and the Gulf would eventually then depend largely for defence on the United States Navy.

British Central Africa presented the gravest prospects of racial conflict. Since 1953 the British dependencies of Northern Rhodesia (Zambia) and Nyasaland (Malawi) had been subjected to a federal government dominated by the virtually independent European minority in Southern Rhodesia (Zimbabwe). A quarter of a million whites were consolidating their rule over six million blacks. Reacting to the federal imposition, the Africans organized national parties and worked for black majority rule. In response to the British abdication in West Africa, the Europeans demanded white independence for the whole Federation before they were submerged under an 'uncivilized' African government. By mid-1959 the Colonial Office feared that 'the Federation may simply break up under the mounting pressure of the internal conflict'.[210] At worst, the white Southern Rhodesians would declare independence unilaterally with the support of the South Africans. At best the British hoped that the Federation would become a 'primarily multi-racial community' that could act as a 'shock-absorber' between South African Apartheid and the emerging black states in the north. But, if white domination were maintained by force, 'the whole of the Western position in black Africa, even in those territories (such as Nigeria) which are . . . well-disposed towards us, will be gravely shaken'.[211] Given the possible domino effects of pan-Africanism, questions of local racial collaboration had broadened into great matters of continental balance that involved the interdependent interests of Europe and the United States.

In January 1960 the Prime Minister set out on a tour of African capitals in search of African partners and British influence. Macmillan assured the new rulers in Lagos and Accra that the British were on the side of black Africa. In Cape Town and Salisbury (Harare) he warned the Europeans against resisting the 'Winds of Change' from the North.[212] The intransigent Premier of the Federation, Sir Roy Welensky, suspected that, if need be, Macmillan would break up the Federation to appease pan-Africanism.[213] African appeasement was certainly Macmillan's overriding aim. From this standpoint it seemed to him that 'the Africans are not the problem in Africa, it is the Europeans who are the problem.'[214] As the new Colonial Secretary, Iain Macleod, remarked, 'The pace of events in Somalia, Tanganyika, Uganda, and above all the Congo' was overtaking the time tables of mid-1959.[215] In an effort at saving the Central African Federation, Macleod ended Federal police rule in Nyasaland and Northern Rhodesia. Hastings Banda and Kenneth Kaunda, the African nationalist leaders, were released from prison.[216] But African hatred of the white Federation was such that, within four years, federal government was to end in African rule in independent Malawi and Zambia. Macmillan wanted to avoid a British Algeria in Central Africa. But in 1965 Premier Ian Smith was to declare independence unilaterally to perpetuate white supremacy in Southern Rhodesia, with disastrous consequences for British relations with the Afro-Asian members of the Commonwealth.

Early in 1960 Macmillan and Macleod promoted a compromise to clear the way for independence in Kenya. If the settlers would accept African majority rule, the Africans would guarantee the Europeans' land and commercial stake in the country. Michael Blundell, the leader of the multi-racial New Kenya Party, was chosen to persuade the settlers. Macmillan told him that 'if the multi-racial approach failed the likelihood was that the whites would be driven out of Africa and this could only be of profound detriment to the black.'[217] In March 'a tacit conspiracy'[218] between Macleod and Julius Nyerere's unrivalled TANU party led to Tanganyikan independence in 1961. Uganda followed a year later after a federal compromise between the dominant Baganda and the rest of the country.[219] After one year more, the suspected Mau Mau leader Jomo Kenyatta was to rule in Nairobi.[220] The British were scrambling out of colonialism before anarchy invited Soviet penetration in conjunction with pan-Africanism and pan-Arabism.[221] The collapse of Belgian rule and its consequences in the Congo lent speed to British heels.[222]

By the summer of 1960 the darkest scenario of Anglo-American planning was realized in the Congo (Zaire). Western relations with a score of newly or prospectively independent African governments were at stake in the crisis. If the Congo disintegrated, radical anti-Western Congolese factions would bid for Soviet support, which would have repercussions in western, eastern, and southern Africa. The supreme test of Anglo-American solidarity in Africa would be to hold the Congo together and to keep it aligned with the West. After prohibiting political activity for decades, in 1959 the Belgian administration, faced with riots and revolts, offered self-government within four years. Diverse political parties emerged. The anti-colonial coalition that insisted on independence in June 1960 soon fell to pieces. Premier Patrice Lumumba's radical centralists quarrelled with President Kasavubu's federalists who represented various ethnic and provincial societies. When the *Force*

Publique dismissed its Belgian officers and mutinied, civil order broke broke down entirely. Belgian troops returned to protect the lives of the 100,000 Europeans. Shortly thereafter Moise Tshombe declared the secession of Katanga province taking with him the bulk of the country's revenue and mineral wealth.

The rump of the Congolese government in Leopoldville required foreign aid if its authority were to be restored. Yet the divided ministers favoured different helpers. Justin Bomboko (Foreign Minister) welcomed the return of the Belgians and looked to Brussels for assistance.[223] Lumumba excoriated the Belgian return, and the Katanga secession, as a Western capitalist plot for a colonial reoccupation. At first Lumumba fruitlessly solicited aid in Washington. The Americans took the initiative in assembling a UN peace-keeping force, chiefly from African states, and called upon the Belgians to withdraw. Afro-Asian opinion sided with Lumumba. Anti-imperial resentment against the Belgian invasion was sapping the good will of black Africa that the West had cultivated so sedulously. The Belgian forces merely withdrew to their bases and the Belgians remained in Katanga. When the United States and the United Nations failed to respond to Lumumba's plea to throw the Belgians out immediately, he called for Soviet aid and appealed to the non-aligned powers for support. Brussels protested that the 'US was seeking [to] cut Belgium off and out from [the] Congo entirely, and injuring NATO in [the] bargain'.[224] General de Gaulle supported the Belgians. The activities of the UN officials in the Congo represented an Afro-Asian menace to the influence of the French over their neighbouring ex-colonial territories. King Leopold's Congo Free State had been set up in 1885 to exclude international rivalry from the heart of Africa. In reverse, the disintegration of the state brought about the alliance of indigenous factions with rival powers and involved the whole of tropical Africa in one way or another in the cold war.

Eisenhower and Macmillan agreed that Lumumba must be removed or 'fall into a river full of crocodiles' before he handed over the richest country in the region to Russian managers and technicians.[225] Covert plans to ensure his disappearance were laid.[226] Meanwhile there was another possibility that tested Macmillan's resolve to placate black nationalism at European expense in Central Africa. Katanga formed part of a multinational mineral empire (much of it British and American and controlled by interlocking directorships) that ran by rail to the Zambian copper belt and the Johannesburg gold mines. The company directors were influential in the right wing of the Conservative party. Welensky saw the chance of allying Tshombe's Katanga with his Federation. Why not back the secession and leave the shell of the Congo to Lumumba and the Soviets? Washington also kept the possibility open as a last resort.[227]

For a time, the Americans vetoed the entry of UN forces into Katanga in an attempt to restore unity in NATO. In the end, Eisenhower and Secretary Christian Herter stood for the integrity of the Congo. Not to be tempted, Macmillan stood with them. Like his Foreign Secretary, Lord Home, he feared that the Congo would become another 'Korea'. According to Home:

> The great danger of the Congo situation has always been the danger of outside intervention & the creation of a situation very similar to that which occurred in the Spanish Civil War & Korea . . . the only hope of averting that was intervention by U.N. & our line has been to give complete support to Mr Hammarskjold.[228]

The Under-Secretary at the Foreign Office, Lord Lansdowne, who served as envoy to the Congo, wrote: 'I cannot emphasise too strongly how unrealistic . . . is the theory that an independent Katanga can exist along side a truncated Congo.'[229] The Congolese could not afford to lose Katanga. The Americans would not tolerate such a disastrous move in the cold war. Independent black Africa as a whole would be alienated.[230] The British, after much debate on the dilemma of the wealth of the copper belt versus the larger issue of the Congo and the cold war, did not want to risk their chances of informal empire in black Africa.[231] The Congo crisis showed that the interdependent interests of the Western allies could all be lost if they were to act independently. Post-colonial sway in Africa would have to be concerted as part of the Western coalition under American leadership.

The Congo held together. Zaire became, for better or worse, a vast client state of the United States. The Congolese type of breakdown, however, was soon matched in the Nigerian civil war and later with Sino-Soviet intervention in Portuguese Africa and Rhodesia. Latter-day Lumumbas abounded. Castro, as Macmillan remarked, became Eisenhower's and Kennedy's Nasser,[232] and Panama their Suez. Cuban forces were to fight in Angola. The cold war fed upon internal instability, whether through colonial or ex-colonial proxies.

VII

In conclusion, we have given an account of what officials believed was happening to the Empire. Their evidence has its limitations. Groping among their illusions for the reality at times of crisis, they did not always find it where they expected. For all that, where the estimates proved unrealistic they were soon corrected. It is the corrections that offer the surest evidence of how the Empire was being made, unmade, and remade.

If the assessments of Attlee and his Treasury advisers in 1945 are credible, the collaborative basis of the pre-war Empire went down in the Second World War. The calculus of Bevin and Marshall suggests that the post-war system regenerated on American wealth and power. Compared with this reinforcement, the loss of India in the imperial Great Game seems almost derisory.[233] With economic recovery and a brief respite from overseas payments deficits, the system under Churchill and Eden regained a tentative dynamism of its own, until in 1956 Eisenhower jolted Eden into realizing that imperial dynamics were still reciprocal. Until the late 1950s British prosperity relied on an imperial economy of which the discriminatory integrity required American toleration, dollar underwriting, and strategic protection. In all these ways, the post-war Empire represented not a continuation, but a more formidable and a more vulnerable innovation. If the system were to succeed in securing and developing the sterling area, it had to operate as a project of the Anglo-American coalition. Such was the common prayer in Whitehall and Downing Street from Attlee to Macmillan.

By comparison the liturgy in Washington dissented in faith and conformed in works. Imperialism was Beelzebub. Ancient antagonism and historic bonds underlay the arguments of exclusive national interest that ostensibly justified the imperial coalition. From ingrained prejudices the Americans were reshaping the Empire in the revolutionary image of the Thirteen Colonies in 1776. The British were welcoming the Americans back into the British family of nations and, informally at least, into the Commonwealth, to which the shared tradition of civil liberties had contributed. Anti-colonialism constrained both sides. For a time, however, American cold war aims ran broadly parallel with British imperial purposes despite the rifts over Communist China and Suez. Committed heavily in the Far East and Europe, and anxious to keep their major allies, Washington depended on imperial proxies in other regions. For all the 'holier than thou' attitudes of the Americans, the British and French Empires were propped up in the democratic cause of saving the global free market from communist annexation. The Americans looked forward in the long run to turning Europe's colonies and client regimes into alliances with national states. So did the British in their own good time. One by one the imperial barriers tottered. Only then did Washington invest its power directly and exert effective influence in local management. Even then the Americans backed the British and French in their efforts at exchanging formal control for informal tutelage. None of the Western powers intended to 'decolonize' their dependencies because they feared 'neo-colonization' by the communists. The relationship between Britain and the United States largely offset British decline in the international system. But at the local level, as Bevin foresaw in 1949, the more American aid was required in competing with the Sino-Soviet bloc for nationalist good will, the more British imperial areas came under American influence.[234]

It follows that the dismantling of the visible Empire is not to be explained in monolithic terms of metropolitan infirmity. With American support or acquiescence, the British had resources enough to deal with local insurgency. Coercion was often threatened. Force was used in Cyprus, Aden, and Malaya with Washington's blessing, and without it in Kenya, Suez, and the Buraimi oasis. The Americans restored much of the British oil fief in Iran, and they refrained from interfering with those in Iraq and the Gulf emirates. In British calculations the necessity for heading off resistance and for winning local collaboration governed the colonial retreat at different speeds in different territories. Just as local imperial authority had multiplied through divided indigenous alliances, so it dwindled in the face of popular national organization. The process had long historical roots. Pre-war power-sharing contracts expired in South Asia without significant superpower intervention, but in Palestine there was American interference. The collaborative arrangements in Egypt had come to an end before the Soviet irruption into the Middle East. Post-war colonial contracts were reaching their term in Ghana and Nigeria before the Russian aid offensive in tropical Africa. Until 1956 the presence of superpowers was by no means the imperative for imperial retreat. Soviet and at times American competition thereafter helped to frustrate the conversion of British pre-war clientships into informal tutelage in most of the Middle East. In tropical Africa after 1958 the danger of Soviet sponsorship multiplied the weight of black nationalism and hastened the dismantling of white supremacy in the eastern and central regions. After Suez, the British concurred with the Americans at last in setting their sights on the post-colonial era. To assert colonial power became counter-productive when it came to bidding against the Soviets for nationalist alliances after independence. According to Anglo-American calculations, the strategic significance of pan-Arabism, of pan-Africanism, and of the non-aligned nations in the cold war motivated the final dismantling of formal empire.

It should be a commonplace, therefore, that the post-war Empire was more than British and less than an *imperium*. As it survived, so it was nationalized and internationalized as part of the Anglo-American coalition. It operated more like a multinational company that, after taking over other peoples' countries, was hiving them off again, one by one, as associated concerns. In this at least, the Empire after 1945 hewed to its original mid-Victorian design. Like the Americans, the Cobdenites in their day had worked for a revolutionary commercial republic of the world, held together by economic attraction rather than by political subordination.[235] Long before Truman and Eisenhower, Palmerston and even Gladstone had discovered that the international economy required imperial protection. Combining the two principles, Victorian imperialism withdrew from countries as reliable economic links and national organizations emerged – while it extended into others in need of development. Such was the genius of British free trade imperialism.[236]

The formal Empire contracted in the post-war years as it had once expanded, as a variable function of integrating countries into the international capitalist economy. Under Anglo-American auspices, the remains of the system were progressively nationalized and in tropical Africa, if not in India and the Middle East, informalized. Only now the American economy would drive the economic development of the system. The ex-colonial powers would share the dividends and the burdens. Most of the new states would have to co-operate with one side or the other in the cold war if they were to fulfil their national aspirations. Though some might choose aid from the Soviet bloc, prospects of development generally depended on the superior economic capacity of the West. After 1956 the British fell in with the American design for Western alliances with freer trade and free institutions. Such was the imperialism of decolonization.

The prescription for British informal sway worked well enough so long as sterling remained central to the economies of many under-developed countries. It was ill-suited to the 1950s and 1960s when the rouble and the dollar were contending for the economic and military contracts as well as the doctrinal loyalty of the third world. Competition devalued, if it did not entirely debase, the currencies of informal sway. President Kennedy's 'New Frontier' began where Europe's imperial frontiers had ended. In competition with communist political economics, the 1960s were dedicated to Third World development under the aegis of the United Nations and the World Bank. As things turned out, the new world order needed a good deal of old-fashioned imperial and financial intervention along with the economic attraction. Visible empires may be abolished; the thraldom of international economy remains. There was no conspiracy to take over the Empire. American influence expanded by imperial default and nationalist invitation.

Austin and *Oxford*, and *Cambridge*

NOTES

1. Paul Kennedy, *The Rise and Fall of the Great Powers* (New York, 1987), e.g. 367 ff. For themes of 'decline' directly relevant to the present article, see John Darwin, 'Imperialism in Decline? Tendencies in British Imperial Policy between the Wars', *Historical Journal*, 23 (1980), 657–79; B.R. Tomlinson, 'The Contraction of England: National Decline and Loss of Empire', *Journal of Imperial and Commonwealth History*, XI (Oct. 1982), 58–72; R.F. Holland, 'The Imperial Factor in British Strategies from Attlee to Macmillan, 1945–63', *JICH*, XII (Jan. 1984), 165–86; and W.W. Rostow, 'Beware of Historians Bearing False Analogies', *Foreign Affairs*, 66 (Spring 1988), 863–8. See also especially the major new work by P.J. Cain and A.G. Hopkins, *British Imperialism*, 2 vols. (London, 1993). We are generally in agreement with their interpretation of the issue of decline (e.g. II, 311 ff.) but, as will be seen, we do not agree with their explanation of the motives of British imperialism (II, 297; also e.g. I, 393, 395).

2. John Darwin provides a shrewd analysis of the historiographical problem in *The End of the British Empire* (Oxford, 1991) and in *Britain and Decolonisation* (London, 1988). See also R.F. Holland, *European Decolonization 1918–1981* (London, 1985); and John D. Hargreaves, *Decolonization in Africa* (London, 1988).

3. See especially Roger Owen and Bob Sutcliffe (eds.), *Studies in the Theory of Imperialism* (London, 1972); and Wolfgang J. Mommsen and Jürgen Osterhammel (eds.), *Imperialism and After* (London, 1986).

4. On the sterling area, a useful recent article with extensive bibliography is Gerold Krozewski, 'Sterling, the "Minor" Territories, and the End of Formal Empire, 1939–1958', *Economic History Review*, XLVI (1993), 239–65. Works essential to our argument are: Alec Cairncross and Barry Eichengreen, *Sterling in Decline* (London, 1983); Susan Strange, *Sterling and British Policy* (London, 1971); J.O.N. Perkins, *The Sterling Area the Commonwealth and World Economic Growth* (Cambridge, 1970); Diane Kunz, 'British Postwar Sterling Crises' (British Studies Distinguished Lecture: Austin, Texas, 1992); and, of lasting value in the context of Empire, J.D.B. Miller, *Survey of Commonwealth Affairs: Problems of Expansion and Attrition 1953–1969* (London, 1974), especially Ch. 12.

5. In the post-war years between 36 per cent and 49 per cent of global merchandise trade was conducted in sterling. Imanuel Wexler, *The Marshall Plan Revisited* (Westport, Conn, 1983), 166.

6. On the collaborative system, see Ronald Robinson, 'Non-European Foundations of European Imperialism', in Owen and Sutcliffe, *Studies in the Theory of Imperialism*. On the origins of the idea, see Anil Seal's preface to John Gallagher, *Decline, Revival and Fall of the British Empire* (Cambridge, 1982), viii ff.

7. War Cabinet Memorandum by L.S. Amery, 'Notes on Possible Terms of Peace', G.T. -448, Secret, 11 April 1917, CAB 24/10. W.R. Louis, *In the Name of God Go! Leo Amery and the British Empire in the Age of Churchill* (New York, 1992), 68. All references to ADM, CAB, CO, DEFE, DO, FO, PREM, T, and WO classifications refer to documents at the Public Record Office, London.

8. It seems to us that Cain and Hopkins overstate the case by arguing that 'Gentlemanly Capitalism' was the primary cause of British expansion and contraction. The stock exchange is obviously an entrepreneurial business, the success of which depends on partnerships on the periphery. *British Imperialism, passim.*

9. W.R. Louis and R.E. Robinson, 'The United States and the Liquidation of the British Empire in Tropical Africa 1941–1951', in Prosser Gifford and W.R. Louis (eds.), *The Transfer of Power in Africa* (New Haven, Conn., 1982), 31–55.

10. Attlee to Truman, 1 Sept. 1945, *Foreign Relations of the United States, 1945* (US Government Printing Office, Washington, DC), VI, 115 (*FRUS* hereafter).

11. Cabinet Memorandum by Lord Keynes, 13 Aug. 1945, CAB 129/1, CP (45) 112, in *British Documents on the End of Empire* (General Editors D.J. Murray and S.R. Ashton), Series A, Vol. 2: *The Labour Government and the End of Empire 1945–*

1951, Ronald Hyam (ed.), Part II (HMSO, London, 1992), 1–5 (hereafter *BDEEP – Labour Government*). For further British documentation see A.N. Porter and A.J. Stockwell (eds.), *British Imperial Policy and Decolonization*, 2 vols. (London, 1987 and 1989). For the economic context see W.K. Hancock and M.M. Gowing, *British War Economy* (London, 1949), Ch. XIX; Richard N. Gardner, *Sterling-Dollar Diplomacy* (Oxford, 1956); Sir Richard Clarke (Sir Alec Cairncross, ed.), *Anglo-American Economic Collaboration in War and Peace 1942–1949* (Oxford, 1982); and, especially for our argument, L.S. Pressnell, *External Economic Policy since the War*, Vol. 1: *The Post-War Financial Settlement* (London, 1986). See also Robert A. Pollard, *Economic Security and the Origins of the Cold War, 1945–1950* (New York, 1985); Robert M. Hathaway, *Ambiguous Partnership: Britain and America, 1944–1947* (New York, 1981); and Alan P. Dobson, *The Politics of the Anglo-American Economic Special Relationship 1940–1987* (New York, 1988).

12. Quoted in M.W. Kirby, *The Decline of British Economic Power since 1870* (London, 1981), 93.

13. See A.K. Cairncross, *The British Economy since 1945: Economic Policy and Performance* (Oxford, 1992), Ch. 2.

14. Minute by R.W.B. Clarke to Sir David Waley, 'What happens if we do not get the US Loan?', 15 Feb. 1946, Clarke, *Anglo-American Economic Collaboration*, 147.

15. Minute by Lord Keynes to Sir David Waley, 'If Congress rejects the Loan', 22 Feb. 1946, Clarke, *Anglo-American Economic Collaboration*, 152.

16. On the ethnic opposition to the loan in the United States and the countering anti-communist argument, see John Rourke, *Congress and the Presidency in U.S. Foreign Policymaking: A Study of Interaction and Influence. 1945–1982* (Boulder, Colorado, 1983), 43–8.

17. On American motives for the loan, see specially *FRUS, 1945*, VI, 54, 110 ff. For British reactions, see Alan Bullock, *Ernest Bevin: Foreign Secretary 1945–1951* (London, 1983), 201–5.

18. Memorandum by Attlee, 'Future of the Italian Colonies', 2 March 1946, DO (46) 27, CAB 131/2.

19. Memorandum by Bevin, 13 March 1946, DO (46) 40, CAB 131/2.

20. Attlee to Bevin, 1 Dec. 1946, FO 800/475, *BDEEP – Labour Government*, Part III, 222.

21. Memorandum by J.S. Bennett, 'International Aspects of Colonial Policy – 1947', 30 April 1947, CO 537/2057, *BDEEP – Labour Government*, Part II, 418–19. For the antecedents of these themes in the wartime period, see W.R. Louis, *Imperialism at Bay* (Oxford, 1977). For domestic politics, Stephen Howe, *Anticolonialism in British Politics: The Left and the End of Empire 1918–1964* (Oxford, 1993).

22. Marginal note by Poynton on Bennett, *idem*, 12 May 1947, ibid., 418.

23. ·For the ministerial discussion on the Mediterranean issue, see *BDEEP – Labour Government*, Part III, 215–348.

24. In October 1949 Bevin reported that 'American policy towards the Middle East has for some time past been crystallising on lines similar to our own . . . The United States Government has undertaken to help His Majesty's Government to maintain their position in the Middle East.' Cabinet Memorandum by Bevin, 'The Middle East', 19 Oct 1949, CAB 129/37/1, CP (49) 209, *BDEEP – Labour Government*, Part III, 383.

25. See John Gallagher, Gordon Johnson, and Anil Seal (eds.), *Locality, Province and Nation* (Cambridge, 1973); Sarvepalli Gopal, *Jawaharlal Nehru* (Vol. 1, Delhi, 1975); B.R. Tomlinson, *The Indian National Congress and the Raj* (London, 1976); R.J. Moore, *Escape from Empire: the Attlee Government and the Indian Problem* (Oxford, 1983); Ayesha Jalal, *The Sole Spokesman: Jinnah, the Muslim League and the Demand for Pakistan* (Cambridge, 1985); Anita Inder Singh, *The Origins of the Partition of India 1937–47* (Delhi, 1987).

26. For documentation see Nicholas Mansergh *et al.* (eds.), *Constitutional Relations*

between Britain and India: The Transfer of Power 1942–1947, 12 vols. (London, 1970–83).

27. See Cabinet Minutes on India's future relations with the Commonwealth, 8 Feb-27 April 1949, BDEEP – Labour Government, Part IV, 187–203; R.J. Moore, Making the New Commonwealth (Oxford, 1987).

28. In 1941 the Indian Army had 418,000 personnel of whom 155,000 (37 per cent) were Muslim, and 263,000 Hindus and other religions, including 51,000 Sikhs. (General R.M. Lockhart, Memorandum, 25 Feb. 1942, India Office Library, L/PO/6/106b). The Muslim element was greatly expanded during the war. See Gowher Rizvi, Linlithgow and India: A Study of British Policy and the Political Impasse in India, 1936–43 (London, 1978), 176.

29. Though the British attempted to retain as much influence as possible over the defence policies of both Pakistan and India. See the important article by Partha Sarathi Gupta, 'British Strategic and Economic Priorities during the Negotiations for the Transfer of Power in South Asia, 1945–47', Bangladesh Historical Studies, VII (1983), 39–51.

30. See the chapter by W.R. Louis in W.R. Louis and R.W. Stookey (eds.), The End of the Palestine Mandate (Austin, Texas, 1986); Michael J. Cohen, Palestine: Retreat from the Mandate (London, 1978); and Palestine and the Great Powers (Princeton, 1982); Martin Jones, Failure in Palestine: British and United States Policy after the Second World War (London, 1986); and Ritchie Ovendale, Britain, the United States, and the End of the Palestine Mandate, 1941–1948 (Woodbridge, Suffolk: Royal Historical Society, 1989).

31. Bernard Wasserstein, Herbert Samuel: A Political Life (Oxford, 1992), 262, 266–7.

32. Parliamentary Debates (Commons), 31 Jan. 1947, column 1347.

33. For documentation see BDEEP – Labour Government, Part I, 31–79 et passim.

34. Message from Attlee to Truman, 15 Nov. 1948, FRUS, 1948, V, Part 2, 1585–9. For earlier discussions of the danger see ibid., 865–1038. On the British side, see e.g. Bevin to Amman and other posts, Top Secret, 12 July 1948, FO 371/68572. For themes of the war relevant to our argument, see Mary C. Wilson, King Abdullah, Britain and the Making of Jordan (Cambridge, 1987); Benny Morris, The Birth of the Palestinian Refugee Problem, 1947–1949 (Cambridge, 1987); Avi Shlaim, Collusion across the Jordan (Oxford, 1988); for the consequences, see Ilan Pappé, Britain and the Arab-Israeli Conflict, 1948–51 (London, 1988).

35. Account of conversation with the President, Lewis Douglas to Acting Secretary of State, 12 Nov. 1948, FRUS, 1948, V, Part 2, 1572.

36. Acting Secretary of State to US Representative (McDonald) in Israel, 30 Dec. 1948, ibid., 1704.

37. Acting Secretary of State to Stabler in Amman, 3 Jan. 1949, FRUS, 1949, VI, 604. For the British side see especially minute by Sir Orme Sargent (Permanent Under-Secretary), 17 Jan. 1949, FO 371/76336.

38. Hearings in Executive Session on Vandenberg Resolution and the North Atlantic Treaty, 2 June 1949, Senate Committee on Foreign Relations, 81st Congress, 1st session, 1949, 256. According to an estimate by the Central Intelligence Agency in 1947: 'Existing British overseas commitments are so extensive and important that their precipitate liquidation would create conditions prejudicial to security interests of the United States.' CIA, Office of Reports and Estimates, 'Review of the World Situation', 26 Sept. 1947, Secret, in Michael Warner (ed.), CIA Cold War Records: The CIA under Harry Truman (Center for the Study of Intelligence, CIA, Washington, DC, 1994), 144–5.

39. On the origins of US support, see Clayton's memorandum, 27 May 1947, FRUS, 1947, III, 230–2. On the British side, see Alec Cairncross (ed.), The Robert Hall Dairies 1947–53 (London, 1989), 138–9, 269–71.

40. A work that helps to correct the bi-polar vision of the cold war as a purely American-Soviet conflict is Anne Deighton (ed.), Britain and the First Cold War (London,

1990). See especially the chapter by John Kent, 'The British Empire and the Origins of the Cold War'. See also Ritchie Ovendale, *The English-Speaking Alliance: Britain, the United States, the Dominions and the Cold War, 1945–51* (London, 1985). On the American side we have found especially useful John Lewis Gaddis, *The Long Peace* (Oxford, 1987); and Melvyn P. Leffler, *A Preponderance of Power: National Security. The Truman Administration, and the Cold War* (Stanford, 1992).
41. Agreed State Dept.-Joint Chiefs memorandum, endorsed by Truman; James F. Schnabel, *The History of the Joint Chiefs of Staff*, Vol. 1 (Wilmington, Del., 1979), 93 and Ch. III.
42. See Top Secret Minutes of 7th Meeting of the Policy Planning Staff, 24 Jan. 1950, *FRUS, 1950*, III, 617–22. According to George Kennan: 'the dissolution of the [British] empire was not in our interest as there were many things the Commonwealth could do which we could not do and which we wished them to continue doing,' ibid., 620.
43. *Hall Diaries 1947–53*, 20 July 1951, 161.
44. Quoted in Strange, *Sterling and British Policy*, 274.
45. See Alan S. Milward, *The Reconstruction of Western Europe 1945–51* (Berkeley, 1984); and Michael J. Hogan, *The Marshall Plan: America, Britain and the Reconstruction of Western Europe 1947–1952* (Cambridge, 1987).
46. Summary of Pentagon Talks, 16 Oct.–7 Nov. 1947, in Bullock, *Bevin*, 468–75; Kennan memorandum, 24 Feb. 1948, *FRUS, 1948*, V, Part 2, 655–57; key British files FO 371/61557–59.
47. See *FRUS, 1949*, VI, 50 ff. There were 'points of asymetry' in individual countries, but they were 'superimposed on an area of broad agreement.' Ibid., 62. See also minute by Michael Wright, 14 Nov. 1947, FO 371/61559.
48. Richard Clarke memorandum, 'The World Dollar Crisis', 16 June 1947, Clarke, *Anglo-American Economic Collaboration*, 168–74.
49. H.W. Brands, *The Devil We Knew: Americans and the Cold War* (Oxford, 1993). 'The ideological gulf between the United States and the Soviet Union gave the geopolitical rivalry unprecedented urgency' (32).
50. Though it was so argued at the time: 'After all,' Sir Roger Makins of the Foreign Office wrote, 'they [the Americans] are paying the piper, and in the last analysis we are dependent on general American support for our security.' (Makins memorandum, 'Some notes on British foreign policy', 11 Aug. 1951, FO 371/124968, *BDEEP – Labour Government*, Part II. 375, note 1). The Foreign Secretary at the time, Herbert Morrison, disliked the emphasis on US dependence. The sentence in the official version of the note was deleted.
51. Cabinet memorandum by Bevin, 'European Policy', CAB 129/37/1, CP (49) 208, 18 Oct. 1949, *BDEEP – Labour Government*, Part II, 344, 347.
52. Ibid., 346.
53. For the background see Dennis Austin, *Politics in Ghana* (London, 1964); Richard Rathbone, 'Political Intelligence and Policing in Ghana in the late 1940s and 1950s', in David M. Anderson and David Killingray (eds.), *Policing and Decolonisation: Politics, Nationalism and the Police, 1917–65* (Manchester, 1992), 84–104. A useful work for comparative perspective is John Kent, *The Internationalization of Colonialism: Britain, France, and Black Africa, 1939–1956* (Oxford, 1992).
54. See Anglo-American official and ministerial talks, *FRUS, 1950*, III, 950–3, 1097–1103. Creech Jones to Creasy, 18 March 1948, CO 537/3558, *BDEEP – Labour Government*, Part III, 38–9.
55. Cabinet memorandum by Creech Jones, 'Gold Coast Constitution', 8 Oct. 1949, CAB 129/36/2, CP (49) 199, ibid., Part III, 46–9. For the origins of the new African policy, see ibid., 38–69. See also Ronald Robinson, 'Andrew Cohen and the Transfer of Power in Tropical Africa', in W.H. Morris-Jones and G. Fischer (eds.), *Decolonisation and Africa* (London, 1980); R.D. Pearce, *The Turning Point in Africa* (London, 1982); and Ronald Hyam, 'Africa and the Labour Government, 1945–

'1951', in Andrew Porter and Robert Holland (eds.), *Theory and Practice in the History of European Expansion Overseas* (London, 1988), 148–72.

56. Or, in the Foreign Office's more general statement of the proposition applicable to all of the non-western world, the British would attempt 'to prevent nationalism getting out of control . . . by creating a class with a vested interest in cooperation.' FO memorandum on 'The Problem of Nationalism', 21 June 1952, CO 936/217, in *British Documents on the End of Empire*, Series A Volume 3, *The Conservative Government and the End of Empire 1951–1957*, David Goldsworthy (ed.), Part I (HMSO, London, 1994), 18 (hereafter *BDEEP – Conservative Government 1951–1957*).

57. Report of the Committee on the Conference of African Governors, CO 847/36/1, 22 May 1947, Appendix II, *BDEEP – Labour Government*, Part I, 199.

58. For documentation see *BDEEP – Labour Government*, Part IV, 246–374 *et passim*. On the motives for confederation see Ronald Hyam, 'The Geopolitical Origins of the Central African Federation: Britain, Rhodesia and South Africa, 1948–53', *Historical Journal*, 30 (1987), 145–72.

59. Acheson to Douglas, 20 July 1949, *FRUS, 1949*, IX, 50. Acheson had a good working relationship with Bevin and, on the whole, admired the Labour Government for its moderation and for its resistance to 'jingo pressures'. Dean Acheson, *Present at the Creation* (New York, 1969), 508.

60. See Top Secret messages between Acheson and Bevin, 10–15 July 1950, *FRUS, 1950*, VII, 347–90. A work relevant for our argument is: Callum MacDonald, *Britain and the Korean War* (Oxford, 1990), especially 95–6. See also D. Clayton James, *Refighting the Last War: Command and Crisis in Korea, 1950–1953* (New York, 1993); Bruce Cumings, *The Origins of the Korean War* (Princeton, 1981); and I.F. Stone, *The Hidden History of the Korean War* (New York, 1952), especially 192–8. Stone makes the point that the right wing in Britain was the first to question British involvement in the fall of 1950.

61. *Hall Diaries 1947–53*, 8 Dec. 1950, 135. The Central Intelligence Agency foresaw that a UN military conquest of North Korea would split the Allies and convince Asians 'that the US is, after all, an aggressive nation pursuing a policy of self-interest in Asia. The invading forces might become involved in hostilities with the Chinese Communists.' (CIA memorandum, 18 Aug., 1950, *FRUS, 1950*, VII, 601.) For British documentation see Roger Bullen and M.E. Pelly (eds.), *Documents on British Policy Overseas*, Series II, Vol.II (London, HMSO, 1987).

62. Bruce to Acheson, 5 Dec. 1950, *FRUS, 1950*, VII, 1387–9. See Alan Bullock's analysis of the European context in *Ernest Bevin*, Chs. 21 and 22.

63. US Delegation Minutes of Fifth Meeting of President Truman and Prime Minister Attlee, Top Secret, 7 Dec. 1950, *FRUS, 1950*, VII, 1449–62. Alex Danchev, *Oliver Franks: Founding Father* (Oxford, 1993), Ch. 6 is essential on the British side. Franks was Ambassador in Washington.

64. From the British perspective, however, if the Anglo-American combination held then it would give the British opportunity to consolidate their position in the Middle East. According to a Foreign Office minute of September 1950: 'because we have a base in Egypt we ought to take the initiative and bear the initial burden if any operation has to be undertaken in the Eastern Mediterranean similar to the Korean undertaking.' Minute by A. Rumbold, 27 Sept. 1950, FO 371/81967.

65. On this point see especially Kenneth O. Morgan, *Labour in Power, 1945–1951* (Oxford, 1984), 430 ff.

66. *Hall Diaries 1947–53*, 136, 139, 142, 150–3.

67. The merging of priorities might have been taken one step further had a proposal been accepted to appoint Lord Mountbatten as British High Commissioner for the Far East. He was described by John Strachey (Secretary of State for War) in a letter to Attlee as 'a man who is, at one and the same time, strong and yet is genuinely and

at heart in sympathy with the new Nationalism of Asia.' Attlee considered but did not act on Strachey's suggestion. (Strachey to Attlee, 11 Dec. 1950, PREM 8/1406/2, *BDEEP – Labour Government*, Part III, 204–5).

68. 'Present World Situation', Top Secret, 25 July 1950, *FRUS, 1950*, III, 1658 ff.
69. It is useful on this point to compare Thomas McCormick, ' "Every System Needs a Center Sometimes" ' An Essay on Hegemony and Modern American Foreign Policy', in Lloyd C. Gardner (ed.), *Redefining the Past* (Corvallis, Oregon, 1986), 195–220. See also William Appleman Williams, *The Contours of American History* (New York, 1973 ed.) and, by the same author, *Empire as a Way of Life* (New York, 1980). For our purpose, significant works on similar themes are: Emily S. Rosenberg, *Spreading the American Dream* (New York, 1982); and Michael J. Hogan, 'Corporatism', *Diplomatic History*, X (Fall 1986), 363–72.
70. Quotations from staff paper by George Kennan, PPS/51, 29 March 1949, *The State Department Policy Planning Staff Papers, 1949*, Vol. 3 (New York, 1983), especially 42–4; revised version *FRUS, 1949*, VII, Part 2, 1128 ff.
71. See the analysis by Miles Kahler, who encapsulates the ambivalence of American policy towards the subjects of colonial empires in three images – those of counter-revolutionary ally, imperial rival, and anti-colonial spokesman. 'The United States and the Third World: Decolonization and After', in L. Carl Brown (ed.), *Centerstage: American Diplomacy since World War II* (New York, 1990), 104–20.
72. See Cabinet memorandum by Bevin, 'Review of International Situation in Asia', 30 Aug. 1950, CP (50) 200, CAB 129/41. For these themes see especially Robert J. McMahon, *Colonialism and Cold War: The United States and the Struggle for Indonesian Independence, 1945–49* (Ithaca, New York, 1981); George McT. Kahin, *Intervention* (New York, 1986). On Malaya, especially A.J. Stockwell, 'Policing during the Malayan Emergency, 1948–60: Communism, Communalism and Decolonisation', in Anderson and Killingray, *Policing and Decolonisation: Politics, Nationalism and the Police*, 105–26. For South-East Asia generally, see Nicholas Tarling, *The Fall of Imperial Britain in South-East Asia* (Oxford, 1993).
73. The division of the Indian Army, however, had shattered the original British plan for the defence of South and South-East Asia: 'the standard [of the Indian Army] has deteriorated considerably, and inevitably so. The division of the Indian Armed Forces between India and Pakistan caused very serious problems. . . . the Indians have yet to show that they can produce a standard of leadership comparable to that provided by the British officer.' Sir Archibald Nye (High Commissioner in India) to Lord Ismay, Secret, 16 Nov. 1951, FO 371/92870.
74. Anglo-American official talks, Washington, 12 Sept. 1949, *FRUS, 1949*, VII, Part 2, 1199. There was good reason for American influence to remain as inconspicuous as possible. According to Sir Archibald Nye, the High Commissioner in Delhi: 'The power of America has drawn on to her much of the odium that formerly attached to Britain as the ruler of this part of the world, and there is deep suspicion of American capitalism.' (Nye to Gordon Walker, Top Secret, 17 May 1951, DO 35/2976).
75. Memorandum of conversation with the Ambassador of Netherlands, 11 Jan. 1949, *FRUS, 1949*, VII, Part I, 139.
76. Report on 'U.S. National Interests in South Asia', Top Secret, 19 April 1949, *FRUS, 1949*, VI, 8–31 (the quotations are on pp. 14 and 28).
77. See National Security Staff Study, 17 May 1951, *FRUS, 1951*, VI, Part 1, 44–5. For ramifications of the idea of India as a buffer, see e.g. Nye to Gordon Walker, Top Secret, 17 May 1951, DO 35/2976; see also especially the book by Olaf Caroe, *Wells of Power* (London, 1951). Caroe's book helped to popularize the view that Western (or American) defence of the Middle East should be based on Pakistan, just as British defence had previously been based on control of the subcontinent.
78. See memorandum for Cabinet Economic Committee, 22 March 1950, CAB 134/225, *BDEEP – Labour Government*, Part II, 142 ff. A key file at the Public Record Office for the evolution of this problem is: PREM 11/2726.
79. See *U.S. Overseas Loans and Grants and Assistance from International Organiz-*

ations: Obligations and Loan Authorizations, July 1, 1945-September 30, 1989,
CONG-R-0105 (Agency for International Development, 1989), 16.

80. But see Michael Lipton and John Firn, *The Erosion of a Relationship* (London, 1975), for the gradual deterioration of the economic connection between Britain and India.

81. Memorandum of 19 Jan. 1959, *FRUS, 1958–60*, XV, 154.

82. See Robert J. McMahon, *Cold War on the Periphery: The United States, India, and Pakistan* (New York, 1994); Ayesha Jalal, 'Towards the Baghdad Pact: South Asia and the Middle East Defence in the Cold War, 1947–1953', *International History Review*, XI (Aug. 1989), 409–33; and especially for the strategic dimension, Richard Aldrich and Michael Coleman, 'Britain and the Strategic Air Offensive Against the Soviet Union: The Question of South Asian Bases, 1945–49', *History*, 74 (Oct. 1989), 400–26. See also Richard J. Aldrich (ed.), *British Intelligence, Strategy and the Cold War, 1945–51* (London, 1992).

83. *U.S. Overseas Loans*, Statistical Annex 1, 26.

84. See *BDEEP – Labour Government*, Part III, 414–19.

85. See David Lee, 'Australia, the British Commonwealth, and the United States, 1950–1953', *Journal of Imperial and Commonwealth History*, 20 (Sept. 1992), 445–69.

86. See W.R. Louis, *The British Empire in the Middle East, 1945–1951* (Oxford, 1984).

87. Memorandum by Loy Henderson, 28 Dec. 1945, *FRUS, 1946*, VII, 2. In the Foreign Office, Sir Orme Sargent (Permanent Under-Secretary) had written a few months previously, in almost a mirror-image of mutual suspicion, of 'the uphill task of maintaining ourselves as a world power in the face of the United States, who now for the first time is prepared to assume this position with the help of the almighty dollar, export surpluses . . . civil aviation, and all the other instruments which they can if necessary use in order to "penetrate" the world' (Minute by Sargent, 1 Oct. 1945, FO 371/44557). For the immediate post-war crisis see Fraser J. Harbutt, *The Iron Curtain: Churchill, America, and the Origins of the Cold War* (New York, 1986).

88. Anglo-American Pentagon Talks of 1947, Top Secret, Oct.–Nov. 1947, *FRUS, 1947*, V, 575–625. Louis, *British Empire in the Middle East*, 109–12. It was the emergency in Greece that caused the Americans to be more favourably disposed to the general position of the British in the Middle East. 'The principal result of the Washington [Pentagon] talks is that for the first time American policy has crystalised on the lines of supporting British policy.' Minute by Michael Wright, 20 Jan. 1948, FO 371/68041.

89. See especially Irvine H. Anderson, *Aramco, The United States and Saudi Arabia: A Study of the Dynamics of Foreign Oil Policy, 1933–1950* (Princeton, 1981), Ch. 6.

90. The Aramco precedent had repercussions throughout the world and in areas other than the petroleum industry. Though the nationalization at Abadan was not a Colonial Office concern, it alarmed the Colonial Secretary, Oliver Lyttelton, and caused him to consider abolishing royalties in mining and other enterprises (for example hydro-electric development) in favour of local investment. See Colonial Secretary to Governors, 13 May 1952, *BDEEP – Conservative Government 1951–1957*, Part III, 163.

91. See James A. Bill and W.R. Louis (eds.), *Musaddiq, Iranian Nationalism, and Oil* (Austin, Texas, 1988).

92. Confidential Annex to Chiefs of Staff (51) 86, 23 May 1951, DEFE 4/43.

93. Confidential Annex, COS (51) 84, 21 May 1951, DEFE 4/43; Cabinet Conclusions, 12 July 1951, CAB 128/20. See also *BDEEP Labour Government*, I, 87–96; and James Cable, *Intervention at Abadan: Plan Buccaneer* (London, 1991).

94. For American fears that Iran would become 'another Korea' if the British did not accommodate Iranian claims to a greater share of the profits of the Anglo-Iranian Oil Company, see State Department memoranda, 21 Sept.–20 Dec. 1950, *FRUS, 1950*, V, 593–635. British assessments tended to be more cautious, with assumptions based on Soviet unwillingness to embark on global war during the time of the Korean

conflict. See, for example, memorandum by Pierson Dixon, 18 May 1951, FO 371/
91459.

95. Acheson to State Department, 10 Nov. 1951, *FRUS, 1952–54*, X, 279.

96. Acheson to Defense Secretary Lovett, 4 Nov. 1952, ibid., 512.

97. Memorandum of discussion, National Security Council, 4 March 1953, ibid., 695. In
the view of Anthony Eden (Foreign Secretary in the Churchill government 1951–55),
Eisenhower was 'obsessed' with the danger of a communist Iran. See Eden's minutes
in FO 371/104613 and 104614.

98. Memorandum of National Security Council discussion, 11 March 1953, *FRUS, 1952–
54*, X, 713. The British welcomed Dulles's attitude, but there was considerable
scepticism on how long it would last. Some British observers of the different
branches of the American government found the CIA much more inclined to adopt a
firm line, but in the State Department, according to C.M. Woodhouse of MI6, there
was a lingering 'silliness' that Mussadiq could be appeased. C.M. Woodhouse,
Something Ventured (London, 1982), 118, 121.

99. See Mark J. Gasiorowski, 'The 1953 Coup d'État in Iran', *International Journal of
Middle East Studies*, 19 (Aug. 1987), 261–86; and Moyara de Moraes Ruehsen,
'Operation "Ajax" Revisited: Iran, 1953', *Middle Eastern Studies*, 29 (July 1993),
467–86. The Americans were 'agog for action', the British Ambassador in Washington reported in the run up to the coup (Franks to Eden, Secret, 24 Aug. 1952, FO
371/98694).

100. Douglas to Sir William Fraser (AIOC), 24 Oct. 1953, FO 371/104642. For the
consortium see Daniel Yergin, *The Prize* (New York, 1991), 475–8; David S.
Painter, *Oil and the American Century* (Baltimore, 1986), 192–8; and especially for
the Iranian side, Mostafa Elm, *Oil, Power and Principle: Iran's Oil Nationalization
and Its Aftermath* (Syracuse, NY, 1992).

101. Minute by Salisbury, 22 Aug. 1953, FO 371/104577.

102. At talks in Washington in January 1952, Churchill had stressed that Anglo-American
cooperation in the Middle East would 'divide the difficulties by ten'. Truman had
declared that 'US-UK agreement was necessary for any settlement of Middle Eastern
problems.' *FRUS, 1952–54*, IX, Part 1, 176.

103. Memorandum of National Security Council discussion, Top Secret, 6 April 1954,
FRUS, 1952–54, XIII, Part 1, 1259. The Foreign Office essentially agreed with this
assessment and with the American view of the magnitude of the threat. Colonial
Office officials were more sceptical. 'We are having a lot of difficulty,' a Foreign
Office official wrote somewhat later, 'in convincing the Colonial Office . . . that the
Communist threat to Africa is as serious as we believe it to be.' (I.T.M. Pink to Sir C.
Stirling, FO 371/118677, *BDEEP – Conservative Government 1951–1957*, Part I,
240)

104. National Security Council memorandum, 24 June, 1954, *FRUS, 1952–54*, II, Part 1,
694–5. In May 1953 Bedell Smith (Under Secretary of State) observed: 'our relations
with the British Government [are] . . . worse than at any time since Pearl Harbor'
(ibid., IX, Part II, 2076). On Dulles see Richard H. Immerman (ed.), *John Foster
Dulles and the Diplomacy of the Cold War* (Princeton, 1990).

105. Cabinet memorandum by R.A. Butler, 'The Balance of Payments Outlook', C (52)
172, 23 May 1952, CAB 129/52; *BDEEP – Conservative Government 1951–57*, Pt.
III, 37–43.

106. Memorandum by Macmillan, 'Economic Policy', 17 June 1952, ibid., 47–50.

107. Ibid., 50.

108. Ibid., 44.

109. Macmillan remarked: 'I doubt . . . whether the American attitude to such a Sterling
Area policy will be determined . . . mainly by economic considerations. The real
interest of the United States is that Britain should make the maximum contribution
to the common defence and that the British Commonwealth should be strong.' Ibid.,
49.

110. 'The largest source of investment capital is, of course, the U.S.A. . . . . [w]e should

spare no effort in trying to persuade the Americans . . . to back it [Sterling area development].' Ibid., 48.

111. American official aid increasingly played this role from 1955 onwards in India, Pakistan, and other Colombo Plan countries as well as in the Middle East and eventually in Africa. American aid to the development of British colonies, however, remained small through the 1950s. In 1951 the Colonial Office did not expect 'U.S. assistance to be more than marginal nor would it be desirable politically for them to play the principal part.' Nevertheless, 'Help to U.K. or sterling area enables U.K. to help Colonies.' American aid to the colonies was thus considerable but indirect. See 'Colonial Development', CO brief for Churchill, Dec. 1951, CO 537/7597, ibid., 159.

112. Or, as Macmillan put it, 'If we decide to reject, as essential to our economic needs, G.A.T.T. (and all that G.A.T.T. implies), it is all the more important that we should be true to N.A.T.O.' Ibid., 45.

113. Foreign Office memorandum on 'The Problem of Nationalism', Secret Guard [Guard = not for American eyes] 21 Nov. 1952, CO 936/217, with extensive CO minutes. See David Goldsworthy, 'Keeping Change within Bounds: Colonial Policy during the Churchill and Eden Governments, 1951-57', Journal of Imperial and Commonwealth History, XVIII (Jan. 1990), 81-108.

114. For the British side of issue, and for defence policy generally, see especially David R. Devereux, The Formulation of British Defense Policy Towards the Middle East 1948-56 (New York, 1990). For changing naval strategy see E.J. Grove, Vanguard to Trident (London, 1988).

115. For the reluctance of the Eisenhower administration 'to fight in the Arctic and in the Tropics; in Asia, the Near East, and in Europe; by sea, by land, and by air; with old weapons and with new weapons', see H.W. Brands, 'The Age of Vulnerability: Eisenhower and the National Insecurity State', American Historical Review, 94 (Oct. 1989), 963-89 (quotation from Dulles on 973).

116. The military side can be followed in the files of the Chief of the Imperial General Staff series WO 216; for naval dilemmas in the wake of the thermonuclear tests in Bikini in March 1954 see 'Future Strategy', 6 May 1954, in the First Sea Lord's Records ADM 205/102. On the base negotiations see W.R. Louis, 'The Anglo-Egyptian Settlement of 1954', in W.R. Louis and Roger Owen (eds,), Suez 1956: The Crisis and its Consequences (Oxford, 1989), 43-71; and Ritchie Ovendale, 'Egypt and the Suez Base Agreement', in John W. Young (ed.), The Foreign Policy of Churchill's Peacetime Administration 1951-1955 (Leicester, 1988), 135-58. On the American side, especially Peter L. Hahn, The United States, Great Britain, and Egypt, 1945-1956 (Chapel Hill, No. Carolina, 1991); and Steven Z. Freiberger, Dawn over Suez: The Rise of American Power in the Middle East, 1952-1957 (Chicago, 1992).

117. See especially Brian Holden Reid, 'The "Northern Tier" and the Baghdad Pact', in The Foreign Policy of Churchill's Peacetime Administration, 159-79.

118. 'In any show-down with Egypt, the control Uganda gives us of the source of the White Nile must clearly be of paramount importance.' Minute by Alan Lennox-Boyd (Colonial Secretary), 23 Nov. 1955, CO 822/1195.

119. C.D. Jackson to President's Special Assistant, Nelson Rockefeller, 10 Nov. 1955, FRUS, 1955-57, IX, 8.

120. President to Secretary of State, 5 Dec. 1955, FRUS, 1955-57, IX, 10-12. In this momentous confrontation, Eisenhower even more than Dulles had to mute his aversion to British imperialism, which is ironic because to the British it was Dulles who seemed to personify the spirit of anti-colonialism. In the words of a contemporary critic, Dulles had a 'hypocritical obsession with the evils of British colonialism.' Hugh Thomas, The Suez Affair (London, 1986 ed.), 174.

121. Dulles, Report to National Security Council, 21 Nov. 1955, FRUS, 1955-57, XIV, 797.

122. See, for example, Trevelyan to Macmillan, Secret, 24 Oct. 1955, FO 371/113680.

123. Eden to Eisenhower, 26 Nov. 1955, FO 371/112739. This was a recurrent theme in

Eden's thought: 'If the Russians get the contract we have lost Africa.' Quoted in Robert Rhodes James, *Anthony Eden* (London, 1986), 430. See also especially David Carlton, *Anthony Eden: A Biography* (London, 1981), *passim*.

124. National Security Council memorandum, 28 June 1956, *FRUS, 1955–57*, XII, 308.
125. Quoted in David Reynolds, *Britannia Overruled* (London, 1991), 203.
126. See especially Keith Kyle, *Suez* (London, 1991), Ch. 5.
127. Dulles's statement at a meeting of the National Security Council, 21 Nov. 1955, *FRUS, 1955–57*, XIV, 797.
128. Memorandum of conference with the President, 31 July 1956, *FRUS, 1955–57*, XVI, 62–8.
129. Quoted in Diane B. Kunz, 'The Importance of Having Money', in *Suez 1956*, 215. See also the same author's *The Economic Diplomacy of the Suez Crisis* (Chapel Hill, No. Carolina, 1991). According to a Foreign Office minute: 'If Middle East [oil] supplies are cut off altogether . . . it is difficult to see how we could manage to avoid major economic disaster' (Minute by Denis Wright, Top Secret, 27 Aug. 1956, FO 371/120799).
130. Memorandum by Macmillan, Top Secret, 7 Aug. 1956, E.C. (56) 8, CAB 134/1217.
131. For Macmillan and the crisis see Alistair Horne, *Macmillan 1894–1956* (London, 1988), Ch. 15.
132. See 'Sterling', 19 Nov. 1956, T 236/4189. See also especially the minutes in T 236/4188 and T 236/4190.
133. See Diane Kunz, *Economic Diplomacy*, Ch. 7. George Humphrey, Secretary of the Treasury, remarked that 'if the United Kingdom did not look out, it would bust itself to a point of bankruptcy and of no return' (National Security Council discussion, 8 Nov. 1956, *FRUS, 1955–57*, XVI, 1077). On the British side of the financial crisis see especially Alec Cairncross (ed.), *The Robert Hall Diaries, 1954–61* (London, 1991), 85–7; and, specifically on the Treasury, Lewis Johnman, 'Defending the Pound: the Economics of the Suez Crisis, 1956', in Anthony Gorst and others (eds.), *Post-War Britain, 1945–64* (London, 1989).
134. Eisenhower remarked: 'The British realized that it [the Russian threat] is partly a propaganda effort but nevertheless they are scared.' The risk was too great to 'discount the possibility that the Russians would actually move into the area with force.' (Memorandum of 7 Nov. 1956, *FRUS, 1955–57*, XVI, 1049) On the weakness of the Soviet position, see Galia Golan, *Soviet Policies in the Middle East* (Cambridge, 1990), 47–53. For the British assessment, 'Soviet Motives and Objectives in the Middle East', Secret, 2 Oct. 1957, FO 371/127737; PREM 11/2404. For the American appreciation, see Special National Intelligence Estimate, 'Soviet Actions in the Middle East', Secret, 29 Nov. 1956, in Scott A. Koch (ed.), *CIA Cold War Records: Selected Estimates on the Soviet Union 1950–1959* (CIA, Center for the Study of Intelligence, Washington, DC, 1993), 147–52.
135. Memorandum on National Security Council discussion, 1 Nov. 1956, *FRUS, 1955–57*, XVI, 906.
136. *FRUS, 1955–57*, XVI, 910. Dulles stated: 'We had almost reached the point of deciding today whether we think the future lies with a policy of re-asserting by force colonial control over the less developed nations, or whether we will oppose such a course of action by every appropriate means' (*idem*, 906).
137. Eden had noted on the eve of the Suez crisis: 'we must now cut our coat according to our cloth. There is not much cloth.' P.R. (56) 11, 13 June 1956, CAB 134/1315. For Macmillan's explanation at Bermuda, see *FRUS, 1955–57*, XXVII, 749–52.
138. Northern European Chiefs of Mission Conference, 19–21 Sept. 1957, *FRUS, 1955–57*, IV, 610. On the need for the United States to support sterling, see State Department memorandum, 26 Nov. 1956, *FRUS, 1955–57*, XXVII, 668–72. For the British Treasury's view of the problem in the aftermath of Suez, T 236/4189.
139. Dulles on agenda for Washington Talks, 17 Oct. 1957, *FRUS, 1955–57*, XXVII, 789–91.
140. Macmillan to Eisenhower, 10 Oct. 1957, *FRUS, 1955–57*, XXVII, 785. Implicit in the

new British approach was a subtle lesson from Suez on the use of force. According to Sir Harold Caccia, the British Ambassador in Washington: 'In American eyes the use of force by others is justifiable in almost any circumstances when it can be shown to be directed against communism; but that, conversely, when the connection cannot be clearly shown, there are almost no circumstances in which they can be counted on to support it openly.' Caccia to Hoyer Millar, Secret and Guard, 10 Sept. 1957, FO 371/ 126888.

141. Memorandum by Merchant for Dulles, 19 Oct. 1957, *FRUS, 1955–57*, XXVII, 795.

142. For the consequences of the Eisenhower doctrine in the Middle East, see especially Malcolm Kerr, 'The Lebanese Civil War', in Evan Luard (ed.), *The International Regulation of Civil Wars* (New York, 1972) especially 72–4. British officials viewed the Eisenhower doctrine as a loosely worded statement designed to win Congressional support for the American initiative in the post-Suez era. They were amused but not comforted when Dulles described it as 'an attitude, a point of view, a state of mind'. As recorded in Caccia to Lloyd, 23 April 1957, FO 371/127896.

143. See National Intelligence Estimate, 'British Position in Persian Gulf and Arabian Peninsula', 19 Feb. 1957, *FRUS, 1955–57*, XIII, 486–8. On the British side, Bernard Burrows, 'The Future of the Persian Gulf States', Secret, 27 May 1957, FO 371/ 126916. Burrows was Political Resident in the Gulf and played a key part in these events. See his memoir, *Footnotes in the Sand: The Gulf in Transition. 1953–1958* (Wilton, Salisbury, 1990).

144. As anticipated by Dulles in agenda for Washington Talks, 17 Oct. 1957, *FRUS, 1955–57*, XXVII, 791.

145. President to George Humphrey, 22 July 1958, *FRUS, 1958–60*, XI, 365.

146. As described by William M. Rountree (Assistant Secretary of State), 14 July 1958, *FRUS, 1958–60*, XI, 228. The British Ambassador in Baghdad, however, believed initially that 'it is essentially an Administration of liberal reformers.' Sir Michael Wright to Lloyd, Secret, 23 July 1958, FO 371/134200.

147. The British assessment of the revolution in relation to the United States is particularly instructive: 'The question arises as to whether a Communist controlled Iraq would be more inimical to our interests than a Nasserite controlled Iraq, the point being that against a Communist controlled Iraq American help could be rallied, and perhaps the whole Arab Nationalist movement turned into a patriotic anti-Communist feeling.' Minutes of a meeting at 10 Downing Street, 21 Dec. 1958, PREM 11/2735. For the Iraqi revolution in this context see Robert A. Fernea and W.R. Louis (eds.), *The Iraqi Revolution of 1958* (London, 1991).

148. Sir Gerald Templer, Chief of the Imperial General Staff, believed that Arab nationalism in general 'had become a tool of Soviet policy'. 12 Aug. 1948, COS (58) 71, ADM 205/116; see also Templer's minutes in WO 216/917. Sir Michael Wright, however, offered this assessment: 'There is no one in sight, other than Abdul Karim Qasim . . . able to keep Iraq independent and united. This is so important not only for the benefit of the Iraqis but also for the future of the oil industry, for British interests generally in the Arab world and for the staving off of the Russian advance into the Middle East that it seems desirable to give Qasim the benefit of the doubt.' Wright to Lloyd, Confidential, 4 Dec. 1958, PREM 11/2735.

149. Nuri, too, had threatened Kuwait. See Macmillan's comment, 9 June 1958, *FRUS, 1958–60*, XII, 302. On the vital importance of Kuwait oil to sterling, see Frank Brenchley, *Britain and the Middle East: An Economic History* (London, 1989), Ch. 12. For Qasim's attack on Kuwait in 1961 and the consequent British intervention, see Mustafa M. Alani, *Operation Vantage: British Military Intervention in Kuwait 1961* (Surbiton, Surrey, 1990).

150. For American reactions to the Iraqi coup, see Editorial Note, *FRUS, 1958–60*, XII, 307–8; 'Briefing Notes by Director of Central Intelligence', 14 July, 1958, ibid., 308–11.

151. Memorandum of Conversation between President and Vice-President, 15 July 1958, *FRUS, 1958–60*, XI, 244.

152. Conference with President, 14 July 1958, ibid., 214.
153. Conference with President, 16 July 1958, ibid., 310.
154. Conference with President, 14 July 1958, ibid., 214–15.
155. Conference with President, 14 July 1958, ibid., 213.
156. Telephone conversations and messages between Eisenhower and Macmillan, 14–15 July 1958, ibid., 231–42. The British records of these conversations are in PREM 11/2387.
157. Memorandum of National Security Council discussion, 24 July 1958, *FRUS, 1958–60*, XI, 384. According to the Foreign Office: 'Like Nuri, Qasim also wants an independent Iraq, in which Kurds and Arabs, Shias, Sunnis and other minorities will be united and which will be developed in accordance with a long-term economic plan, financed from the oil royalties paid by the Iraq Petroleum Company.' Annual Report for Iraq, 1958, FO 371/140896.
158. See National Intelligence Estimates: 'The Outlook for Lebanon', 10 May, 1960, *FRUS, 1958–1960*, XI, 649–53; 'The Outlook for Jordan', 10 March 1960, ibid., 681–7.
159. Memorandum of conversation with President, 21 March 1957, *FRUS, 1955–57*, XXVII, 710.
160. See Jill Crystal, *Oil and Politics in the Gulf* (Cambridge, 1990), 81–6. For the political side of the Kuwaiti crisis of 1960 see especially George Middleton (Bahrain) to Sir Roger Stevens, Secret, 10 Sept. 1960, FO 371/152120: 'We cannot see the Americans taking over the lead from us [in the Gulf], for they even more than we are tarred with the capitalist brush and are objects of peculiar suspicion.'
161. Record of conversation between Lloyd and Dulles, 4 Feb. 1959, FO 371/141841; memorandum of conversation between Eisenhower and Macmillan, 22 March 1959, *FRUS, 1958–60*, 216.
162. The Soviets offered no alternative market for Iraq's oil until 1969. See Michael E. Brown, 'The Nationalization of the Iraqi Petroleum Company', *International Journal of Middle Eastern Studies*, 10 (1970), 107–24.
163. Memorandum by Legal Adviser (Hager) to State Department, 11 April 1960, *FRUS, 1958–60*, IV, 630–3. For an earlier assessment, see British and American joint review of 'Middle East Problems Bearing upon the Supply of Oil to the Free World', *FRUS, 1955–57*, X, 682–89.
164. See memorandum of National Security Council discussion, 9 May 1960, *FRUS, 1958–60*, VI, 633–6.
165. 'The *official* policy of the State Department is not unfriendly towards the maintenance of British interests. At the same time . . . the American oil companies are fiercely competitive . . . and, since we do not have the same . . . economic resources as the Americans, we tend to lose ground all along the line.' George Middleton to A.D. Ross, Personal and Confidential Guard, 20 Dec. 1956, FO 371/121238.
166. Cabinet memorandum by Burke Trend, 1 March 1957, PREM 11/2582. For the changing naval dimension of the problem see Peter James Henshaw, 'The Transfer of Simonstown: Afrikaner Nationalism, South African Strategic Dependence, and British Global Power', *Journal of Imperial and Commonwealth History*, XX (1992), 419–44.
167. Memorandum by Lennox-Boyd, 'Aden Colony and Protectorate', Secret, 14 Aug. 1959, C.P.C. (59) 12, CAB 134/1558. See especially Glen Balfour-Paul, *The End of Empire in the Middle East: Britain's Relinquishment of Power in Her Last Three Arab Dependencies* (Cambridge, 1991).
168. A comment made by W.L. Gorrell Barnes of the Colonial Office reveals how the interplay of local and international circumstances had to be born in mind while assessing the strategic aim in Aden: 'Our own general [colonial] policy and the fashion of anti-colonialism is of course a factor, but only insofar as local conditions create a situation which these considerations can exacerbate.' Minute by Gorrell Barnes, 24 April 1959, CO 1015/1912.

169. See Ronald Robinson and John Gallagher, *Africa and the Victorians: The Official Mind of Imperialism* (2nd ed., London, 1981).
170. Minutes by Burke Trend, 1 March 1957, and 20 Nov. 1958, PREM 11/2582.
171. Record of conference between East African Governors and Secretary of State, Entebbe, 7–8 Oct. 1957, Secret, CO 822/1807. In the event of the Sudan falling under Nasser's sway, 'the threat will reach to the borders of Uganda and Kenya'. Minute by Trend to Prime Minister, 20 Nov. 1958, PREM 11/2582.
172. Lennox-Boyd to Macmillan, Secret and Personal, 12 Feb. 1959, PREM 11/2582; 'Policy in Aden and Somaliland', Secret, 17 Nov. 1958, C.P.C. (58) 19, CAB 134/1557. It is of interest that Lennox-Boyd had no clearer idea than had his predecessors at the time of the First World War and Peace Conference about the status of Somalia or Tanganyika in international law. 'Incidentally,' he once asked, 'where does "sovereignty" lie. . .? The Queen is not Queen of Tanganyika under international law is she?' Minute of 11 July 1957, CO 926/1054.
173. Even the more diehard Colonial Governors had begun to recognize, in the words of Sir Edward Twining in Tanganyika, that there would be a time 'when we pass out of the phase of control into the phase of influence' – though he thought that it would be 'a generation or so before control gives way to influence.' Twining to Gorrell Barnes,12 Nov. 1956 CO 822/912, *BDEEP – Conservative Government 1951–1957*, Part II, 272. The principle, however, had long been established in the Colonial Office. For example, one official wrote in 1953: 'as the Secretary of State progressively loses direct control of the Colonies, he must increasingly rely on influence and advice to them'. Minute by A.E. Drake, 3 Oct. 1953, ibid., III, 306.
174. Cabinet memorandum by Arthur Creech Jones, 'Gold Coast Constitution', 8 Oct. 1949, CAB 129/36/2 (*BDEEP – Labour Government*, Part III, 46–9).
175. Arden-Clarke to Cohen, Personal, 5 March 1951, CO 537/7181. For the full story see Richard Rathbone (ed.), *British Documents on the End of Empire* (Series B, Volume I): *Ghana* (London, 1992), Part I, 1941–1952, *passim* (henceforth *BDEEP – Ghana*).
176. 'We have only one dog in our kennel, all we can do is to build it up and feed it vitamins and cod liver oil'; it could only be replaced with one 'of even more extremist nationalist tendencies.' Arden-Clarke to Cohen, 12 May 1951, quoted in Hyam's note on Cohen minute, 11 June 1951, *BDEEP – Labour Government*, Part II, 73–4.
177. To obtain Nkrumah's collaboration, the Governor, Sir Charles Arden-Clarke, promised to consider virtual internal self-government within five years, and to make him Prime Minister with control over all domestic departments. The Governor's object was to win time for the emergence of a moderate political party that would win the next election. Sir John Macpherson, Governor of Nigeria, commented: 'The thought that two or three years . . . would be sufficient to achieve this, seems the dreamiest [pipe dream] I have ever heard of.' Macpherson to Lloyd, 8 Jan. 1952, CO 967/173. For the policy of constitutional advance in Ghana and Nigeria generally, see *BDEEP – Labour Government*, Part III, 38–78; for Ghana, see *BDEEP – Ghana*, Part II, *passim*.
178. 'Africa: The Next Ten Years', Interdepartmental Report, June 1959, FO 371/137972.
179. Home hoped that 'the emergence of Nigeria . . . will cut him down to size.' Memorandum by Home, 1 June 1959, PREM 11/2588.
180. C. de Brabant, 'Anglo-French Colonial Cooperation, Principally in West African Affairs' (unpublished M. Litt. thesis, Oxford University, 1989).
181. See Ronald Hyam's preface to Cabinet memorandum by James Griffiths (Colonial Secretary), 'Nigerian Constitution', 3 May 1950, CAB 129/39, CP (50) 94, *BDEEP – Labour Government*, Part III, 52 ff.
182. The phrase of Iain Macleod in a minute to Macmillan, 9 May 1960, PREM 11/3047.
183. Sir Anthony Rumbold in Paris wrote at the time of Algerian independence: 'There are not wanting Frenchmen today to evoke memories of Fashoda. . . . We must

particularly avoid giving any ground for ever-present French suspicions of an Anglo-Saxon drive to replace their influence in Africa.' Rumbold to Lord Home, Confidential, 23 May 1962, FO 371/161371.

184. 'Statement of U.S. Policy Toward Africa South of the Sahara', 23 Aug. 1957, *FRUS, 1955–57*, XVIII, 79–80; see also assurances to Macmillan at Bermuda Conference, 23 March 1957, ibid., 55–7. Despite the consensus, the British were worried that the client states would attempt 'to play us and the Americans off against each other . . . It is not always easy to get the Americans to discuss these things with us.' Minute by A.D.M. Ross, 19 March 1957, FO 371/127755.

185. See *FRUS, 1955–57*, XVIII, 219–302 for American frustration over the situation in Algeria. For the British side, e.g FO 371/161371.

186. Until 1956 the Americans had usually refused in principle to adopt joint policies with Britain and France in colonial and quasi-colonial affairs to avoid the taint of imperialism. As a result, the Europeans were free to divert forces, and incidentally American aid, to regional imperial purposes, and involve the United States in Soviet confrontation without Washington's authorization. After Suez, Dulles pressed with little success for European policies in the 'peripheral regions' to be coordinated in the NATO Council of Ministers. Otherwise, he feared, NATO would be torn apart. (*FRUS, 1955–57*, IV, 78 ff; 109; 200–1; 265 ff.) For explanation of the genesis of the alignment of views on Africa in a meeting between Dulles and Selwyn Lloyd at the Brize Norton airfield in October 1958, see minute by Adam Watson, 15 June 1959, FO 371/137952.

187. For the turning point in 1955 and the beginning of the debate in the Colonial Office about a possible 'Anglo-Greek-Turkish condominium' or 'even a N.A.T.O. solution' see minutes in CO 926/257.

188. See *FRUS, 1958–60*, X, 564–835. For the key British files on Cyprus in relation to other dependent territories, CAB 134/1558 and CAB 134/1559 (Colonial Policy Committee, 1959 and 1960). For recent interpretation of Cyprus in the 1950s, see Robert Holland, 'Never, Never Land: British Colonial Policy and the Roots of Violence in Cyprus, 1950–54', and David M. Anderson, 'Policing and Communal Conflict: The Cyprus Emergency, 1954–60', both in *Journal of Imperial and Commonwealth History*, XXI (Sept. 1993), 148–207.

189. 'Africa: the Next Ten Years', June 1959, FO 371/137972. For the interdepartmental discussions see CAB 134/1353. The quotations are from the copy in FO 371/137972, which is a complete document, but see CO 936/572 and PREM 11/2587.

190. 'This is the first time,' the head of the African Department of the Foreign Office noted, 'that an effort has been made to see the picture as a whole. . . . Hitherto the different areas of Africa have been regarded as largely in water-tight compartments.' Minute by Adam Watson, 15 June 1959, FO 371/137952. Christopher Eastwood of the Colonial Office recognized the urgency of 'high level talks with the Americans' in his minute of 3 July 1959, CO 936/572.

191. 'Africa: the Next Ten Years', June 1959, FO 371/137972.

192. Notably Lord Hailey in *An African Survey* (London, 1957 ed.); see John W. Cell, *Hailey: A Study in British Imperialism, 1872–1969* (Cambridge, 1992), 301–2.

193. Colonial Office officials went on to draw the lesson they had learned from the Iraqi revolution: 'we would gain nothing by trying to back authoritarians against public opinion.' Minutes of a meeting at the Colonial Office, Secret, 20 May 1959, CO 936/572.

194. 'Africa: the Next Ten Years', June 1959, FO 371/137972, 6.

195. Ibid., 29.

196. See National Security Council 5818: 'US Policy Toward Africa South of the Sahara', approved by President, 26 Aug. 1958, *FRUS, 1958–60*, XIV, 23–37.

197. See especially CO 1032/144, CO 1032/146, and CO 1032/147.

198. Cf. Cain and Hopkins, *British Imperialism*, II, 281 ff.

199. Agreed U.S.-U.K paper, 'Means of Combatting Communist Influence in Tropical Africa, 13 March 1957', *FRUS, 1955–57*, XXVII, 759.

200. 'Africa: the Next Ten Years', June 1959, FO 371/137972, 25–6.
201. The interest of the Americans in Africa was rapidly increasing: 'Their main concern is political and strategic. . . . If we are prepared to co-operate with the Americans, we have an opportunity to influence their thinking and benefit from their growing interest in Africa, which is bound to become a major factor in the future of the continent.' 'Africa: The Next Ten Years', June 1959, FO 371/137972, 19–20. This optimistic assessment was in marked contrast to the view held two years earlier: 'United States investment in tropical Africa . . . will naturally depend on economic as well as political factors – the investment must look profitable as well as secure against expropriation. It seems unlikely that there would be any great rush of American capital. . . .' R.W. Bailey to Adam Watson, Confidential, 20 March 1957, FO 371/125304. In 1952 the Colonial Secretary, Oliver Lyttelton, had written that it was important to lure American capital into Africa but not to hold out false hope: 'Lead the horse to the water', he admonished the Colonial Governors in Africa, '. . . but do not lead him up the garden path.' Circular despatch by Lyttelton, 22 Aug. 1952, CO 537/7844, *BDEEP – Conservative Government 1951–1957*, III, 168.
202. For the stalemate in American policy over aid to Africa, March-Dec. 1960, see *FRUS, 1958–60*, XIV, 93–171 *et passim*.
203. One danger remained the bedrock American anti-colonial mentality, now manifested 'by the negro vote'. The Afro-Asian bloc vote at the United Nations was another. 'Africa: the Next Ten Years', 19, 29–30.
204. 'Africa: the Next Ten Years', 23.
205. For the background see Ronald Robinson, 'The Colonial Office and the Settler in East-Central Africa, 1919–63', in E. Serra and C. Seton Watson (eds.), *Italia E Inghilterra Nell'Eta Dell Imperialismo* (Milan, 1990), 195–212.
206. 'Africa: the Next Ten Years', 16.
207. Minute by Ramsbotham, 27 Feb. 1959, FO 371/137951.
208. Macleod to Macmillan, 9 May 1960, PREM 11/3047.
209. Minutes by War Office and Air Ministry, 11 May 1960, PREM 11/3047.
210. 'Africa: the Next Ten Years', FO 371/137972, 17.
211. Ibid., 18.
212. Significantly, Eisenhower had used this metaphor for the national aspiration of underdeveloped countries in his second Inaugural Address in January 1957. Dwight D. Eisenhower, *The White House Years: Waging Peace, 1956–1961.* (New York, 1965) 103. In the Suez crisis, Eisenhower and Dulles had feared that the British and the French might 'commit suicide by getting deeply involved . . . in an attempt to impose their rule by force on the Middle East and Africa.' Memorandum of conversation with Dulles, 24 Oct. 1956, *FRUS, 1955–57*, XVI, 774. By 1959 this concern had become part of Macmillan's creed.
213. Through a leak in the intelligence supplement to *The Economist*, Welensky had learned something of the contents of 'Africa: the Next Ten Years' and of Anglo-American discussions about it. Record of Meeting with Welensky, 20 Jan. 1960, PREM 11/3065.
214. Minute by Macmillan, 28 Dec. 1959, PREM 11/3075.
215. Macleod to Macmillan, Secret, 8 Feb. 1960, PREM 11/3030.
216. Macleod had written to Macmillan: 'If we go on with this emergency which as you know rests on the shakiest of grounds, political conditions are bound to worsen.' 27 Jan. 1960, PREM 11/3030; see also 3 April 1960, PREM 11/3076.
217. Note of Meeting, 17 Feb. 1960, PREM 11/3031.
218. John Darwin's phrase: see his account in *Britain and Decolonisation*, Ch 6. See also Cranford Pratt, *The Critical Phase in Tanzania 1945–1968* (Cambridge, 1976); and John Iliffe, *A Modern History of Tanganyika* (Cambridge, 1979).
219. See D. Anthony Low and R. Cranford Pratt, *Buganda and British Overrule* (London, 1960).
220. See Gary Wasserman, *Politics of Decolonization* (Cambridge, 1976); B. Berman and J. Lonsdale, *Unhappy Valley: Conflict in Kenya and Africa* (London, 1992).

221. See Colonial Secretary's account of progress in Africa, Cyprus, Malta, and West Indies: Minute by Macleod to Macmillan, 31 May 1960, PREM 11/3240.

222. For the connection between the Congo and the independence of the British East African territories, see CO 822/1451, especially minutes of a meeting of 16 Nov. 1959 at the Colonial Office: 'There had been a great upward surge of nationalism in the Belgian Congo which had not been foreseen . . . On the whole these developments had not greatly influenced the thinking of the leading political people in Tanganyika because their minds had been directed to their own internal political problems. But if H.M.G. failed to produce an acceptable answer to those problems, then it could not be expected that Tanganyika would remain immune from the trend of events elsewhere in Africa.'

223. Herter to US Congo Embassy, 12 July 1960, *FRUS, 1958–60*, XIV, 299. Madeleine G. Kalb, *The Congo Cables: The Cold War in Africa – From Eisenhower to Kennedy* (New York, 1982) remains essential. For the memoirs of the British Ambassador, see Ian Scott, *Tumbled House: The Congo at Independence* (London, 1969). For the United Nations and the Congo, the magisterial and revealing account by Brian Urquhart, *Ralph Bunche: An American Life* (New York, 1993), Chs 22–4.

224. US Mission at United Nations to State Department, 14 July 1960, *FRUS, 1958–60*, XIV, 305.

225. Memorandum of conversation between the President and Lord Home, 19 Sept. 1960, *FRUS, 1958–60*, XIV, 495; memorandum from Board of National Estimates to Director CIA, 22 Aug. 1960, ibid., 435–42. The evidence on the British side is fragmentary, but see minute by H.F.T. Smith in the Foreign Office on 'ensuring Lumumba's removal from the scene by killing him'. Minute of 28 Sept. 1960, FO 371/146650.

226. Director CIA to Station Officer, 26 Aug. 1960, *FRUS, 1958–60*, XIV, 443; cf. memorandum on National Security Council discussion, 18 Aug. 1960, ibid., 421 footnote 1.

227. Memorandum on National Security Council meeting, 18 Aug. 1960, *FRUS, 1958–60*, XIV, 424.

228. Minute by Home, c. 14 Sept. 1960, FO 371/146644.

229. Memorandum by Lansdowne, 26 Sept. 1961, PREM 11/3/91.

230. National Estimates memorandum, 22 Aug. 1960, *FRUS, 1958–60*, XI, 435–42.

231. See Cabinet Conclusions 74(62), 11 Dec. 1962, CAB 128/36/2.

232. Macmillan to Eisenhower, 22 July 1960, *FRUS, 1958–60*, VI, 1005, note 6. For a major reassessment see 'The Future of Anglo-American Relations', 5 Jan. 1960, FO 371/152112.

233. Cf. D.A. Low, 'The Asian Mirror to Tropical Africa's Independence', in Gifford and Louis, *Transfer of Power in Africa*, 3.

234. For the geographic spread of American military and economic aid, see *U.S. Overseas Loans and Grants*.

235. See Bernard Semmel, *The Rise of Free Trade Imperialism* (Cambridge, 1970).

236. See John Gallagher and Ronald Robinson, 'The Imperialism of Free Trade', *Economic History Review*, Second Series, VI (1953), 1–15. For a critique, W.R. Louis (ed.), *Imperialism: The Robinson and Gallagher Controversy* (New York, 1976).

Determination versus Drift: The Anglo-American Debate over the Trusteeship Issue, 1941–1945

JOHN J. SBREGA

The author is a member of the faculty in Tidewater Community College.

A key issue plaguing Anglo-American relations during World War II stemmed from differing views about the future of dependent peoples and the thorny problem of colonialism. Some Americans, notably President Franklin D. Roosevelt, insisted that "independence" was the goal for all dependent peoples, while Prime Minister Winston Churchill reflected the British view that "self-government"—which allowed for a loose association, or commonwealth of states—should be the proper goal. Of course, neither the American nor British leader recognized any need to consult the diverse groups arbitrarily lumped together under the category "dependent peoples" about their wishes and dreams for the future.

Americans voices frequently assailed the evils of colonialism, or rather dark American perceptions of European-style colonialism. Since his views on the subject were well known, Churchill served as a lightning rod for American criticisms. On the other hand, British officials were often irritated by what they considered unfounded American allegations. Recognizing the overriding need for Anglo-American harmony,

British leaders set out to educate Americans on the actual workings of their colonial system and thereby lead the Americans to an appreciation of the British point of view.

To date, the historical literature on the trusteeship issue reflects mainly the pathbreaking contributions of Christopher Thorne and William Roger Louis.[1] In his remarkable survey, Thorne looked at colonialism as only one part of the larger complexities affecting the Anglo-American relationship. His title—*Allies of a Kind*—was used, in particular, to call attention to shared racial assumptions in the United States and Britain. Thorne touched on several key issues affecting the Allied partnership in the war against Japan, among them trusteeship, but he did not undertake an in-depth analysis of the subject. Louis carefully analyzed every nuance in the development of British policy regarding dependent areas and traced its path beginning in the late nineteenth century. In his research, Louis made extensive use of Colonial Office records. This study differs, in part, because of the greater use of the papers of the Prime Minister and the Foreign Office as well as important private collections, such as the papers of General the Lord Ismay, George C. Marshall, and Joseph C. Grew. In this context, a direct connection, heretofore relatively unappreciated, exists between the furor surrounding the 1942 visit of Chiang Kai-shek to India and the renewed determination by the United States government to defend the interests of dependent peoples. I also place new emphasis on the little known interplay between the United States and the Soviet Union at the San Francisco Conference in 1945 when the Americans sought support in their conflict with the British over the stated purpose of the international trusteeship system.

In analyzing the development of the concept of international trusteeship during World War II, a general pattern of

---

1. Christopher Thorne, *Allies of a Kind: The United States, Britain, and the War Against Japan, 1941–1945* (New York, 1978); William Roger Louis, *Imperialism at Bay: The United States and the Decolonization of the British Empire, 1941–1945* (New York, 1978).

American vacillation and British resolve emerges. The Americans, less decisive than the British, eventually bowed to pragmatic arguments about the wisdom of preserving the British Empire—a process which I characterize here as a "non-policy of determined drift."

The first major wartime statement on colonial policy by the British surfaced in 1940. The War Cabinet approved a proposal by Malcolm Macdonald, colonial secretary under Neville Chamberlain, for a subsidy to promote colonial development. Macdonald promised cooperation and assistance from London without any "spirit of dictation."[2]

Other British actions early in the war indicated a genuine desire to introduce administrative reforms throughout the Empire. For example, official declarations in 1940 held out the prospect of dominion status for Burma and India; in March 1941 the new Colonial Secretary, Lord Lloyd, established a special committee on postwar colonial problems chaired by Lord Hailey. Progressive ideas discussed in Parliament particularly sparked American attention. Colonial Under-Secretary Harold MacMillan, in June 1942, outlined for the House the interdependence of the colonial relationship, emphasizing especially the idea of military-economic partnership. This enlightened statement earned praise inside the State Department.[3]

Yet American anti-imperialist barbs continued to trouble British officials. In one typical episode, Sumner Welles made casual references to racial equality and an end to imperialism in the soaring rhetoric of his 1942 Memorial Day address. Welles's remarks particularly angered British Ambassador Lord Halifax, Foreign Secretary Anthony Eden, and Dominions Secretary Clement Attlee. Attlee protested to Churchill:

---

2. Macdonald memorandum, "Statement of Policy on Colonial Development and Welfare and on Colonial Research," WP(G)(40)44, Feb. 13, 1944, War Cabinet Papers, CAB 67/4, Public Record Office, London (hereafter cited as PRO).

3. H. Freeman Matthews to Cordell Hull, July 31, 1942, file: 841.00/1601, Records of the U.S. Dept. of State, Record Group 59, National Archives, Washington, D.C. (hereafter cited as RG 59); J. H. Peck (secretary in the Prime Minister's Office) memorandum, May 26, 1942, PREM 4–42/9, Premier Papers, PRO; *Parliamentary Debates* (House of Commons), 5th ser., vol. 380, 2002–2042.

The High Commissioners are considerably exercised in their minds as to the habit of prominent Americans including members of the administration of talking as if the British Empire was in the process of dissolution. It will be well for Americans . . . to be aware that the British Colonial Empire is not a kind of private possession of the old country, but is part of a larger whole. . . .[4]

The Atlantic Charter in 1941 represented the first serious attempt at a joint Anglo-American accord on the subject, but fundamental problems about imperial preference and later qualifications by Churchill on the scope of the applicability of the Charter's principles to the British Empire left the whole issue in doubt. Another splendid opportunity arose one year later during a conversation between Secretary of State Cordell Hull and Halifax, in which the ambassador revealed that the Colonial Office was preparing a policy statement intended to ward off uninformed foreign criticism. Hull pleasantly surprised Halifax by suggesting that a joint declaration might carry more weight. He proposed an American-British-Chinese-Dutch announcement embodying "a very clear expression against officious intervention from outside with affairs which were responsibility of parent State."[5]

After digesting Halifax's report of this discussion, the new Colonial Secretary, Colonel Oliver Stanley, appealed to Churchill for permission to pursue the joint declaration Hull and Halifax had contemplated. With the approval of the Prime Minister and the collaboration of Attlee, Eden, and Stafford Cripps, Stanley submitted a memorandum on colonial policy which earned tentative approval from the War Cabinet.[6]

The authors prepared two draft texts for Halifax to deliver to Secretary Hull. The first set out general policy guidelines

4. Halifax (reporting Welles's remarks) to Foreign Office, June 11, 1942, PREM 4-42/9, PRO; Attlee to Churchill, June 16, 1942, and Eden to Churchill, June 15, 1942, *ibid.*

5. Halifax to Eden, Aug. 25, 1942, WP(42)544, Dec. 5, 1942, CAB 66/31, PRO; OSS memorandum, "British Colonial Policy," April 28, 1944, file: OSS R&A 1398, RG 59; OSS memorandum, April 24, 1944, file: OSS 71664-C, RG 226.

6. Stanley, Attlee, Cripps, Eden memorandum, "Colonial Policy," WP(42)544, Dec. 5, 1942, CAB 66/31, PRO; Stanley to Churchill, Dec. 1, 1942, PREM 4-42/9, PRO.

looking to conditions of security and prosperity for all, including dependent areas not yet ready to share the burdens of responsibility for preventing a reoccurrence of the existing aggression. Consequently, there was a duty "for all parent States to enter into general defense schemes designed to ensure freedom from fear for all peoples." Then, after international security arrangements had been established, the "parent States" would work to develop the social, economic, and political well-being "of peoples who are unable without dangers to themselves and to others to assume full responsibility for their affairs." This first draft declaration closed with a call for organizing and marketing the natural resources of dependent areas "not for the promotion of purely commercial ends, but in the best interests of the peoples concerned and of the world as a whole."

The second draft message to Halifax addressed the practical application of these general principles, but it was to be presented only if Hull agreed with the first proposed text. In this section, the authors desired to explore the type of machinery for consultation and collaboration that could be made available. Regional commissions, composed of representatives of parent states and nations having a major defense or economic interest in the region, were mentioned, yet it was clearly spelled out that each parent state retained full responsibility for its own territories. The authors concluded by identifying Southeast Asia as the best region for early efforts at Anglo-American agreement because (a) the Japanese occupied the entire area, (b) the need for common defense was most urgent there, and (c) the United States had some practical experience in colonial administration in the region.

The War Cabinet approved the memorandum, subject to the endorsement of the Dominions. Churchill appended a message stressing the importance of the project to each of the four Dominion Prime Ministers. He welcomed American interest in the British Empire and wanted the United States, through such cooperative ventures, to continue to look outward rather than inward. Moreover, Churchill believed that the proposed Joint Declaration would help "clamp down the restless, irresponsible and ignorant criticisms which have been prevalent in America."[7]

The responses from the Dominion leaders, however, fell below the War Cabinet's expectations. Without exception, the four Dominion Prime Ministers protested the undue emphasis on defense in the draft declaration. For example, Jan Christian Smuts of South Africa urged deemphasizing any hint of the United States defending the British Empire. Furthermore, Canadian Prime Minister Mackenzie King, Australian Prime Minister John Curtin, and New Zealand Prime Minister Peter Fraser joined Smuts in advocating wider representation on the regional commissions—possibly to include native peoples.[8]

Although unsolicited, the Viceroy of India, Lord Linlithgow, interjected his views in a personal message to Churchill. The Viceroy admitted that, for the present, Churchill and President Franklin D. Roosevelt would undoubtedly work in close harmony; nevertheless, the Viceroy remained apprehensive about the future. He warned that "a weak P.M. here and an indifferent, hostile or electioneering President in U.S.A. might put us badly at a disadvantage." In addition, the Dominions Office received unfavorable reactions to the proposed Joint Declaration from each of the four British High Commissioners in the Dominions. They, too, recommended less emphasis on defense and security arrangments. Eden alerted Halifax to these views. The Foreign Secretary suggested that the British proposals be presented as an effort to work out Hull's own ideas and to apply the principles of the Atlantic Charter.[9]

---

7. Churchill circular message, Dec. 11, 1942, PREM 4–42/9, PRO; WM(42)166, Dec. 9, 1942, CAB 65/28, PRO.

8. Dominions Secretary Attlee summarized the four replies for the Cabinet in WP(43)6, Jan. 4, 1943, CAB 66/33, PRO. The full text of each reply (from Curtin, Fraser, King, and Smuts) may be found in PREM 4–42/9, PRO.

9. Eden to Halifax, Dec. 14, 1942, PREM 4–42/9, PRO; Linlithgow to Churchill, and Linlithgow to Secretary of State for India Leo Amery, Jan. 2, 1943, *ibid.*

Halifax agreed that the draft text contained too great an emphasis on defense. He pointed out that Americans believed in the need to solve the social and political inequities among dependent peoples, which created conditions leading to exploitation and intervention by other powers. Thus, the standard of living and the political status of such peoples represented key elements of security. Completing his second year in the United States, Halifax revealed a growing awareness of the American character. His advice to the Foreign Secretary was to concentrate more on the form rather than the substance of the proposed declaration. "Tradition leads Americans to attach great value to general statements of rights and principles," Halifax explained. Consequently, he advocated providing Hull with only "the broad heads" of the proposed policy statement because the "preamble of any declaration in which we ask them to join will in their eyes be of almost equal importance to the articles which follow." Halifax confirmed that Secretary Hull had expressed interest in the raising of social standards for dependent peoples. Shortly thereafter, Halifax apparently elicited the approval of President Roosevelt for the concept of regional commissions, for at least that was the impression relayed to London.[10]

After digesting the various critiques, Stanley, Attlee, Eden, and Cripps presented a revised draft declaration on colonial policy to the War Cabinet in early January 1943. Citing the basic need to prevent future aggression which, in turn, required assurances to all peoples of "security, prosperity, equal status and equal opportunity," this draft text identified the duty of "parent States" to contribute to the social, economic, and political development of colonial peoples "until they were able, without damage to themselves and others, to discharge the responsibilities of government." Although this newer version did embody a call for general defense schemes, it put much more emphasis than the original statement on guidance

---

10. See Halifax telegrams to Eden, Dec. 24 and 26, 1942, WP(43)8, Jan. 5, 1943, CAB 66/33, PRO.

and development. For example, the resources of dependent areas would be organized and marketed for the service of the indigenous population and general global welfare rather than imperial commercial interests. Also, the regional commissions were given a broader base to include native peoples as well as the "parent States" and other nations which had a major interest in the area. The declared goal of this regional cooperative machinery was "to promote the advancement of the Colonial peoples and the general welfare of mankind."[11]

The War Cabinet approved this revised draft—after striking out the reference to "equal status" and substituting the term "Parent or Trustee States" in place of "parent States." The reactions from the Dominions were generally favorable, and Halifax gave his endorsement to the proposed text in the confidence that the duty of guidance would appeal to Americans. Upon incorporating stylistic changes suggested by various readers (in what amounted to a third draft), the four authors obtained support from the Prime Minister at the Casablanca Conference and approval from the War Cabinet of this third draft text for submission to Secretary Hull.[12]

Halifax presented the British proposal to Hull on February 4, 1943, but the State Department waited almost two full months before answering with a draft text of its own. It was handed to Eden in Washington in late March. Despite the apparent lassitude on this issue, American thinking about dependent areas had, in fact, evolved to a fairly mature stage by the time of Eden's visit to the United States. By mid-1942, for example, the State Department had established a monitoring system to follow ideas advanced within the international community

---

11. WP(43)8. Jan. 5, 1943, CAB 66/33, PRO.
12. See WM(43)4, Jan. 7, and WM(43)12, Jan. 20, 1943, CAB 65/33, PRO. Cabinet Secretary E. E. Bridges collected the various comments on the first draft text for Churchill, who was by then considering a second draft. These included the comments of Amery, WP(42)575; Bevin, WP(42)606; Cripps, WP(42)614; the four Dominions, WP(43)6; Stanley, WP(43)7; and the Viceroy of India, WP(43)9. The responses from Halifax and the Dominions to the second draft are annexed to the third draft, Jan. 19, 1943, CAB 65/33, PRO.

concerning dependent areas in the postwar era. In addition, internal State Department arrangements for postwar studies produced fruitful discussions about American policies.[13]

Although some influential Americans, including Roosevelt, voiced concern about the general subject of the future of dependent peoples, their interest quickened considerably during 1942 as a result of a diplomatic explosion over the specific case of India. When Generalissimo and Madam Chiang Kai-shek visited India in February 1942, Mahatma Gandhi told them: "[The British] will never voluntarily treat us Indians as equals; why, they do not even admit your country to their staff talks." After Chiang tried to enlist Roosevelt's aid in interceding to promote self-government for India (and Roosevelt was obviously sympathetic to the idea), Churchill became incensed. On August 29, 1942, Churchill lectured Chiang: "I think the best rule for allies to follow is not to interfere in each other's internal affairs. . . . I should like to place on record the fact that no British Government of which I am the head, or a member, will ever be prepared to accept such mediation on a matter affecting the sovereign rights of His Majesty, the King Emperor."[14] The episode warned Americans about the depth of British resistance to any tinkering with their Empire. Thus, by mid-1942, the United States government renewed its determination to seek mutual understanding and accommodation with the British on the future of colonialism, especially through joint studies of dependent areas.

13. Hull to Ambassador Clarence Gauss (in China), July 21, 1942, U.S. Dept. of State, *Foreign Relations of the United States, 1942*, Vol. VII: *China* (Washington, D.C., 1956), 733; H. Notter, P. Moseley, C. Rothwell memorandum, T-15, July [10?], 1942, box 31, Harley A. Notter Files, (hereafter cited as Notter Files) RG 59; Harold Shantz (U.S. Embassy in London) to Secretary of State, Mar. 25, 1942, file: 841.00/1547, RG 59; Hull memorandum of conversation with Halifax, Feb. 4, 1943, box 4, Leo R. Pasvolsky Files, RG 59.

14. PREM 4–45/4 and PREM 3–167/1, PRO; file: "PM's Telegrams—1942," General the Lord Ismay Papers, King's College, London; John J. Sbrega, *Anglo-American Relations and Colonialism in East Asia, 1941–1945* (New York, 1983).

Earlier in August, the Political and International Organization (PIO) Subcommittee had prepared a detailed analysis of a system of international trusteeship for dependent peoples. This plan evisioned an executive authority within a projected international organization which would supervise all dependent areas and determine when the goal of self-government had been attained. Regional supervisory councils would administer specific dependent areas on a day-to-day basis and report periodically to the executive authority. All administrative officials would be confirmed by the executive authority only after they swore a loyalty oath to the international organization (as opposed to their native—imperial—countries). Although this version and subsequent revisions failed to consider enemy possessions and smaller states possibly rendered dependent because of regional security arrangements, State Department planning at this stage persistently emphasized the important point that all colonial powers, while retaining administering authority, had to place their colonies under international trusteeship. The PIO memorandum enumerated specific supervisory and administrative guidelines, which included (1) preparation for self-government, (2) economic and social justice, (3) equal economic opportunity for all, and (4) contributions toward a general international security system. Finally, this planning memorandum reaffirmed the ultimate goal of self-government for dependent peoples but asserted that this goal would be compatible with a partnership of free membership on a federal, or commonwealth, basis.[15]

Hull and the State Department, in November 1942, significantly altered the scope of the territories scheduled to come

---

15. Unsigned memorandum, "International Trusteeship," PIO-29a, Aug. 28, 1942, box 117, Notter Files RG 59. For other versions of this plan, see Clarke M. Eichelburger, B. V. Cohen, James T. Shotwell memorandum, PIO-29, Aug. 28, 1942; B.O. Gerig memoranda, PIO-30 and 30a, Sep. 4, 1942; Eichelburger memorandum, PIO-29e, Oct. 22, 1942; unsigned final draft, PIO-29i, April 15, 1943 (all in *ibid.*); also folder "PIO Minutes 1–40," box 138, *ibid.*

under the postwar trusteeship system being planned. They recommended first the inclusion only of presently mandated territories (i.e. League of Nations) and any areas detached from enemy states and second the exclusion of existing (i.e. prewar) colonial arrangements. Hull suggested that "the colonial powers would undertake a pledge to observe specified principles to administration and would publish essential information regarding their colonial administrations."[16] How the Churchill cabinet and other interested parties, such as the French and the Dutch, would have enjoyed hearing that news!

Somewhat earlier, in another indication of American thinking about dependent areas, Roosevelt emphasized the key role of the Big Four in developing the machinery for trusteeship. He told a British diplomat that any specific trusteeship arrangement would probably have an initial term of ten years, with perhaps a possible renewal for another ten years.[17] Thus, despite Hull's assertion to Halifax that the proposal for a joint declaration had been made entirely on the secretary's own responsibility,[18] American plans about trusteeship had, in fact, significantly matured by the time the British draft statement was under consideration in Washington and the conversations with Eden had begun in March 1943.

Meanwhile, prior to 1944, there were no credible voices in official American circles calling for the United States to embark on a postwar policy of imperialism.[19] Notwithstanding some grandiose remarks by one naval officer[20] (who did not represent the consensus views of the group), the special inter-

16. Hull to Roosevelt, Nov. 17, 1942, box 1, ibid.
17. Sir Ronald I. Campbell (British Embassy in Washington) to Sir Alexander Cadogan (Permanent Under Secretary of State for Foreign Affairs), Aug. 6, 1942, PREM 4–42/9, PRO.
18. Halifax to Foreign Office, Jan. 6, 1943, ibid.
19. See, for example, Notter to Welles, Mar. 15, 1943, box 3, Notter Files RG 59.
20. Captain H. L. Pence advocated taking over the Japanese Mandated Islands, which he referred to as "aircraft carriers." His views, frequently expressed, received no support among the other postwar planners. See, for example, minutes of meeting #20, June 16, 1943, box 79, Notter Files RG 59.

departmental subcommittee on dependent areas never seriously entertained the prospect of territorial aggrandizement for the United States. In fact, one position paper written by Rupert Emerson, and approved by the subcommittee, explicitly called for "the abandonment of imperialist pretensions."[21]

On the basis of the British proposal, Hull and the State Department modified their November memorandum on March 9. The American draft statement submitted first to Roosevelt, distinguished clearly between mandated or detached enemy territories, on the one hand, and colonial possessions, on the other. Hull strongly advised Roosevelt to include in the trusteeship system only the former. Incorporating the British idea of regional commissions for dependent areas, the American draft stipulated that colonial peoples should be granted progressive measures of self-government on a fixed time schedule aimed at complete independence. According to the American version, the proposed United Nations organization would be responsible not only for cooperating with the designated dependent peoples in preparation for independence but also for influencing the imperial powers to adopt similar policies toward their colonies.[22]

Although there had been no opportunity to explore the American counter proposal during his visit to the United States, Eden reported to the War Cabinet that he found the American draft unsatisfactory in several respects. Specifically, he criticized the imposition of time-table deadlines, the lack of distinction between dependent areas and territories which had lost their independence, and, perhaps most important, the announced goal of complete independence. The American draft remained the basis for unofficial conversations about trustee-

---

21. Rupert Emerson memorandum, Mar. 9, 1943, box 36, *ibid.*

22. State Department memorandum, Mar. 9, 1943, enclosed in Hull to Roosevelt, Mar. 17, 1943, box 1, Notter Files RG 59; Cordell Hull, *The Memoirs of Cordell Hull* (2 vols., New York, 1948), II, 1234–1236; Ralph Bunche memorandum, "The Background of Recent Department Policy Regarding Dependent Areas," Jan. 3, 1945, box 275, Notter Files RG 59; unsigned, undated memorandum, "International Trusteeship," box 22, *ibid.*

ship by the President at QUADRANT (Quebec, August 1943) and the secretary of state at the Moscow Conference of Foreign Ministers in October 1943; however, the topic was not formally discussed at either meeting. Privately at QUADRANT, Eden told Hull that the term "independence" could never have a satisfactory meaning to cover what various governments might have in mind in their use of the term.[23]

Official British statements on colonial policy, meanwhile, dispelled all doubts that His Majesty's Government would retain the Commonwealth system. Colonial Secretary Stanley, for example, delivered two important speeches in which he frankly declared that "the administration of the British colonies must continue to be the sole responsibility of Great Britain" and that the British goal for colonial peoples was "self-government within the framework of the British Empire."[24]

Until the spring of 1944, planners in London and Washington seemed to be passing on different rails. Each group had labored on the project of trusteeship peripherally and apparently only dimly aware of the depth of the ideas of the other. The British persistently emphasized the concepts of "Commonwealth" and regional groupings (to consult on common problems as well as security arrangements). This twin emphasis complemented concurrent postwar planning for a world organization since the British had always upheld the doctrine of accountability. Thus, the general power of supervision implied in a world organization could still be detached from specific administrative responsibility within, say, the British Commonwealth of Nations.[25]

---

23. Hull memorandum, Aug. 31, 1943, box 284, Notter Files RG 59; WM(43)53, SSF, April 13, 1943, CAB 65/34, PRO.

24. Unsigned memorandum, "British Colonial 'Partnership,'" Nov. 29, 1943, box 91, Notter Files RG 59. For more on British statements of colonial policy, see W. J. Gallman (U.S. Embassy in London) to Hull, Jan. 11, 1943, file: 841.00/1614, RG 59; Gallman to Hull, March 17, 1943, file: 841.00/1643, RG 59; Ambassador John G. Winant (in London) to Hull, July 14, 1943, file: 841.00/1654, RG 59; press reports collected in FO 371.35917, F 1589/877/61, in papers of the Foreign Office (hereafter cited by file and piece numbers), PRO, and PREM 4–43A/5, PRO.

25. See, for example, Lord Hailey memorandum, "The Future of Colonial Peoples," enclosed in Hailey to Churchill, March 24, 1944, PREM 4–42/9, PRO.

American ideas about dependent areas lacked an overall integration. American planners could accept regional machinery but strongly opposed the fragmentation of general security responsibilities spread over various regional arrangements. Leo Pasvolsky, special assistant to Hull, led a vocal faction within the State Department calling for a supervisory coordinating agency created by the United Nations coalition.[26] And, of course, there remained the perplexing problem of the ultimate goal of trusteeship. Was it independence or self-government?

American policy planning failed to shift out of these early abstractions into more practical assessments without abandoning the desired goals ascribed in Washington to trusteeship. To accept an unfettered doctrine of accountability might mean the revival of prewar colonial evils; to accept regional groupings might mean a relapse into the parochialism and passivity that plagued the prewar period. A general system of international trusteeship appeared to hold the solution, at least for American planners, to the problem of dependent territories. The British were equally lax in planning specific arrangements, but they seemed to stand on more sure ground since they were merely advocating a system of colonial administration and accountability that had already proved viable within the British Commonwealth.

Nevertheless, despite the mutual suspicions and heated rhetoric, elements of a compromise did exist. The State Department's Committee on Colonial Problems pointed to American policy concerning Puerto Rico and argued that, like the British, the United States viewed its dependent territories as "permanent adjuncts of the national domain." Moreover, a special Pasvolsky subcommittee on war aims noted the vast area of agreement in British and American objectives with regard to the administration of dependent areas. These mutual objectives included "the improvement of economic, social, and

---

26. Pasvolsky memorandum, "International Activities in Which the United States Must Participate," Aug. 9, 1943, box 284, Notter Files RG 59.

educational standards and conditions in colonial areas and the progressive development of dependent peoples toward self-government."[27] Although these elements of compromise did exist and might have helped bring about an agreement eventually, a real breakthrough in the joint formulation of the trusteeship concept came during the visit to London in April 1944 of a State Department group headed by Under-Secretary of State Edward R. Stettinius, Jr.

Aware that the British regarded the draft declaration proposed in March 1943 by Hull as vague and impractical, the Stettinius Mission set out to settle specific problem areas such as Italian Somaliland, Libya, and the Japanese Mandated Islands. As these conversations progressed, mutual suspicions regarding the general topic of international trusteeship gradually diminished. Colonial Secretary Stanley and Isaiah Bowman took the lead in arriving at a common understanding.

To be sure, not all disagreement evaporated. Yet the dialogue concerning trusteeship emphasized congruence rather than conflict. At the conclusion of the discussions, Stanley presented four guidelines which everyone agreed would serve as the basis for further exploration. Stanley's four points were: (1) any statement on colonial policy should become part of the structure of the world organization rather than a joint declaration; (2) regional commissions, made up of parent states and states with major interests in such areas would study, recommend, and advise but would not be actual administrative bodies; (3) functional branches of the world organization (health, nutrition, labor, etc.) would be linked to the work of the regional commission; and (4) all colonial powers would submit annual published reports to the world organization.[28]

Point two on regional commissions, of course, undermined the hopes of the more idealistic planners in the State Department, but it did reflect the preference of Secretary Hull. In fact,

27. Pasvolsky subcommittee memorandum, "British Peace Aims," Mar. 29, 1944, box 15, *ibid.*; minutes of CP meeting #2, Sep. 30, 1943, box 183, *ibid.*
28. Stettinius report to Hull, May 22, 1944, box 87, *ibid.*

American attention to trusteeship before the Yalta Conference remained within the general framework of Stanley's four points. Various State Department working papers transformed regional supervisory commissions into regional advisory commissions accountable to the world organization. Meanwhile, the goal for dependent peoples shifted to self-government "on the basis either of independence or of autonomous association with other peoples within a state or grouping of states."[29]

To the surprise of the British, the United States bypassed a splendid opportunity for valuable consultations by eliminating the subject of trusteeship from the agenda for the Dumbarton Oaks Conference in 1944. The explanation lay in the desire of the Joint Chiefs of Staff, at least for the time being, to avoid the awkwardness that would surely emerge in realistic and frank discussions of postwar security arrangements and trusteeship. Army Chief of Staff General George C. Marshall pointed out that conversations about trusteeship necessarily affected two major military considerations: first, the vital importance of an early Russian entry into the Far Eastern war; and second, the profound changes in the military strengths of the major powers at this stage in the war (e.g., a powerful Soviet Union and a considerably weakened British Commonwealth). Another consideration of major importance was the growing conviction that postwar national security required American control, if not possession, of the Japanese mandated islands. Thus, the original American concept in 1942 had suffered considerable erosion by early 1945.[30]

Throughout this gradual change in policy, however, Roosevelt remained constant in his rhetoric of idealism. He

---

29. See the unsigned State Dept. memoranda: "Regional Advisory Councils," n.d. [Aug. 1944?], box 22, *ibid.*; "Trusteeship," n.d. [Dec. 1944?], box 39, *ibid.*

30. Pasvolsky memorandum, "Questions Left Unsettled at Dumbarton Oaks," Nov. 15, 1944, box 246, *ibid.*; Bunche memorandum, "Background of Recent Department Policy Regarding Dependent Areas," Jan. 3, 1945, box 275, *ibid.*; Alger Hiss memorandum, Aug. 5, 1944, box 65, *ibid.*; Joint Chiefs of Staff memorandum, enclosed in Marshall to Hull, Aug. 3, 1944, U.S. Dept. of State, *Foreign Relations of the United States, 1944,* (7 vols., Washington, D.C., 1966), I, 699–703.

affirmed his definite desire to hold to the principle of international trusteeship. In London, meanwhile, this idealistic strain in the United States (reflected also in the recommendations of the State Department about the postwar international structure) was generally accepted at face value. Although some British officials suspected that American criticism of British colonial practices was a ruse to supplant prewar European imperialism with a postwar American version,[31] British planning, as noted, proceeded on the generally accepted belief that Americans were simply misinformed or unreasonable about the theory and practices of the British Commonwealth.

Rather than fret over possible imperialist tendencies and acquisitive instincts in the United States after the war, most British officials, in fact, expressed quite an opposite concern—namely, the probability that Americans would lapse into the same isolationism that had paralyzed American policy in the inter-war period. The British wanted the United States to stay actively involved in international affairs and to assume the global responsibilities befitting a superpower. This policy would not only ease the anticipated postwar burdens on the strained resources of the Empire but also position the United States around the globe in ways that would buttress British interests. The "special relationship," consequently, would continue to benefit Britain.

Therefore, most British policymakers—even the skeptical Oliver Stanley—encouraged American participation on the postwar global scene. Churchill promoted this spirit when he advised the four Dominion prime ministers: "We should do well not to resent but rather to welcome American interest in the British Colonial Empire, and there would be advantages in so

---

31. See, for example, Victor Cavendish-Bentinck memorandum, Dec. 22, 1943, FO 371.35921, F 6656/1422/61, PRO; A. L. Moffat memorandum, Nov. 10, 1944, file: 740.0011PW/11–1044, RG 59; Roosevelt to Stettinius, Nov. 24, 1944, file: 740.0011PW/11–2444, RG 59; Charles Taussig memorandum of conversation, Jan. 16, 1945, box 52, Charles Taussig Papers, Franklin D. Roosevelt Library, Hyde Park, New York (hereafter cited as Taussig Papers).

arranging our affairs that the United States joins in public acceptance of a line of policy towards Colonial peoples and their development."[32] Where British criticism or ill-feeling against Americans existed, it was not out of suspicions of United States imperialism (as is argued by some contemporary historians) but rather out of more mundane motives, such as blind frustration because of the war[33] and the malevolent influence of notable American anglophobes, such as Leo Crowley,[34] Monsignor Francis J. Spellman,[35] and the Lauchlin Currie-Owen Lattimore connection.[36]

An episode in late 1944 indicated the depth of British sensibilities—especially those of the Prime Minister—about genuine or perceived outside interference in imperial affairs. In December, Halifax reported that the State Department not only wanted trusteeship discussed at the forthcoming Yalta Conference but also expected the British to initiate concrete proposals in preparation for that meeting. Immediately after reading this message, an anxious Churchill addressed the Foreign Secretary:

How does this matter stand? There must be no question of our being hustled or seduced into declarations affecting British sovereignty in any of the Dominions or the Colonies. Pray remember my declaration against liquidating the British Empire. If the Americans want to take Japanese islands which they have conquered, let them do so with our blessing and any form of words that may be agreeable to them.

---

32. Churchill circular message, Dec. 11, 1942, PREM 4–42/9, PRO; Benjamin O. Gerig memorandum of conversation, Jan. 8, 1942, box 3, Notter Files RG 59.

33. For example, the House of Commons erupted in a sudden outburst of anti-American rhetoric on Jan. 8, 1942. See *Parliamentary Debates* (House of Commons), 5th ser., vol. 379, 82–174; T. C. Achilles to Secretary of State, Jan. 9, 1942, file: 711.41/523, RG 59.

34. Ray Atherton to H. Freeman Matthews, Feb. 10, 1944, box 1, H. Freeman Matthews Files, RG 59.

35. Sir D'Arcy Osborne (British Minister to the Vatican) to Foreign Office, March 1, 1943, FO 371.37543, R 2044/912/57, PRO.

36. Sir Ronald I. Campbell to Foreign Office, Sept. 5, 1943, FO 371.35994, Z 9726/2/17, PRO.

But "Hands off the British Empire" is our maxim and it must not be weakened or smirched to please sob-stuff merchants at home or foreigners of any hue.[37]

Eden promptly reassured the Prime Minister that the State Department did not contemplate liquidating the Empire. Eden provided Churchill with a copy of a War Cabinet memorandum Stanley had drawn up on the basis of the four points worked out with Stettinius. In fact, Eden suggested that Stanley visit Washington and show the memorandum to the State Department. Still unconvinced, but preoccupied with more immediate problems, such as the Ardennes campaign and the perplexing Polish question, Churchill refused to be rushed into an official declaration that might undermine his beloved Empire. Obviously uncomfortable that he had not had sufficient time to study the implications of the Stanley proposal, Churchill referred to another trusted opinion—that of his principal private secretary, John M. Martin. Far from a danger to the Empire, Martin advised, the four points seemed to promise other nations a means of legitimate inquiry into colonial and dependent areas without infringing on British sovereignty (or that of another colonial power).[38]

Although the Prime Minister said he accepted Martin's views, he could not shake his concern. After Eden and Stanley reevaluated the British position, Eden relayed more soothing words to the Prime Minister. In a revealing summary of British colonial planning on the eve of the Yalta Conference, Eden told Churchill that the four points did not jeopardize the Empire. By seizing the initiative, Eden hoped to prevent the State Department from circulating its own colonial schemes which might endanger the Empire. Eden suggested that, if Roosevelt raised the topic at Yalta, the Prime Minister might state that the British

---

37. Halifax to Foreign Office, Dec. 30, 1944, PREM 4–31/4, PRO; Churchill to Eden, Dec. 31, 1944, *ibid.*; Stanley and Attlee memorandum, "Colonial Policy," WP(44)738, Dec. 14, 1944, CAB 66/59, PRO.

38. The Churchill-Martin correspondence may be found in PREM 4–31/4, PRO; see also Eden to Churchill, Jan. 8, 1945, *ibid.*

were preparing a plan of trusteeship and that, in the meantime, perhaps the Americans would hold off their own proposals.[39]

At Yalta, the issue of international trusteeship, which had seemed a potential powderkeg, sailed through to unanimous agreement with surprising ease—save for one brief explosion by the Prime Minister. At a meeting of the foreign ministers on February 9, Secretary of State Stettinius incorporated in a report to the heads of state a draft proposal by Alger Hiss that the Big Five should consult on territorial trusteeship and dependent areas prior to and during the forthcoming United Nations Conference. As Stettinius was reading his report, the Prime Minister interrupted to say that he would never consent to "forty or fifty nations thrusting interfering fingers into the life's existence of the British Empire." He shouted that he would never agree to have a British representative placed in the dock to defend the Empire, and he repeated the words: "never, never, never." Presidential aid Harry Hopkins said later that he could hardly follow the excited and rapid speech of the Prime Minister. Stettinius tried to explain that the trusteeship system was not meant to be applied to the British Empire, but Churchill insisted it should be so stated if that was the case. He suddenly turned to Stalin and inquired how the Soviet leader would feel about a suggestion to internationalize the Crimea for use as a summer resort. Coolly, Stalin replied that he would be delighted to offer the Crimea as a place to be used for meetings of the Big Three. There was a brief recess at this point.

During this intermission Stettinius asked Hiss to jot down a summary of the proposed trusteeship system. The Hiss memorandum affirmed that trusteeship would be applied only to (1) existing League of Nations mandates, (2) territories detached from enemy countries, and (3) "any other territory that may *voluntarily* be placed under trusteeship." Hiss also left to subsequent agreements the matter of identifying which territo-

---

39. See in *ibid.:* Churchill to Martin, Jan. 4, 1945; Churchill to Eden, Jan. 18, 1945; and Eden to Churchill, Jan. 24, 1945.

ries within the three categories would be placed under trusteeship. Stettinius showed this hastily written note to Churchill who indicated his agreement before the plenary session reconvened. The wording was substantially embodied in the final "Protocol of Proceedings."[40] By acquiescing in the idea of voluntary submission to trusteeship authority, the United States virtually ensured that the colonial powers would retain control over their prewar possessions.

What had caused this retreat from the original American ideal of a comprehensive system of trusteeship to promote independence for all dependent peoples? The State Department and President Roosevelt had followed the path of least resistance since the ambitious—and idealistic—planning days of 1942. Roosevelt never abandoned his intention to thwart the postwar restoration of prewar colonial controls, but he never threw the full weight of the United States behind his scheme. At Cairo and Tehran, the President enlisted the support of Chiang Kai-shek and Stalin, yet he delayed making a final policy decision for so long that events virtually preempted his options. By the summer of 1944, the presidential firmness had dissipated. The Joint Chiefs persuaded Roosevelt and the State Department to drop trusteeship from the Dumbarton Oaks agenda to avoid adding yet another flashpoint to Russo-American relations. The State Department was split between "idealists," who anticipated the end of colonialism, and "realists," who believed that postwar cooperation among the

40. U.S. Dept. of State, *Foreign Relations of the United States: The Conferences at Malta and Yalta* (Washington, D.C., 1956), 844–977; James F. Byrnes, *Speaking Frankly* (New York, 1947), ix–x; Robert Sherwood, *Roosevelt and Hopkins: An Intimate History* (New York, 1948), 865–866; Lord Moran, *Winston Churchill: The Struggle for Survival, 1940–1965* (London, 1966), 228–229; Edward R. Stettinius, Jr., *Roosevelt and the Russians* (Garden City, 1949), 238–239; Sir Llewellyn Woodward, *British Foreign Policy in the Second World War* (London, 1972), 536; Earl of Avon, *The Memoirs of Anthony Eden: The Reckoning* (London, 1965), 595; see also Louis, *Imperialism at Bay;* Thorne, *Allies of a Kind;* Sbrega, *Anglo-American Relations;* Robert Dallek, *Franklin D. Roosevelt and American Foreign Policy, 1933–1945* (New York, 1979).

powers—including the British and other imperial nations—was a prerequisite to international stability.[41]

Zealous American officials had pressed more idealistic notions of territorial trusteeship on the reluctant British at Malta and again at Yalta; however, these efforts ended with the notes hastily composed by Hiss. The Yalta Protocol, therefore, marked the virtual demise of any hopes for a progressive postwar readjustment in the treatment of colonial dependencies. The earnest efforts of the British, who upheld the principle of accountability, to develop a solution to the problems of colonialism had the unfortunate effect of removing the practices by other colonial powers from direct international supervision through a world organization. Accountability, consequently, was seriously undermined as one possible safeguard for dependent peoples. In addition, presidential procrastination served to erode liberal and humane aspirations concerning colonialism. Roosevelt pursued what might be called a "non-policy of determined drift," and, to that extent, he unwittingly contributed to the gradual erosion of his original concept of international trusteeship. Shortly before his death, Roosevelt insisted that "independence" not "self-government," remained his ultimate goal for dependent peoples,[42] but events had far outpaced this wishful thinking.

Ironically, at the San Francisco Conference, the Chinese, on May 8, and the Russians, on May 14, 1945, introduced draft resolutions which supported the eventual "independence" of the trusteeships. Russian delegate A. Sobolev observed, apparently with a straight face, that the term independence was "very useful to inhabitants of trust territories because it clearly recog-

---

41. See, for example, the testimony of Abbott Low Moffat in U.S. Congress, Senate, Committee on Foreign Relations, *Hearings . . . Causes, Origins, and Consequences of the Vietnam War* (Washington, D.C., 1972), 161–165; Bunche memorandum, "Arrangements for International Trusteeship," box 273, Notter Files RG 59.

42. Taussig memorandum, March 15, 1945, box 49, Taussig Papers; also Taussig's report of Roosevelt's views and events at the San Francisco Conference in Taussig memorandum of conversation with Eleanor Roosevelt, Aug. 27, 1945, box 52, *ibid.*

nizes on behalf of these people, those principles and aims which are included among the basic purposes of the Organization."[43]

The angry British delegation threatened to abandon the issue entirely. The Chinese and Russian proposals rocked the American delegation, which was already divided because of sharp differences in Washington. Bitter exchanges had erupted on the eve of the conference when the State Department resisted military-naval leaders who argued for complete American control of strategic Pacific islands. Even the Department of Interior entered the fray, with the contention that American trusteeships should come under its civilian control. The American delegation maneuvered around domestic liberal sentiment by arranging to differentiate certain "strategic" trusteeship territories from other trusteeship territories. The "strategic" trusts were to come under the Security Council (and United States influence), while the General Assembly exercised supervisory functions for the other trust territories through a Trusteeship Council. British anxieties that this formula might jeopardize imperial defense schemes were eased when the Americans successfully produced an amendment exempting from the supervision of the Trusteeship Council those imperial arrangements which contributed to "the maintenance of international peace and security."[44]

The American position became even more awkward after the Chinese and Russians advocated "independence" as the proper goal for dependent peoples. Charles Taussig and Harley Notter supported those proposals, but Harold Stassen, John Foster Dulles, Stettinius, Pasvolsky, and Isaiah Bowman argued against them. Stassen labelled independence a "provocative word." Bowman wanted to cultivate the postwar friendship of the British, French, and Dutch because he be-

---

43. Minutes of Trusteeship Committee, box 273, Notter Files RG 59.

44. *Ibid.;* see also minutes of the United Kingdom delegation meetings, May 8 and 12, 1945, CAB 21–1611–16/17/1, PRO; Lord Cranborne (in San Francisco) to Stanley, May 12, 1945, PREM 4–31/4, PRO.

lieved an "inevitable struggle" would take place between the United States and the Soviet Union.[45]

A compromise formula emerged to avoid embarrassment over the term "independence." The final draft on trusteeship incorporated the language of the Atlantic Charter by identifying the ultimate goal as "the freely-expressed wishes of the people concerned." Russian resistance persisted, but after an extraordinary personal approach by Stettinius to Andre Gromyko, the Trusteeship Committee reached agreement on June 8. Twelve days later, this section of the United Nations Charter passed "without objection" through Commission II (Under President Jan Christian Smuts), which was acting in behalf of the full membership.[46]

Thus, the original American ideals of international trusteeship for all dependent peoples evaporated. Ambitious projects to prevent a continuation of prewar imperial exploitation fell before the skillful maneuvering of those nations with a vested interest in colonialism. Even the limited concept of international controls for mandated areas and ex-enemy territories crumbled against the perceived security needs of the United States.[47]

Ironically, a tragic postwar twist saw the United States gradually become identified with the other colonial powers as suppressors of the legitimate aspirations of dependent peoples for independence. In the absence of strong, clear leadership from

---

45. Minutes of United States delegation meeting, May 18, 1945, box 272, Notter Files RG 59.

46. For a report on Stettinius's approach to Gromyko, June 2, 1945, see "Stettinius Diary—San Francisco Conference," box 283, Notter Files RG 59; also related correspondence and memoranda in the Edward R. Stettinius Papers, University of Virginia.

47. Secretary of War Henry L. Stimson, for instance, advocated obtaining the Japanese Mandated Islands. He argued, "They are not colonies; they are outposts, and their acquisition is appropriate under the doctrine of self-defense," box 172, Henry L. Stimson Papers, Yale University. At San Francisco, Senator Tom Connally asserted, "I don't want to be morally in the wrong, but I want to keep those islands," in minutes of meeting, June 1, 1945, box 283, Notter Files RG 59.

the White House, American wartime policy concerning dependent areas floated aimlessly. The ill-effects of this uncertainty proved even more harmful in the face of resolute action by the colonial powers to protect their imagined imperial interests. How prophetic was Churchill's remark in 1942 that Americans "were not above learning from us, provided that we did not set out to teach them."[48] The praiseworthy objectives that had marked American postwar planning early in the war were subsequently drowned in a "non-policy of determined drift."

48. WM(42)8, Jan. 17, 1942, CAB 65/29, PRO.

The Anglo-American Alliance, 1941-45

By G.D. Sheffield

Writing in 1950 about the wartime Anglo-American Alliance, Winston Churchill asserted, "There never was a more serviceable war machinery established among allies, and I rejoice that in fact if not in form it continues to this day."[1]

This is a statement that reveals much and conceals much. It reveals an essential truth about the solidity of the alliance, for rarely, if ever, has there been such a close and successful coalition of independent states. But it also conceals the tensions that existed within the Alliance: the arguments over strategy, the personality clashes, and the divergent war aims of the coalition partners. Above all, the statement reveals Churchill's desire to minimize wartime tensions at a time when the Anglo-American Alliance was being reforged as the core of NATO in the face of the growing Soviet threat. Churchill largely succeeded in his aim. A generation of historians saw the Anglo-American Alliance of 1941-45 through his eyes, and for the most part the general public on both sides of the Atlantic still do. This brief paper can do no more than summarize the main issues and highlight some of the most important works on the subject, but, at a time when the current Anglo-American relationship is

G.D. SHEFFIELD is senior lecturer in the Department of War Studies, Royal Military Academy, Sandhurst, England, and Senior Research Fellow at De Montfort University, England. An earlier version of this piece was presented to the annual meeting of the Mississippi Historical Society in Columbus, Mississippi, on March 3, 1995. The author wishes to thank the Mississippi Historical Society and the British Studies Program based at the University of Southern Mississippi for their support of the paper delivered at that conference.

[1] Winston S. Churchill, *The Grand Alliance* (London, 1950), 609.

undergoing reassessment, it is helpful to cut through the myth to view the reality of the wartime alliance.

It is important to remember that the Anglo-American Alliance was just one part, albeit an important one, of a wider coalition. By carrying the main burden of the war against Nazi Germany on the Eastern front, the USSR gave the British and American decision-making elites the luxury of time to have disagreements over strategy. Many smaller powers participated in coalition. The Allied campaign in Italy from 1943 to 1945 involved not only American and British troops but also French, Poles, Indians, New Zealanders, South Africans, Canadians, and even Brazilians. Nevertheless, the Anglo-American relationship lay at the core of the Western coalition.

After fifty years of the close alliance, first in the Second World War and then in NATO, it is all too tempting to think of the Anglo-American Alliance as being "natural," since Britons and Americans speak (approximately) the same language, and the decision-making elites, if not the ordinary peoples, share a common cultural background. This has led to the notion, at least in Britain, that the two states enjoyed and continue to enjoy a "special relationship."[2] This cozy view has been challenged in recent years. Now most historians would agree that from 1941 to 1945 the U.S. and Britain were, in Christopher Thorne's words, "Allies of a kind."[3]

In 1941 the idea of an Anglo-American Alliance was a distinct and not entirely welcome novelty. The two states were economic rivals. The Boxer rebellion of 1900 aside,[4] the two states had participated together in a military coalition only once before, in 1917-18, and this was not a particularly happy experience for either side.[5] For Americans, Britain was the traditional enemy. Much as eighteenth-century Englishmen and Scots forged a concept of "Britishness" in the face of the military threat from France, Americans defined themselves, at least in part, by

---

[2] The phrase is most closely associated with Churchill, who used it in his "iron curtain" speech at Fulton, Missouri, in 1946. However, see also John Baylis, *Anglo-American Defence Relations 1939-1984* (London, 1994), xvi and John Dickie, *"Special No More"—Anglo-American Relations: Rhetoric and Reality* (London, 1994), x.

[3] Christoper Thorne, *Allies of a Kind: The United States, Britain and the War Against Japan, 1941-1945* (London, 1978).

[4] Benjamin Franklin Cooling, "Some Considerations of Allied Operational Cooperation in World War II," *Revue Internationale d'Histoire Militiare*, No. 63 (Freiburg, 1985), 142-45.

[5] David F. Trask, The AEF and Coaltion Warmaking, 1917-1918 (Lawrence, KS, 1993).

being different from the old colonial power. To this heady brew must be added the other currents that contributed to "isolationism," including anti-British sentiments of Irish-and German-Americans; the opposition to British imperialism that was expressed by Americans from President Franklin D. Roosevelt downwards; and, not least, the feeling that the American Expeditionary Force had beaten Germany in 1918 but the U.S. was robbed of the just spoils of war by their allies.[6]

The feeling of social and cultural inferiority that a surprising number of otherwise hard-boiled American soldiers—Stillwell, Patton, Mark Clark—appeared to have felt when faced with their British counterparts can perhaps be seen as a parable of republican New World resentment of monarchical Old World condescension and snobbery. Cultural factors, the disdain of the aristocrat for the parvenu, also help to explain the lack of enthusiasm of some Britons for the American alliance. Sheer mutual ignorance was also a factor. Few British generals, for instance, had visited the U.S.A. before the war, and many seem to have gained their opinions of Americans from watching Hollywood movies. As Thorne has suggested, a common language facilitated the unconscious supposition that Americans thought and behaved like Britons, and vice-versa.[7] When this proved not to be the case, it made disagreements especially bitter.

The Anglo-American Alliance was the product of "an unforeseen and unique crisis": the rapid conquest of France by Germany in May-June 1940. Up to that point the British "special relationship" had been with the other major European democracy, France.[8] Since 1688, the British had lost only one major war, the American War of Independence or

---

[6] See the views of two Mississippians on participation in the European conflict. The first, a veteran of the AEF, expressed disillusionment with the U.S. intervention in 1917-18, while the second suggested that the U.S. should take Canada and British possessions in the West Indies in return for U.S. aid. Frank D. Montague to Hon. William Colmer, June 12, 1940, and F. E. Montgomery to Hon. William Colmer, January 23, 1941. William M. Colmer Dapers, University of Southern Mississippi. I owe these references to Professor Kenneth G. McCarty.

[7] Thorne, 91-122; Brian Holden Reid, "Tensions in the Supreme Command: Anti-Americanism in the British Army, 1939-45" in Brian Holden Reid and John White, eds., *American Studies: Essays in Honour of Marcus Cunliffe* (London, 1991), 272-85.

[8] David Reynolds, "Roosevelt, Churchill, and the Wartime Anglo-American Alliance, 1939-1945: Towards a New Synthesis," in William Roger Louis and Hedley Bull, eds., *The "Special Relationship": Anglo-American Relations Since 1945* (Oxford, 1986), 20-21. This

Revolutionary War of 1775-83. This was one of only two major wars that Britain had attempted to fight without allies, and the British elite learned the obvious lesson.[9] In 1940, the Churchillian rhetoric of standing "alone" against Nazi Germany disguised a desperate realization that without American intervention Britain could not win and might even lose. Previously, Britain had believed that it could manage with American resources. Now it needed American military power too.

Fortunately for the British, the summer of 1940 also marked the greatest "strategic crisis" in American history.[10] The security of the United States had depended upon the British and the French containing Hitler. With the fall of France, the defeat of Germany became imperative for U.S. security. The United States began to extend considerable help, albeit in an incremental fashion, to the beleaguered British in a distinctly un-neutral way, especially following Roosevelt's re-election in November 1940. Lend-Lease, the exchange of U.S. destroyers for British bases, the escorting of British convoys by U.S. warships—all these are symbols of America's proxy war with Nazi Germany. Even then, it took the wholly gratuitous declaration of war by Germany on December 11, 1941, to get the United States involved in the European conflict, an act of strategic folly that rates alongside Hitler's decision to invade the Soviet Union. Without Hitler's intervention, it is possible that America would have found itself at war in the Pacific, but not in Europe, FDR being unable to risk asking Congress to declare war on Germany. [11]

The U.S.A. and Britain held one war aim in common: to defeat Germany and Japan, in that order. Otherwise, their war aims diverged. In very general terms, the Americans viewed war as a departure from normality, an interference with the usual course of events. In the case of the war with Nazi Germany, Americans aimed to defeat the aggres-

article is the best concise analysis of the wartime Alliance. See also David Reynolds, *The Creation of the Anglo-American Alliance, 1937-41: A Study in Competitive Co-operation* (London, 1981). For the Anglo-French alliance see Brian Bond, *Britain, France, and Belgium, 1939-40* (London, 1990) and Correlli Barnett, "Problems of Coalition Warfare," in *Journal of the United Services Institution* (hereinafter cited as *JRUSI*) vol. 126, no. 3, September 1981, pp. 7-8.

[9] David French, *The British Way in Warfare, 1688-2000* (London, 1990), 234.

[10] David Reynolds, "The United States and European Security from Wilson to Kennedy, 1913-1963: A Reappraisal of the "Isolationist" Tradition, *JRUSI*, vol. 128, no.2 (June 1983), 20.

[11] Stephen E. Ambrose, *Rise to Globalism* (Harmondsworth, 1976), 36.

sors and then go home. British aims were perhaps more complex and were founded in long experience of fighting to preserve the balance of power in Europe. However, from 1940 onwards British aims included the very survival of Britain as a great power.[12]

The Greek question demonstrated the incompatibility of American and British aims. In 1943 the British wanted to occupy Greece and restore the pre-war elite to forestall a communist putsch when the Germans evacuated their forces. This would have involved the extension of Allied, and not just British, operations in the eastern Mediterranean, which in turn risked postponing Operation OVERLORD, the Allied invasion of France planned for May 1944. Eisenhower and the Joint Chiefs of Staff balked at using U.S. troops to support what they saw as British anti-Soviet machinations that might have delayed the defeat of Hitler. The British eventually moved in to Greece at the end of 1944, but without U.S. support.[13]

The differing American and British views on imperialism were another source of conflict between the Allies. American suspicion of British war aims led to SEAC's (South-East Asia Command) acronym being translated as "Save England's Asian Colonies." Some of the British elite discerned more than a trace of hypocrisy in this American attitude, for the U.S. also had an empire, albeit a largely informal one. FDR's views on imperialism led to some fierce clashes with Churchill, most notably over India in 1942-43.[14] Ultimately, by making some concessions such as the dispatch of the Cripps Mission to India in March 1942, and by making clear his depth of feeling over the issue, Churchill fought off the American challenge.[15] This helped to preserve the stability of the Alliance but did little to preserve the British empire, which was fatally undermined during the Second World War.

---

[12] Maurice Matloff, "Allied Strategy in Europe, 1939-1945," in Peter Paret, ed., *The Makers of Modern Strategy from Machiavelli to the Nuclear Age* (Oxford, 1986), 679-80.

[13] Ambrose, *Rise to Globalism*, 64-66.

[14] For a flavor of the opposing views, see Churchill to Roosevelt, March 7, 1942 (letter C-39), and Roosevelt to Churchill, March 10, 1942 (letter R-116), both in Warren F. Kimball, *Churchill & Roosevelt: The Compete Correspondence*, Vol. III (London, 1984 paperback edition), 388-89, 402-04.

[15] See Thorne, *Allies of a Kind*, especially 233-48, and Reynolds, "Wartime Anglo-American Alliance," 27-29. For a wider perspective see D. Cameron Watt, *Succeeding John Bull: America in Britain's Place 1900-1975* (Cambridge, 1984), 194-252.

The British found themselves in an unenviable situation in the Second World War. They desperately needed American aid, but in accepting it they were accelerating the replacement of Britain by the U.S.A. as a great power. If some Americans feared that they were fighting to prop up British imperialism, the British elite knew that they were allied with an economic and political rival with an economic philosophy diametrically opposed to the imperial trade bloc created by the Ottawa agreement of 1932.[16] The memory of 1914-18 was still fresh. In the First World War Britain's economic autonomy had been undermined by the mobilization of her society and economy to fight a total war, an effort that was made possible only by the financiers and factories of the United States. After 1916, Britain's ability to carry on the struggle with Germany rested to an alarming degree on American goodwill.[17]

Thus, a factor in British appeasement of Germany in the 1930s was the fear that war would lead to economic dependency on the U.S.A., which would threaten the sterling bloc and imperial preference. However, U.S. help was recognized as essential if war did break out with Germany. It has been argued that a major success of the much-maligned Chamberlain government was to insure that when Britain went to war in 1939, she did so with the sympathetic support of the United States and her president.[18] The British attitude towards this voluntary move into the embrace of her major economic rival was summed up by a British diplomat, when he rather undiplomatically told a Nazi official that Britain would rather become an American dominion than a German province.[19] It was the lesser of two evils.

In John Maynard Keynes's words, the British 'threw good housekeeping to the winds" during the Second World War. On September 22, 1940, the War Cabinet had to choose between making peace with Germany or accepting American aid on terms that were likely to be highly unfavorable. The British decided to fight on, and the arrival of a U.S. warship

---

[16] Reynolds, *Creation of the Anglo-American Alliance*, 291.

[17] David French, *British Strategy & War Aims 1914-1916* (London, 1986) 121-22, 228, 248.

[18] Ritchie Ovendale, "Appeasement"and the English Speaking World (Cardiff, 1975), 320. See also C.A. MacDonald, *The United States, Britain and Appeasement, 1936-39* (New York, 1981).

[19] Paul Kennedy, "The Continental Commitment and the Special Relationship in 20th Century British Foreign Policy," *JRUSI*, Vol. 128, No. 3 (September 1983), 12.

at Capetown in December 1940 to pick up £50m of Britain's last gold reserves symbolizes both British economic impotence and American asset-stripping. By the end of the war Britain was victorious but impoverished. She was the world's largest debtor nation, having lost about twenty-five percent of her pre-war wealth, the profits of 200 years of imperialism having been spent in one six-year spree.[20] The United States emerged from the war as the richest nation on earth, the value of its exports having risen from $4 billion to $14.2 billion in the period from 1940 to 1944. The contrast with Britain, which had become an American economic and political client, was stark.[21]

The rise of the U.S.A. and the decline of Britain should, of course, be placed in context. The war of 1939-45 accelerated this process but did not initiate it.[22] There was no reason why the U.S. should not take full advantage of her rival's predicament. Britain had achieved greatness through the destruction of economic rivals, even those, like the Dutch, whom they were fighting alongside in time of war. Ironically, during the Second World War Churchill found himself in much the same position as the Dutch leaders during the war of the Spanish Succession, and, had his biography of the Duke of Marlborough been written after 1945, he might have written of their activities a little more sympathetically.[23] Moreover, Lend-Lease was, as Churchill stated in the House of Commons on March 12, 1941, a "monument of generous and far-seeing statesmanship"[24] and, just beyond the war period, Marshall Aid was to help rebuild the British economy and pay for the British welfare state. Even the reappearance of a multilateral economy was acceptable to the British under the right conditions—if, that is, the U.S. took the lead in promoting it by offering loans and lowering her own tariffs.[25]

The British cushioned the change in their relationship with the U.S.A. by a deft readjustment of their views about their place in the

[20] Paul Kennedy, *The Realities Behind Diplomacy* (London, 1981), 316-18; Clive Ponting, *1940: Myth and Reality* (London, 1991 paperback edition), 4-10.

[21] I.C.B. Dear and M.R.D. Foot, eds., *The Oxford Companion to the Second World War* (Oxford, 1995), 1286.

[22] For a stimulating discussion of British decline, see Correlli Barnett, *The Collapse of British Power* (London, 1972).

[23] J.R. Jones, *Marlborough* (Cambridge, 1993), 228-29.

[24] Martin Gilbert, *Finest Hour: Winston S. Churchill 1939-41* (London, 1989 paperback edition), 1033.

[25] Reynolds, "Wartime Anglo-American Alliance," 30-33.

world. In 1945 the ruling elite and the common people alike believed
that Britain continued to be a great power, and Britain did indeed play
a global role for another twenty years. The British also persuaded
themselves that they had a "special relationship" with the Americans.
According to a piece of scurrilous British doggerel, the Americans may
have had "the moneybags, but we have the brains."[26] Whether the
Americans shared this assumption of a "special relationship" with
Britain is, to put it mildly, doubtful.

The divergence of war aims between the two major Western allies
was mirrored in their views on strategy. The British favoured "the
indirect approach": using British seapower and airpower to weaken
Germany by blockade and strategic bombing, while conducting military
operations in peripheral areas such as the Mediterranean and encouraging resistance movements in occupied countries. This was the mid-
twentieth century version of the traditional "British way in warfare."
The other important element was a large continental army to take on
the bulk of the enemy forces. During the latter stages of the war against
Napoleon, Russia, Prussia and Austria provided this force, leaving
Wellington free to fight a successful secondary campaign in Spain and
Portugal, and between 1941 and 1945 the Red Army served this function. In the latter part of the First World War the British Empire itself
had raised a continental-scale army, and thus had suffered one million
dead. Churchill, one of the foremost critics of the strategy of 1914-18,
was determined to avoid a repetition of the Western Front.[27]

The Americans had a Clausewitzian rather than a Fabian approach.
Drawing upon the strategic legacy of Grant and Sherman, the U.S.
favored a direct approach: to build a mass army (215 divisions were
planned in 1941), to get to Germany by the shortest possible route, which
was by an invasion of France launched from England, and to smash the
German army. While at the lower levels of operations and tactics both
armies did have much in common—both emphasized massive firepower,
for instance—this strategic dichotomy was to bedevil wartime Anglo-
American relations.[28]

---

[26] A. Roberts, *The Holy Fox* (London, 1991), 297.

[27] For British strategy, see Alex Danchev, "Great Britain: The Indirect Strategy," in
David Reynolds, Warren F. Kimball, A. O. Chubarian, eds., *Allies at War: The Soviet,
American and British Experience, 1939-45* (London, 1994), 1-26; John Keegan, "Churchill's
Strategy" in Louis and Blake, *Churchill*, 327-52.

There were four major strategic controversies that beset the Anglo-American alliance: first, the decision to go for "Germany First," that is, to give priority to the European Theatre while conducting a holding operation against the Japanese; second, the British preference for a peripheral, Mediterranean strategy, against the American preference for a direct assault from Britain across the English Channel; third, the U.S. desire for an amphibious assault in the south of France in conjunction with the landings in Normandy, against the protests of the British; fourth, Eisenhower's decision, against the wishes of the British, not to race the Soviets for Berlin in 1945.

Broadly speaking, the British had the upper hand in the Alliance until the end of 1943. Preliminary discussions in Washington in January 1941 (that is, before the U.S. entered the war) established the principle of "Germany First," a decision reaffirmed at the Arcadia Conference held after Pearl Harbor. In 1942, the British also won the debate that mattered: Anglo-American forces were committed to an invasion of North Africa in November of that year (Operation TORCH) rather than an assault on France. This outcome was partly the result of superior negotiating skills and the fact that the British were still the senior partner in terms of troops "on the ground"; but the intervention of Roosevelt, who supported the British position rather than that of the U.S. military, was crucial. The President was all too aware that the American public was inclined to view the Pacific conflict as "their" war, and TORCH ensured that American forces would be fighting German troops by the end of 1942. The invasion of North Africa led to an extension of the Mediterranean strategy, to invasions of Sicily in July 1943 and the Italian mainland in September. Despite these apparent signs of continuing British dominance, during 1943 the balance of influence within the alliance gradually shifted, as the American war economy expanded rapidly and large numbers of American servicemen and their equipment began to arrive in Europe. At the Teheran conference of November 1943 the British were effectively caught in a pincer movement between the Americans and the Soviets, both of whom favoured an invasion of France in 1944. This was a warning of the shape of things to come. In 1944-45 the U.S. war effort dwarfed that of the

---

[28] Russell F. Weigley, *The American Way of War* (Bloomington, IN, 1977 paperback edition), 313-59; Matloff, "Allied Strategy," 685.

British, and as a consequence the Americans dominated Alliance decision making. Churchill's failure to persuade the U.S. to abandon the
landing in the south of France in August 1944 was symbolic of the
reduced British status within the Alliance.[29] By the time of the Yalta
conference in February 1945, Churchill was describing the British as a
small lion sandwiched between "a huge Russian bear and a great
American elephant."[30] The analogy was all too apt.

Brian Holden Reid has suggested a "model" for discussing Anglo-
American strategic controversies. The U.S. "navalist" stance, personi-
fied by Admiral Ernest J. King, was "anti-British" and wanted to change
"Germany First" to "Japan First," which would of course involve an
increase in the role and influence of the U.S. Navy. The mirror image of
this approach was the "British Way in Warfare" of which Sir Alan
Brooke, the Chief of the Imperial General Staff (CIGS), was a leading
proponent. This approach sought to preserve British supremacy by
committing the alliance to a traditional British method of warfare—amphibious operations—in a traditional British area of influence, the
Mediterranean. Finally, there was the "diplomatic" approach of British
Field Marshal Sir John Dill and the American General Dwight D.
Eisenhower, who sought to maintain "Germany First," and "to place
Allied co-operation above national prejudice." Appropriate administrative machinery was developed to ease the way of this happy course. This
model is particularly helpful in displaying the subtleties in the strategic
debates. "Germany First," for instance, united the British and the U.S.
Army against the U.S. Navy.[31]

The strategy of the war against Japan throws the limitations of
British influence in the Alliance into sharp focus. The British had few
forces in the Pacific theatre, and it was the Australians, not the British,
who acted as junior partners to the Americans. The major strategic
controversies were fought out between the U.S. Army and Navy, with
the British very much on the periphery. Only in Burma did the British
have the predominant role in the formulation of strategy, and even here
British and U.S. objectives (the reconquest of a lost colony as a stepping-

---

[29] Matloff, "Allied Strategy," 683-96; Reynolds, "Wartime Anglo-American Alliance,"
23-27.

[30] This analogy was recorded by Churchill's private secretary in his diary entry of
February 24, 1945.

[31] Holden Reid, "Tensions in Supreme Command," 286-87.

stone to the recapture of Singapore for the former, the succour of China for the latter) were in conflict. The story of the British Pacific Fleet of 1944-45 demonstrates all too clearly the restricted nature of British power east of Suez. It was allowed into the Pacific on sufferance, much against the will of Admiral King, only after Churchill had pressured FDR at the 1944 Quebec Conference. The BPF had to be logistically self-supporting, and was allocated to Nimitz's spearhead drive in the Central Pacific only after considerable lobbying. It eventually operated as a weak task force—TF57—of the U.S. Fifth Fleet.[32]

Much writing about the Anglo-American Alliance has focused on the leaders of the two states: Franklin Delano Roosevelt and Winston Churchill. As with so much else to do with this subject, Churchill himself set the historical agenda in his war memoirs. Writing at a time of increasing east-west tension, Churchill glossed over or excluded examples of Anglo-American friction. He also depicted himself as reprising his Cassandra act of the 1930s, when (according to the Churchill legend, assiduously cultivated by the man himself) he warned of Nazi expansionism, only for his warnings to fall on deaf ears. This time, Churchill warned the Americans of Soviet expansionism, only for the idealistic and politically myopic Roosevelt to disregard his warnings; FDR wanted to win the war first, and only then think about the post-war settlement.

This is, of course, a caricature. As Warren F. Kimball has argued, Roosevelt had a shrewd grasp of the realities of geopolitics. FDR had a "vision," albeit "vague," of the situation he wanted to see after the war, a vision "he pursued with remarkable consistency." FDR wanted the U.S. to take the lead in the post-war world, which would mean collaboration not just with Britain but also with the Soviet Union. Unlike Churchill, he was not obsessed with the forward march of "bolshevism," and he saw, through Soviet revolutionary rhetoric, Stalin the cautious geopolitician. In short, Roosevelt wanted "peace accompanied by positive, systemic reforms," while Churchill seemed to be advocating "a mere armistice that only set the stage for the next confrontation." Here is not the place to debate the origins of the Cold War, except to say that in the tense atmosphere of the late 1940s and early 1950s it was all too easy to subscribe to Churchill's view. Yet without the benefit of 20/20 hind-

---

[32] Colin Bruce and Terry Charman, "The British Pacific Fleet of 1944-45, and Its Newspaper, *Pacific Post*," in *Imperial War Museum Review*, No. 8, 16-19.

sight, Roosevelt's policy, which by 1943 was supported from pragmatic motives by his senior military advisors, made much sense. It recognized the reality of Soviet power. The U.S.S.R. was bearing the brunt of the war against Germany, and the victory of the Red Army, which was desirable in the interests of saving American lives, would inevitably lead to the states of Eastern Europe falling like ripe plums into Stalin's lap.[33]

Historians have also begun to look more critically at Churchill's role in the Alliance. Here is a clear case of a divorce between "popular" and academic thought, for the vast bulk of the British and U.S. publics continue to see Churchill as he wished to be seen, as a heroic figure, the savior of his country. A storm of controversy erupted when John Charmley's critical biography *Churchill: The End of Glory* appeared in 1993. Charmley argued that in July 1945 Churchill's policies lay in ruins. The threat of Hitler had been removed, only to be replaced by that of Stalin; the British Empire had been fatally undermined; Britain was reduced, economically and politically, to a dependency of the U.S.A.; and Churchill's Conservative Party had been decisively defeated by Labour. Churchill, in short, was a political failure.[34]

Whilst Charmley's book served a valuable purpose in debunking uncritical "Winston Worship," this author cannot agree with his views on Churchill's wartime leadership. Nazi Germany, if not uniquely evil, was a very unpleasant regime that needed to be destroyed. It was a rare act of moral and physical courage for Britain to fight a total war knowing the likely cost (although *pace* Clark, there was probably no real alternative to fighting on). Given these circumstances, any prime minister would have to have pursued broadly similar policies. Churchill made mistakes, but on the whole he made skillful use of a bad hand. It is unlikely that an alternative prime minister could have achieved much more. Moreover, in 1945 Britain's moral prestige was high, and her people were about to benefit from the construction of a welfare state.

---

[33] This paragraph is largely based on Warren F. Kimball, "Franklin Roosevelt: 'Dr. Win-the-War,'" in Joseph G. Dawson, ed., *Commanders-in-Chief: Presidential Leadership in Modern Wars* (Lawrence, KS, 1993), 87-105. The quotations are from p. 95. See also Kimball's *The Juggler: Franklin Roosevelt as Wartime Statesmen* (Princeton, NJ, 1991), 84-105.

[34] John Charmley, *Churchill: The End of Glory* (London, 1993), 649. Fuel was added to the fire by Alan Clark, a maverick Tory politician, who suggested in a review of Charmley's book that Britain should have made peace with Hitler in 1941. *The Times*, January 2, 1993, p. 12.

The year 1945 might not have been Churchill's finest hour, but it was the British people's.[35]

Kimball has disputed the notion of what Churchill himself called an "intimate comradeship" between the President and the Prime Minister. While they did develop a rapport, their wartime association was not characterized by absolute frankness.[36] The increasing dominance of the U.S.A. within the Alliance also colored the relationship; from 1943 onwards, the Anglo-American relationship was not one of equals.[37] If there was a period when Churchill was indispensable, it was May-June 1940. The news that Churchill rather than the "appeaser" Lord Halifax succeeded Neville Chamberlain as prime minister[38] sent a signal to Washington that British resistance would continue after the defeat of France. Thereafter, the Alliance would probably have functioned well enough under the leadership of President Willkie and Prime Minister Bevin, the latter offering a kind of working class version of Churchill's bulldog leadership. The wartime Anglo-American relationship emerged and flourished for rather more complex reasons than a personal friendship between Churchill and Roosevelt.

If FDR and Churchill have moved towards the wings, historically speaking, another partnership has moved to center stage. George C. Marshall's pivotal role has long been recognized, but, thanks to Alex Danchev's work, we now see the importance of his relationship with Field Marshal Sir John Dill. Dill was the head of British Joint Staff Mission in Washington, the representative of the British Chiefs of Staff on the Combined Chiefs of Staff (CCS). He was also an "amateur ambassador" acting for Churchill in the latter's role as Minister of Defence. Dill and Marshall struck up an excellent working relationship and a genuine friendship, which contrasted strongly with Dill's rather

[35] For a work that supports this view, see Peter Hennesy, *Never Again: Britain 1945-51* (London, 1993); for a book fiercely critical of the "New Jerusalem" approach, see Correlli Barnett, *The Audit to War: The Illusion and Reality of Britain as a Great Nation* (London, 1986).

[36] Warren F. Kimball, "Wheel Within a Wheel: Churchill, Roosevelt and the Special Relationship," in Robert Blake and William Roger Louis, eds., *Churchill* (Oxford, 1993), 291-307. Quotation is taken from p. 300.

[37] See Robin Edmonds, *The Big Three: Churchill, Roosevelt and Stalin in Peace & War* (London, 1991), 371-78.

[38] See, however, Andrew Roberts's defense of Halifax's record on appeasement in *The "Holy Fox."*

frosty relations with Churchill, who had sacked him as the Chief of the Imperial General Staff in 1941. The CCS was an unparalleled attempt to integrate the war efforts of two sovereign states. Dill and Marshall acted in concert to smooth over—or if possible, prevent—inter-allied crises. Paradoxically, Dill's lack of intimacy with Churchill enhanced his value in dealing with the Americans. Dill's willingness to stand up to Churchill, his realistic assessment of the weakness of the British position, and Marshall's trust in Dill played an invaluable role in holding the Alliance together.[39]

The relationship of Dwight David Eisenhower, Supreme Commander, Allied Expeditionary Force, and his principal British subordinate, Bernard Law Montgomery, did not work as smoothly. Eisenhower's grasp of coalition war, of the need to hold together a group of disparate parties united only by the desire to defeat Germany, made him one of the greatest assets the Alliance possessed. An important influence on Eisenhower's appreciation of the nuances of coalition warfare was his association with Major-General Fox Connor, a Mississippian who had served as Pershing's Operations Officer in the First World War.[40] Eisenhower's talents as a military politician, a modern-day Schwartzenburg, were not matched by his skill as a battlefield commander. In his memoirs, Montgomery criticized Eisenhower's "broad front strategy" of 1944-45, claiming that, by allowing a number of poorly co-ordinated thrusts towards Germany, he left the Allies open to a German counterstroke, which was duly delivered in December 1944 in the Ardennes. This criticism has some validity. By contrast, Montgomery's plan for a "narrow front" thrust—commanded, of course, by himself—was politically naive. To give the starring role in a potentially war-winning offensive to a British commander would have been politically unacceptable to Americans from Roosevelt and Marshall downwards, as Eisenhower knew only too well. Eisenhower's sensitivity towards his British ally is also demonstrated by the license he allowed

---

[39] Alex Danchev, Very Special Relationship: Field Marshal Sir John Dill and the Anglo-American Alliance 1941-44 (London, 1986); A Special Relationship: Field Marshal Sir John Dill and General George C. Marshall, *JRUSI*, Vol. 130, No. 2, pp. 56-61.

[40] Stephen E. Ambrose, *The Supreme Commander: The War Years of General Dwight D. Eisenhower* (London, 1971), 588; Stephen E. Ambrose, "Dwight David Eisenhower" in Peter Dennis and Adrian Preston, eds., *Soldiers as Statesmen* (London, 1976), 114-15; Stephen E. Ambrose, *Eisenhower The Soldier 1890-1952* (London, 1983), 73-74, 76-77.

Montgomery, a British national hero, whose insubordination and rude-
ness tried even Ike's legendary patience.[41]

Much of this paper has discussed tensions within the Anglo-American alliance. In concluding, we must redress the balance. For all its
faults, the alliance was both close and effective.[42] Moreover, as one
examines previous coalition wars, the remarkable nature of the Alliance
becomes clear. In 1914-18, the French and the British co-operated—up
to a point—but effective machinery for coalition warfare was created
only in late 1917. The appointment of a supreme allied commander had
to wait for a moment of extreme crisis in April 1918, when the British
feared that the Alliance was about to disintegrate and hastily agreed to
a French generalissimo. Similarly, the worst moments of the Anglo-
American Alliance offer nothing as bad as the disastrous command,
characterized by extreme inter-allied mistrust, exercised by the Anglo-
French coalition in the 1940 campaigns. Churchill's claims may have
contained a fair measure of hyperbole, but the Anglo-American Alliance
of 1941-45 was one of the most cohesive and effective partnerships in
the history of warfare.

[41] Montgomery of Alamein, *The Memoirs of Field-Marshal Montgomery* (London, 1958,
book club edition), 248-65, but see Ambrose, "Dwight David Eisenhower," 115-16.
Montgomery's plan would also have encountered severe logistic problems: Russell F.
Weigley, *Eisenhower's Lieutenants: The Campaigns of France and Germany 1944-1945*
(London, 1981), 277-83.

[42] For cooperation on the atomic bomb and Ultra, see Margaret Gowing, *Britian and
Atomic Energy, 1939-1945* (London, 1964); Baylis, *Anglo-American Defense Relations*,
15-22; F. H. Hinsley *et al*, *British Intelligence in the Second World War*, vol. II (London,
1981), 41-58.

Mission to America: Maksim M. Litvinov in the United States, 1941–43

HUGH PHILLIPS*

On 7 December 1941, Maksim M. Litvinov arrived in the United States to begin his turbulent and frustrating tenure as the Soviet ambassador. The ambassadorship marked the climax of a diplomatic career that began in 1918, when Litvinov was the Bolshevik representative in Great Britain. Subsequently he had been deputy commissar for foreign affairs in the 1920s and commissar for foreign affairs from 1930 to 1939. As commissar, he had been a leading advocate of collective security as a defense against the expansionism of Nazi Germany. He also had been the chief Soviet negotiator in the talks that led to diplomatic recognition of the Soviet Union by the United States in 1933. He was, in short, a well-known figure on the international scene.

As ambassador to the United States, Litvinov had relatively little influence on the formulation of Soviet policy, but he was nonetheless a highly important intermediary between Washington and Moscow. Although his dispatches by no means tell the whole story of the early wartime coalition, they do shed light on some major issues, including President Franklin D. Roosevelt's views on Soviet participation in the Pacific war; the opening of a second front (a pivotal concern for Moscow); and Roosevelt's basic assumption about the roles of the United States, the Soviet Union, and Britain in the postwar world. Moreover, Litvinov's views on Soviet-American cooperation have an intrinsic interest for historians because he was the foremost advocate of good relations between Moscow and the West. It is highly significant that, although he felt very bitter toward America during much of his tenure as ambassador, Litvinov left Washington convinced that there would be no

*It is a pleasure to acknowledge the generous support I have received from the following organizations in the preparation of this article: the Research Institute of the University of Alabama in Huntsville, the Kennan Institute for Advanced Russian Studies, and the International Research and Exchanges Board. A special note of thanks is due to the staff of the Slavic and East European Reading Room of the Sterling Library at Yale University.

261

genuine obstacle to Soviet-American cooperation after the victory of the Grand Coalition.

Litvinov had been interested in the United States from the beginning of his service to the Soviet state. He clearly understood that the country had assumed a new importance in world affairs as a result of World War I, and in 1918 he asked the founder of the new Soviet state, Vladimir I. Lenin, to send him to Washington. Lenin agreed, but the American embassy in London refused to grant Litvinov a visa.[1] In the 1920s he headed the Western section of the Foreign Commissariat and did his best to keep a line open to Washington and to maintain his contacts in the United States, occasionally meeting with Americans visiting the Soviet Union.[2] Finally, in 1933, he arrived in America. He succeeded in obtaining diplomatic recognition of the Soviet Union, but the period of rapprochement between the two nations was brief, and by 1941 the two future superpowers were scarcely on speaking terms.[3] All of this changed, of course, when the United States and the Soviet Union were forced into an alliance against Nazi Germany.

On 6 November 1941, with the Wehrmacht approaching the suburbs of Moscow, the Soviet government announced Litvinov's appointment as ambassador to the United States. The reaction in Washington was favorable. According to the *New York Times,* American officials considered Litvinov the Soviet Union's "ablest and most forceful diplomat," a man who "could exert real influence" on the administration.[4] This assessment was only partially accurate. Litvinov was certainly a forceful diplomat. Indeed, Assistant Secretary of State Sumner Welles, who dealt frequently with and admired Litvinov, described him as "blunt" and "often brutal."[5] He did not like platitudes or generalities and worked tirelessly to get specific information on American policy. Some tension between him and Roosevelt was inevitable, for the president did not always like to be specific in his policy declarations. At the same time, Litvinov would prove unable to exert much influence in Washington, and his ability to sway Joseph Stalin, the Soviet leader, turned out to be equally limited. His primary goal was to push for the speedy opening of a second front in Western Europe, and it is unlikely that his frequent complaints about the postponement of this operation advanced the launching of the D-day invasion.

Almost as soon as he arrived in Washington, Litvinov received a telephone call from Roosevelt informing him of the Japanese attack on Pearl Harbor. According to Litvinov, Roosevelt seemed "almost glad" that Amer-

---

[1]Ivan Maisky, *Journey into the Past* (London, 1962), 67.

[2]Teddy J. Uldricks, *Diplomacy and Ideology: The Origins of Soviet Foreign Relations, 1917–1930* (London, 1979), 81. See also Hugh Phillips, "Between the Revolution and the West: A Political Biography of Maksim M. Litvinov" (Ph.D. diss., Vanderbilt University, 1985), chap. 5.

[3]Thomas R. Maddux, *Years of Estrangement: American Relations with the Soviet Union, 1933–1941* (Tallahassee, 1980).

[4]*New York Times,* 7 November 1941.

[5]Sumner Welles, *The Time for Decision* (New York, 1944), 31.

ica was finally in the war, and at the end of their conversation he said "Praise God," which Litvinov thought was "curious."[6] After speaking with Roosevelt, Litvinov told his friend, Joseph E. Davies, the former American ambassador to the Soviet Union, that he was "not so sure" it was a good thing for the United States to become a belligerent. Davies took this remark to mean that the ambassador feared that the new situation would mean a reduction in American aid to the Soviet Union.[7]

On 8 December, Litvinov had his first meeting as ambassador with Roosevelt. The president appeared "fatigued and preoccupied," and Litvinov conjectured that American losses had been greater than official public reports indicated. Roosevelt was indeed grim; he expressed grave doubts about the ability of the United States to hold the Philippines. But what the president wanted most to discuss was the often forgotten American campaign for a "second front" in the Pacific. He asked Litvinov rather vaguely if the USSR expected "to participate" in the Pacific war. Litvinov replied that he doubted it. He certainly did not expect a Japanese declaration of war on the Soviet Union, for that would not be "in the interests of Japan itself." Roosevelt then raised the issue of American bombers using the Soviet port of Vladivostok as a resupply point for missions from Manila to Japan.[8] Litvinov does not indicate whether he answered Roosevelt's query, but he already had told Davies that it was Soviet policy to treat Japan "gingerly . . . to avoid a two-front war," and a Soviet authority on World War II diplomacy has confirmed that "one of the tasks of Soviet diplomacy was to avoid attempts to draw the USSR into the Far Eastern war."[9]

Litvinov requested a formal answer to Roosevelt's question from Moscow. It was not long in coming. In a typically terse telegram, Viacheslav Molotov, Litvinov's successor as commissar for foreign affairs, told the ambassador on 11 December that "it is impossible at present for us to go to war with the Japanese and we are forced to assume a position of neutrality." He explained that Japan had given the Soviet Union no reason to break the

---

[6]Grigorii N. Sevost'ianov, *Diplomaticheskaia istoriia voiny na Tikhom Okeane* [A diplomatic history of the war in the Pacific] (Moscow, 1969), 21. Professor Sevost'ianov's source for this telephone conversation is the Arkhiv Vneshnei Politiki SSSR [Foreign Policy Archive of the USSR]. My requests for access to that and other Soviet archives were denied.

[7]Joseph E. Davies (former ambassador to the USSR) memorandum of conversation, 7 December 1941, U.S. Department of State, *Foreign Relations of the United States, 1941* (Washington, 1956), 4:731 (hereafter *FRUS*, with year and volume).

[8]Litvinov to the People's Commissariat for Foreign Affairs (Narkomindel), 8 December 1941, Ministerstvo Inostrannykh Del SSSR [Ministry of Foreign Affairs of the USSR], *Sovetsko-amerikanskie otnosheniia vo vremia Velikoi Otechestvennoi voiny, 1941-1945gg.: dokumenty i materialy v dvukh tomakh* [Soviet-American relations during the Great Patriotic War: documents and material in two volumes], 2 vols. (Moscow, 1984), 1:143-44. This work, which consists mostly of documents from the Soviet Foreign Policy Archive and covers Soviet-American relations during World War II, contains a wealth of previously unavailable material and has not been utilized fully by Western diplomatic historians.

[9]Davies memorandum, 7 December 1941, *FRUS, 1941* 4:731; Sevost'ianov, *Diplomaticheskaia istoriia,* 39.

neutrality pact signed in April 1941 and that because of the German invasion, the Soviets had transferred half of their Far Eastern troops to the German front. The commissar affirmed the basic tenet of Soviet wartime policy when he concluded by emphasizing that "our main common enemy is Hitlerite Germany."[10]

Immediately upon receipt of Molotov's instructions, Litvinov visited Roosevelt. According to the ambassador, the president said that he "regretted the decision but in our place he would have done the same." Roosevelt asked if Litvinov would issue a joint communiqué with Secretary of State Cordell Hull to the effect that the Soviet Union "might at any time take any decision in relation to Japan." Litvinov refused, because he believed such an action would be a direct provocation to Tokyo. As Litvinov was leaving, the president told him that Moscow's decision on the Far East "would probably prolong the war with Japan but there was nothing to be done about it."[11]

There is some evidence that the Soviet Union's absorption in its struggle with Germany was not the sole reason for its refusal to take on the Japanese. On 16 December, Jan Ciechanowski, the Polish ambassador in Washington, told Sumner Welles that Litvinov had said that Russia "had no intention of doing anything with regard to Japan . . . until it saw whether the United States was actually able and determined to undertake a major and effective offensive against [that country]." Litvinov had added that Soviet intervention would "relieve the United States of the need to incur losses itself."[12] It is difficult to understand why Litvinov would have made such a cynical remark to a virtual stranger who was certain to convey it immediately to the Americans, and it would be easy to conclude that Ciechanowski was being less than truthful with Welles. Yet only a few days earlier T. V. Soong, the personal envoy of the Chinese leader Jiang Jieshi, told Welles that the Soviet military attaché in Chongqing (Chungking) had said that Russia would not go to war with Japan for fear that if it did, "the United States would not be willing to concentrate its full war effort upon Japan and thus hold Japan in check."[13] These stories could hardly have been coincidental. Plainly the Soviet leadership welcomed American belligerence in the Far East because it would tie down Japanese forces and relieve the USSR of its fear of a two-front war. The pact of April 1941 between Moscow and Tokyo did guarantee mutual neutrality in the event that one of the signatories became involved in war. But Stalin had just received an object lesson on the value of neutrality pacts from Adolf Hitler.

On 13 December, Litvinov gave his first major presentation to the press. He emphasized that Germany was the main enemy and asserted that after Germany had been defeated the other Axis powers could be "polished

---

[10]Molotov to Litvinov, 11 December 1941, *Sovetsko-amerikanskie otnosheniia* 1:144.
[11]Litvinov to Narkomindel, 11 December 1941, ibid., 145.
[12]Sumner Welles (undersecretary of state) memorandum of conversation, 16 December 1941, *FRUS, 1941* (Washington, 1958), 1:665.
[13]Welles memorandum of conversation, 9 December 1941, ibid. 4:738.

off without trouble." He explained that the Soviet Union "naturally" would like to see a second front established in Europe, but added diplomatically that it "took into consideration" the difficulties involved in such an operation.[14]

Shortly after Litvinov's press conference, British Prime Minister Winston Churchill arrived in Washington to confer with Roosevelt. From these discussions, in which Litvinov played no part, the decision emerged to concentrate Western military operations on West Africa. It was a triumph for Churchill's Mediterranean strategy. Both leaders also made certain that they recognized the vital contribution the Red Army was making to the defeat of Hitler, and they resolved to do their utmost to keep aid flowing to Russia.[15]

On 27 December the president invited Litvinov and Churchill to breakfast at the White House. Litvinov, who was angry at not having been consulted earlier, reported that the Western leaders gave him only a partial account of their negotiations. Roosevelt explained to him that recent delays in aid shipments to Russia were due to the "unexpectedness of America's entrance into the war and the needs on the West coast," and both leaders pledged to redouble their efforts to get aid to his country.[16] Roosevelt then told the ambassador of an informal proposal for a general declaration by all the states at war with the Axis, and he read a draft text that included both an obligation not to sign a separate peace and a reference to freedom of religion. Litvinov said that the Kremlin would probably prefer "freedom of conscience" to "freedom of religion." Roosevelt was adamant, however, explaining that he had suffered severe criticism because the Atlantic Charter had contained no provisions on freedom of religion.[17] In the end Moscow conceded Roosevelt his reference to "freedom of religion."

Next it was Litvinov's turn to be stubborn. Churchill wanted to add the words "and authorities" after the word "governments" in the phrase "governments signatory hereto." This change, he said, would allow the Free French to adhere to the declaration. According to Harry Hopkins, Roosevelt's close adviser, Litvinov told the president and prime minister that he had "no power to agree to the inclusion of that word . . . and no ambassador of Russia has the power to agree to any textual change." Churchill asserted that the change was "inconsequential," but Litvinov was unconvinced; he

---

[14]*Washington Post*, 14 December 1941.

[15]Mark Stoler, *The Politics of the Second Front: American Military Planning and Diplomacy in Coalition Warfare, 1941–1943* (Westport, 1977), 22–24; Vilnis Sipols, *The Road to Great Victory: Soviet Diplomacy, 1941–1945* (Moscow, 1984), 64–66; George C. Herring, Jr., *Aid to Russia, 1941–1946: Strategy, Diplomacy, the Origins of the Cold War* (New York, 1973), 52–53.

[16]Litvinov to Narkomindel, 27 December 1941, *Sovetsko-amerikanskie otnosheniia* 1:145. It must be noted that Roosevelt made this pledge at a time when "the War Department was stripping ships of guns and planes originally intended for the U.S.S.R." Herring, *Aid to Russia*, 53. According to Litvinov, no mention was made of the decisions on African operations.

[17]Litvinov to Narkomindel, 27 December 1941, *Sovetsko-amerikanskie otnosheniia* 1:146. See also Robert E. Sherwood, *Roosevelt and Hopkins: An Intimate History* (New York, 1948), 448–49.

clearly believed the change could have significant consequences. Churchill became somewhat abusive, telling Litvinov that he "wasn't much of an ambassador if he didn't have the power even to add a word like this" and reminded the Russian that they "were at war and there was no time for long-winded negotiations." The ambassador "stuck to his point," however, and the declaration was issued without the word "authorities." Litvinov later told Hopkins that after the meeting he cabled Moscow for permission to insert the word at issue, but approval came too late.[18]

The declaration, which was signed on 1 January 1942 and became known as the United Nations Declaration, continued to trouble the Soviets, who wanted to ensure that certain countries would not be admitted as adherents to it. Litvinov spoke of this concern in a meeting with Roosevelt and Hopkins on 12 January. In a telegram to Moscow he wrote that when he "began to speak about additional adherents to the Declaration . . . Roosevelt burst out laughing concerning the quantity of points I raised." Among those "points" were "Lithuania, Latvia and others." Hopkins immediately said that every country that was unacceptable to the USSR could be excluded from the declaration. Litvinov pressed the matter further, saying that he wanted a promise from America that no more adherents to the declaration would be admitted without consultation with the Soviet Union. "Roosevelt immediately agreed, saying . . . that discussions ought to take place among the four chief participants, i.e., the U.S.S.R., the U.S.A., Great Britain and China."[19] For all practical purposes, the concessions that Litvinov won from Roosevelt at this meeting constituted American recognition of Moscow's absorption of the Baltic states. Even clearer assurances on that score would be forthcoming.

By coincidence, on the day after Litvinov met with Roosevelt, Loy Henderson of the State Department issued a memorandum counseling against a policy of Big Four unanimity. He argued that if the Russians obtained "veto power" over future signatories, they would probably oppose all but "those which have a Communist center or are willing to work for specific Soviet aims."[20] His memorandum came too late to affect Roosevelt's decision, however.

On 20 January, Litvinov turned his attention once again to the war and sent a substantial telegram to Moscow assessing the military situation. He conceded that the struggle with Germany soon would be entering its most crucial phase. The Germans, he wrote, were "gathering their last reserves in the occupied lands in order to throw them on our front" and were "counting on moving the rest of the Hungarian Army (and maybe Bulgarian)" into

---

[18]Sherwood, *Roosevelt and Hopkins*, 449–51. The Soviets also were careful to be certain the declaration carried no obligations for them vis-à-vis Japan. Cordell Hull (secretary of state) memorandum of conversation, 29 December 1941, *FRUS, 1942* (Washington, 1960), 1:18–19.

[19]Litvinov to Narkomindel, 12 January 1942, *Sovetsko-amerikanskie otnosheniia* 1:147.

[20]Loy W. Henderson (assistant chief, Division of European Affairs) memorandum to Ray Atherton (acting chief, Division of European Affairs), 13 January 1942, *FRUS, 1942* 1:34–35.

Russia for a spring offensive. "A Japanese attack at that time can not be excluded," he declared. He accurately observed that Roosevelt's promises of imminent and substantial aid were "illusions," because the United States was also getting pressure for military support from Australia and China, not to mention Latin America, and he suggested that another talk with the president was in order.

> In view of this [situation] ought we not put directly before [the United States and Britain] the issue of rendering direct military aid by the creation of a second front on the European continent. In Britain there is an army of two million and in the U.S.A. one-and-a-half million and neither are doing anything. Why can't they land 500,000 men in Holland, Belgium, France or even Norway? They refer to the absence of transportation but, before April . . . if they desired, it would be possible to prepare the necessary means. If . . . they have the means to transfer American troops to the Near East, to Northern Ireland and to Murmansk, as Roosevelt proposed, then why can't they use such craft for a more serious goal. If America is still not prepared to take part in military operations, then American troops could be dispatched for the defense of Britain and then British troops could cross the Channel. . . . Maybe this has been discussed with [British Foreign Secretary] Eden, but I do not know. In any case is it not time for me to discuss this matter seriously with Roosevelt, the point of departure being the nonfulfillment of Roosevelt's promises about our supplies and the difficulties that will be before us in the spring? If they can't help by means of military materials, let them help with people. . . . To talk about this with Roosevelt is not enough, it is necessary for me to prepare public opinion and that requires time. I will await your speediest answer.[21]

Clearly Litvinov had thought the issue through. He wanted to get an immediate commitment from the Allies to land in Europe, before they dispersed their forces and energies too broadly. Sixteen days after he made his proposals, Litvinov received Molotov's "speediest answer." In four crisp sentences the commissar put Litvinov in his place: Moscow "would welcome" a second front in Europe, but as Litvinov well knew, such a request had been denied three times before, and Molotov did not want a fourth refusal. "Therefore you are not to place before Roosevelt the issue of a second front. We will await the moment when maybe our allies will put the issue before us."[22]

---

[21]Litvinov to Narkomindel, 20 January 1942, *Sovetsko-amerikanskie otnosheniia* 1:149–50. On 12 January, Roosevelt, in characteristic fashion, tossed out the idea of American troops landing at Murmansk, freeing Soviet forces there to move to the front. He emphasized that it was just an idea and wanted to know Moscow's opinion. See Litvinov to Narkomindel, 12 January 1942, ibid., 148.
[22]Molotov to Litvinov, 4 February 1942, *Sovetsko-amerikanskie otnosheniia* 1:150–51. Molotov failed to follow his own advice, and in talks with the British and Americans in the spring of 1942 the commissar repeatedly raised the issue of the second front. Robert Dallek, *Franklin D. Roosevelt and American Foreign Policy, 1932–1945* (New York, 1979), 341-42.

Molotov's cable confirmed Litvinov's worst fears. He would not be able to influence policy in Moscow. Then, in a meeting on 12 February, Roosevelt told Litvinov that there was no plan for a landing in Western Europe; instead, the Allies would open a second front in North Africa, to be followed by landings in "Yugoslavia and other points." The president said a landing in Europe was "too complicated" and would be endangered by the sizable German forces near Aachen. Litvinov replied bitterly that there were "no serious forces near Aachen and to get German troops to Western France would demand no less time than their transfer to Yugoslavia where Hitler could also send Bulgarian, Hungarian, and other forces." He gave no account of Roosevelt's response but noted that the president looked "very weary." Angry with both the American government and his own, the ambassador also heatedly pointed out to Moscow that he was forced repeatedly to remind Roosevelt that he had no instructions from his government and no proposals to give but "could only speak of [his] personal judgments."[23]

On 12 March a mysterious meeting took place between Roosevelt and Litvinov, no record of which has been found in U.S. archives.[24] According to Litvinov's account of the meeting, Roosevelt informally made some very significant concessions to the Soviet Union on its border demands. Essentially the Soviets wanted the Allies to recognize their borders as they existed in June 1941. The Americans had refused officially to discuss the specifics of this issue until the peace settlement—a stance that could only have aroused Stalin's suspicions. Now Litvinov told Moscow that although Roosevelt was "worried" about the Baltic States and the former Romanian territories of Bessarabia and Bukovina (areas the Soviet Union had either "seized" or "regained" between 1939 and 1941, depending upon one's viewpoint), he did not differ from them on any significant issue.

> He does not foresee any difficulties regarding our border desires after the war. But the conclusion of a secret agreement disturbs him. Public opinion in America is not prepared. The issue may cause undesirable discussions and the president may be reminded about the Atlantic Charter where it mentions self-determination. He himself had always thought it had been a mistake to separate provinces from Russia after the war and he thought Wilson had also been opposed to this. And therefore he assures Stalin in a personal way that he absolutely agrees with us.

Litvinov told Roosevelt that the Baltic States had "constitutions" and that "Estonia already had self-determination." He then asked the president if he had any objections to "some kind of secret agreement" between Britain and the USSR, presumably on the border question.

> Roosevelt answered that he would not be against such an agreement if it remained a secret even from him. Roosevelt clearly desires that an

[23]Litvinov to Narkomindel, 13 February 1942, *Sovetsko-amerikanskíe otnosheniia* 1:152.
[24]Warren F. Kimball, ed., *Churchill and Roosevelt: The Complete Correspondence*, 3 vols. (Princeton, 1984), 1:420.

agreement should be oral and not formal. I pointed out that such an
agreement usually only binds the contracting individuals . . . and that
Churchill and Eden are not immortal. Roosevelt understood the allusion
and, smiling, said he hoped to stay in his place until the end of the war.
He asked me to give Stalin his thoughts and proposed that he take the
matter under consideration.[25]

Roosevelt concluded with a request, made to Litvinov "at almost every
meeting," to confer personally with Stalin. He felt that both he and Stalin
were "realists" and that they could therefore "easily" achieve a meeting of
minds. Litvinov told Stalin that Roosevelt suggested they meet "maybe after
the war somewhere in the Aleutian Islands," and added that he himself
jokingly suggested Berlin, where "the climate is better." Litvinov concluded
his dispatch on a serious note, observing that the president expected "some
sort of answer from us regarding the Baltic."[26]

If Litvinov's account of this meeting and the territorial concessions
Roosevelt made is correct, there can be little wonder why no record of the
conversation has been found in American archives. But Litvinov's dispatch
cannot be accepted without reservation, because Roosevelt gave the British
ambassador, Lord Halifax, a different account of the meeting. According to
Halifax, Roosevelt denied indicating that the United States would recognize
the 1941 borders, although he did say that he favored the Soviet Union
obtaining "complete security after the war."[27] The two accounts are not
wholly contradictory, yet neither are they wholly complementary. It is difficult to understand why either Litvinov or Halifax would have lied to his
government. Nor was there any obvious reason for Roosevelt not to tell
Halifax what he told Litvinov, for Roosevelt's acceptance of the 1941 borders
would have delighted Churchill, who, with Stalin's knowledge, was at that
time pressing for just such a policy.[28] Still, it seems likely that it was the
president who misrepresented matters, not the two ambassadors, neither of
whom had anything to gain by misleading his government.

The affair will probably always remain something of a mystery. It is
possible that the president simply changed his mind. However, another interpretation is consistent with two of Roosevelt's basic assumptions about
changing realities. First, the president believed that "postwar stability would

---

[25]Litvinov to Narkomindel, 12 March 1942, *Sovetsko-amerikanskie otnosheniia* 1:155.
If Litvinov's account is correct, this territorial concession on the part of Roosevelt was made
earlier than Western specialists previously had believed. See, for example, Keith Eubank,
Summit at Teheran (New York, 1985), 115; John Lewis Gaddis, *Russia, the Soviet Union, and
the United States: An Interpretive History* (New York, 1978), 160; and Herring, *Aid to Russia*,
104. On the basis of Western sources, these three scholars have written that Roosevelt resigned
himself to the Soviet absorption of the Baltic States only in the spring of 1943.

[26]Litvinov to Narkomindel, 12 March 1942, *Sovetsko-amerikanskie otnosheniia* 1:156-
57.

[27]Eubank, *Summit at Teheran*, 38.

[28]Ibid. See also Winston S. Churchill, *The Second World War*, vol. 4, *The Hinge of Fate*
(Boston, 1950), 327.

require a Soviet-American accord."[29] He also believed that Britain's days as a great power were over.[30] By secretly making specific border concessions to Litvinov, Roosevelt may have hoped to gain Soviet goodwill, to facilitate a meeting of the two "realists," and ultimately to promote postwar cooperation with Moscow. At the same time, by telling Churchill that he would not recognize the Soviet Union's 1941 borders, Roosevelt may have hoped to convince the prime minister to take a similar stand. If Churchill did so, he would antagonize Moscow, but Roosevelt would welcome a London-Moscow rift, because it would have promoted a bilateral Soviet-American solution to the territorial issue.

After the March meeting with Roosevelt, Litvinov told Stalin that the president was ready to accept the borders of June 1941. Molotov cabled a rather curious reply on 23 March. In typically laconic fashion the commissar wrote that, in effect, the issue did not concern Roosevelt. The president's remarks were "informational," he said, and did not "require a response."[31] Clearly Moscow already intended in early 1942 to retain the borders of 1941, and Stalin knew that both Churchill and Roosevelt had accepted this demand, even if only informally.

Litvinov went on the stump for a second front in mid-March, making speeches on 16 March and 10 April.[32] At about the same time, Roosevelt invited Molotov to Washington for "an exchange of views." The president stressed that he did not want "to go over the head of my friend, Mr. Litvinov, in any way."[33] In fact, however, that was precisely what he wanted to do. By now he was convinced that Litvinov lacked any real power or influence.[34] Litvinov's inability to get an answer to Roosevelt's demarche of 12 March would appear to have contributed greatly to the president's loss of interest in the ambassador.

When Litvinov learned of Roosevelt's intention to invite Molotov to Washington, he was dismayed. He did not think it boded well for the opening of a second front. He told Molotov that it would not make sense for him to come to America if there were any concrete plans for an invasion. "Coordination of action" would have to be discussed with London rather than Washington. "The troops landing on the continent would be English and the leadership would be English, not Roosevelt," Litvinov wrote. "I suppose therefore that by inviting you the president has in mind a proposal relative to Soviet-Japanese relations." Litvinov added pointedly that Roosevelt would

---

[29]Dallek, *Franklin D. Roosevelt*, 533.

[30]Eubank, *Summit at Teheran*, 488-89.

[31]Molotov to Litvinov, 23 March 1942, *Sovetsko-amerikanskie otnosheniia* 1:158.

[32]Sevost'ianov, *Diplomaticheskaia istoriia*, 98.

[33]"Personal Message from the President to Mr. Stalin" [received on 12 April 1942], Ministry of Foreign Affairs of the USSR, *Correspondence between the Chairman of the Council of Ministers of the U.S.S.R. and the Presidents of the U.S.A. and the Prime Ministers of Great Britain during the Great Patriotic War of 1941-1945*, vol. 2, *Correspondence with Franklin D. Roosevelt and Harry S. Truman (August 1941-December 1945)* (Moscow, 1957), 23.

[34]See Roosevelt to Churchill, 27 May 1942, in Kimball, *Churchill and Roosevelt* 1:490.

"want probably to discuss also such questions as the Baltic, Poland, Finland, aid to China, an airline to Alaska and other issues which he has been unable through me to get any kind of clarification and sometimes even an answer."[35]

The formal invitation to Molotov arrived in Moscow on 12 April. Two days later the Soviet government instructed Litvinov to visit the White House to find out exactly why the president wanted to speak directly with the commissar. Roosevelt was evasive, saying he only wanted to discuss a second front. But when Litvinov replied that his answer was "too general" and that it was "desirable to know something concrete," the president relented. He said that by a process of elimination the United States had decided that the best way to help the USSR was a "landing in France . . . by September." Hopkins and General George C. Marshall were then in London to explain that an invasion was "absolutely necessary." Roosevelt had not yet received a detailed report from Hopkins, but he thought that Molotov's visit might "help and strengthen" Washington in dealing with London. Litvinov told Moscow that what Roosevelt really wanted was a visit that would help him in the opinion polls by showing that he was "undertaking something new." He also believed Roosevelt wanted to "make an impression on Japan." Litvinov then repeated the long list of items about which he was unable to enlighten the president and concluded by saying that, in his opinion, it would be difficult for Molotov to reject the invitation unless he were to "bring forward a counter-proposal for a meeting in London." Accordingly, Stalin informed Roosevelt on 20 April that Molotov would accept his invitation.[36]

On 21 April, Litvinov sent Molotov bad news. The president had told him that the Marshall-Hopkins mission had failed and that "Churchill and the War Cabinet favored a second front, but the General Staff was against it." The generals had pointed to British reverses in North Africa, Malta, Ceylon, Burma, and the Indian Ocean. Litvinov asked Roosevelt what the relationship was "between all this and a second front for which there are sufficient forces on the British Isles." Roosevelt "agreed that there was no connection" and proceeded to blast the British as "rotting from inactivity" and "bungling" in their actions near Ceylon. He added that "in principle the British favor a second front," and with that remark, Litvinov noted, he "began to roar with laughter." The president concluded the meeting by repeating that the Americans wanted an immediate invasion, whereas the British, he believed, wanted to postpone a second front in Europe until 1943.[37]

This meeting was in many ways analogous to the meeting of 12 March. Once again Roosevelt used the occasion to emphasize America's sympathy with Moscow's wishes while working to keep the Russians and the British at

---

[35]Litvinov to Molotov, 11 April 1942, *Sovetsko-amerikanskie otnosheniia* 1:159.

[36]Litvinov to Molotov, 14 April 1942, ibid., 162–63. See also Stalin to Roosevelt, 21 April 1942, ibid., 164.

[37]Litvinov to Molotov, 21 April 1942, ibid., 164. Churchill never actually agreed to an invasion in 1942. See Churchill, *The Hinge*, 324.

odds. He reminded Litvinov that he too regarded Churchill's advocacy of an invasion "in principle" as meaningless. It should not be surprising that Litvinov came to the conclusion that Britain was indeed the major obstacle to the fulfillment of Moscow's pressing need for a second front in Europe. Yet two days after his meeting with Roosevelt, Litvinov received a very different view of the situation in Britain. Hopkins told the ambassador that he "considered his mission to London a success" and believed that the English would land on the Continent "comparatively soon." Apparently confused by Litvinov's reports about Anglo-American intentions vis-à-vis a second front, Stalin decided that Molotov should stop in Britain en route to Washington.[38]

Molotov signed a treaty of alliance in London but got nothing in writing on a second front or on Soviet border demands. Churchill believed that the Soviets dropped the borders issue because they were confronted by "solidarity of view between the British and American governments," but that was hardly the case.[39] Having received Roosevelt's concessions of 12 March, the Soviet dictator probably saw no need to press the British.

In Washington, Molotov discussed the borders issue with Roosevelt, who was pleased to hear that Churchill had put nothing in writing on that subject. On three occasions the president repeated his promise that the Allies would open a second front in 1942. Litvinov, much to his annoyance, was excluded from many of the discussions between Roosevelt and Molotov, and at the sessions he did attend he was openly bored.[40] He found his lack of authority increasingly galling, and Molotov, whom Litvinov detested, apparently went out of his way while he was in Washington to emphasize Litvinov's subordinate position.[41]

The ambassador's bitterness was not reserved solely for his superiors. On 22 July 1942, Litvinov met with Roosevelt to discuss the Anglo-American decision to undertake an offensive in North Africa, which Litvinov dismissed as unimportant. The following day he expressed the anger that many Russians certainly felt:

> The Americans and the English consider the [present] situation ideal with the Germans beating on us and driving us back as long as there is some kind of front somewhere, if only in Western Siberia, which is tying down German forces. . . . The Soviet Union ought to be, in their estimation, so weakened that it will not be able to speak loudly at the conclusion of peace.[42]

---

[38]Litvinov to Molotov, 23 April 1942, *Sovetsko-amerikanskie otnosheniia* 1:166. See also Igor' N. Zemskov, *Diplomaticheskaia istoriia vtorogo fronta v Evrope* [A diplomatic history of the second front in Europe] (Moscow, 1982), 68.

[39]Churchill, *The Hinge,* 336.

[40]Eubank, *Summit in Teheran,* 50-52; Sherwood, *Roosevelt and Hopkins,* 556-58, 561.

[41]Tat'iana Litvinov, interview with author, Hove, England, 30 March 1981; Sherwood, *Roosevelt and Hopkins,* 571.

[42]Litvinov to Narkomindel, 23 July 1942, quoted in Zemskov, *Diplomaticheskaia istoriia vtorogo fronta,* 119-20.

In October, Litvinov again met with Roosevelt and reported that the president had become "more firm" in his rejection of a European invasion because of the difficulties with operations in North Africa. The ambassador felt this policy was a complete victory for Churchill, who had the president "in tow" on North Africa and on the "majority" of other issues, but he believed that the Soviet Union should not let the push for a second front "die down for a moment."[43] He clearly doubted that a second front would be opened soon, however. After the decisive Soviet victory at Stalingrad, he reiterated his belief that the United States and Great Britain were "striving for maximum exhaustion and wear-and-tear on the forces of the Soviet Union for the purpose of lessening its role in the solution of postwar problems."[44]

Litvinov's hostility toward the United States seems to have begun to abate by the spring of 1943. He had come once again to put a high priority on Soviet-American cooperation in the postwar world. It is impossible to say precisely why Litvinov's hostility toward America lessened, but some clues may be found in his last conversations with American officials before his return to Moscow.

On 16 March 1943, Litvinov met with Hopkins for a discussion of specific border issues. Hopkins asked Litvinov point-blank what he believed Russia's demands would be at the "Peace Table." According to Hopkins, Litvinov said that

> the Soviets would, of course, want the Baltic states; that Russia considered them now part of the U.S.S.R.; that they had always been historically part of Russia, apart from the fact that they were essential to them for security reasons. Litvinov said he thought Russia had no desire to occupy all of Finland . . . but that Russia would insist on moving the [border] line about to a point where the Russian armies were at the end of the Finnish war.

The ambassador believed that Russia would not object if East Prussia was given to Poland, but the Soviets would insist on the right to determine the Polish border. He added that he did not "anticipate any great difficulty with Poland about this" but thought that "Poland would make outrageous demands" and that "Great Britain and the United States [and presumably the Soviet Union] should decide what was to be done about Poland and tell them rather than ask them." He concluded by saying that Russia should keep Bessarabia and that Germany should be dismembered.[45]

These demands were not in themselves remarkable; they were more or less the same demands the Soviet leadership had been making for some time. What is significant is that there is no record of Hopkins raising any objection

---

[43]Litvinov to Narkomindel, 13 October 1942, *Sovetsko-amerikanskie otnosheniia* 1:252.

[44]Litvinov to Narkomindel, undated [early 1943], quoted in Zemskov, *Diplomaticheskaia istoriia vtorogo fronta*, 148. It is not surprising that, hearing such opinions from Litvinov, the Soviet press and Stalin should have made particularly bitter comments on the Western allies at this time. Herring, *Aid to Russia*, 68–69.

[45]Sherwood, *Roosevelt and Hopkins*, 713.

to them—a point Litvinov surely appreciated. He could reasonably assume that what he considered to be the USSR's basic postwar goals would not meet with American resistance.

That assumption was confirmed in a conversation on 29 March with Anthony Eden, who told Litvinov that the issue of the Soviet Union's western border would not meet serious difficulties in Washington. The Soviet ambassador was concerned by rumors of "America's strivings to create reactionary governments in Europe and [America's] relations with rightist elements of the European political emigration." Eden assured him that Roosevelt "decisively disavowed any such efforts." On the positive side, Litvinov observed that there was "a coincidence of views" between the Soviet Union and the United States on the subject of "replacing the League of Nations with a new postwar organization." He envisioned an organization comprised of "dozens of governments or groups of governments, while the ruling and executive authority would reside in the Big Four."[46] He himself endorsed the idea of great-power control and could only have been heartened by what seemed a clear readiness on the part of the West, especially the United States, to cooperate with the Soviet Union in postwar reconstruction.[47]

The change in Litvinov's attitude toward the United States was evident in his last interview before his return to Moscow. He spoke with Welles about his hopes for Soviet-American relations. Welles reported the ambassador to have said that

> the future peace of the world depended very largely upon understanding and cooperation between the Soviet Union and the United States. He said that without the achievement of this, he did not believe that any international organization was conceivable or that the peace . . . could possibly be maintained. . . . [T]he way things were now going, he did not see any prospect of the achievement of that kind of understanding and cooperation. He said it was for this reason that he had insisted that he be permitted to return to Moscow where he intended to do his utmost to persuade Stalin that the policy which [he] had in mind should be followed in the interest of the Soviet Union itself. He said he was far from optimistic as to the outcome of his impending mission and . . . doubted very much that he would be permitted to return to Washington.[48]

Despite his disappointments in the United States, the aged diplomat clung tenaciously to the idea that good relations with America were imperative for the Soviet Union. Even though Molotov and Stalin, by all accounts, were ignoring him, he wanted to return to Moscow to fight for his convictions.[49]

[46]Litvinov to Narkomindel, 29 March 1943, *Sovetsko-amerikanskie otnosheniia* 1:299–300.

[47]Vojtech Mastny, *Russia's Road to the Cold War: Diplomacy, Warfare, and the Politics of Communism, 1941–1945* (New York, 1979), 219–20.

[48]Welles memorandum of conversation, 7 May 1943, *FRUS, 1943* (Washington, 1943), 3:522–23.

[49]There is much evidence to suggest that Stalin placed relatively little value on postwar cooperation with the United States. After Yalta, he rejected even cosmetic adherence to the

Several conclusions may be drawn from Litvinov's account of his experiences in Washington. By the spring of 1942 (not 1943 as previously had been thought), Stalin believed that he had gained the acquiescence of the United States to the retention of the 1941 borders. Therefore, when Roosevelt later attempted to persuade Stalin on the merits of a Baltic "referendum and the right of self-determination" for the region, the Soviet dictator was justified, to some extent, in his belief that the president was stepping back from his March 1942 statements.[50] It is also clear that Roosevelt raised Soviet hopes that a second front would be opened relatively early in the war and then attempted to blame the British when an invasion had to be delayed, even though Churchill had told the president that the earliest practical date was late summer of 1943.

These events support the interpretation of Roosevelt's wartime foreign policy as one designed to placate Russia as much as possible for the eminently sound reason that it was inevitable that after victory that state would resume its status as a great power. In addition, Litvinov's accounts of his meetings with Roosevelt lend support to the thesis that the president believed that Britain's days as a great power were coming to an end. The supplanting of Britain by Soviet Russia in international politics was a complicated and delicate process, and it can be argued that Litvinov shows that Roosevelt grappled with this difficult situation about as well as any American president could have in the context of World War II.

It is surely no coincidence that as Litvinov became disillusioned with the United States and his messages to Moscow became increasingly acerbic, the statements of Stalin and the Soviet press became more acerbic too. However, by mid-1943, Litvinov had returned to his earlier conviction about the necessity of Soviet-American cooperation, and on this point the ambassador's views were then closer to Roosevelt's than to Stalin's. It is certain that Litvinov presented Stalin with arguments in favor of what Vojtech Mastny has described as a policy of "positive, albeit carefully circumscribed, collaboration with the West," although it seems that Litvinov made these points even earlier than Mastny has indicated.[51] For whatever reason, however, Stalin was not interested, and Litvinov's and Roosevelt's hopes for a new world order, established upon the cornerstone of Soviet-American cooperation, were never realized.

Declaration of Liberated Europe as applied to Romania and Poland. See Gaddis, *Russia, the Soviet Union, and the United States,* 166. In 1946, Litvinov told American journalist Richard C. Hottelet that there had never been much hope for Soviet-American cooperation because of the "ideological conception prevailing [in Moscow] that conflict between the Communist and capitalist worlds is inevitable." *New York World Telegram and Sun,* 28 January 1953.

[50]Dallek, *Franklin D. Roosevelt,* 436.

[51]Vojtech Mastny, "The Cassandra in the Foreign Commissariat: Maxim Litvinov and the Cold War," *Foreign Affairs* 54 (January 1976): 376. Mastny's article deals primarily with Litvinov's activities after his return from Washington.

Joseph E. Davies and Soviet–American Relations, 1941–43

ELIZABETH KIMBALL MACLEAN*

Joseph E. Davies is best known for his controversial service as U.S. ambassador to the Soviet Union in 1937–38. His 1941 book, *Mission to Moscow,* and the movie based on that book, provided a highly favorable image of the Soviet Union during World War II, when both the United States and Russia were warring against Nazi Germany. From 1941 to 1943, however, Davies also played a little known but important unofficial role as a personal liaison between the White House and the Soviet embassy in Washington. In that capacity he served as a direct channel through which representatives of the Soviet Union could express their views to President Franklin D. Roosevelt, and in turn the president and his administration could explain American policies to the Soviets. The key to the success of Davies's activities as an intermediary between Soviet and American officials was the awareness on the part of each side that he had the confidence of the other. In 1943, as a result of the trust in him shown by Soviet officials, Roosevelt broadened Davies's role as a liaison by sending him on a personal mission to Soviet Premier Josef Stalin. That later "mission to Moscow" was the high point of Davies's wartime career in Soviet-American relations.

Joseph E. Davies was uniquely qualified to serve as an unofficial liaison between the Soviet embassy and the White House. His role grew out of a special combination of personal and political relationships he had developed over many years with Franklin Roosevelt, on the one hand, and with high officials of the Soviet Union, on the other. Davies and Roosevelt developed a close friendship while serving in the administration of President Woodrow Wilson. They saw much of each other on both a social and political basis, attending biweekly meetings of the Common Counsel Club for Democratic progressives, playing golf, and socializing at family gatherings. The two young men were seen regularly at parties euphemistically

*I would like to thank Dr. Wayne Cole for his valuable suggestions and advice in the preparation of this paper.

73

dubbed "Administration Dancing Classes." Davies treasured a photograph that Roosevelt gave him at the time with the inscription, "to my old side kick."[1]

After World War I, while establishing a lucrative corporate law practice in Washington, Davies kept in touch with Roosevelt, enthusiastically supporting his budding national political career. In 1920 he seconded Roosevelt's nomination for vice president at the Democratic convention. A decade later, he took charge of the Democratic presidential campaign in the West, renewing contacts with Roosevelt's old associates from Wilsonian days and lending his well-established oratorical and organizational skills to the cause. With victory came the offer of a cabinet post, but Davies turned it down; he wanted to rebuild his personal fortune that had been diminished by the 1929 crash. Four years later, with his financial position restored, Davies again contributed his time and a generous share of his substantial income to Roosevelt's campaign. In return, the president appointed him U.S. ambassador to the Soviet Union.[2]

Davies began his ambassadorial mission in January 1937, at a time of growing tension and concern over the threat that Nazi Germany posed to European peace. The president, recognizing that the Soviet Union would play a crucial role in a European crisis, specifically instructed Davies "to win the confidence of Stalin." The new ambassador accepted the assignment with enthusiasm. Arriving in Moscow in January 1937, he immediately launched a vigorous campaign to cultivate the friendship of the Soviets. After exploring the capital, he traveled through south Russia to investigate the condition of Soviet industry and agriculture. Aware that "Stalin would get wind of" his reports to the State Department, Davies highlighted his accounts of Soviet economic progress and military development by commending the work of local directors and praising Moscow officials. He also plunged into the social scene, entertaining the Soviets lavishly and being entertained in return on an unprecedented scale for visiting foreigners. He established close ties with several high Soviet officials, including Vyacheslav Molotov, president of the Soviet of People's Commissars, and Foreign Minister Maxim Litvinov. Even Premier Stalin invited the ambassador to a private meeting, an event Davies believed was "a unique occurrence in [Soviet] diplomatic history."[3]

[1]Joseph Davies Tydings, interview in Washington, DC, 8 October 1978; "Ambassador Davies," *Fortune* (October 1937): 97; Frank Burt Freidel, *Franklin D. Roosevelt: The Apprenticeship* (Boston, 1952), pp. 168–69; Joseph E. Davies, *Mission to Moscow* (New York, 1941), pp. xi–xii; Eleanor Davies Ditzen, interview in Washington, DC, 26 October 1978; "Foreign Service: To the Reds," *Time* 30 November 1936, p. 11.

[2]*Fortune* (October 1937): 212; Freidel, *Franklin D. Roosevelt: The Ordeal* (Boston, 1954), p. 68 and *Franklin D. Roosevelt: The Triumph* (Boston, 1956), p. 211; Ditzen, interview, 26 October 1978; John Lewis Gaddis, *The United States and the Origins of the Cold War, 1941–1947* (New York, 1972), p. 34.

[3]Daniel Yergin, *Shattered Peace: The Origins of the Cold War and the National Security State* (Boston, 1977), pp. 33, 49–50, 417; Ditzen, interview, 26 October 1978; *Fortune* (October 1937): 94, 218, 221; "Russia: Babbitt Bolsheviks," *Time*, 15 March 1937,

Davies's social activities and unconventional methods of collecting data irritated career diplomats at the American embassy. As specialists in Soviet affairs, they were understandably insulted when Davies rejected their expert advice and relied instead on information from British and American journalists. He not only refused to adopt the embassy's hard-line approach to Soviet-American relations but showed at times an undisguised contempt for professional diplomats as a group. He was accused of treating the embassy "staff as hired help." George Kennan, Charles Bohlen, and other diplomats criticized Davies's fitness for the post. The ambassador was a novice on Soviet affairs, schooled only in State Department documents, and, according to Bohlen, "sublimely ignorant of even the most elementary realities of the Soviet system and of its ideology." In the eyes of his critics, Davies was seduced by the flattery of Moscow officials, and his reports to Washington, in Bohlen's opinion, were "incurably optimistic" and misleading. "While containing a good deal of information and shrewd observation, [they] were almost always superficial and heavily slanted." Kennan considered Davies a political opportunist, a publicity hound. He challenged the ambassador's motives for accepting the post and questioned his seriousness regarding the mission. Davies's well-publicized effort to improve the atmosphere in Soviet-American relations, by creating a more positive impression of the Soviet Union for home consumption, was motivated, according to critics, by a desire to enhance his own newspaper image. The more egregious aspects of his personality and his excessive concern with public relations made him a target of ridicule and caused many of his contemporaries as well as later historians to discount his influence.[4]

During the years following his assignment in Moscow, Davies offered to serve the president as an intermediary to the Soviets. It was not until June 1941, however, after Nazi Germany had invaded the Soviet Union, that the Roosevelt administration capitalized on the personal contacts Davies had established with Soviet officials. The president and his advisers became aware of the potential advantages of Davies's position as a result of the vigorous campaign he launched in the summer of 1941 to convince the administration to send aid to the Red Army. In early July, Davies was in and out of the executive offices, pressing his case for aid on Roosevelt's closest advisers. He argued that the Russian front was crucial to the security of the United States. Despite the predictions of military experts, Davies believed the Red Army could hold out against the Nazi

pp. 20–24; Davies, *Mission to Moscow*, pp. 28, 53, 67, 103, 173, 214, 339, 356–57, 403, 408, 411, 599, 617–19, 622.

[4]George F. Kennan, *Memoirs: 1925–1950* (Boston, 1967), pp. 82–84; Charles E. Bohlen, *Witness to History: 1929–1969* (New York, 1973), pp. 44–45, 51–52, 56; Richard H. Ullman, "The Davies Mission and United States-Soviet Relations, 1937–1941," *World Politics* 9 (January 1957): 221–23, 226–30, 236–37; Davies, *Mission to Moscow*, p. 436; Yergin, *Shattered Peace*, pp. 33–34.

onslaught if America sent immediate aid. He warned presidential assistant Harry Hopkins that the administration's failure to take action might force Stalin into signing a separate peace with Hitler. The Soviets had to be assured of American support, both material and psychological, and those assurances, he advised, could best be provided through personal contacts at the highest levels. "Word ought to be gotten to Stalin direct," wrote Davies in a memo to Hopkins, "that our attitude is 'all out' to beat Hitler and that our historic policy of friendliness to Russia still exists."[5]

In his effort to convince the administration to support the Red Army, Davies not only talked with American officials but also took the initiative to sound out the Soviets. He wanted to show Soviet officials that he had a personal interest in their cause. He hoped to gather evidence on the Red Army's capacity to withstand the Nazi attack, which would add weight to his argument for American aid.

On 9 July, over lunch at his home, Davies reestablished his contacts with Soviet Ambassador Constantin Oumansky. The ambassador was sufficiently impressed with Davies's interest in the Russian situation to meet him again several days later at the Soviet embassy. Davies found Oumansky more than willing to furnish specific evidence on the Red Army's capacity to withstand the Nazi invasion. After several conversations, Davies came to the conclusion that he could play a part in improving communications between Soviet officials and the administration, and he requested the State Department's permission to serve unofficially as a liaison to the Soviet embassy. On 15 July, he told Acting Secretary of State Sumner Welles that he "wished to be of every possible help, freely, of course, to the Soviet Embassy." Welles responded positively to the idea, assuring the former ambassador of his "entire confidence," as well as that of the State Department.[6]

Meanwhile, Davies had also hoped to talk with Roosevelt about the aid situation. He had first tried to see the president on 30 June. It was not until 16 July, however, the day after making his request to Welles to serve as a liaison to the Soviet embassy, that Davies finally had an opportunity to meet with the president on the matter. It was the nature of the role Davies could play, as much as the nature of the advice he had given, that sparked Roosevelt's interest in the former ambassador. The idea of a personal liaison to the Soviet embassy may have appealed to Roosevelt for several practical reasons. The president wanted to show the Russians that, despite the State Department's reluctance to support the Soviet cause, he was sincere in his efforts to help. Davies had argued that in order to keep the Soviets fighting they had to be assured of American support, and the

---

[5] U. S., Department of State, *Foreign Relations of the United States, 1939*, 1: *General* (Washington, 1956): 234–36; Ullman, "The Davies Mission," *World Politics* 9: 220–21, 232; Davies, *Mission to Moscow*, pp. 475–76, 487–89; Robert E. Sherwood, *Roosevelt and Hopkins: An Intimate History* (New York, 1950), pp. 306–8.

[6] Davies, *Mission to Moscow*, pp. 489–92.

president may have viewed the former ambassador as a means of providing that reassurance. The president also may have been motivated by personal considerations. He did not like Oumansky and avoided contact with him as much as possible. He may have welcomed the opportunity to have Davies serve as a link to the Soviet ambassador. Davies wrote later in his diary that Roosevelt asked him "to keep in close touch with the Embassy."[7]

It was not unusual for Roosevelt to give an unofficial, but potentially influential, role to a man like Davies. In his formulation of foreign policy, the president tended to rely on individuals who were not professionals or career diplomats. He once told Davies that he, "like Woodrow Wilson, appreciated men who had a 'passion for anonymity.' " Although Roosevelt did not "systematically" circumvent the State Department, his opinion of many of its members was not particularly high. He preferred to have private, informal discussions with trusted individuals rather than formal conferences with State Department officials.[8] Davies's long personal relationship with the president, therefore, contributed to his position of influence after July 1941.

Thus, Davies's unofficial connection with the Soviet embassy helped give him access to the Oval Office, and, throughout the war, he used that opportunity to press his personal views on Roosevelt. In terms of their basic analysis of Soviet-American relations, Davies and the president were in accord to a striking degree. Although Roosevelt's confidence in the evolution of the Soviet Union from a dictatorship into a capitalist democracy never paralleled Davies's heights of enthusiasm, the president believed that American capitalism and Soviet communism eventually might evolve into more similar forms. Like Davies, he did not share the apprehension of the State Department toward Russia's postwar goals. At the beginning of World War II, pragmatic considerations motivated Roosevelt to adopt an approach to Soviet-American relations similar to that of Davies. It was the president's opinion that Nazi Germany threatened the Western world in

---

[7]Ibid., pp. 492–93; Davies, diary, 30 June, 16 July 1941, Joseph E. Davies Papers, Manuscript Division, Library of Congress, Washington, DC. Davies kept most of the records of his activities in either his diary or his journal. Any accounts that he did not specifically designate as diary or journal entries are cited here as "notes." Most of his accounts were typewritten versions of original handwritten journal and diary entries. The later versions served as drafts for a book he planned to write on his wartime experiences. In some cases, such as Davies's 1943 meetings with Roosevelt, the original handwritten accounts are available. I have quoted from the original accounts where they exist, unless they are very brief or sketchy. In such cases, the later accounts help provide more detailed or precise information. William L. Langer and S. Everett Gleason, *The Undeclared War, 1940–1941* (New York, 1953), p. 540; Raymond H. Dawson, *The Decision to Aid Russia, 1941* (Chapel Hill, 1959), pp. 143, 149; Ullman, "The Davies Mission," *World Politics*, 9: 238; James MacGregor Burns, *Roosevelt: The Soldier of Freedom* (New York, 1970), p. 102.

[8]Langer and Gleason, *The Challenge to Isolation*, pp. 2–10; Davies, diary, 16 October 1942; Robert Dallek, *Franklin D. Roosevelt and American Foreign Policy, 1932–1945* (New York, 1979), pp. 532–33.

the summer of 1941, not the Soviet Union. Roosevelt initiated a policy of aid to Russia because, in words echoing those of the former ambassador, "the defense of any country resisting Hitler or Japan was in the long run the defense of our own country." After Operation Barbarossa, the president, like Davies, considered Soviet-American cooperation indispensable.[9]

The policy approaches advocated by Davies in early July were given added momentum later that month by the successful outcome of a series of conversations between Harry Hopkins and Premier Stalin in Moscow. Hopkins seemed impressed by the sincerity of the Soviet premier, as Davies had been earlier. The resolution of several matters involving supplies, which had plagued Soviet-American relations on the lower echelons, reinforced Davies's argument for personal diplomacy at the top levels. The discussions, furthermore, convinced Hopkins that given sufficient aid, the Red Army could hold out through the winter, as Davies had predicted, and could provide a permanent front against the Nazis. Hopkins's visit to Moscow produced a "point of no return" in Roosevelt's determination to provide all-out aid to the Soviet Union. On 1 October the Anglo-American Supply Conference in Moscow issued a formal protocol extending substantial aid to the Red Army with no strings attached. Davies had won his case with the administration.[10]

Meanwhile, changes were taking place in the Soviet embassy that were to solidify Davies's position as a personal liaison. In September 1941 Oumansky informed Davies that he was leaving his Washington post. Davies said he hoped that Maxim Litvinov, with whom he had been on particularly cordial terms during his 1937–38 mission to Moscow, would be appointed the new ambassador. A month after his conversation with Oumansky, Davies indeed learned that Litvinov had been assigned to the embassy post. On 7 December, having been notified beforehand by the Soviet embassy of Litvinov's arrival, Davies greeted the new ambassador at the airport in Washington.[11] Only hours before Litvinov's plane landed, the Japanese had attacked Pearl Harbor. Thus, with America in the war and with his ties to the Soviet embassy cemented by Litvinov's appointment, Davies's efforts to promote cooperation between the Soviet Union and the United States took on new dimensions.

After Pearl Harbor, Davies settled into the role he was to play as a

    [9] Davies, *Mission to Moscow*, pp. 308, 318, 414–15, 496; Gaddis, *Origins of the Cold War*, pp. 40–41; Dawson, *Decision to Aid Russia*, p. 138; George Fischer, "Genesis of United States-Soviet Relations in World War II," *The Review of Politics* 12 (July 1950): 365–66.

    [10] Dawson, *Decision to Aid Russia*, pp. 178–79; Davies, journal, 8 September 1941; Yergin, *Shattered Peace*, pp. 53–54; Herbert Feis, *Churchill, Roosevelt, Stalin: The War They Waged and the Peace They Sought*, 2d ed. (Princeton, 1957), pp. 12–13; Fischer, "Genesis," *Review of Politics*, 12: 368–70, 372–75.

    [11] Davies, *Mission to Moscow*, pp. 500–1; *FRUS, 1941*, 1: *General, The Soviet Union* (Washington, 1958), p. 657; *FRUS, 1941, 4: The Far East* (Washington, 1956), pp. 730–31; Davies, journal, 7 December 1941.

liaison throughout the war. When problems in allied relations were discussed at the Soviet embassy, the former ambassador listened sympathetically to what Litvinov and other Soviet officials had to say and then relayed their opinions to the White House. The liaison worked both ways. Davies spent as much time explaining the American position to the Soviets as he did listening to the Soviet point of view. According to the president, his efforts were "of inestimable help in assessing situations." Roosevelt told Hopkins "to keep in constant touch" with Davies and asked the former ambassador to "come in and see him at lunch or otherwise" whenever he "thought it necessary." Davies shuttled messages and opinions back and forth from the Soviet embassy to the White House, occasionally meeting with both Hopkins and Litvinov on the same day.[12]

Davies functioned as an intermediary in several areas. During 1942 his primary responsibility was to maintain Soviet confidence in the American supply effort, a job that involved soothing ruffled nerves and egos on both sides. When the Russians complained, for instance, that American manufacturers were "stalling" in order to avoid completing Soviet supply orders, Davies assured Litvinov that there were good reasons for the delays and that Roosevelt had informed him that the United States would be "caught up" on deliveries "by the end of April." Soviet complaints remained an habitual topic of discussion in his meetings with Hopkins. Lower echelons on the American side also had grievances that Davies relayed to the Soviet embassy. Early in the year, apparently with the supply problem in mind, Roosevelt considered offering Davies his old post as ambassador to the Soviet Union. He wrote Secretary of State Cordell Hull that "Joe would be really persona grata, would have access to Stalin, and in a couple weeks could get into complete touch with the airplane and tank situation." Davies, however, declined the post for health reasons, and instead the appointment was given to Admiral William H. Standley.[13]

In the spring of 1942 Stalin offered his Western allies another opportunity to demonstrate their sincerity in support of the Soviet war effort. The Soviet premier wanted Great Britain and the United States to recognize his claim to certain eastern European territories acquired during the period of the Nazi-Soviet Pact. Particularly controversial was his demand for a section of Poland east of the Curzon Line, a boundary established by Britain's Curzon Commission after World War I. Prime Minister Winston Churchill was willing to acknowledge Stalin's claim, but Roosevelt and Hull were not. Davies feared that the American stand threatened to destroy Soviet confidence in the West. His unofficial position as a liaison gave him the unique opportunity to encourage some form of understanding.

Davies discussed the issue of the Curzon Line with Soviet, British,

---

[12] Davies, diary, 16 October 1942.
[13] Ibid., 20, 29 March, 29 October 1942; Davies, journal, 15 October 1942; Elliott Roosevelt, ed., *F.D.R.: His Personal Letters, 1928–1945* (New York, 1950), 2:1273.

and American officials. In conversations with Litvinov, he became convinced that the Soviet argument for the Curzon Line was sound, but he cautioned the ambassador not to press the issue. The American public, he warned, would not understand the Soviet demand. He counseled patience; the matter would resolve itself in time.[14]

In the meantime, Britain's Ambassador Lord Halifax, who had been denied an interview with the president, took up the subject of the Curzon Line with Davies. The British at that time were completing the draft of a twenty-year treaty of alliance with the Soviet Union. Halifax wanted to know whether Davies thought the British should officially recognize Stalin's territorial claim by incorporating it in the treaty. If Britain resisted, would Stalin sign a separate peace with Hitler? Davies said he believed not. Stalin would continue to fight as long as he was certain the West would give him "effective" help. He warned Halifax, however, that by refusing to recognize Stalin's claim, the Western allies "would seriously prejudice [Soviet] confidence in allied judgement and good faith." That refusal would have serious repercussions on allied unity during the war and on cooperation between the Soviet Union and the West after the war.[15] Davies thus counseled Litvinov to be patient, while he advised the British to accept Stalin's claim without delay.

In reporting his conversation with Halifax to Welles and Roosevelt, Davies urged each of them to recognize the Soviet claim to the Curzon Line, but he found them both adamantly opposed. Though the president "understood" the security argument behind the Soviet demand, he maintained that "it was not necessary nor wise to bring it up now." Roosevelt did not want the territorial provision incorporated in the Anglo-Soviet treaty, believing that the matter would solve itself in time. At the peace conference it might "ultimately be done, in equity and good conscience," he said, but it must "not be projected and established through or during military operations." The president was confident that if he and Stalin could have a personal talk, the Soviet premier "would appreciate the value of not offending world public opinion now."[16] Roosevelt had made his position clear; Davies did not initiate a discussion of the topic again in 1942. Not until the early spring of 1943, after Roosevelt failed to convince Stalin to meet with him, did Davies find the president more receptive to his views on the territorial issue.

Meanwhile, the president set in motion a plan designed to postpone the question of Stalin's territorial claim by offering the Soviet premier something he needed more, a second front. After Hopkins acquired Churchill's agreement "in principle" to a 1943 invasion of Europe, with a possible emergency landing in 1942 if necessary, Roosevelt invited Soviet Foreign Minister Vyacheslav Molotov to Washington. Molotov arrived in

---

[14] Davies, diary, 8 January 1942; Davies, journal, 6 April 1942.
[15] Davies, journal, 6 April 1942.
[16] Ibid., 6, 7 April 1942.

May 1942, after stopping first in London to sign the Anglo-Soviet Treaty of Alliance. The treaty omitted the crucial clause regarding the Soviet claim to the Curzon Line. With an impending Nazi offensive in mind, the Soviets had decided to avoid any action that might prejudice Roosevelt's plans for an early second front. Having given in to the president, however, Molotov had reason to expect a quid pro quo when he arrived in Washington.[17] At their meeting on 30 May, Roosevelt informed his Soviet guest that he could expect a second front that year. Molotov, however, demanded more than a private pledge from the president; he wanted a firm, public commitment to an invasion of Europe in 1942.[18]

During their discussion the previous evening, the president had asked Molotov if there were any Americans he wanted to see while he was in Washington. The foreign minister had replied that he wished to "exchange greetings" with Joseph Davies. Meeting at the Soviet embassy a few days later, Davies found the Soviet minister particularly concerned about the Anglo-American plans for a second front. Molotov may have been trying to encourage Davies to use his influence to induce the Roosevelt administration to make a more definite commitment to a 1942 invasion. He told Davies that the Red Army "desperately needed" the front. In light of the impending Nazi offensive, "his government needed a definite date so they could coordinate their plans. . . . His Government had to be definitely advised."[19] A few days later Molotov did obtain Roosevelt's commitment, in the form of a public joint communique, to a second front in Europe in 1942. Davies, however, left no record of a meeting with the president during the remainder of Molotov's stay in Washington, so it is unlikely that he had a direct influence on the president's final decision.[20]

Molotov returned to England to obtain Churchill's endorsement of the joint communique, but the prime minister refused to sign. He had never committed himself fully to a 1942 front in Europe. By mid-July he succeeded in convincing Roosevelt to agree to an alternate strategy for 1942, an invasion of North Africa, code named "Torch." Soviet resentment of the new Anglo-American plan was clearly reflected in Litvinov's remarks to Davies. The ambassador had told Davies earlier that "right or wrong, the Soviet people believed that they had received a definite promise" in the joint communique. After the decision on Torch, Litvinov

---

[17] Sherwood, *Roosevelt and Hopkins*, pp. 525–28, 534–38; Feis, *Churchill, Roosevelt, Stalin,* pp. 61–64; Dallek, *Roosevelt and American Foreign Policy,* pp. 339–41. See also Davies, journal, 24 February 1943.

[18] Sherwood, *Roosevelt and Hopkins*, p. 575; Dallek, *Roosevelt and American Foreign Policy,* pp. 343–44; Burns, *Soldier of Freedom,* p. 234.

[19] Sherwood, *Roosevelt and Hopkins,* p. 561; Davies, diary, 29 May 1942. Davies's diary entry is dated 29 May. It was not until that evening, however, that Molotov told Roosevelt he wanted to see Davies. The weight of the internal evidence, though contradictory, suggests that the Molotov-Davies conversation took place on 1 June. At their luncheon meeting, Molotov told Davies that he had just come from seeing the president. The only day on which Molotov met with Roosevelt exclusively in the morning was 1 June.

[20] Sherwood, *Roosevelt and Hopkins*, p. 577.

"grumbled bitterly" that the Red Army was doing all the fighting, while the British and Americans were making the decisions and presenting them to the Soviets as a "fait accompli." Davies urged that they had no "time to stop to pick up pins." They had to maintain confidence in each other, but as he wrote later, "it didn't go over."[21]

During the Anglo-American discussions on Torch, Litvinov's complaints became increasingly anti-British and anti-Churchill in nature. His attitude reflected a long history of Anglo-Soviet friction, stemming from the Bolshevik Revolution itself and from Britain's intervention in the Russian civil war. Churchill, who was instrumental in that intervention, remained an implacable foe of the communist regime throughout the twenties. With the rise of Nazi Germany, however, Churchill led the opposition to appeasement and endorsed collective security measures against Hitler. Old hostilities and suspicions were revived, nonetheless, when negotiations for an alliance against Germany broke down and Moscow and Berlin signed the Nazi-Soviet Pact. In 1941, when the Germans attacked the Soviet Union, Litvinov was convinced, as he later told Davies, "that the British fleet was steaming up the North Sea for [a] joint attack of the British with HITLER." In early 1942 an unpleasant personal encounter between Litvinov and the prime minister could have scarcely encouraged cordial relations between the two men. Churchill had "rather impatiently upbraided" the Soviet ambassador for his handling of a matter involving the UN declaration. According to what the president later told Davies, Churchill's "language bordered on the insulting." When the prime minister pressed for the invasion of North Africa, Litvinov insisted that Churchill opposed the cross-channel invasion "for political and Empire reasons."[22] The argument began to appeal to Davies.

The president, unwittingly, may have reinforced Litvinov's views. In several conversations with Davies, Roosevelt complained about Churchill's "mid-Victorian attitude" toward the British Empire. The prime minister refused to endorse the mandate system, and he opposed Roosevelt's call for colonial independence after the war. The president feared that peace would be threatened by the existence of colonial empires. "The tail," he said, "could not continue to wag the dog." He told Davies that he had informed the prime minister that he was prepared to take the problem "up personally with his King and his advisers." He was confident, however, that in the long run Churchill himself would "lead the way."[23]

During the summer, the former ambassador began to interpret Soviet-Western diplomacy in terms of the historic friction in Anglo-Soviet relations. That bias influenced his analysis of a series of conversations

---

[21] "Russia's Desperate Defense," box 11, Davies Papers; Davies, diary, 20 July 1942.
[22] Davies, diary, 23 June 1941, 8 January, 17 June 1942. See also Sherwood, *Roosevelt and Hopkins*, p. 449.
[23] Davies, journal, 6 April, 23 July 1942; Davies, diary, 23 July, 29 November 1942.

between Churchill and Stalin in Moscow. In August 1942 the prime minister went to the Soviet Union to personally explain the Anglo-American decision on Torch to the indignant Soviet premier. Though cordiality dominated the final meeting of the two leaders, Davies became convinced that the general tone of their conversations clearly revealed the deep distrust with which Stalin regarded the British prime minister. He began to assume that Churchill could not serve as a mediator to restore Soviet confidence in the Western allies. Only Roosevelt could do that.[24]

The president's confidence in his own ability to win Stalin's trust paralleled that of Davies. He had expressed that faith with brutal frankness in a letter to Churchill the previous spring. "Stalin hates the guts of all your top people. He thinks he likes me better, and I hope he will continue to do so." By August, however, the premier had rejected all Roosevelt's invitations for a meeting, and the president made no secret of his growing concern. He told journalists Arthur Krock and Mark Sullivan that he had instructed Ambassador Standley in Moscow to propose the idea of a meeting to the Soviet premier, but Standley "had received a 'brush-off.'" Krock and Sullivan discussed the problem with Davies late in the summer. They suggested that he "try to do something about it."[25]

Not surprisingly, Davies responded to the suggestion. Throughout the fall of 1942, using his access to the Soviet embassy and the White House, he encouraged the Soviets to trust Roosevelt, while advising Hopkins and the president to give first priority to a private meeting with Stalin. In conversations with the Soviet ambassador, Davies was forced to submit to a barrage of complaints that reinforced his conviction that a Roosevelt-Stalin meeting was imperative. As Hitler's armies marched toward Stalingrad, Litvinov became desperately worried. "Why—why, . . . do you not take some of the weight 'off the back' of our Army," he demanded. Although Litvinov sympathized with Roosevelt's predicament regarding the joint communique, he said that the Soviet people could not accept a broken promise. Davies suggested that the African invasion and air bombing of Germany were in "compliance with the spirit of the [joint] communique," but Litvinov "would have none of it." He criticized Churchill's motives and warned that the Soviets were losing faith in America's "ability to resist British influence." Davies said he "had no need to worry about F.D.R." He urged the Soviet ambassador to assure Stalin that Roosevelt's prime objective was to keep allied unity in order to defeat Hitler.[26]

---

[24] "Russia's Desperate Defense," box 11, Davies Papers.

[25] Winston S. Churchill, *The Second World War: The Hinge of Fate* (Boston, 1950), p. 201; Davies, diary, 20 July, 23 August, 18 September 1942. For Standley's account of the proposal to Stalin, see William H. Standley and Arthur A. Ageton, *Admiral Ambassador to Russia* (Chicago, 1955), pp. 152–53.

[26] Davies, diary, 20 September, 29, 30 October 1942.

In conversations with Hopkins, Davies emphasized the need to restore Soviet confidence in the United States. The Russians were suspicious, he said, because of Roosevelt's opposition to the Curzon Line as well as his failure to carry out the promise of the joint communique. However, the main problem, he told Hopkins, was Churchill. The Soviets thought he was "only using them to beat off a mad dog, until, thereafter, [he could] discard them as no longer necessary. That is, of course, crazy, . . . but that is what the 'tops' are thinking as I read them." As a solution, Davies recommended a private meeting between Stalin and Roosevelt. There was no reason why Churchill should serve as "a friendly broker" in Soviet-American relations, especially when Stalin "distrusted the broker more than he did the other party." The argument seemed to appeal to Hopkins, who suggested that Davies explain it to Roosevelt.[27]

Davies volunteered the suggestion to Roosevelt, but he did not press it. Early in November 1942 British and American troops invaded North Africa. Military considerations required a meeting of the leaders of the three allied governments to plan future strategy. There could be no question of omitting Churchill. As plans for a top-level conference proceeded, Roosevelt was careful to avoid any action that might suggest to Stalin that the president and the prime minister were settling matters between themselves before conferring with the Soviet premier. With that in mind, Roosevelt rejected Churchill's request for a preliminary Anglo-American conference.[28]

Arranging a meeting for the three leaders proved elusive. Roosevelt wrote three invitations to the Soviet premier and received three rejections before he became convinced that Stalin was not interested in a meeting with his two Western allies. In early December the premier's final message on the subject implied that there was nothing to talk about, that all the West had to do was open a second front in Europe in the spring. The president had no choice but to settle for a conference alone with the prime minister.[29] Thus, in 1942 Roosevelt failed to establish personal contact with Stalin. The groundwork had been laid, however, for a presidential initiative the following spring, which would directly involve Davies in the arrangements for a private meeting between the president and the Soviet premier.

Soviet-Western relations continued to deteriorate in early 1943. In January, at the Casablanca Conference, Roosevelt and Churchill agreed to delay the cross-channel invasion a second time in order to attack Hitler from the south through Sicily. Litvinov complained bitterly to Davies when he learned of the decision and scorned Churchill's plan to "attack by way of

---

[27] "Serious Soviet Misunderstanding," 29 September 1942, Davies Papers; Davies, diary, 3 October 1942; Davies, journal, 30 September, 1942.
   [28] Davies, diary, 16 October 1942; Sherwood, *Roosevelt and Hopkins*, p. 661; Dallek, *Roosevelt and American Foreign Policy*, p. 368.
   [29] Feis, *Churchill, Roosevelt, Stalin*, pp. 99–101.

the 'soft underbelly of the axis.' "[30] In March, Soviet-American relations were further chilled when Ambassador Standley accused Soviet officials of concealing information from the Russian people on America's Lend-Lease contribution to the war effort. Responding to the situation, the London *Times* suggested that Britain should serve as a friendly broker to ease the tensions in Soviet-American relations. On 12 March, when Foreign Minister Anthony Eden arrived in Washington, it was rumored that he had come to serve as a mediator to "patch up" relations between the United States and the Soviet Union. Roosevelt resented the idea that he needed Britain's help to restore harmony in his relations with the Soviets.[31]

On 13 March, the president began to formulate a rudimentary plan that could, in its final stages, simultaneously restore Soviet confidence in the United States and disqualify Britain as a broker. In a meeting with Davies, he outlined his concerns about the deterioration in Soviet-American relations. The president "knew Stalin was bitter over the second front"; Standley's criticism had made the situation worse. The ambassador "had messed things up," Roosevelt said, and was no longer of use in Moscow. He would have to come home. The president wanted Davies to return to Russia to take up his old post as ambassador. Davies was the best man "to straighten out that situation." According to Roosevelt's advisers, the former ambassador was his " 'Ace in the Deck.' " The assignment appealed to Davies, but he reminded the president that his doctors would oppose any plans for a long stay in the Soviet Union. Roosevelt recommended a physical checkup. If the medical test results showed that Davies could not stay in Moscow for an extended period, the president wanted him to go for about "four or six weeks."[32]

The two men discussed Foreign Secretary Eden's visit to Washington "and the idea being circulated that it required the intervention of G. B. as a friendly broker or 'go between' to bring about understanding between the U.S.S.R. and the U.S.A." Davies admitted that at that moment relations between Moscow and London appeared to be more stable than relations between Moscow and Washington. The former ambassador was convinced, however, that despite the good will produced by the Anglo-Soviet treaty, "legacies of old suspicions" continued to plague relations between Britain and Russia. The Soviets harbored a deep "mistrust of British Imperialism" and of Churchill's motives in prosecuting the war. Roosevelt was suspect, warned Davies, because the Soviets thought that he and Churchill "were great cronies." The president believed it was essential that "there should be no differences now to divide the allied strength against Hitler. He wanted Stalin to know that [the United States

---

[30] Davies, diary, 23 January 1943.

[31] Ibid., January 1943, 4, 9 February, 11, 12 March 1943; Sherwood, *Roosevelt and Hopkins*, pp. 705–6; Burns, *Soldier of Freedom*, p. 368.

[32] Davies, diary, 13 March 1943; Davies, "notes," 14 March 1943. See also Sherwood, *Roosevelt and Hopkins*, p. 733.

was] on the level—had no axes to grind, and [was] concerned first with winning the war." Possibly as a result of Davies's analysis of Soviet opinion, the president kept the Soviets fully informed of his discussions with Eden and made it clear that the United States was party to no decisions on the status of postwar Europe. Roosevelt wanted to convince the Soviets that the United States was not "in a secret combination with the British."[33]

Roosevelt reviewed the efforts that he and Churchill had made to convince Stalin to agree to a meeting of the three leaders. All had failed. The president believed "it was vitally necessary that" he meet with the Soviet premier. He was certain that "if he and Stalin could have a face to face talk," he could clear up the misunderstandings. He instructed his envoy to "talk the whole situation" over with Stalin and "to arrange for a meeting." Davies was to make "a general exploration of all matters affecting the war and the peace," and "to see where the ideas of the Pres. and Stalin might be in accord and wherein there might be difference[s]." Roosevelt did not want the Soviet premier to fear that in the event of a meeting of the three powers, Stalin "would be in the 'nutcracker' and at a disadvantage." Roosevelt did not suggest at that time that he wanted Davies to arrange a meeting without Churchill. The former ambassador was left with the impression that the president had devised a new strategy to convince Stalin to agree to a meeting of the three heads of state.[34]

On 16 March, Davies was admitted to Boston's Lahey Clinic. He underwent a series of tests that proved that his condition was benign, but confirmed his earlier suspicion that he could not remain in Moscow for an extended period. "You silly, old idiot," cabled Roosevelt when he heard the news, "why did you think that you could have a condition other than benign after suffering from it for fourteen years! For the love of Pete take care of yourself first and when that is done, come to Papa at the White House."[35]

On 2 April, while still resting in the hospital, Davies sent a memo to Hopkins and Roosevelt, analyzing Britain's diplomatic role as a friendly broker. "Ironical" though it was, wrote Davies, in 1943 Churchill was being "heralded as the 'good broker' to patch up differences between" the Soviet Union and the United States. That recently achieved stability in Anglo-Soviet relations was due to London's "realistic" approach to foreign policy. "Without blinking," Britain had recognized Stalin's claim to the Curzon boundary and had signed a treaty of alliance with the Soviets, both of which the United States had refused to do. The situation was "not good," warned Davies. Washington had to adopt a similarly

---

[33]Davies, "notes," 14 March 1943; Davies, journal, 14 March 1943; Feis, *Churchill, Roosevelt, Stalin,* p. 125.

[34] Davies, journal, 14 March 1943; Davies, "notes," 14 March 1943.

[35] Davies to Hopkins, 23 March 1943; Roosevelt to Davies, 26 March 1943, Davies Papers.

realistic approach to relations with Moscow. After the war, "the world 'set-up' [would] be radically changed." England would "be faced with bank-ruptcy," and only the United States and the Soviet Union would have sufficient resources to finance world reconstruction. Peace and stability would then depend on their ability to cooperate. In view of the cordial relations that had existed between Russia and the United States before the war, there was no reason why present or future differences "could not be rationally composed." The same, however, could not be said for England. With the defeat of Hitler, latent tensions in Anglo-Soviet relations over Churchill's desire to control the balance of power in Europe and to maintain the empire and command of the seas would surface and lead to clashes of interest that could threaten world peace. The United States would then be called on to assume the role of broker in Anglo-Soviet rela-tions. In the meantime, Davies concluded, it was essential "in the face of Stalin's bitterness toward Churchill, bred at Versailles and thereafter, and recently intensified, . . . that the President should personally step into the breach to at least establish confidence in our good faith and purposes."[36]

On 12 April, just after Davies returned to Washington, he and the president met again. Their discussion that afternoon covered a wide range of topics from domestic politics to the structure of the postwar peace. Regarding Roosevelt's instructions for the mission, Davies left only a brief and incomplete note. The president wanted him to "arrange for a meeting either ———or———."[37] In a later, more detailed account of their discus-sion, however, Davies made it clear that the president had definitely abandoned his original plans for a three-power meeting. His new instruc-tions were explicit. "If you are able to arrange this meeting, after some thought I think it would be better at the outset if it were confined to Stalin and myself. . . . 'Three is a crowd,' " he said, "and we can arrange for the Big Three to get together thereafter. Churchill will understand. I will take care of that."[38]

The president's ideas regarding the arrangements for the meeting with Stalin continued to evolve. On 29 April, in a final conference with Davies, Roosevelt said he had come to the conclusion that the best way to broach the subject of the meeting with Stalin was to address a letter from himself directly to the premier. In that case, replied Davies, there was no need to send a special envoy to Moscow. Ambassador Standley could give Roosevelt's message to Stalin. But the president said no and that he specifically wanted Davies to deliver the letter, as he knew the Soviets "had confidence in what [Davies] would say." The former ambassador, moreover, could present his "own views which [the Soviets] knew would have weight" with Roosevelt. Davies would also be in a position to obtain Stalin's ideas for the president's use. Roosevelt was certain that if a

[36] "Memorandum to Hopkins for the President," 2 April 1943, Davies Papers.
[37] Davies, "notes," 12 April 1943.
[38] Davies, diary, 12 April 1943.

meeting could be arranged, "he could convince Stalin of the advisability of doing things in a way that would not give offense to the public. . . . He was sure that 'Uncle Joe' (as he called him) and he would understand each other."

The president said that Hopkins had told him about the brief that Davies had prepared on the subjects he would need to explore with Stalin. Roosevelt "felt that this had covered the ground thoroughly." The president was referring to Davies's brief entitled "Complaints I May Have to Confront," which outlined possible responses to questions Stalin might raise. On the matter of the Curzon Line, Davies planned to tell Stalin: "We think you are entitled to the Curzon Line, but think it unwise to insist upon it now." The evidence suggests that the president was authorizing the former ambassador to inform Stalin that the United States would take a positive stand on the Soviet Union's crucial claim to the Curzon Line. According to Davies's notes on the meeting, however, Roosevelt never made that authority explicit.

The two men discussed a possibly site for the meeting. The president recommended a secluded place, possibly on a ship. Checking his desk globe, he decided that Alaska seemed to be about halfway between Moscow and Washington. The former ambassador could suggest that site to Stalin.[39]

Davies left Washington on 6 May 1943, arriving in Moscow thirteen days later. On the evening of 20 May, Davies and Ambassador Standley were ushered into Stalin's conference room in the Kremlin where they were greeted by Stalin, Molotov, and the interpreter Pavlov. Standley formally presented Davies to the premier and then excused himself saying he had "guests at the Embassy." Davies had informed Standley earlier that the president believed "more could be accomplished" if Davies were "unaccompanied when he delivered the President's letter." Roosevelt had told his envoy in March that the Soviet leaders "would talk on a more frank and friendly basis" if Standley were not present.[40]

Davies spent two and a half hours with Stalin. He presented Roosevelt's letter, which Pavlov translated. The president requested a meeting with the premier that summer; Churchill was not to be invited. Roosevelt wanted a "completely simple visit," without large staffs, so the two leaders could have " 'a meeting of the minds.' " During the translation, Stalin, "doodling" on a piece of paper, remained silent and "grim." Davies said that the president was concerned about the deterioration in Soviet-American relations, which "had become acute when there developed the recent unfortunate incident precipitated by a statement made by our Ambassador here." If Stalin and Roosevelt could meet, the problems

---

[39] Ibid., 19, 29 April 1943.

[40] Standley to Secretary of State Cordell Hull and Roosevelt, 21 May 1943, File No. 121.861/160, Record Group 59, Department of State Records, National Archives, Washington, DC; Davies, diary, 14 March, 20 May 1943.

between them could be ironed out. "I am not so sure," Stalin replied. It took Davies "a long time to penetrate a suspicious, almost hostile attitude." Finally, however, the Soviet premier agreed to meet with the president.[41]

During the course of their discussion, Davies offered Stalin some insights into the relationship between Roosevelt and Churchill. Despite mutual respect and loyalty, he said, Roosevelt did not agree with Churchill on several issues. The president's "ideas as to post-war conditions, in some respects, particularly with reference to colonial and backward peoples, for instance, differed from those of the Prime Minister." Churchill was "more representative of British Imperial policy than of the American point of view." Davies's description of the Churchill-Roosevelt relationship was based on several conversations he had had with the president during the past year.[42] There is no evidence, however, that Roosevelt gave his emissary the authority to discuss his relationship with the prime minister in such detail with Stalin.

Davies said that Roosevelt did not believe that the United States needed a friendly broker in its relations with the Soviet Union, and that it was essential that Soviet and American leaders work out their own problems. The former ambassador predicted that after the war Britain would be exhausted, and world peace would depend on the ability of the United States and the Soviet Union to cooperate. The Soviets, Davies suggested, could do their part in reducing tension between the two countries by abolishing the Comintern.[43] The suggestion may have had no direct influence on the matter, but two days later the Soviet Union abolished the Comintern.

 Davies followed the general outline of his April brief in presenting the American position on the major issues of controversy. On the question of the Curzon Line, he assured the premier that recognition of the Soviet claim would come "as a natural and necessary decision at the Peace Table." For the moment, however, he said, "our Public Opinion had to be considered." Roosevelt was "concerned that there should not even be suspicion that the Principles of the Atlantic Charter were not being now sustained by the Three Allies." Stalin could be assured that the president, a realist as well as an idealist, was cognizant of the fact that "the millenium had not yet arrived," and in the meantime the great powers would have to take whatever steps were necessary to maintain their vital securities.[44] It has generally been assumed that Stalin did not learn of Roosevelt's position on the Curzon Line until the Tehran Conference in December 1943. It would appear, however, that Davies provided Stalin with that information seven months earlier.

---

[41] *FRUS, 1943: The Conferences at Cairo and Tehran* (Washington, 1961), pp. 3–4; Davies, diary, 20 May 1943; Davies, "notes," June 1943.
[42] Davies, diary, 20 May 1943, 23 July, 29 November 1942.
[43] Ibid., 20 May 1943.
[44] Ibid.

A week later, Stalin presented Davies with a formal written reply to Roosevelt's invitation. The Soviet premier agreed that a conference was "necessary," and suggested they meet sometime "in July or August." He recommended Fairbanks, Alaska, as a site.[45] Having accomplished the primary goal of his mission, Davies left Moscow two days later. His plane had been spruced up for the journey home. Painted on the outside in large yellow letters in both English and Russian were the words: "Mission to Moscow."[46]

Arriving in Washington on 3 June, the former ambassador went directly to the White House to report to the president. Roosevelt read Stalin's written reply and questioned Davies in detail about the premier's oral response to the invitation. Davies explained the code that Stalin had suggested should be used for any further correspondence related to the Fairbanks meeting. Based on his discussions with Stalin and several other officials in Moscow, the presidential envoy then presented his own analysis of the state of Soviet opinion. Much of the report confirmed his earlier impressions of Soviet attitudes based on conversations before the mission with officials at the Soviet embassy in Washington.[47]

In an official written report for the president, Davies described the Soviet attitude toward Britain as "cordial and strong." He wrote that the Russians placed "great reliance upon the May 26, 1942 treaty with Great Britain." In his unofficial, oral report to the president, however, Davies described the Soviet attitude in less positive terms. Talks with Stalin, Molotov, and other Soviet officials had confirmed his earlier impression that the Russians did not trust Churchill. They feared that his first concern was to protect the British empire and to maintain control of the balance of power in Europe. They were suspicious of British attempts to build a federation out of eastern European countries that would serve in the future as a possible "cordon sanitaire" against the Soviet Union. A small group of Soviet "isolationists" feared that Britain planned to let the Soviet Union and Germany fight each other until both were exhausted, so that Britain could control the terms of peace.[48]

Davies had found the Soviets critical of American policy as well.

---

[45]*FRUS: Cairo and Tehran*, pp. 6–7.

[46]Standley and Ageton, *Admiral Ambassador*, p. 380.

[47]Davies, diary, 3 June 1943. Davies gave the president an oral report on 3 June and supplemented that with a written report dated 29 May. See *FRUS, 1943, 3: The British Commonwealth, Eastern Europe, The Far East* (Washington, 1963), pp. 657–60. Davies's specific account of his oral report to the president on Soviet attitudes is brief. In his diary for 3 June he wrote that he gave the president a "complete report on all the significant talks," and that his written "report and general memoranda were generally covered." Therefore, it is most likely that his conversation with the president was based partially on the official written report and partially on a series of notes and impressions that he recorded in his journal while he was still in Moscow, as well as on the journey back to Washington.

[48]*FRUS, 1943*, 3:660; Davies, diary, 3 June 1943; Davies, journal, 25, 26, 28 May, June 1943.

Stalin had stated emphatically that his claim to the territory in Poland east of the Curzon Line was not open to discussion; he "held that to be settled." The Soviets did not accept the Anglo-American campaign in Africa as a true second front. "They were suspicious," said Davies, "and stated flatly that commitments had been broken." Davies believed that his mission "had relieved [the] fear and suspicion somewhat as to the President himself." The Soviets, however, "were still convinced that if he [could] help it, Churchill [would] never consent to a Cross-Channel crossing." If the allies failed to establish a front in western Europe in the summer of 1943, Davies concluded, it would "have far reaching effects" on the Soviet attitude toward "the prosecution of this war and in their participation in the reconstruction of peace."[49]

The mission was finished. Davies had spent twenty-seven days traveling almost 26,000 miles at a cost of $25,000 from the president's emergency fund. Roosevelt complimented his friend on a job well done and told him to go home for a well-deserved rest.[50]

What had the mission accomplished? Davies's personal assessment was predictably positive. He concluded that the mission served as a "transitional period in Soviet-American relations. President Roosevelt had taken the initiative, and Marshall Stalin had responded. . . . Stalin had come out of his shell." Roosevelt had replaced Churchill as the friendly broker.[51] On the surface, Davies's conclusions may have been justified. Stalin had finally responded positively to Roosevelt's request for a meeting, and Soviet-American relations, threatened earlier by the Standley incident, appeared to be more cordial. Symbolic of that new atmosphere was the decision to abolish the Comintern and the manner in which the Soviets treated Davies during his mission. His reception "was the warmest given any visiting foreigner." *Pravda* allotted him "more prominence than even Winston Churchill received."[52]

In the long run, however, the mission may have had other more subtle effects on relations among the allies, particularly in regard to Stalin's approach to the United States. Since June 1941 the Red Army had been on the defensive, pleading for support from the West. Then in early 1943 the victory at Stalingrad had turned the tide. The Soviets were feeling "pretty cocky" after their victory, Hopkins later told Davies. They "don't need the West to beat Hitler, if they have to."[53] It was just at that time that the president sent his personal envoy halfway around the world to entreat the

---

[49]Davies, diary, 20 May, 3 June 1943; Davies, journal, 28 May 1943; *FRUS, 1943,* 3:658–59.

[50]Howland Shaw to Harold D. Smith, Bureau of the Budget, 3 May 1943, File No. 121.861/40A, Record Group 59, Department of State Records; "Second Mission to Moscow," *Life,* 4 October 1943, p. 87; Davies, diary, 3 June 1943.

[51]Davies, diary, 20 May 1943; Davies, journal, 9 December 1944.

[52]*Life,* 4 October 1943, p. 90.

[53]Davies, diary, 7 June 1943.

Soviet leader to join him in a private meeting, a meeting without Prime Minister Churchill. Stalin must have been impressed with his seemingly improved status vis-à-vis his two Western allies. Davies's assurances on the Curzon Line and the information he provided concerning Roosevelt's relationship with Churchill could have only reinforced that impression.

The mission also created tension in Anglo-American relations. Roosevelt did not inform Churchill of his purpose behind the mission until after Davies had returned from Moscow. The prime minister at first responded angrily to the news, although in the long run he grudgingly gave his assent to a Roosevelt-Stalin meeting. The president later denied that he had proposed the idea of a private meeting with the Soviet premier. He wrote Churchill that it was Stalin who had "assumed" that the meeting would not include the prime minister.[54] That the strain in Anglo-American relations was kept to a minimum was more to Churchill's credit than to that of Roosevelt.

The mission may have reinforced Roosevelt's confidence in the personal approach to Soviet-American relations. Events seemed to prove that Stalin could be reached through informal personal contacts. Hopkins's trip to Moscow in the summer of 1941 had clearly demonstrated the benefits of such an approach. Davies's mission in May 1943 seemed to confirm them; personal diplomacy had succeeded, after every other approach had failed, in convincing Stalin to meet with the president.

In the end, the mission did not succeed in its purpose; the meeting at Fairbanks never took place. While Davies was in Moscow, the British and American Joint Chiefs of Staff met in Washington and agreed to again delay the cross-channel invasion. Stalin reacted by withdrawing his ambassadors from London and Washington and by calling off the Fairbanks meeting. Roosevelt's carefully planned strategy had failed. The president could conclude, however, that it had not failed because of any fault in Davies's personal diplomacy, but because of a military decision entirely divorced from the activities of the former ambassador.

The mission to Moscow in 1943 was the high point of Davies's career as an unofficial intermediary between leaders of the Soviet Union and the United States. It was not the last time, however, that the administration relied on Davies's services. When the Fairbanks meeting was called off, Roosevelt again turned privately to the former ambassador for help in arranging a meeting with Stalin. After establishing his own personal relationship with the Soviet premier at the Tehran conference in December 1943, the president depended on Davies's services on fewer occasions. The former ambassador continued to function as a liaison but during the remainder of Roosevelt's administration, it was the State Department, rather than the president, that took advantage of Davies's connections with Soviet officials.[55]

---

[54]*FRUS: Cairo and Tehran*, pp. 10–12.

[55]Davies, diary, 27 September, 2, 5, 6 October 1943; *FRUS, 1944*, 4: *Europe* (Washington, 1966), pp. 1224, 1229–30, 1232–33, 1235–39.

In April 1945, when Harry S Truman became president, he turned for advice to Davies and Roosevelt's other old advisers. The new president also capitalized on Davies's position as an intermediary to the Soviets. Truman's decisions to send the former ambassador on a mission to London in May 1945 and to take him as an adviser to the Potsdam conference in July of the same year were largely based on the advantages stemming from Davies's personal connections with Soviet officials.[56] The rapid decline of Davies's influence in the administration after the Potsdam conference reflected the changes then taking place in Truman's approach to Soviet-American relations. Davies's position as an unofficial liaison had rested on two assumptions: the United States needed to have the confidence of the Soviets, and Stalin could be trusted. As the two former allies turned into adversaries, it became clear that the Truman administration no longer accepted those assumptions. In the atmosphere of the Cold War, there was no place for a Joseph E. Davies.

---

[56]Davies, journal, 30 April, 13, 21 May, 16 July 1945; Davies, diary, 21 May, 15, 16 July 1945; Davies, diary-journal, 15 July 1945.

Spheres of Influence in Soviet Wartime Diplomacy*

Albert Resis
Northern Illinois University

After three decades, a Europe partitioned into two opposing blocs has become a fact of international life, a division that the principal states have "normalized." Yet this east-west division of Europe, which solidified in the postwar period, was desired by neither the Soviet Union, nor Britain, nor by the United States. For, if the Big Three agreed on any postwar aim at all, it was—apart from the obvious desire to prevent a resurgence of an aggressive Germany—their aim to prevent the realignment of Europe into rival or hostile coalitions. Such a realignment, the Big Three leaders believed, would repeat the doleful history of pre-1914 Europe and make a third world war probable, perhaps inevitable.

Each member of the Big Three had, in addition, his own special reasons for opposing a postwar partition of Europe. Stalin feared the formation of a non-Soviet bloc in Europe, believing that such a bloc would spearhead a global, anti-Soviet, united front that would haunt the Kremlin even as the Allies waged war in close unity. Churchill feared a division of Europe that would leave Britain alone to face the USSR on the continent, or one that would grind Britain between the US and USSR and strip Britain of empire. Roosevelt feared that separate blocs would shatter the "One World," the global "Open Door" Washington believed essential for America's postwar prosperity. More immediately, he feared that US recognition or acquiescence in British recognition of the Soviet Union's frontiers of 1941 and other Soviet claims in eastern Europe would shatter America's unity-for-victory campaign and reinforce isolationist sentiments.

These concerns shaped the attitude of the U.S. government towards spheres-of-influence agreements.—What more certain way to split the world into hostile coalitions than divide Europe into separate spheres? Washington's opposition to such agreements respecting Europe stemmed largely from the assumption that spheres of influence were synonymous with hostile blocs. This assumption was

*This article is based on a paper delivered at the 1979 Meeting of the American Historical Association, 29 December 1979, in New York City. I would like to thank Robert C. Tucker and Vojtech Mastny for their helpful comments on the paper.

Journal of Modern History 53 (September 1981): 417–439]
© 1981 by the University of Chicago. 0022-2801/81/5303/003$01.00

not, however, shared by Stalin or Churchill. If the division of Europe into two antagonistic blocs had led to the Great War then in their view the failure to form an anti-German defense bloc in the 1930s caused the Second World War. And even Washington's abhorrence of such agreements did not prevent a neutral US from extending its hemispheric defense line almost into European waters, a sphere of interest euphemistically, but justifiably, called a "security zone" against Axis aggression. Despite the glaring disparity between US practice in the western hemisphere and US preachments to Britain against spheres in Europe, the vast extension of the US security zone between 1939 and 1941 was of course enthusiastically aided by Churchill. And by the spring of 1941, even Moscow halted its attacks on "Monroe Doctrine" imperialism and tacitly supported U.S. action.[1]

Still, the U.S. refused Britain and the USSR a similar free hand in their respective security zones. Consequently Churchill and Stalin, too, were forced to take equivocal positions regarding spheres of influence in their respective zones of security. To placate Washington, the British and Soviet governments disingenuously disclaimed any intention of concluding spheres-of-influence agreements even as they sought such agreements. Despite Moscow's insistence since 1940 that London recognize the Soviet Union's sphere in eastern Europe and London's conditional willingness to do so, USSR Commissar for Foreign Affairs Viacheslav Molotov and Foreign Secretary Anthony Eden denied at the Moscow Conference of Foreign Ministers in October, 1943, that their governments desired to establish special areas or zones of responsibility or influence.[2] In fact however each was still

---

[1]The US Ambassador in Moscow was impressed by the strong emphasis and the objective tone of Soviet press reports on the US defense program and aid to Britain. The Soviet press, he believed, had been instructed to refrain from publishing material critical of the US defense efforts. ("Steinhardt to Hull. Moscow, 7 May 1941." *Foreign Relations of the United States: Diplomatic Papers [FRUS]*, 1941, 1:614). In 1945 Soviet historians described President Roosevelt's policy of consolidating hemispheric defenses and extending them eastward as "perspicacious." (*Istoriia diplomatii*, ed. V.P. Potemkin [Moscow, 1941–45], 3:712.)

[2]*Foreign Relations of the United States [FRUS]*, 1943, 1:638–41. Also, the recently published Soviet record of the Moscow Conference of Foreign Ministers contains more detail on these points than the aforementioned American papers: *Moskovskaia Konferentsiia Ministrov Inostrannykh Del SSSR, SShA i Veliko-Britanii. 19–30 oktiabr' 1943 g. Sbornik dokumentov.* (Moscow, 1978), 192–4 and 261–2. This is volume one of six volumes projected in the series *Sovetskii Soiuz na mezhdunarodnykh konferentsiiakh perioda Velikoi otechestvennoi voiny 1941–1945 gg.*

True, USSR Ambassador Ivan Maisky told Eden in August 1943 that after the war the USSR and the Anglo-Americans each could have a sphere of influence in Europe, the Soviet Union in the east and Britain and America in the west. But the Soviet government preferred to regard Europe as one, each of the Big Three admitting each other's right to an interest in all parts of the continent. Eden said that, too, was

planning to do just that. The British plan had been unfolded by Churchill in Washington in May 1943, when he proposed that Europe, under a "Supreme World Council" consisting of the United States, Britain, the Soviet Union, and perhaps China, be reorganized into some twelve regional federations, confederations, and states, including a Danubian and a Balkan Federation. These would constitute a "Regional European Council" or "United States of Europe" to be policed mainly by Britain, seconded by the USA. As for Russia, Churchill merely stated that Poland and Czechoslovakia "should stand together in friendly relations with Russia." Because Churchill's project to foster regional federations in Europe lacked strong US support, Soviet opposition and the westward advance of the Red Army forced Churchill in October 1944 to change tack: Soviet expansion in Eastern Europe might also be curbed by a secret Anglo-Soviet agreement delimiting their respective spheres of influence in Eastern Europe.[3]

Britain's preference. (Anthony Eden. *The Reckoning* [Boston, 1965], pp. 469–70.) On the eve of the capitulation of Italy, while the Soviet army was still fighting to liberate Soviet territory, it is not surprising that the Soviet ambassador should assert a right to an interest in all parts of the continent. In any event, these professions can not be taken seriously, since at no time during the war did any of the three allies evince great willingness to admit the other partners' right to a substantial interest in his own zone of security.

On the problem of wartime spheres of influence, see Vojtech Mastny, *Russia's Road to the Cold War: Diplomacy, Warfare, and the Politics of Communism, 1941–1945.* (New York, 1979), pp. 97–110, 117–18, 207–11 and 214. Also see his "Spheres of Interest and Soviet War Aims in 1943," in *Eastern Europe in the 1970's* ed. S. Sinian, I. Deak, and P. C. Ludz (New York, 1972), pp. 87–107. Still outstanding is William Hardy McNeill's *America, Britain, and Russia: Their Cooperation and Conflict, 1941–1946.* (London, 1953; reprinted by Johnson Reprint Corporation, New York and London, 1970), pp. 309–10, 316–23, 332, 356–7, 405–11, 424–5, 462–4, 479–80, 493–7, and 723.
[3] Winston Churchill, *The Second World War,* vol. 4, *The Hinge of Fate* (New York, 1962), pp. 696–700. See also footnote 44, below. McNeill regarded Churchill's scheme as designed to form a European political unit that "could hold a balance between Russian and American power." But Churchill was forced by American opposition to abandon this approach. (McNeill, *America, Britain, and Russia,* pp. 322–3.) In fact, however, Churchill and the Foreign Office still persisted in the hope that various kinds of European regional or federal organization might come about. (Llewellyn Woodward, *British Foreign Policy in the Second World War* [London, 1976], 5:59, 90–1, 117–19, 122, and 124.) Moscow, without attacking Churchill directly, violently denounced his proposals on federations in eastern Europe as "anti-Soviet"; they negated the Anglo-Soviet Alliance and the necessity of friendship and cooperation between the USSR and its Allies in the postwar period. ("Chto skryvaetsia za proektom Vostochno evropeiskoi federatsii ili konfederatsii? Po stranitsam inostrannoi pechati." *Voina i rabochii klass.* No. 4, [July 15, 1943] p. 27.) This blast was followed up a few months later by "K voprosu o federatsiiakh 'malykh' gosudarstv v Evrope," *Izvestiia,* November 18, 1943. On the Anglo-Soviet spheres-of-influence secret agreement, see Albert Resis, "The Churchill-Stalin Secret 'Percentages' Agreement on the Balkans, Moscow, October, 1944," *American Historical Review,* (April, 1978), 83:368–87.

Stalin and Molotov, for their part, surmised as early as 1942 that they had found an ideal spheres-of-influence policy. It would, they hoped, prevent a revival of German military power and abort, not generate, a potential anti-Soviet bloc in Europe, thus maximizing Soviet security and Soviet political influence abroad. And, if British participation and American acquiescence in such arrangements were secured, the Grand Alliance could be continued indefinitely into the postwar era in the form of a Big Three global condominium.

In this article I propose to recount the development of this spheres-of-influence policy from inception in the German-Soviet Non-Aggression Treaty of August 23, 1939, to birth in the Anglo-Soviet Treaty of Alliance of 26 May 1942, and to adduce some of its immediate consequences, a study greatly facilitated by the release to the public of Britain's wartime diplomatic papers.[4]

We should note at the outset that Soviet spokesmen indignantly deny that Soviet diplomacy ever engaged in spheres-of-influence arrangements respecting Eastern Europe with the Germans, or the British, or any one else. In such matters Moscow is obliged to reckon with Lenin's axiom that any sphere-of-influence agreement under imperialism, however congenial the initial agreement, makes war inevitable.[5] Since 1939, however, Lenin's successors have been stuck with a fundamental contradiction between Leninist theory and Stalinist practice in Soviet diplomacy. Hence the angry refusal by Soviet spokesmen to acknowledge the elementary facts about Soviet policy towards Eastern Europe since that date.

The glaring disparity between Soviet claim and reality regarding spheres of influence in Europe was born in August 1939. Twice, on

---

[4] I have used for this article "British Foreign Office: Russia Correspondence, 1781–1945, Microfilmed for Scholarly Resources by the Public Record Office, London, England" (Wilmington, Delaware: Scholarly Resources, Inc., 1978), comprising "British Foreign Office, Collection 371, General Correspondence, Political" for each year. All documents deposited in the Public Record Office (PRO) which are used in this article are drawn from this collection unless otherwise stated. Crown copyright of these PRO documents is hereby acknowledged.

[5] V. I. Lenin, *Polnoe sobranie sochinenii* [*PSS*] (5th ed.; Moscow, 1960–1970), 27: 416–17. Lenin's doctrine of imperialism was embodied in the 1919 program of the Russian Communist Party (Kommunisticheskaia Partiia Sovetskogo Soiuza v rezoliutsiiakh i resheniiakh s'ezdov, konferentsii i plenumov TsK. [8th ed.; Moscow, 1970], 2, 39–40), which passage is based on Lenin's draft (*PSS*, 38, 106–07). Soviet scholarship defines "spheres of influence" as a form of colonial dependence embodied in a contractual agreement based on the mutual recognition of the primacy of the interests of the imperialist contracting parties in their respective territories. "Sphere of influence" is applied to political aims, "sphere of interest" to economic and commercial aims. (*Diplomaticheskii slovar*, ed. A. A. Gromyko et. al. [3rd ed.; Moscow, 1971–1973], pp. 3, 437). But Soviet diplomacy used both terms interchangeably.

August 3 and again on the 15th, the German government offered
Moscow an agreement that would delimit the interests of both powers
all along the line "from the Black to the Baltic Seas." Soviet historians claim that Moscow rejected these offers. Moscow then signed a
nonaggression treaty with Germany on 23 August 1939, only after all
hope for an escape-proof, mutual-defense alliance and military convention with Britain and France was lost. The treaty, which was
published, said nothing about agreement on territorial changes. But
the "Secret Additional Protocol" attached to the treaty called things
by their right name, stating that the northern border of Lithuania
constituted the frontier of the German-Soviet "spheres of interest" in
the Baltic area. In Poland the frontier would follow the line of the
Narew, Vistula, and San Rivers. Concerning southeastern Europe,
the USSR expressed its interest in Bessarabia, Germany its disin-
terest.[6]

On September 15, two weeks after the Germans invaded Poland,
Foreign Minister von Ribbentrop prodded the USSR to occupy the
sphere allotted it in Eastern Poland. Unless the Red Army moved up
to the agreed line in Poland, he warned, German troops might have to
pursue the retreating Poles to the existing Soviet frontier. Molotov
replied that the Red Army would move westward "perhaps tomorrow
or the day after."[7] In fact Moscow had delayed, because the Red
Army was already engaged in an undeclared war to repel the
Japanese-Manchukuon invasion of the Mongolian People's Republic.
The Japanese, still reeling under the shock of Berlin's signing the
nonagression treaty with Moscow, themselves signed a cease-fire
agreement with Moscow, to take effect September 16.[8] On the next
day, the Red Army entered Poland.

Devising a political cover for this invasion, Molotov notified Ribbentrop that Moscow would inform the Poles that the Red Army had
entered Polish territory in order to protect Ukrainian and Belorussian brethren in a Poland that had "disintegrated." True, this explanation might jar German sensibilities, Molotov admitted, but Moscow
saw no other plausible justification. The Soviet note bearing this
message to Poland was drafted by Stalin, who also drafted a joint

---

[6] *Documents on German Foreign Policy 1918–1945* [*DGFP*], Series D (Washington,
1949–1964), 6:1049–1050, 1059–62, and 7:63, 76–7, 88–90, 115–16, and 245–7. For the
Soviet claim that Moscow rejected the German offers see *Istoriia Velikoi Otechestvennoi Voiny Sovetskogo Soiuza 1941–1945*. [*IVOVSS*], ed. P. Pospelev (Moscow, 1960–
65), 1:174–5. This claim is not confirmed in the German documents.
[7] *DGFP*, 8:69, 76–7.
[8] *Soviet Documents on Foreign Policy*, ed. Jane Degras (London, 1951–1953) 3:373–
74.

German-Soviet communique, which the Germans accepted in place of Ribbentrop's draft. Molotov had rejected that draft because it presented the facts "too frankly." The Stalin draft substituted the phrase, "the interests of Germany and of the Soviet Union," for Ribbentrop's reference to "German-Soviet natural spheres of interest." The phrase "respective national interests" was employed in the German-Soviet Boundary and Friendship Treaty signed September 28. The secret protocols, however, referred to "spheres of influence."[9]

In short, Moscow's eagerness to conceal the German-Soviet spheres-of-interest agreements matched Berlin's eagerness to proclaim them. To this day, the Soviet government has not acknowledged the authenticity of the secret protocols attached to the treaties of August-September 1939.[10]

The shock, bewilderment, and rage the German-Soviet treaties aroused in the antifascist public need no description here. Many observers in the West regarded the treaties as an alliance. More seasoned observers, however, saw in them quite the opposite. On 1 October 1939 Winston Churchill, First Lord of the Admiralty in the Chamberlain government, said in a radio report on the war that he could not forecast the action of Russia, since "it is a riddle wrapped in a mystery inside an enigma." But we should note that Churchill went on to say, "perhaps there is a key. That key is Russian national interest." He wished only that Russia stood on its present line as allies of Poland instead of as invaders. In any event this line was "clearly necessary for the safety of Russia against the Nazi menace." Churchill not only expressed his understanding and approval of Soviet action in Poland; he also surmised that Ribbentrop had just been summoned to Moscow to learn that "Nazi designs upon the Baltic States and the Ukraine must come to a dead stop." Russia had also drawn a line in southeastern Europe against Germany, for it could not "be in accordance with the interest or safety of Russia that Germany should plant itself upon the shores of the Black Sea, or that it should

---

[9] *DGFP*, 8:79-80, 95-7, 105, 113-14, and 164-67. Soviet historians assail Molotov's contemptuous dismissal of the Polish Republic as "the misshapen offspring of the Versailles Treaty." Molotov's language is, apparently, the only aspect of Soviet conduct toward Germany in 1939-1940 that Soviet authorities find discreditable or mistaken. (*IVOVSS*, 1:249.)

[10] The existence of the secret protocol of August 23, which was found in the archives of the German Foreign Ministry captured by American and British armies, became public knowledge at the Nuremburg Trial of War Criminals in 1946. The protocol was denounced as a forgery by the Soviet Prosecutor at the main trial. (Gerhard Weinberg, *Germany and the Soviet Union, 1939-1941* [Leiden, 1954], p. 47.)

overrun the Balkan States and subjugate the Slavonic peoples of southeastern Europe. That would be contrary to the historic life interests of Russia." Thus, Churchill concluded, Russia's vital interests made her a natural ally of Britain and France whose interest coincided with Russia's in preventing Germany from carrying the war into the Balkans and Turkey.[11]

Nor was Churchill's qualified endorsement of Soviet action mere idiosyncrasy. Prime Minister Chamberlain declared on October 26 in the House of Commons that there was nothing in Mr. Churchill's "personal interpretation" of events that was at variance with the view of the government.[12] The Churchill-Chamberlain statements of October were tantamount to an official but gratuitous invitation for Moscow to extend a Soviet protectorate over the Baltic states, precisely what Moscow was setting up at the moment and would presently attempt to set up in the Balkans.

Stalin breathed not a word in public of his spheres-of-influence agreement with Hitler. Meanwhile, each dictator used the secret agreements to his best advantage in dealing with other states. Stalin, for example, on October 3 told the Latvian foreign minister in Moscow that Latvia had best permit the USSR to build military and naval bases in Latvia, because Latvian resistance would find no support from Germany. Germany had signed a spheres-of-interest agreement with the Soviet Union and as far as Germany was concerned, "we could occupy you."[13]

Hitler had no ideological qualms about such agreements. Countering Churchill's contention that the USSR had closed Germany's path to the east, Hitler claimed a German-Soviet community of interests in

---

[11] Winston Churchill, "The First Month of the War," in *Winston Spencer Churchill, His Complete Speeches*, ed. Robert Rhodes James (New York, 1974) 6:6161, and Churchill, *The Gathering Storm* (New York, 1961), p. 399. The abridged text in the latter omits reference to the Baltic States and to the community of Allied and Soviet interests in the Balkans.

[12] House of Commons, *Parliamentary Debates, Commons*, Fifth Series, 1938–1939, 352, cols. 1570–71. The Roosevelt administration, too, interpreted Soviet action in September and October as directed against Berlin. (Robert Dallek, *Franklin D. Roosevelt and American Foreign Policy, 1932–1945* [New York, 1979], p. 208.)

[13] Boris Meissner, *Die Sowjetunion, die Baltischen Staaten und das Völkerrecht* (Cologne, 1956), p. 62; quoted by Edgar Thomson, "The Annexation of the Baltic States," in *The Anatomy of Communist Takeovers*, ed. Thomas T. Hammond (New Haven, 1975), p. 219. But, according to Soviet sources, Stalin also told the Latvian Minister of Foreign Affairs that the possibility of a German attack on the USSR could not be ruled out. The sudden shift in German policy favorable to the USSR could not be relied upon; therefore timely preparations for another shift would have to be made. (Soviet Archives of Diplomatic History quoted in V. Ia. Sipols, *Sovetskii soiuz v bor'be za mir i bezopasnost'* 1933–1939 [Moscow, 1974], page 404, n. 289.)

eastern Europe. In his Reichstag speech of 6 October 1939 Hitler boasted that Germany and the USSR had agreed on a clearly marked boundary between "their two spheres of interest." Since the two great powers had agreed that Poland would never rise again, continuation of the war by Britain and France for the restoration of Poland made no sense.[14]

By June 1940 the USSR had extended its rule over the territories specifically allotted it under the secret protocols of August-September 1939. Five new Soviet Socialist Republics entered the USSR: the Karelian, Estonian, Latvian, Lithuanian, and Moldavian Republics. Northern Bukovina and eastern Poland were absorbed in the Ukrainian and Belorussian Republics. Soviet diplomacy then aimed to win London's *de jure* recognition of these gains, the Baltic States in particular, and Berlin's nonencroachment on the Soviet sphere. The USSR, treated more or less as an international pariah in the old collective security days, now found itself a much-aggrandized neutral, ardently wooed (at least briefly) by the principal belligerents. Moscow's aversion for spheres-of-influence agreements had no doubt abated greatly; they could be used to divide the imperialist world against itself and enable the USSR to emerge from the war as the *tertius gaudens*.

The British, fighting on alone since the fall of France, sought through Ambassador Cripps in Moscow a Soviet neutrality toward Britain as benevolent as that toward Germany, one which would culminate in an Anglo-Soviet nonaggression treaty. In exchange, Britain offered *de facto* recognition of the USSR's territorial gains. *De jure* recognition would be given sympathetic consideration by Britain in consultations regarding a postwar settlement. After the war Britain would pledge not to enter into any anti-Soviet agreement if the USSR abstained from anti-British action. Ambassador Cripps' negotiations with Moscow broke down, however, because the USSR made *de jure* recognition of Soviet sovereignty over the Baltic States the precondition for any further agreements.[15]

Thus, the British government offered British recognition of Soviet gains in eastern Europe—but at a price. That price was too high for

---

[14] The Times (London), October 7, 1939.
[15] Llewellyn Woodward, *British Foreign Policy in the Second World War* (London, 1970–1976), 1:492–96; I. M. Maisky, *Vospominaniia sovetskogo posla. Voina 1939–1943* (Moscow, 1965), pp. 130–132. Cripps asked Deputy Commissar for Foreign Affairs Andrei Vyshinsky whether the USSR intended to allow a German hegemony in the Balkans. Vyshinsky replied that it was not the habit of the Soviet government to give away anything, especially if such action were in conflict with their interests. (Woodward, 1:496.)

Moscow. The British offer, if accepted, would have entailed worsening of German-Soviet relations and the likelihood of war with Germany. In any case the immediate threat to the Soviet position in eastern Europe came from the Wehrmacht, not from British diplomacy.

By spring 1940, the Germans were rapidly encroaching on the ill-defined Soviet sphere in the Balkans. To strengthen the Soviet bargaining hand against this action, Molotov informed Berlin on 13 July 1940 that Ambassador Cripps had on July 1 suggested to Stalin that the USSR provide the leadership required to block the German advance into the Balkans. Stalin told Cripps that he did not think that the Germans sought control of the area. Moreover, "no power had the right to an exclusive role in the consolidation and leadership of the Balkan countries. The Soviet Union did not claim such a role either . . ." although she was "interested" in Balkan affairs.[16] Moscow thus hoped that Stalin's disclaimer of any intention to secure control over the Balkans might persuade the Germans to stay out of the area. Alternatively, Cripps' suggestion might serve to warn Hitler that continued German encroachments on the Balkans could provoke the USSR into entering the area with British backing. Both ploys failed.

Shortly after the signing of the Tripartite Pact on 27 September 1940, Ribbentrop invited Molotov to Berlin in order to share with Germany, Italy, and Japan the historical mission of "delimiting their interests on a world scale." Moscow accepted the invitation. In Berlin, Molotov was informed on November 12 by Hitler and Ribbentrop that the time had come to parcel out the "bankrupt estate" of a defeated Britain and for the Soviet Union to sign a four-power pact with Germany and its two major partners. The Germans invited the Soviet Union to move southward in the direction of the Indian Ocean, which would constitute the Soviet sphere. They also offered to seek replacement of the Montreux Convention by an agreement giving unrestricted right of passage through the Turkish Straits to the warships of the Soviet Union and other Black Sea powers exclusively. Germany would claim central Africa, Italy northern and northcentral Africa, and Japan east Asia as their respective spheres. But Molotov pressed Hitler and Ribbentrop to explain German troop movements in Finland and Rumania. The next day Ribbentrop offered Molotov an added inducement to sign the draft four-power pact: Germany might prevail upon Japan to recognize Outer Mongolia and Sinkiang as a Soviet sphere, if the Soviet Union would sign a nonaggression pact

---

[16] *DGFP*. 10:207–08. Cripps' letter to Collier, Moscow, July 16, 1940. N 6526/30/38. FO 371/24845. PRO.

with Japan and reduce its military aid to China. Spurning these blandishments, Molotov doggedly pursued the question of German action in Finland and the Balkan states. Existing agreements, he insisted, must be fulfilled before taking up proposals for new spheres of influence. No definite reply to the German offer could be given until the matter was discussed by the Kremlin.[17]

On 25 November 1940, Molotov gave his government's reply. The USSR would sign the German draft four-power pact of November 13 if Germany acceded to the following conditions: One, Germany must immediately withdraw its troops from Finland. Two, the USSR must acquire military and naval bases within range of the Turkish Straits and conclude a mutual assistance treaty with Bulgaria, "which geographically is situated inside the security zone of the Black Sea boundaries of the Soviet Union." Three, "the area south of Batum and Baku in the general direction of the Persian Gulf" shall be recognized as the center of Soviet aspirations. Four, Japan shall renounce her coal and oil concessions in northern Sakhalin.[18]

The Soviet counteroffer to the Germans clearly reflected Stalin's main security concerns: First, German military penetration of Finland and southeastern Europe constituted the most immediate threat to Soviet security interests. Second, the Soviet Union preferred the establishment of Soviet bases at the Straits to Axis guarantees as the means of ensuring free passage of the Straits for warships of the Black Sea powers exclusively. Third, Moscow ignored Berlin's invitation to move against India, because such a move would risk provoking war with Britain over an area still marginal to Soviet security interests. Moscow preferred instead the risk of expanding in a primary security zone, in the direction of eastern Turkey, the Levant, the Arabian Peninsula, and western Iran. (It will be recalled that Britain and France had planned during the Soviet-Finnish War in 1939–40 to bomb the Soviet Union's Baku oil fields from Allied air bases in the Middle East.) Finally, Moscow appeared to be confident after the defeats it inflicted on Japan in the undeclared wars of summer 1938 and 1939 that Japan no longer posed an immediate threat to the Soviet far east.

Three weeks after Molotov transmitted the Soviet counteroffer to Germany, Hitler signed "Operation Barbarossa," his directive for the German invasion of the USSR scheduled for 15 May 1941. But Bar-

---

[17] *Nazi-Soviet Relations, 1939–1941*, ed. R. J. Sontag and J. S. Beddie (Washington, 1948), p. 213. A slightly different translation from the German, "delimitation of their interests for the ages," is in *DGFP*, 11:296–97. Ibid., 542–45, 551–56, 558–61, 565–570.
[18] *DGFP*, 11:714–15.

barossa was not inspired by Moscow's insolent counteroffer—it represented the culmination, not the starting point, of German planning for war on Russia. Indeed, Hitler had used the Berlin talks with Molotov to divert Soviet attention to Asia and away from the Balkan and Finnish spheres claimed by the USSR. Stalin clearly underestimated the danger Germany posed to Soviet security in these spheres because he refused to recognize Germany's moves there for what they were: preparations for invasion of the Soviet Union. For Stalin was blinded by the suspicion that the British might already be collaborating with Germany in a deal at Soviet expense,[19] or the fear that they might push the Russians into a needless war with Germany even as he resisted German efforts to embroil the USSR in a needless war with Britain over India.

Early in 1941 the Soviet government mixed cajolery with vociferous protests to curb German encroachments in the Soviet Union's Balkan sphere. On 17 January 1941 Molotov asked Ambassador Schulenburg why Berlin had not responded to the Soviet note on Soviet terms for adhering to the draft four-power pact. Molotov then said that if German troops concentrating in Rumania should enter Bulgaria, Greece, and the Straits area, the British would surely attempt to forestall them, thus turning the Balkans into a theater of war. The Soviet government had stated repeatedly to the German government that Moscow considered the territory of Bulgaria and of the Straits as ''a security zone'' of the USSR. It was therefore the duty of the Soviet Government to give warning that it would ''consider the appearance of any armed forces on the territory of Bulgaria and of the Straits as violation of the security interests of the USSR.''[20]

Meanwhile, the British were trying to swing the USSR away from Germany. Churchill hoped that the USSR would (with active British aid) combine with Turkey, Rumania, Bulgaria, and Yugoslavia in January 1941 to form a Balkan front to stop Hitler. But, Churchill wrote, Moscow lost this golden opportunity to enter the war with a second front already in existence. Thus, Stalin and his commissars showed themselves at this moment ''the most completely outwitted bunglers of the Second World War.''[21]

Nevertheless, the British, in order to secure closer military ties

---

[19] *Istoriia diplomatii,* ed. A. A. Gromyko et al. (Moscow, 1959-), 4:150–51.

[20] *DGFP,* 11:1122–23 and 1124–25. Also *Istoriia diplomatii,* 4:154–55, which does not allude to Molotov's query.

[21] Churchill, *The Grand Alliance* (New York, 1962), pp. 298–99. But Churchill also speculated that a British-sponsored united front in the Balkans might prompt Hitler ''to take it out of Russia.'' (Ibid., pp. 142–3.)

with the USSR, were almost prepared on the eve of the Nazi invasion of the USSR to recognize Soviet sovereignty over the Baltic states.[22] The German invasion on 22 June 1941 temporarily ended such Anglo-Soviet bargaining. On that evening Prime Minister Churchill announced on the BBC Britain's unstinting support for her new ally despite all ideological differences.

But Churchill received no direct acknowledgment from Stalin until Stalin's broadcast of July 3. Then, to break the ice, Churchill sent Stalin two personal messages on July 7 and 10 but again received no direct reply.[23] Stalin in the meantime, however, proposed to Ambassador Cripps an Anglo-Soviet alliance, which they signed on July 12. The Anglo-Soviet Agreement on joint action against Germany provided that the two governments mutually undertake to render each other all kinds of assistance and support during the war against Hitlerite Germany. Neither ally would negotiate or conclude a separate armistice or peace treaty except by mutual consent. The agreement said nothing, however, about Soviet frontiers.[24]

Now having an alliance with Britain, Stalin on July 18 replied to Churchill's personal messages of support and encouragement. Stalin turned directly to a defense of his non-aggression treaty with Germany. Hinting at the secret protocol on spheres of interest, he argued that the USSR's desperate military situation would have been immeasurably worse if the invaders had jumped off at the Soviet border of 1 September 1939, instead of the border of 22 June 1941. Implying that this border was now Britain's, too, he implored Churchill to open a second front in Northern France and in Norway.[25]

But Stalin attempted more than exculpation of his dealings with Hitler: he was also setting the stage for negotiations with Britain concerning Soviet frontiers. His first step, however, was to obtain fighting alliances with the other victims of Nazi aggression. Talk of frontiers could come later. On July 3, the day Stalin had emerged from his self-imposed seclusion, Moscow instructed Ambassador

---

[22] "Welles Conversation with Halifax, June 15, 1941," *Foreign Relations of the United States,* 1941, 1:760–61.

[23] Woodward, 2:10–13. Churchill, *Grand Alliance,* pp. 322–25. *Correspondence Between the Chairman of the Council of Ministers of the USSR and the Presidents of the USA and the Prime Ministers of Great Britain During the Great Patriotic War of 1941–1945* (Moscow, 1957), 1:11–12.

[24] Woodward, 2:14. At the July 10 meeting of Cripps with Stalin to negotiate the alliance, Molotov had attempted to interject questions affecting third countries, but Stalin summarily silenced him. ("Steinhardt to Hull, Moscow, 11 July 1941," *FRUS,* 1941, 1:183.)

[25] *Correspondence,* 1:12–13.

Maisky to begin negotiations for alliances with the émigré Polish, Czechoslovak, and Yugoslav governments. According to those instructions, the USSR favored the restoration of the independence of these countries and regarded their political regimes as a purely internal matter. In mid-July Maisky was instructed to conclude with Poland and Czechoslovakia an alliance modeled on the one just signed with Britain.[26]

A mutual assistance agreement with Czechoslovakia was quickly concluded on July 18. Poland, however, was another matter. The Poles insisted on the restoration of their prewar eastern frontiers, the Soviets on their western frontiers of June 1941, modified for "a national Poland, including cities and regions that had recently passed to the USSR." In order to get a mutual assistance agreement signed, Maisky and Premier Sikorski of Poland were constrained to defer the frontier problem. In the agreement they concluded on July 30, the USSR recognized as nugatory the German-Soviet treaties of 1939 respecting territorial changes in Poland. The Polish government declared that it was not bound by any anti-Soviet agreement with a third power.[27]

But the question of future frontiers, peace, and security could not be deferred for long. Soviet insistence on its 1941 frontiers in negotiations with Poland raised for President Roosevelt the specter of the secret treaties of the Great War, as did the Anglo-Soviet agreement. Hence the proclamation of the Atlantic Charter by Roosevelt and Churchill on August 15, 1941[28] on the heels of the Soviet-Polish agreement. The Charter might well be cited to bar the restoration of the 1941 boundaries of the USSR. For it opposed territorial aggrandizement and territorial changes effected without consent of the peoples concerned and favored the restoration of sovereignty and self-government to those peoples forcibly deprived of them. Moreover, the Charter seemed to aim at disarmament of all nations except the US who would join Britain in policing the postwar world. Or, so Churchill interpreted the final point.[29]

As German armies pressed toward Moscow for the kill, Stalin was hardly in a position to challenge parts of the Charter he might deem "anti-Soviet." Ambassador Maisky, in the name of the Soviet gov-

[26] *Dokumenty i materialy po istorii Sovetsko-Pol'skikh otnoshenii* (Moscow, 1963-), 7:1939–1943 gg., 7:198. Maisky, *Vospominaniia*, p. 152.
[27] Maisky, *Vospominaniia*, pp. 153–7. Edward Rozek, *Allied Wartime Diplomacy: A Pattern in Poland* (New York, 1958), pp. 50–65.
[28] William L. Langer and S. Everett Gleason, *The Undeclared War 1940–1941* (New York, 1953), p. 679.
[29] Churchill, *Grand Alliance*, p. 375.

ernment, enthusiastically praised the principles of the Charter, then attached an "interpretation" that enabled the USSR to construe the Charter any way Moscow wished:

Considering that the practical application of these principles will necessarily adapt itself to circumstances, needs, and historical peculiarities of particular countries, the Soviet government can state that a consistent application of these principles will secure the energetic support of the . . . Soviet Union.

Lest his point be missed, Maisky stressed that the principle of respect for the sovereign rights of peoples had always marked Soviet domestic and foreign policy.[30] In short, the Soviet government endorsed the Charter only insofar as the terms were compatible with the Soviet frontiers of 1941.

By September, the USSR had signed mutual assistance military agreements with Britain, Czechoslovakia, and Poland and had established close ties with DeGaulle. But these agreements covered only the war period and provided no guarantees of the Soviet frontiers of 1941. All appeals to Britain to open a second front proved unsuccessful, and Allied military cooperation remained uncoordinated. Anglo-Soviet relations were still crippled by mutual suspicion, Stalin contended, because the USSR and Britain had no understanding on war aims, or plans for the postwar organization of the peace, or treaty of mutual military assistance against Hitler.[31] While the German army hammered at the gates of Moscow, Stalin sought a treaty of alliance with Britain that would strengthen their military cooperation, provide guarantees against a resurgent warlike Germany in the postwar era, and recognize the Soviet frontiers of 1941, all to be embodied in an Anglo-Soviet spheres-of-influence agreement.

Stalin, therefore, accepted Churchill's proposal that Stalin receive Foreign Secretary Eden in Moscow. Eden undertook the visit to allay Stalin's suspicions that Britain and the US intended to exclude the Soviet Union from the postwar peace settlement and that they planned to treat a defeated Germany leniently. Eden hoped to strengthen Anglo-Soviet ties of alliance without Britain's entering into commitments, secret or open, respecting frontiers, and he sought to secure Stalin's approval of Britain's war aims in Europe: one, the disarmament of Germany; two, the reorganization of Europe in conformity with the Atlantic Charter ("no aggrandizement, territorial or

---

[30] "Declaration by the Government of the USSR at the Inter-allied Conference at London," in *Soviet Foreign Policy During the Great Patriotic War, Documents and Materials,* ed. and trans. Andrew Rothstein (London, 1944–45), 1:96–98.

[31] "Stalin to Churchill, November 8, 1941," *Correspondence,* 1:33.

other'') and with Stalin's speech of 6 November 1941 (''no intervention whatever in the internal affairs of other peoples''); and three, ''the encouragement of confederations of the weaker European states.''[32]

In their first conversation, held 16 December 1941, Stalin offered Eden two draft treaties, one on wartime military cooperation and the other on cooperation in the postwar peace settlement. Since both drafts were for publication and contained nothing specific on frontier questions, they were quite acceptable to Eden; but he was not empowered to sign an agreement in the form of a treaty, which Stalin insisted upon.[33] Then Stalin without warning pulled out of his pocket a draft protocol that laid out a grand plan for the postwar arrangement of all Europe, including details on frontier changes. On the following evening. Stalin said that what really interested him most was British recognition of the USSR's frontiers of 1941.[34]

Stalin's aims and the terms he set for the postwar territorial settlement and for continental security were:[35]

One, Stalin told Eden that he regarded the question of the USSR's western frontiers as ''the main question for us in the war''; Eden inferred that Stalin regarded British recognition of the Soviet frontiers of 1941 as the ''acid test'' of the sincerity of his British ally. The USSR must, Stalin said, have the three Baltic states and the Finnish border of March 1940 with Petsamo returned to the USSR: Bessarabia and northern Bukovina; and the territory to the east of the Curzon Line with slight variations. He proved willing, however, to put the question of the Soviet-Polish frontier in abeyance.

Two. in order to prevent the postwar revival of a German military threat and to punish Axis aggression, the allies should dismember

---

[32] Anthony Eden, *The Reckoning* (Boston, 1965), 328–9. ''Winant to Hull. London, 21 December 1941,'' *FRUS*, 1941, 1:201–203 and *FRUS*, 1941, 4:759–60. ''Winant to Hull, London, December 4, 1941,'' *FRUS*, 1:192–4. Secretary of State Hull had informed Eden that while discussions of postwar settlement might proceed between Eden and Stalin in Moscow, no specific commitments should be entered into respecting individual countries. ''Above all there must be no secret accords.'' (''Hull to Winant, Washington, 5 December 1941,'' Ibid., 194–95.)

[33] Woodward, *British Foreign Policy*, 2:221–25. Eden, *The Reckoning*, pp. 344–36.

[34] ''Memorandum by Secretary of State [Eden] on Conversations with M. Stalin, December 16–20, 1941,'' Moscow, 25 December 1941. N 1880/5/38. FO 371/ 32879. PRO. Maisky, *Vospominaniia*, p. 208.

[35] ''Record of Interview between Foreign Secretary and M. Stalin, 16 December 1941, at 7 p.m.,'' W. P. (42) 8. 5 January 1942. CAB 66/20 PRO. ''Record of a Meeting between the Foreign Secretary and Stalin, on the night of December 17, 1941,'' Ibid. The microfilmed ''Correspondence'' states that these records were ''missing.'' In fact, however, they are available in the Cabinet papers just cited and are microfilmed by the PRO.

Germany and require her to pay reparations in kind, and they should reduce her allies territorially in favor of the victims of aggression. Accordingly, he said, transfer east Prussia to Poland and extend Poland's western frontiers to the Oder.[36] Add Tilsit and Germany north of the Niemen River to the Lithuanian SSR. Detach the Rhineland from Prussia, perhaps accord Bavaria independence, and restore Austrian independence. Return the Sudetenland to Czechoslovakia. Transfer territories from Hungary to Czechoslovakia and to Rumania, who would cede Bessarabia and Northern Bukovina to the USSR. Add the Italian Islands and certain coastal towns of the Adriatic to a restored Yugoslavia.

Three. Stalin proposed that the USSR and Britain should each set up its own sphere of influence in Europe, although he did not use that term, and the British did not yet have plans to establish military bases on the continent. To secure the western approaches to the USSR, Stalin desired alliances with Finland and Rumania, who would allow Soviet naval military and naval bases on their territory. Stalin would have no objections to Britain's taking similar measures. "If France is not restored or revived as a great power in the near future," Stalin said, "it would be in [Great Britain's] interest to have on the French Coast some military and naval bases, such as Boulogne and Dunkirk." To guarantee the independence of Holland and Belgium, Britain should be in open alliance with them, Britain having the right to maintain naval and military bases, and, if necessary, troops in those countries. Nor would the Soviet government object to Britain's acquiring naval bases in Norway or Denmark, but the USSR would like an international guarantee regarding the entrances to the Baltic Sea.

Four. Stalin also implied that the Soviet and British spheres of influence should be separated by a large buffer zone. This would consist of a dismembered Germany and the smaller states who would recover their national independence. Czechoslovakia should be restored with her pre-Munich frontiers slightly enlarged at Hungarian expense. An independent Yugoslavia should be restored and somewhat enlarged at Italian expense. Albanian independence should be revived. Turkey should receive the Dodecanese Islands and extend its European frontier at Bulgarian expense. Greece should receive additional islands in the Aegean and should be reestablished as an independent state, as should all other occupied countries, within prewar frontiers.

---

[36] The Oder is not mentioned, however, in Foreign Office papers I have seen, e.g., minutes on the meeting with Sir Orme Sargent on April 21, 1942, to examine Stalin's ideas on the future map of Europe. N 2182/G FO 371/32880. PRO.

Five, there remained the matter of the peace and security of post-war Europe against a revived, expansionist Germany. Eden proposed to Stalin at their first meeting that they ought to encourage the federation and confederation of the weaker states. Stalin replied that if certain countries of Europe wished to federate, then the Soviet Union would have no objection. But he also suggested that postwar peace and security be preserved by a military alliance of the "democratic countries," who would form an international peace-keeping military force. Thus two projects for multilateral security organization, which would soon come into conflict, were proposed: the British scheme for political federations of weak states, opposed by the Soviet proposal for military alliance of democratic countries headed by the USSR and Britain.

In sum, Stalin, as these conversations reveal, came forward as a conservative nationalist prepared to make frontiers in Europe coterminous with ethnographic boundaries, except where the punishment of Germany and her associates and where the security of Britain and the USSR were concerned. Perhaps he already discerned the possibility of the USSR's emerging from the war as the preponderant power in all Europe. Mastny has suggested that as early as July 1941 Stalin's desire for land was limitless, because "his craving for security was limitless." In fact, however, Stalin came forward as a Soviet "isolationist" advancing (at least for the present) relatively modest territorial claims. Eden, on his return to London, assessed Stalin's demand that Britain recognize the Soviet Union's frontiers of 1941 as "very reasonable" when one recalls how much Stalin might have demanded: for example "control of the Dardanelles; spheres of influence in the Balkans; a one-sided imposition on Poland of the Russo-Polish frontier; access to the Persian Gulf; access to the Atlantic involving cession of Norwegian and Finnish territory." President Roosevelt for his part did not find Soviet demands unreasonable although he did stigmatize the Eden-Stalin conversations as "provincial."[37] We might add that Stalin did not yet suggest that the "World Police" force Roosevelt and Churchill envisaged as an Anglo-American body needed a third "policeman," the USSR. Moreover Stalin had, in deference to his Anglo-American partners, abandoned

---

[37] Mastny, *Russia's Road*, p. 41. Memorandum by the Secretary of State for Foreign Affairs [Eden], "Policy Towards Russia." W.P. (42) 48. 28 January 1942. FO 371/32875. Roosevelt granted that the USSR was entitled to obtain "full and legitimate security," but that question could not be settled until after the war. Meanwhile he would take up the matter directly with Stalin. "Memorandum of Conversation, by the Under-Secretary of State [Welles]," 20 February 1942. *FRUS*, 1942, 3:521.

for the duration of the war at least Moscow's stock antiimperialist rhetoric. He asserted no Soviet interest in the western hemisphere or in the British Empire. He would leave western Europe in the custody of his partners and acknowledge central Europe, rendered harmless by the dismemberment of Germany, as a buffer zone—or field of east-west contention, depending on circumstances. He even carefully recognized Britain's special interest in Greece, Turkey, and Yugoslavia[38] by proposing that they be aggrandized territorially, while he made no claims on them. Thus Rumania's southern frontier would constitute the line setting off the Soviet and the British spheres of influence in Southeastern Europe. He was even willing to shelve for the present the question of the Polish-Soviet frontier. All that Stalin asked in exchange was that his partners concede him the free hand in the USSR's eastern European sphere that he was willing to concede them in their western European, Mediterranean, and north Atlantic spheres. In short, as early as 1941–42, Stalin assumed that the future peace and security of Europe and the postwar fate of the Grand Alliance hinged on each ally's recognizing and honoring his partner's core security zones, while the Anglo-Soviet allies, assisted by their smaller allies, policed the continent.

An Anglo-Soviet treaty of alliance was not concluded in Moscow. Without consulting London, the Dominions, and Washington, Eden could not sign Stalin's secret protocol endorsing the Soviet frontiers of 1941 let alone the secret protocol encompassing Stalin's grand plan. Stalin, for his part, made recognition of the 1941 frontiers, except for Poland, the precondition for an alliance. The result was a deadlock.

Six months of assiduous but fruitless efforts to reach agreement ensued, in the course of which Moscow raised its demands. Moscow reverted to the requirement that London accept Stalin's proposals for Anglo-Soviet spheres of influence as well as recognize the 1941 frontiers of the USSR, except for Poland.[39] And now Moscow would not accept London's minimum condition, the provision that the allies agree to encourage the formation of federations and confederations in

---

[38] Elisabeth Barker, *British Policy in South-East Europe in the Second World War* (London, 1976), p. 129.

[39] "Eden to Kerr, London, 1 May 1942," N 2336/86/G FO 371/32880. PRO. When Eden again replied that he could not sign the secret protocol, Maisky exclaimed "let it be public!" ("Eden to Kerr, London 5 May 1942," N 2385/86/G FO 371/32880. PRO.) London vainly did its best to persuade Washington to acquiesce in a British alliance with the USSR that would recognize the Soviet frontiers of June 1941, except for the Soviet Polish boundary the question of which would be left in abeyance. Churchill, *The Hinge of Fate* (New York, 1962), pp. 284–92. Maisky, *Vospominaniia*, pp. 238–44, 246–48.

Europe. Stalin and his lieutenants had concluded that the British proposal prefigured a new *cordon sanitaire* against the USSR, despite Eden's indignant denials to the contrary.[40] Each party for the moment wearily gave up efforts to have his desiderata accepted by the other. Just when all hope for agreement seemed doomed, the British offered Molotov, who had come to London, a simple, long-term, draft treaty of alliance that contained neither the British nor the Soviet minimum conditions. To the amazement of Maisky, the Kremlin, when consulted by Molotov, readily scrapped its previous proposals and approved the draft.[41] The treaty was signed on 26 May 1942.

Part One of the treaty was identical with the 1941 alliance agreement, except that the treaty called for joint struggle against Germany's associates in Europe as well as against Germany. Part Two concerned the postwar aim of preventing a repetition of aggression by Germany or states associated with her. The allies declared their desire to unite with other like-minded states in common action to preserve peace and resist aggression. Pending such a union, the two allies would do all in their power to render impossible such aggression. If either ally became the victim of an attack by Germany or a state associated with her, the other ally would forthwith give its partner all possible military and other support. The allies pledged not to enter into an alliance or coalition directed against the other. Unless superseded by the aforementioned union for common action, the treaty would remain in force for a period of twenty years.[42]

After bitter resistance to anything less than recognition of the USSR's frontiers of 1941, why did Moscow for the moment drop this demand? For one thing, another summer offensive by the Germans was in the offing and an Allied second front in France assumed greatest urgency for Stalin. Signing the alliance might smooth the way for the Anglo-American allies to stage in 1942 the second front they had promised. In any event, it must have become clear to Stalin, as it was to Eden, that if the war ended with Soviet troops occupying the territories the Soviet government claimed, the Allies would hardly try to drive them out.[43] In short the Soviet frontier problem would be

---

[40] Molotov said he had information that some federations might be directed against the USSR. Eden replied that the British government "would never be parties to any scheme directed against the Soviet Union; that was the very opposite of their policy. They were interested only in the formation of federations as a defense against Germany." ("Second Meeting with the Soviet Delegation at No. 10 Downing St. 21 May 1942," N 2902/G FO 371/32882. PRO.)

[41] Maisky, *Vospominaniia*, p. 247.

[42] For the text of the treaty, see *Soviet Foreign Policy*, ed. Rothstein 1:158–60.

[43] Eden Memorandum, "Policy Toward Russia," 28 January 1942. W.P. (42) 48. FO

solved by the Red Army, not by the Commissariat of Foreign Affairs. Given future military success, Moscow would nevertheless still need a timely means of checking the movement toward European federation and confederation Churchill designed to maintain a future balance of power against the USSR.[44]

Ironically, the political means by which the USSR might block Churchill's plan to build a new anti-Soviet equilibrium was suggested by the Anglo-Soviet treaty of alliance, which the British themselves had drafted. If the USSR could conclude similar treaties of alliance with the smaller states of Europe, Germany would be "encircled," eliminating the menace of future German aggression. And to bar any "anti-Soviet" federation or confederation, the USSR could invoke Article Seven, which stated that each party pledged not to conclude an alliance and not to take part in any coalition against the other party. Accordingly, Moscow now sought similar mutual defense alliances with the weaker European states. The British were thus hoist by their own petard.

And the British quickly realized it, but too late. When Molotov, on 9 June 1942, stopped off in London en route home from Washington, Eden asked that Molotov not conclude a treaty of alliance, then under discussion, with the exiled government of Yugoslavia. Feigning surprise, Molotov asked, if alliance with Britain, why not with Yugoslavia? Eden replied that a long-term Soviet alliance with Yugoslavia, which would support Yugoslav territorial claims, might start a treaty-making race between Britain and the USSR for favor of minor allies. A whole network of conflicting treaties would then arise to entangle the postwar peace conference. To avert that complication, Eden proposed a "self-denying ordinance": the British and Soviet governments should pledge not to conclude a mutual assistance treaty with a minor ally without prior agreement between London and Moscow. Molotov agreed to consult his government on Eden's proposal.[45]

371/32875. PRO. Eden found harmonizing relations with the allies difficult, because "Soviet policy is amoral: United States policy is exaggeratedly moral, at least where non-American interests are concerned."

[44] Churchill considered European confederation crucial to bar the "measureless disaster if Russian barbarism overlaid the culture and independence" of Europe. ("Churchill to Eden, 21 October 1942," Churchill, *Hinge of* Fate, p. 488.) He thought that a Danubian Federation and a Balkan Federation, and the recreation of a strong France, were particularly necessary "for the prospect of having no strong country on the map between England and Russia was not attractive." (Ibid., p. 697.)

[45] "Seventh Meeting with the Soviet Delegation Held at the Foreign Office at 3:30 p.m. on June 9, 1942." N 3000/G FO 371/32882. PRO. On the fate of the "self-denying ordinance," see Woodward, *British Foreign Policy*, 2:595–99.

For the next seventeen months the British tried fruitlessly to win Soviet agreement to their "ordinance" and confederation plan. But the Soviet leaders had correctly assessed this plan as one designed to counterweigh Soviet power in Europe. At the Moscow Conference of Foreign Ministers, Molotov in effect killed the "self-denying ordinance" and the confederation scheme proposed by the British. The Soviet delegation stated that it had not given, and could not give, its assent to a requirement that the USSR and Britain consult before a long-term alliance could be concluded with a bordering state, e.g., Czechoslovakia.[46] Eden had proposed a joint declaration, which stipulated that the Big Three powers should seek neither to create nor recognize any separate spheres or areas of responsibility in Europe, and they should assist other states in forming federations or confederations. Molotov assailed the declaration as premature, dangerous, and superfluous. The three great powers should not artificially force the pace of federation; after all, the plan could be reexamined when the time was more ripe. The plan was dangerous, because it projected a new *cordon sanitaire* against the USSR, and superfluous since there was no disposition on the part of the Soviet government, or, as far as he knew, on the part of the British, to divide Europe into separate spheres of influence. The declaration was not acted upon.[47]

Moscow did not sign a mutual assistance treaty with the Royal government of Yugoslavia. By war's end, however, the USSR did sign an anti-German treaty of mutual assistance with Czechoslovakia (12 December 1943), France (10 December 1944), Tito's Yugoslavia (11 April 1945), and Poland (21 April 1945).[48] Thus Churchill's federation scheme proved stillborn, and Stalin and Churchill reached a secret agreement dividing southeast Europe into spheres of influence. The triumph of Soviet arms was accompanied by the triumph of Soviet diplomacy, whose degree of success can be gauged by reference to the aims Stalin formulated back in December 1941.

---

[46] "Statement of the Soviet Delegation on Point 8 of the Agenda," *FRUS*, 1943, 1:726–27.

[47] "Draft of Declaration on Joint Responsibility for Europe," Ibid., 736–7. [Molotov,] *Moskovskaia konferentsiia*, p. 192 and *FRUS*, 1943, 1:762–3. A few days later, Maxim Litvinov, Molotov's deputy, asked the conferees why Eden's declaration covered only Europe (ibid., p. 680), thus reminding Eden and Hull of the existence of the British Empire and of the Monroe Doctrine.

[48] For the texts of the treaties, see *War and Peace Aims of the United Nations*, ed. Louise W. Holborn (Boston, 1948), 2 vols: 2:761–63; 780–81; 783–84; and 784–86. All four treaties contained virtually the same language with regard to hostile alignments as that included in article Seven of the Anglo-Soviet Treaty: "Each High Contracting Party undertakes not to conclude any alliance and not to take part in any coalition directed against the other High Contracting Party." Deferring to the British desire for

Most of these aims had been achieved and more. But Stalin had yet to fulfill his grand plan for postwar security: an alliance of European states to keep Germany down. On the eve of the founding meeting of the United Nations Organization in San Francisco, Stalin studiously ignored the embryonic UN and bluntly placed his faith in such an alliance system. For he hailed the signing of the Polish-Soviet Treaty as completing an eastern united front "from the Baltic to the Carpathians" against German imperialism. If that were now supplemented by a similar grouping in the west, that is, by an "alliance between our countries and our Allies in the west," German aggression would not be free to run amok. Therefore, he did not doubt that the western Allies would welcome this new treaty.[49]

But quite the contrary proved true. Stalin's intention of enlarging the Soviet alliance system only heightened fears in the west of a *Pax Sovietica*. From November 1944, therefore, Eden remonstrated with Churchill that Britain must immediately proceed to organize a western defense bloc, including a rearmed France, ostensibly in order to restrain Germany but also to guard against potential Soviet expansion. Otherwise, Britain's western European allies, especially the French, might get the impression "that their only hope lies in making defense arrangements not with us, but with the Russians." Thus was conceived the idea that led to the Brussels Pact in 1948 and the North Atlantic Treaty Organization in 1949.[50] In short, the very success of Soviet wartime diplomacy recoiled on Moscow by generating the western political-military alliance that Soviet diplomacy was designed to forestall.

Irony of ironies, Stalin, a classical balance-of-power practitioner, had in the meantime reverted to Leninist theory on "spheres of influence" to explain the widening split. On 9 February 1946, Stalin

---

Polish-Czechslovak federation, Moscow adjoined to its treaty with Czechslovakia a protocol permitting adherence of Poland, which would make it a trilateral alliance. (Woodward, *British Foreign Policy*, 2:597–99. Barker, *British Policy*, pp. 136–37).

But none of these treaties contained both parts of an important proviso found in article Five of the Anglo-Soviet Treaty: the signatories "will act in accordance with the two principles of not seeking territorial aggrandizement for themselves and of noninterference in the internal affairs of other states." The Soviet alliance with Czechoslovakia (article Four) and with Poland (article Two) did, however, pledge friendly cooperation between the two countries in accordance with the principles of mutual respect for their independence and sovereignty and non-intervention in the internal affairs of the other state.

[49] I. F. Stalin, "Rech' pri podpisanii dogovora mezhdu sovetskim soiuzom i pol'skoi respublikoi. 21 aprelia 1945 g," in Stalin, *Sochineniia*, ed. Robert H. McNeal (Stanford, 1967), 3 vols. 2 (15):186.

[50] Eden, *The Reckoning*, pp. 572–73. Elisabeth Barker, *Churchill and Eden at War* (London, 1978), pp. 116–7, 215–17, and 290–91.

asserted in an "election" speech that neither the First World War nor the Second was caused by "accidents" or by "mistakes" committed by statesmen, though mistakes were made. Such conflicts inevitably break out, because the group of capitalist states "which considers itself worse provided than others with raw materials and markets usually makes attempts to alter the situation and repartition the 'spheres of influence' in its favor by armed force. The result is a splitting of the capitalist world into two hostile camps and war between them." Stalin implied that this process was leading to a third imperialist war, now among his former allies. Nevertheless, the USSR, he decreed, needed at least another three or more five-year plans to guarantee itself against "all possible accidents."[51]

But Stalin's projection of a new intra-imperialist war did not materialize. Instead, the USSR found itself confronted by NATO, a western bloc that embodied some of Stalin's worst fears. In sum, Soviet postwar diplomacy, basing itself on the great gains scored from 1939 to 1945, had failed in the end to prevent the breakup of the wartime alliance and to avoid an east-west partition of Europe. Historians have yet to establish conclusively the share of responsibility each ally must bear for this split, and statesmen have yet to make the old world one again.

[51] I. V. Stalin, "Rech' na predvybornom sobranii izbiratelei stalinskogo izbiratel'nogo okruga goroda moskvy. 9 fevralia 1946 g," in Stalin, *Sochinenaniia.* 3 (16):2–4, 20.

East European Quarterly, XX, no. 4
January 1987

DEATH AND POLITICS:
THE KATYN FOREST MASSACRE AND
AMERICAN FOREIGN POLICY

Crister S. and Stephen A. Garrett
Monterey Institute of International Studies

In April, 1943, the German army was absorbed in trying to stabilize its position on the Russian front after the disaster of Stalingrad when Wehrmacht officers in the vicinity of Smolensk were told by local peasants of the existence of mass graves in the nearby Katyn Forest. Given the record of German atrocities in Russia, the Wehrmacht authorities might have been expected to shrug off yet another piece of evidence of the draconian activities of the SS in the occupied territories. In fact, the Germans had their own reasons for investigating the veracity of these reports. After a brief search, they located the site of the graves and discovered the bodies of some 4100 Polish officers. The cause of death without exception was a shot to the back of the head. The hands of the officers had been tied behind their backs with binder cord. A few of the bodies had four-edged bayonet wounds.[1]

Josef Goebbels, Reich Propaganda Minister, wasted no time in informing the world of the outrage and explicitly condemned the Soviet government for the barbarous act. The Russians, not surprisingly, placed the blame elsewhere. Radio Moscow replied two days after the Goebbels announcement that the Polish officers had died when they "fell into the hands of the German-Fascist hangmen in the summer of 1941, after the withdrawal of the Soviet troops from the Smolensk area."[2] The Russian statement went on to say that "beyond doubt Goebbels' slanderers are now trying by lies and calumnies to cover up the bloody crimes of the Hitlerite gangsters."[3] The Polish government-in-exile in London, in its initial reaction to the Katyn development, combined expressions of horror at the discovery itself with a careful attempt at this early stage not to associate itself openly with the German position on culpability. "No Pole can help but be deeply shocked by the news of the discovery of the bodies of Polish officers," a communique out of London announced, which went on to state that "the Polish government denies to the Germans any right to base, on a crime they ascribe to others, arguments in their own defense."[4]

The Katyn affair had a particular sensitivity since the Polish officers could have been regarded as a critical component of a reconstituted post-war Polish state. The victims were largely reservists, who in civilian life had been doctors, lawyers, priests and teachers—in other words, those holding a natural position of leadership in Polish society. There was another sensitive aspect to the Katyn revelations that soon developed, however, one which was not unrelated to the above circumstance, and which introduced complications which are the main theme of this essay. As specific information began to emerge following the discovery of the Katyn graves, the only reasonable conclusion was that the Soviet Union had indeed, for reasons of its own, systematically executed a large percentage of the Polish officers who had fallen into its grasp following the Soviet invasion of Poland in late September, 1939.

The evidence on Soviet culpability for the Katyn massacre is extensive, and for purposes of this essay need only be summarized here. It is suggestive, in the first place, that both the Poles and the Germans extended an invitation to the International Red Cross to conduct an independent investigation at the gravesite in order to determine the facts, but the Soviets spurned the Red Cross's involvement. Instead, they waited until January, 1944, four months after Russian forces had recaptured the area around Smolensk, to form their own "investigative commission", which would settle once and for all the Katyn dispute. This commission, after due deliberation, concluded that in the autumn of 1941 "the German occupation authorities carried out mass shootings of Polish prisoners of war."[5]

It can be presumed that had the Germans known their own guilt in the Katyn affair, they would hardly have extended an invitation to the International Red Cross to conduct an on-site investigation of the Katyn Graves. Also lending credence to the German protestations of innocence was the fact that once a role for the Red Cross was rejected by that organization (on the grounds that the Soviet Union had not agreed to its participation), the Germans hastily formed their own investigative commission composed of experts in medical jurisprudence and criminology from European universities in Belgium, Denmark, Switzerland and the Netherlands. The commission dissected hundreds of the exhumed bodies in an attempt to determine the date of death. Clues were sought in letters, diaries and newspapers found on the bodies, as well as the condition of the corpses themselves. The final conclusion of the commission was that the men had died sometime in March or April of 1940.[6] The implication was obvious: the Germans had not invaded Russia until late June, 1941, and had not reached the Smolensk area until September, 1941.

Taken collectively, the evidence assembled by the commission was compelling. When they examined the bodies, they found numerous Russian newspapers in the coat pockets of the corpses. None were dated later than April, 1940. There was also the matter of the overcoats. According to the Soviet commission, the men had died probably in September, 1941. At that time of the year in the Smolensk area, the temperature ranges between sixty-five and seventy-five degrees Fahrenheit. It seems highly unlikely that the Polish officers would have worn heavy winter coats in such conditions. Several American newspaper correspondents in fact queried the Soviet authorities at the time on the apparent contradiction. One of them recalled that "the Soviets were stunned with that question. They did not know exactly what to answer and it took them several days to figure out an answer."[7] The eventual "solution", according to the Soviet authorities, was that perhaps the men had been executed in December rather than September, 1941.

Still another variation on the creative Soviet explanation of the Katyn affair was that possibly the Germans had disinterred bodies from other locations in the spring of 1943, brought them to the gravesite at Katyn, put them face down in the graves, and planted newspapers from the spring of 1940 on the bodies. Aside from the inherent difficulties in this account— assembling, for instance, thousands of Russian newspapers issued in the spring of 1940—there was a macabre medical consideration arguing against such a scenario. The International Medical Commission noticed that the bodies they examined were stuck together because of a "human glue" secreted by the dead bodies. To reach this state of decomposition, the bodies needed to be buried for over a year. Yet only a month or two had passed between the time the Russians claimed the Germans had transferred the bodies and the German announcement of their discovery at Katyn.[8]

None of this is to deny that the Germans would have been quite capable of massacring the Polish officers. As noted, the Nazi regime had already done much worse by the time of Katyn. It is simply to suggest that in this particular instance the Soviet authorities seemed almost certainly to have taken a page out of their rivals' handbook of atrocities. Soviet representatives at the later Nuremberg Trials initially attempted to include the Katyn massacre amongst the charges leveled against the German defendants, but the facts supporting such an indictment were so thin that eventually the Russian presecutor quietly, allowed the Katyn affair to be struck from the list of particulars in the indictment. Perhaps the most poignant testimony to the real circumstances—and the real date—of the Katyn massacre was contained in the diary of a certain Polish Major Adam Solski found at the gravesite. Major Solski wrote:

April 8. 1940, 3:30 a.m. departure from Kozielsk station, moving west.

April 8. Since 12 noon we have been standing in a railway siding at Smolensk.

April 9. In the morning some minutes before five, reveille; in the prison trucks, and preparations to leave. We are to go somewhere by car, and what next?

April 9 (later). It has been a strange day so far. Departure in prison coach in cells, terrible, taken somewhere in a wood.[9]

The motivations behind a Soviet execution of over four thousand men of the Polish officer corps are not hard to determine. Ever the cold-blooded geopolitician, Stalin clearly intended to reduce Poland to a subordinate status after victory over the Germans as a strategic buffer against potential future attack from the West. For a leader who by some estimates presided over the deaths of approximately ten million of his own countrymen in the terrible purges of the late 1930's, the slaughter of a few thousand Polish officers in order to weaken post-war Polish resistance to Soviet designs must have seemed a mere trifle. A major question surrounding Katyn, however, was whether others not directly involved in the affair would be content to regard it as only a "trifle", in particular the United States.

American policy toward the Katyn Massacre has to be seen in the broader context of American diplomacy toward Eastern Europe generally and Poland specifically. That diplomacy had always had something of a paradoxical character. In *objective* terms American strategic and economic links with Eastern Europe had always been distinctly marginal. American trade with the region during the 1920's and 1930's, for example, had never exceeded more than five percent of the net sum of American imports and exports.[10] Moreover, it is instructive that until very late in World War I President Woodrow Wilson hardly offered any new vision of political rearrangements in the region. On the contrary, his policy was to work for the continuation of the pre-war Austro-Hungarian Empire, albeit with some concessions made to greater autonomy for the ethnic groupings within the Empire. Wilson held off a declaration of war against Austria-Hungary until eight months after the initiation of American hostilities against Germany, and even then he assured Vienna that "we do not wish in any way to impair or to rearrange the Austro-Hungarian Empire. It is no affair of ours what they do with their own life, either industrially or politically. We do not propose or desire to dictate to them in any way."[11] The subsequent development of full sovereignty for the peoples of the Empire such as Hungary, Czechoslovakia and Yugoslavia derived basically out of the general collapse of Austrian military and political cohesion.

Subjectively, however, the United States for a long time prior to Katyn had fancied itself as in some way the special ally of the East European peoples in their struggle for self-determination and basic human rights. Certainly in terms of mass opinion in this country, there was a continuing sentimental affinity for the valiant, if at times seemingly hopeless, struggle of the Eastern Europeans to control their own destiny. When the Hungarian patriot Louis Kossuth traveled to the United States in 1852 following the abortive Hungarian revolution of four years earlier, for example, Daniel Webster spoke for many when he enthusiastically proclaimed that the "world has waited for nearly eighteen hundred years to see his like."[12] Some one hundred thousand people lined the railroad tracks in Ohio as Kossuth made a triumphant procession to the state capital of Columbus to address the legislature. The reception which Kossuth enjoyed was matched when the Czech leader Thomas Masaryk arrived in the United States in May, 1918. Masaryk was interested in getting Wilson's recognition of the provisional Czech government, but at first his impact on Wilson was less momentous than on the American people. Huge crowds attended his every movement and at Pittsburgh he signed an agreement with Slovak representatives which has popularly been considered as the "Declaration of Independence" for the new Czech state. American enthusiasm for the Czech cause was increased by romantic reports of the attempted exodus of the so-called "Czech legion" from Bolshevik Russia in 1918. Teddy Roosevelt regarded the struggle of the Czech legion as a "great and historic feat. . . literally unparalleled, so far as I know, in ancient or modern warfare."[13]

If the United States had historically felt a special connection to the nations of Eastern Europe, this feeling was especially observable in this country's attitude toward Poland. Undoubtedly this sense of a "special relationship" derived in part out of the fact that during the so-called New Immigration from approximately 1890 to 1924 Poland had provided more emigrants to the United States than any other Eastern European nation (on the order of two and a half million). The presence of a large Polish-American community virtually ensured that the fate of Poland would continue to be a politically powerful issue in the United States. This was reflected in Wilson's own Fourteen Points, which specifically listed an independent Poland as one of America's goals in any postwar settlement. For most Americans, whether of Polish extraction or not, the brutal Nazi assault on the Polish state in September, 1939 served to reinforce the widespread sympathy for the long suffering of the Polish people.

The news that four thousand men of the Polish officer corps had been murdered, in sum, seemed destined to arouse a strong reaction in the United States, even in the midst of many other horrors of the conflict, including Nazi occupation policy in Poland itself. Nevertheless, the melancholy argument advanced here is that Washington in fact never approached the Katyn massacre in its own terms either during or after the war. Instead, it was simply one element in a larger complex of political and military considerations. While World War II raged, the basic American strategy was to ignore or downplay the Katyn events. When the Cold War began to emerge between the United States and the Soviet Union after 1945, Katyn suddenly became a very convenient device by which the Soviets could stand accused before the bar of world and American public opinion. Perhaps it would be naive to expect that an issue such as Katyn could ever have been divorced from the more fundamental ebbs and flows of international politics. Nevertheless, an analysis of evolving American policy toward the Katyn affair says a certain amount about the realities of the American "commitment" to Eastern European interests and self-determination generally and that of Poland specifically. Perhaps the ultimate point of studying Katyn is to demonstrate the gulf that has separated the sentimental aspirations of the American people in foreign policy from the hard realities that in actuality have been the prime determinant of that policy.

KATYN AND THE AMERICAN WAR EFFORT

Undoubtedly the single most important factor conditioning the overall American response to the Katyn affair was the Roosevelt Administration's belief that the maintenance of the Grand Alliance between the United States, Great Britain and the Soviet Union was essential to the successful prosecution of the war as well as hopes for a satisfactory world order following victory over Germany and Japan. The fundamental point is that news of the Katyn massacre had the potential seriously to affect what the Roosevelt Administration saw as critical political and military objectives.

Roosevelt was particularly sensitive to Russia's military contribution to coalition war objectives. He saw the value of Soviet participation "in terms of dead Germans and smashed tanks."[14] He also thought the Soviet Union could provide important military assistance for the American campaign against Japan once the allies defeated Germany. According to Roosevelt's military advisers, Russia's participation in the Asian theater could save untold thousands of American lives.[15]

Symptomatic of President Roosevelt's attitude toward Soviet-American wartime cooperation was his stance on an issue that arose several months before news of the Katyn massacre emerged. Moscow announced in January, 1943 that all ethnic Poles in the Soviet Union would perforce be made Soviet citizens. These people represented the some 1,500,000 Poles who had been forcibly deported into the interior of Russia between February and June, 1941. After receiving the Polish government's urgent request for American arbitration on the nationality question, Roosevelt told the Polish ambassador to the United States, Jan Ciechanowski, that the Soviet Union was winning battles while the Western allies were experiencing considerable difficulties in North Africa. Roosevelt explained to Ciechanowski that under the circumstances the United States was reluctant to take any action that might be interpreted as American meddling in Soviet domestic affairs.[16]

Once news of the Katyn massacre became public knowledge, what views did President Roosevelt hold as to who was responsible for the outrage? This is a question of some interest given subsequent American policy concerning Katyn. Roosevelt's actual theory about Katyn is somewhat difficult to ascertain. Shortly after the discovery of the graves of the Polish officers, one Ernst Hanfstaengl, former foreign press chief for Adolf Hitler and later a refugee from the Reich, was providing the American Administration with analyses of current events within Germany. Hanfstaengl concluded from Goebbels' line of propaganda that in this instance the Germans were telling the truth. After reviewing Hanfstaengl's analysis, Roosevelt commented to his close associate Sumner Welles that he was sure Hanfstaengl was "on the level".[17]

One year later, however, the President's opinion seemed altogether different. Presidential aide George Earle presented Roosevelt with evidence suggesting once again Russian guilt. Roosevelt commented, according to Earle, that "this is entirely German propaganda and a German plot. I am absolutely convinced the Russians do not do this."[18] When Earle pointed out that the Germans had invited the Red Cross to investigate Katyn, the President replied, "The Germans could have rigged things up. Those Nazis are very smart, and they could rig it up for the Red Cross."[19]

Whatever Roosevelt's private views eventually were with respect to the Katyn affair, the main thrust of the Administration's policy toward the issue was consistently to downplay its significance and to attempt to exclude it from discussions about "larger" issues. Representative of the American stance was Washington's reaction to Stalin's announcement that he was breaking off diplomatic relations with the Polish government-in-exile in London because of the latter's invitation to the Red Cross to investigate the circumstance surrounding Katyn. Roosevelt replied to Stalin's telegram announcing the break in Polish-Soviet relations by making a cautious plea on behalf of the leader of the London Poles and by offering the hope that Katyn would not unduly upset relations amongst all those united in fighting the fascists. The President stated that "in my opinion Sikorski had in no way acted with the Hitler gang but instead he has made a mistake in taking up this particular matter with the International Red Cross. He concluded by saying that "I do hope that in this present situation you can find means to label your reaction as a suspension of conversations with the Polish Government-in-Exile rather than a complete severance of relations."[20]

When Stalin rejected this plea for moderation, the Roosevelt Administration displayed little sense of urgency over the Polish-Soviet crisis and held to the hope that the whole affair could be resolved without American involvement. The American stance seemed to be infused with a considerable measure of fatalism. As one noted diplomatic historian has commented, American inaction did not mean there was no interest in fostering a reconciliation between the Russians and the Poles but was a simple recognition of the fact that Washington had no "effective chance for bringing this about."[21]

In any case, Roosevelt's approach to the Katyn affair—or rather nonapproach—could be seen in the absence of any American raising of the issue in the various wartime conferences that took place in 1943. Churchill and Roosevelt held bi-lateral meetings first at Washington in May and three months later at Quebec, and in both instances the question of Katyn was noticeably absent from the agenda. During the Teheran conference at the end of the year involving not only Churchill and Roosevelt but also Stalin, British Foreign Minister Anthony Eden was struck by the fact that "the President did not want to get involved in a discussion on Poland, and this, therefore, was entirely an Anglo-Russian affair."[22]

Polish officials who tried to push the issue with Roosevelt came away with little doubt concerning the President's priorities. Stanislaw Mikolajczyk, a leading figure among the London Poles, tried to discuss the Katyn matter with the American Administration, but for a period of months was not allowed even the opportunity to speak directly with Roosevelt. The American position, as described by Mikolajczyk, amounted to the Americans telling the Poles: "You have to settle the problems of the Polish-Soviet relations. These people are dead. You will not help them, but you will spoil the collaboration of the Allies. Therefore, keep silent."[23]

When Mikolajczyk finally did get a chance to meet with Roosevelt, he was introduced to another aspect of the American attitude toward Katyn that deserves separate attention. The President informed the Polish leader that eventually he would indeed become directly involved in the whole range of Polish-Soviet controversies and would "act as a moderator in this problem and affect a settlement." In explaining why he had not so far initiated a compromise, however, Roosevelt told Mikolajczyk that "I haven't acted on the Polish question because this is an election year."[24] The calculations of the President were clear enough. Polish-Americans were a crucial factor in the electoral votes of large industrialized states in the Northeast and Midwest. Roosevelt feared that millions of them might vote against him in the 1944 election if a controversy over Poland erupted and he was forced, because of larger strategic considerations, to publicly support the Russian position on Katyn.

There was another respect in which American public opinion influenced Washington's approach to Katyn quite aside from Roosevelt's concerns about not alienating the Polish ethnic vote. Americans may have had a generalized sympathy for Poland's suffering, and generalized aspirations for the future of Poland, but the Polish government-in-exile in London found it very difficult to translate these abstractions into specific support for its position concerning Katyn. The London Poles were seen as at least partially responsible for the break in Soviet-Polish relations due to their imprudent request to the International Red Cross to investigate Katyn. The Polish authorities recognized this problem in "public relations" when they subsequently withdrew their request to the Red Cross (without, it might be noted, changing Stalin's determination to have nothing further to do with them). Influential representatives of the American media blamed Hitler and Goebbels for concocting the Katyn story to instigate a break in Polish-Soviet diplomatic ties, and the perception was that the London Poles had played into the hands of German strategy. The liberal *Nation* sympathized with Russian anger at Polish actions, and they were joined in this analysis by the august *New York Times*. There was also considerable comment in the American press about the supposedly undemocratic and unrepresentative character of the London Polish government. *The New Republic* went so far as to accuse the Polish government-in-exile of being "as illiberal as the Nazis themselves."[25] In sum, not only did President Roosevelt have his own reasons for avoiding a public commitment to the Polish version of Katyn but there was hardly a groundswell of American public opinion, at least among non-Polish-Americans, to move him in this direction. The President in any case for the remainder of the war years took quite extraordinary steps to insure that any discussion of Katyn sympathetic to the Polish position was excluded from the public domain. A brief consideration of some of these measures merits our attention.

THE RESTRICTED DEBATE OVER KATYN

The basic strategy pursued by Roosevelt, dictated by his concern about the potential effect of a full airing of the Katyn affair on American wartime policy as well as on American domestic politics, was simply to try to eliminate Katyn as a topic of discussion as much as possible. After the first week following the discovery of the mass graves, the President basically ignored the issue in his communications with other Allied leaders. American diplomatic personnel were specifically restrained from raising the Katyn matter in the course of their activities in various foreign capitals. Within the United States, the Administration undertook an aggressive campaign to contain the public debate over Katyn, which had an impact not only on Congressmen but even on commentators for the numerous foreign language radio stations in this country.

Roosevelt's main difficulty in this enterprise was that a number of individuals in and outside the American government were highly suspicious about Russian duplicity in the Katyn affair. Thus it required a coordinated effort amongst agencies such as the War Department, the State Department, and the Office of War Information to enforce the policy of silence. One case that may be taken as representative involved a certain Lieutenant Colonel John Van Vliet.

Colonel Van Vliet had been captured by the Germans prior to April, 1943, and as the Wehrmacht authorities prepared to exhume the bodies at the Katyn gravesite he was transported to the site to witness the proceedings. The Germans evidently felt that if an American officer witnessed the exhuming of the corpses the German story about culpability for the Katyn massacre would receive greater credence. During his stay at Katyn, Van Vliet talked to the International Medical Commission, observed the condition of the bodies, and finally reached the conclusion that the Soviets had undoubtedly been responsible for the tragedy.

After his release from a German POW camp at the end of the war, Colonel Van Vliet went to General Clayton Bissell, Assistant Chief of Staff for Intelligence at the War Department, to report on his knowledge of the Katyn affair. Bissell gave the following instructions to Van Vliet: "Due to the nature of your report and the possible political implications, it is directed that you neither mention nor discuss the matter with anyone in or out of the service without specific approval in writing from the War Department."[26] Bissell then proceeded to place a "Top Secret" classification on the Van Vliet report. He later testified that three months after receiving it he sent a copy of the report to the State Department. Officials at State, however, claimed that they had no record of ever having seen the Van Vliet report, and the Department of the Army could find neither a receipt for the actual transmittal nor a covering letter for the document. The Van Vliet analysis of Katyn remains missing to this day.[27]

Colonel Henry Syzmanski's analysis concerning Katyn met basically the same fate as that which befell the observations of Van Vliet. General George C. Marshall, then the Army Chief of Staff, had instructed Syzmanski, an expert in Eastern European affairs, to compile a report on the facts surrounding Katyn. In May, 1943, Colonel Syzmanski submitted his findings to the Intelligence Service of the War Department. Drawing from information about Polish prisoners-of-war in Russia, a report on prison camps in the Soviet Union, and a summary of the facts concerning the graves themselves, Syzmanski essentially reached the same conclusion on culpability as that offered by Colonel Van Vliet. The response, by Major General Strong of army intelligence, was to write to Colonel Syzmanski's immediate superiors instructing them to tell the Colonel to "avoid political involvement" in the Polish argument about Katyn.[28] Syzmanski's analysis was subsequently ignored by the Department of the Army, the State Department, and the International Military Tribunal at Nuremberg. Word of its existence did leak out to various Congressmen of Polish-American descent, who asked to see a copy. Their request was denied on the grounds of "secrecy." An attempt to discuss the findings of Colonel Syzmanski with President Roosevelt also proved unavailing. Secretary of State Cordell Hull merely assured the Congressmen that he would convey their "message" to the President. Congressman Alvin O'Konski summarized the situation by saying that "our personal intervention did not get anywhere at that time."[29]

In discussing individual instances in which the Roosevelt Administration attempted to control the debate over Katyn within the government, however, it is the case of George Earle that perhaps stands out as most representative. A long-time government servant, Earle had served as Minister to Austria and Bulgaria. In 1943, he was Special Emissary of the President for Balkan affairs, stationed in Turkey. Earle traveled throughout the Balkans gathering intelligence, and through his contacts in Bulgaria and Romania, he received data about the Katyn affair. Earle summarized the information he had gathered, and his own conclusions about Katyn, in a report submitted personally to President Roosevelt in May, 1944.[30]

In a subsequent private conversation with the President, Earle underlined his belief that the Soviets had in fact been responsible for Katyn, and suggested that a neutral Red Cross investigation might after all be advisable. Roosevelt ignored these comments, and instead spent the rest of the meeting with Earle explaining that he wanted him now "to find out something about the veterans of this war, whether they should have a new organization."[31] The President ended the conversation by asking Earle as well to "go out over the country and spend three weeks finding out whether I can be re-elected or not."[32]

After completing his work in America, Earle went back to Turkey. Over the next year he continued to gather information about Katyn from his contacts in Eastern Europe. Finally, in March, 1945, Earle wrote to Roosevelt explaining his intention to write a book on Katyn. The President responded rather decisively:

> I specifically forbid you to publish any information or opinion about any ally that you may have acquired while in office or in the service of the United States Navy.
>
> In view of your wish for continued active service, I shall withdraw any previous understanding that you are serving as an emissary of mine and I shall direct the Navy Department to continue your employment wherever they can make use of your services.[33]

The Navy decided the best place for an expert in Eastern European affairs would be Samoa. In hopes of having his orders changed, Earle tried to explain to Roosevelt the pointlessness of sending someone with his background to Samoa. "I think you had better go," the President replied, "and see what you think of the Pacific War as one of our problems."[34] Upon his return from Samoa, Earle received an apology from the Chief of Personnel of the Navy, who said that the Navy Department had had nothing to do with his being assigned to the South Pacific.[35] President Roosevelt, it appeared, had personally made sure that Earle received orders to a place securely distant from any contact with Eastern European affairs.

The efforts directed by the President to "quarantine" potentially troublesome discussion of the Katyn affair extended outside his own administration. A particular target of these measures was the extensive network of foreign language radio stations in the United States, especially those broadcasting in Eastern European languages and whose personnel were inclined to be somewhat cynical about Soviet policies. During the war there were three organizations responsible for monitoring news about the war coming from the foreign language stations. In addition to the Federal Communications Commission and the Foreign Language Wartime Control Committee, there was the Office of War Information (OWI). The latter, responsible for the dispensing and censoring of war news, took the most direct lead in dealing with radio commentators who expressed anti-Soviet views in the context of the Katyn issue.

In one case, a reporter for the Polish radio station WJBK in Detroit made several remarks indicating Russian guilt in the Katyn massacre. The OWI reacted quickly to this unwelcome expression of opinion. OWI official Alan Cranston spoke to the Chairman of the foreign language committee of the National Association of Broadcasters. Cranston urged the chairman to convince station WJBK to stop making comments concerning Soviet responsibility for Katyn. The station manager agreed to "think it over".[36] An editorialist at WBNY in Buffalo also offered the opinion that the Russians had something to hide concerning Katyn. Soon after, the WBNY manager received a letter from Washington urging appropriate restraint on station employees concerning sensitive issues like Katyn. The editorial commentator was shortly dismissed from his position at the station.[37]

The general position of those charged with supervising the information put out on the public airwaves during the war was in fact that all foreign language stations should avoid expressing openly anti-Soviet views on the air. The Federal Communications Act expressly forbade this effort at censorship, yet those responsible for overseeing the activities of the foreign language radio network "urgently recommended that news and war commentators be requested to cease, immediately, the broadcasting of editorial or personal opinion."[38] To be sure, analysis of the circumstances behind Katyn was not the only target of this directive. Nevertheless, it was Katyn perhaps more than any other issue that spurred the Administration's determination to shield pursuit of its felt wartime needs from any embarrassing complications arising from an open consideration of the real guilt—and potentially the real implications—behind this particular atrocity.

AN EVALUATION

When one considers the record of American wartime silence, and the various attempts to sustain this silence both within and without the government, on the Katyn affair, it is difficult not to conclude that this was a particularly egregious example of cynicism and even hypocrisy in foreign policy. Nevertheless, in arriving at a fair verdict on the Roosevelt Administration's handling of Katyn, it is necessary to consider the essence of the situation as they saw it. Certainly the argument that continued Soviet commitment to the military defeat of Germany was crucial to the Allied war effort can not be disregarded. Churchill himself, reflecting on the great struggle against the Nazis, commented that the Soviet armies "tore the guts out of the German Wehrmacht". To the extent that a Western showdown over Katyn would have vitiated the Soviet military effort, perhaps it is understandable that the tragedy should have been ignored in view of larger interests. The notion that Soviet-Western cooperation was critical to a satisfactory international postwar order is also a proposition that deserves some respectful attention. If dwelling on Soviet culpability in the Katyn affair would indeed have had the effect of undermining chances of such cooperation, there is a case that can be made for President Roosevelt's determination to ignore the relatively smaller tragedy in the effort to avoid a large one—general confrontation after the war between East and West. The fact that events did eventually move in this direction is hardly a basis on which to denounce the President's *bona fides*.

Yet there are legitimate questions that remain. An obvious one concerns the actual effect that a tougher American stance on Katyn was likely to have on the Soviet war effort. It is true that in 1943 there were very preliminary discussions between the Germans and the Soviets on the possibility of a compromise peace which would have taken the Soviet Union out of the struggle against Nazism.[39] On balance, however, the chances that Stalin would have abandoned the effort to crush once and for all the German menace hardly seems credible, even in terms of the information available at the time. To this extent, then, American connivance in ignoring evidence about Katyn can be seen as not only ignoble but also unnecessary.

There is also the fact that the aggressive cover-up within American circles concerning Katyn continued well beyond the period in which the outcome of the war could be considered seriously in doubt. It is instructive to recall that when George Earle informed Roosevelt that he intended to write a book on Katyn, the war hardly had two months to run. Even from the perspective of the President's personal fortunes, Earle's communication came *after* the former had successfully won re-election in November, 1944. Moreover, the Van Vliet analysis of Katyn was given to American authorities after the war had actually ended. The only defense that seemingly can be given for this continued indifference to the real circumstances of Katyn was that the Truman Administration still hoped to enlist Moscow in a general commitment to a stable post-war international order.

Reference to President Truman's stance on Katyn, it must be said, undermines the essentially "instrumental" approach that consistently characterized the American attitude toward the massacre. Despite the rather bizarre attempt by the Soviet Union to raise the Katyn issue at the Nuremberg proceedings, the United States carefully declined to become involved. The main American representative at the war crimes trials, Justice Robert Jackson, told the Soviet delegation that he "would keep hands off and leave the entire contest to the Soviet and German lawyers."[40] In his own defense, Jackson later commented that he knew nothing "at any time during the trial of Colonel Van Vliet or Colonel Syzmanski."[41]

The position of the President, however, changed rather dramatically during the next few years as the Cold War intensified between Moscow and Washington. No longer was there an attempt by the Administration to muffle discussion concerning Soviet culpability for the Katyn massacre. Indeed, the evident Soviet guilt in the matter stood as a powerful piece of evidence to doubtful Congressmen and American public opinion about the legitimacy of the Truman Administration's challenge to a malevolent and aggressive Soviet foreign policy. The turnabout in the official stance on Katyn was symbolized most noticeably when the Congress undertook a formal investigation of the affair in 1951. Truman made sure his Administration complied with all committee requests for documents and information, especially after his former Ambassador to Poland, Arthur Lane, became a prominent supporter of an "objective" investigation of the circumstances of Katyn. The fact that the massacre still was viewed in terms of its political ramifications—in this case, domestic ramifications—reflected at the same time, in Truman's refusal to accept Congressional recommendations following the investigation that the Katyn affair be brought before either the United Nations or the International Court of Justice at the Hague. Clearly, Truman did not care to have Katyn linger as an issue with which his Republican opposition could assault the Democrats during the upcoming 1952 Presidential elections for their record of "indifference" to the fate of the Polish officers.[42]

What, then, may be fairly concluded about American policy toward the Katyn events? An obvious conclusion is that the ostensible American commitment to Eastern European interests and that of Poland specifically has always been a hostage to larger concerns. This phenomenon presents itself not only in the contest of Katyn—the United States was essentially a passive bystander to the Russian crushing of the Hungarian revolt in 1956, and President Johnson was only dissuaded with great difficulty from going ahead with a planned visit to the Soviet Union shortly after Moscow's intervention in Czechoslovakia in 1968. The essential gap between American aspirations for Eastern Europe and the felt constraints on American policy toward the region does not, however, provide much consolation to the Poles who still vividly recollect one of the most calculated and tragic assaults on their national identity. Perhaps symptomatic of the sensitivity of Katyn for the Polish nation is the effort by the Soviet Union itself to erase the historical memory of Katyn.

In 1969, the Russians announced the unveiling of a memorial on the site of the village of Khatyn, located about 160 miles from Katyn itself. The Khatyn with an "h" was one of the 9,200 Byelorussian villages destroyed by the Germans and one of 136 in which all the inhabitants were killed. After erecting the monument, the Russians tried to obliterate Katyn from maps and history books, and replace it with Khatyn.

> 1954— A map of the Minsk Region in the *Large Soviet Encyclopedia* does not show Khatyn at all.
> 1956— A map of the Smolensk area in the *Large Soviet Encyclopedia* shows Katyn.
> 1959— A large atlas of the USSR shows neither Khatyn nor Katyn.
> 1974— A map of the Minsk Region in the *Large Soviet Encyclopedia* shows Khatyn but not Katyn.[43]

The current Polish government led by General Wojciech Jaruzelski has also attempted—or been compelled—to confront the memory of Katyn. In 1981 groups associated with the Solidarity labor movement erected a memorial to the Katyn victims in Warsaw's cemetery for the war dead. The date given for the Katyn massacre on the monument was April, 1940.

Shortly after, the authorities removed the Solidarity monument, but in March, 1985 they erected without prior announcement one of their own on the same site. The inscription on the new monument reads: "To the Polish soldiers-victims of the Hitlerite fascism that arose on the soil of Katyn." The wording obviously was a reflection of the Jaruzelski regime's dependence on the good will of Moscow, yet in a delicate balancing act the monument pointedly omits any date for the Katyn massacre. The fact that the government chose to construct the new memorial at this time was presumably related to the general observance of the fortieth anniversary of then end of the war. The fact that there was no date on the monument and no public announcement of its presence was testament to the regime's sensitivity to the symbolism of Katyn for the Polish people. Whether the new memorial will serve its intended effect may be questioned. Soon after its erection an unknown visitor scrawled "1940-N.K.V.D. [the Soviet secret police]" in the dirt alongside the monument.[44]

In summarizing the American stance on Katyn, it is easy enough to conclude that President Roosevelt's attitude toward the issue was based on an unwarranted optimism about the potentiality of involving the Soviet Union in the construction of a stable, postwar order, given an American willingness to ignore evidence of Stalin's capacity for brutality. Such an analysis may be insensitive to what was after all in its own terms a laudable goal— to create a future world that would be better than the one that gave rise to the war in the first place. Still, it seems hard to ignore the force of the message sent by a British official to Winston Churchill's Cabinet and King George VI to the effect that "we have, in fact, perforce used the good name of England to cover up the massacre."[45] If this was true for Great Britain, it seems equally applicable to the "good name" of the United States. None of this means that this country was an accomplice to the Katyn crime, but it was hardly our finest hour either. After all, World War II was fought for a basically moral purpose: to rid the world of a barbarous creed. Perhaps the ultimate moral of the Katyn affair is that if one fights evil by ignoring still other evils, the strength of one's moral purpose is inevitably compromised.

NOTES

1. U. S., House of Representatives, Select Committee on the Katyn Forest Massacre, *The Katyn Forest Massacre. Hearings before the Select Committee to Conduct an Investigation of the Facts, Evidence, and Circumstances of the Katyn Forest Massacre.* 82nd Congress, 1st and 2nd Sessions, 1951-1952 (Washington: Government Printing Office, 1952), part 1, pp. 11-13; part 5, p. 140 (hereafter cited as *Hearings*).

2. Polish Cultural Foundation, *The Crime of Katyn: Facts and Documents* (New York: McGraw Hill, 1948), p. 113.

3. General Sikorski Historical Institute, *Documents on Polish-Soviet Relations 1939-1945* Volume I, 1938-1943 (London: Heinemann, 1961), p. 524.

4. *Ibid.*, p. 527.

5. *Ibid.*, p. 646.

6. *Hearings*, part 5, pp. 1402-1403.

7. *Ibid.*, part 7, p. 2131.

8. *Ibid.*, part 5, p. 1403.

9. *Ibid.*, part 2, p. 184.

10. Stephen A. Garrett, "The Economics and Politics of American Trade with Eastern Europe," *East European Quarterly* XV (Winter, 1981), p. 496.

11. Victor Mamatey, *The United States and East Central Europe* (Princeton: Princeton University Press, 1957), p. 150.

12. J. W. Oliver, "Louis Kossuth's Appeal to the Middle West—1852," *Mississippi Valley Historical Review* XIV (1928), pp. 481-495.

13. *The Letters of Theodore Roosevelt*, Volume VIII (Cambridge: Harvard University Press, 1954), p. 1364.

14. John Lewis Gaddis, *The United States and the Origins of the Cold War 1941-1947* (New York: Columbia University Press, 1972), p. 6.

15. *Ibid.*

16. Richard C. Lukas, *The Strange Allies* (Knoxville: University of Tennessee Press, 1978), p. 32.

17. *Hearings*, part 7, p. 2248.

18. *Ibid.*, p. 2204.

19. *Ibid.*, p. 2206.

20. United States, Department of State, *Foreign Relations of the United States: The British Commonwealth and Europe, The Far East, 1943.* Volume III (Washington: Government Printing Office, 1963), p. 395.

21. Herbert Feis, *Churchill, Roosevelt, Stalin* (Princeton: Princeton University Press, 1957), p. 194.

22. Roy Doublas, *From War to Cold War, 1942-1948* (New York: St. Martin's Press, 1981), p. 25.

23. *Hearings*, part 7, p. 2173.

24. Stanislaw Mikolajczyk, *The Rape of Poland* (New York: McGraw Hill, 1948), p. 59.

25. "Who Can Speak for Poland?" *The New Republic* 108 (May 10, 1943), p. 623.

26. *Hearings*, part 2, p. 51.

27. *Ibid.*, part 7, pp. 1885-1914.

28. *Ibid.*, p. 1938.

29. *Ibid.*, part 3, p. 499.

30. J. K. Zawodny, *Death in the Forest* (South Bend, Indiana: University of Notre Dame Press, 1962), p. 182.

31. *Hearings*, part 7, p. 2206.

32. *Ibid*.

33. *Ibid*, p. 2201.

34. *Ibid*., p. 2203.

35. *Ibid*.

36. *Ibid*., pp. 2005-2006.

37. *Ibid*., p. 2021.

38. *Ibid*., p. 2027.

39. B. H. Liddell Hart, *History of the Second World War* (New York: G. P. Putnam's Sons, 1970), p. 488.

40. *Hearings*, part 7, p. 1971.

41. *Ibid*., p. 1973.

42. "Memorandum for the President," 22 January 1952, Official File, Harry S. Truman Library (Independence, Missouri), "U.S. Shelves Katyn Issue," *New York Times*, June 18, 1953, p. 13.

43. Louis Fitzgibbon, *Unpitied and Unknown* (London: Bachman and Turner, 1975), p. 484.

44. "New Polish Monument Honors the Katyn Dead," *New York Times*, April 10, 1985, p. 7.

45. "Death in the Forest," *Time Magazine* (July 17, 1972), p. 31.

The Sino-American Alliance During World War II and the Lifting of the Chinese Exclusion Acts

Xiaohua Ma

Nearly sixty years ago, Henry R. Luce envisioned that the twentieth century was "America's first century as a dominant power in the world."[1] His famous vision of "The American Century" showed America's commitment to exert upon the whole world the full impact of American influence. At century's end, it seems appropriate to assess how the United States attempted to exert its influence, particularly to spread American-style freedom and democracy in its foreign policy and to evaluate its relations with East Asia, particularly with China over the last one hundred years. To begin thinking about America's engagement with China historically, World War II provided a special stage for an American image of an American-oriented China. Because of the war, the United States came to embrace a vision of a "strong" and "independent" China emerging in postwar Asia. How did this new vision emerge in the American imagination, and how did it affect America's East Asian policy?

Xiaohua Ma is Associate Professor of the Department of Humanities and Social Studies at Osaka University of Education in Osaka, Japan. Her research and teaching are in American foreign policy and ethnic studies. Her recent book, The Illusionary New Order in the Asian Pacific: The Conflicts of the Sino-American Alliance during World War II, *was published in Tokyo, January 2000.*

American Studies International, June 2000, Vol. XXXVIII, No. 2

This essay examines how the United States transformed its China policy to promote China as an "equal state" in international relations during World War II. In particular, it focuses on the repeal of racially discriminatory legislation against the Chinese in 1943. By examining the process of repeal, we can see that the abolition of the discriminatory laws against the Chinese not only marked a historic turning point in America's China policy in wartime, but also had a great impact on the transformation of America's East Asian policy in the postwar period.

Formation of Chinese Exclusion Policy

The first Asian immigrants to enter the United States were Chinese, lured to California by the Gold Rush of 1848. By 1850 there were over 20,000 Chinese immigrants in the United States, most of them in California. Railroad construction in the United States during the 1860s further accelerated the influx of Chinese laborers. There were 63,199 Chinese in the United States in 1870. Ten years later there were 105,465 Chinese in America, over ninety percent of who settled on the Pacific Coast.[2]

As the number of Chinese increased, however, Caucasian workers in California began to resent Chinese laborers. The Chinese were considered "culturally and racially inferior" and a threat to wage levels and working conditions. By the mid-1870s, the completion of the transcontinental railroad, the growth of the white labor force in the West, and the nationwide economic depression all encouraged white working men to turn against the Chinese. With the development of anti-Chinese sentiment in the Pacific states, especially in California, on May 6, 1882, the U.S. Congress enacted a bill prohibiting Chinese immigrants from entering the United States.[3]

The Chinese Exclusion Act of 1882 was the first racially restrictive immigration law in American history.[4] The emergence of this discriminatory legislation initiated a gradual process of immigration restriction based on race. The enactment of this legislation marked the end of the free immigration era in American history. This discriminatory law not only had long-term repercussions for America's relations with China, but also affected overall immigration policy and internal politics. On the other hand, it can also be considered as merely the first step in the growth of anti-Asiatic legislation. Following enactment of this law, Asian immigration became a constant target of American nativism and racism. Subsequently, the Immigration Act of 1924 stopped the flow of immigrants from Asia into the United States.

Emergence of the Sino-American Alliance

On December 7, 1941, Japan attacked on Pearl Harbor. That sudden attack led directly to a reversal of America's anti-Chinese immigration policy. The day after the attack, the United States together with China declared war on Japan, and the two countries became allies immediately. The special wartime alliance between China and the United States initiated a far-reaching transformation in America's East Asian policy, especially its China policy.

Upon hearing about the attack, Chiang Kai-shek immediately summoned the American Ambassador to Chongqing, Clarence Gauss, and proposed a military alliance of allied nations to fight against the Axis powers.[5] On December 13, Secretary of State Cordell Hull instructed Maxwell M. Hamilton, Chief of the Division of Far Eastern Affairs of the State Department, "to draw up a draft of a declaration to be made by the nations fighting the Axis, which would bind them together until victory and would commit them to the basic principles that we uphold."[6] On January 1, 1942, a Joint Declaration of the United Nations was issued, with China listed as the fourth signatory, following the United States, Great Britain, and the Soviet Union.[7] The inclusion of China as a major power in the Declaration demonstrated that China had become indispensable to America's war strategy.

From the outset of the war, however, the United States adopted a "Europe First Policy." This policy implied that the war in Asia was secondary in America's global strategy. Although the outbreak of the Pacific War altered American concerns and forced the United States to focus on the war in Asia, Washington's primary aim was to "keep China in the war" in order to tie up millions of Japanese troops until the ultimate Allied victory in Europe. As Stanley K. Hornbeck, Adviser to Secretary of State Cordell Hull, pointed out, when the United States decided to lend China 500 million dollars in January 1942, it was "the time for us to tie China into our war (which still is her war) as tight as possible."[8]

oIn order to achieve this goal, the United States aided China. Politically, one of the most important measures taken was to aid China's participation in international affairs, promoting China as a "Great Power" on the world stage. This strategy emerged in the spring of 1942. On May 2, 1942, President Roosevelt declared that "in the future an unconquerable China will play its proper role in maintaining peace and prosperity not only in Eastern Asia but in the whole world."[9] Soon after, in discussions with Soviet Foreign Minister V. M. Molotov in May – June 1942, Roosevelt emphasized the importance of postwar cooperation among the "four policemen," which included China, the United States, Great Britain, and the Soviet Union.[10] In December 1942, in a conversation with Owen Lattimore, former American special adviser to Chiang Kai-shek, Roosevelt stressed the role of China as a member of the "Big Four" after the war.[11] Moreover, the treaty concluded with China on January 11, 1943, to relinquish extraterritoriality, further demonstrated that the Unites States intended to give formal expression to China's "Great Power" status. This superficial alliance, however, did not alter the racially unequal relations that existed between the United States and China. The continuing existence of the Chinese Exclusion Acts was one example of this unaltered inequality. Thus, America's racially discriminatory immigration laws became a vital resource for Japan in its campaign of "Asia for the Asiatics."

After the attack on Pearl Harbor, Japan began to call the war "the Greater East Asia War" and declared that its war aim was to "liberate East Asia from Anglo-Saxon imperialists," and establish "the Greater East Asia Co-Prosperity Sphere," which was to be based on the principle of "racial equality and harmony."[12] In order to reinforce the propaganda effect, in February 1942, an article entitled "A New Step towards Emancipation of Asian Peoples" came out in *Toa Kaijou* [Emancipation of East Asia]. It insisted that the essence of "injustice and inequality" was rooted in American exploitation of the Asian peoples.[13]

Furthermore, with the guidance of the Japanese Army, *FRONT*, one of the most important wartime propaganda magazines, began publication in early 1942, condemning Western oppression in Asia and extolling "racial harmony" in "the Greater East Asia Co-Prosperity Sphere." Japanese propagandists claimed that equality slogans from the United States were "hypocritical" and that the essence of "so-called equality" was the "beast-like treatment or semistarvation pay to the Asiatics."[14] Later, in June 1942, a series of "Open Letters to Asian Peoples" came out in the *Asahi Shumbun*, in which exploitation and oppressions of Asian by the "Anglo-Saxon Powers" was strongly denounced.[15] "Asia must be one – in her aim, in her action and in her future," Japanese propagandists appealed to the Asian peoples; "when Asia becomes one in truth, a new order will be established throughout the world."[16]

MELTING UNDER THE RISING SUN

Figure 1 — A typical Japanese wartime cartoon to condemn Western imperialism in Asia (*The Times Weekly*, March 21, 1943).

American Studies International, June 2000, Vol. XXXVIII, No. 2

In summary, the Japanese propagandists ridiculed the Allied Powers in their newspapers and radio propaganda directed towards Asian peoples, insinuating that Asian peoples would never receive equal and impartial treatment from the Allied Powers. Japanese propagandists also utilized "psychological weaponry," the Chinese Exclusion Acts, to fight against Roosevelt's Four Freedoms, from which racial equality was excluded.

One of the most important reasons for the enactment of the Chinese Exclusion Act in 1882 had been American racism, or the sense of white superiority, which was firmly rooted in the ideology of social Darwinism and late nineteenth-century American nativism. This dominant ideology became the critical factor in the exclusion not only of the Chinese, but also for all Asian races. While explaining the universality of the Atlantic Charter in his address on Memorial Day, 1942, Under Secretary of State, Sumner Welles insisted that "the discrimination between peoples because of their race, creed or color must be abolished," for America was fighting a war to "assure the sovereign equality of peoples throughout the world as well as in the world of the Americas."[17]

Figure 2 — Cartoon published in Japanese Occupied China to denounce American discriminatory laws against the Chinese. Over 16,000 Chinese Americans served in U.S. military in World War II, however, the Chinese who were recruited to join the army began to fight against Roosevelt's Four Freedoms because of their hatred of the Chinese Exclusion Acts. (*Zhongshan Ribao*, December 24, 1942.)

Nevertheless, the racially discriminatory laws against Asians, particularly Chinese, still existed at that time in American legislation. Hereby Japanese propagandists found valuable ammunition for their appeals to other Asians and began to use this "weaponry" to fight against the Allied Powers, since China, America's first cross-racial ally, was not treated as equally as other Allied Powers in American domestic legislation. A typical Japanese propaganda attack, using Chinese exclusion as a weapon, is the following:

> At present the U.S. government has improved the treaties with China. You might think that the overseas Chinese in the U.S. have received good treatment due to the relations of allies. This sweet-worded but ugly-faced U.S. is doing these for the face of Chunking... But facts are contrary. For instance, the U.S. drafted innumerable single Chinese and put them in the army. Talking about singles, the Chinese in the U.S. had to leave their wives in China, because of the Immigration Laws, are classified as singles. Thus denying his wife in China. This is the attitude of the U.S. toward allied peoples who are fighting under the same common principle. Our Japan has never badly treated the Chinese that are in Japan and have never forced the Chinese into army. The difference between the inhuman nature of the Americans and the nature of our Japanese could be seen by facts.[18]

Japanese propaganda, such as this, directed at America's anti-Chinese laws, attempted to appeal to Asians by emphasizing the American racial legislation. In support of Japan's strategy, on June 24, 1943, an editorial entitled "America's Hypocritical and Ugly Face" was published in the *Zhonghua Ribao* [China Daily], a newspaper controlled by the Wan Jingwei Puppet regime. Its author condemned the evils of American democracy and insisted that "if the American government does not abolish the discriminatory laws against the Chinese, Asian peoples can never be treated equally." Finally it appealed to "all Asians to unite together to drive away American and British imperialists from Asia in order to establish a prosperous Asia for the Asiatics."[19]

But was the Japanese new ideal order of the "Greater East Asia Co-Prosperity" was itself based upon equality? In January 1941, the Japanese government unequivocally declared that the foundation for establishing the new order was based on the "Yamato people."[20] On January 16, 1942, Prime Minister Tojo Hideki reiterated the principle in the Imperial Diet that within the new order only the Japanese could be the "meishiu" (master) in "the Greater East Asia Co-Prosperity Sphere."[21]

UNCLE SAM: "OPEN DOOR FOR ME AND CLOSED DOOR FOR YOU"
American immigration policy is subtle in its hypocrisy.

Figure 3 — Japanese cartoon – "American immigration policy is subtle in its hypocrisy" (*The Times Weekly*, July 5, 1943.)

The Campaign to Repeal Chinese Exclusion

Japan's use of the Chinese exclusion to fight a propaganda war against the Allies embarrassed the United States, for China was its most populous ally. Having been battered by Japan's racial propaganda weapon, the United States took the initiative to eliminate this "unfortunate barrier" on the ideological battlefield. There were, however, political preconditions for this shift. Although the outbreak of the Pacific War in 1941 altered America's traditional attitudes towards China, a wholly sympathetic view of China and its people existed among the American public before the Pacific War broke out. This pro-China sentiment originated before Japan's attack at Pearl Harbor and could be traced to a deeper American sense of attachment to the Chinese. When Japan invaded China on July 7,

1937, Americans showed great sympathy for the Chinese. Public opinions polls during the Sino-Japanese War indicated overwhelming popular support for the Chinese. According to a Gallup Poll carried out in August 1937, 43% of Americans sympathized with the Chinese, and the favor rate increased to 74% in 1939.[22]

After the Pearl Harbor attack, American sympathy for the Chinese grew even stronger, for the Chinese were a people who had long been bravely resisting Japanese aggressors. Two days after the attack, an editorial appearing in the *New York Times* argued that if the United States cooperated with China, "a loyal ally with...inexhaustible manpower," it would have "the key to the strategy of the Pacific."[23] In April 1942, another editorial entitled "China's Splendid Fight" came out in the *New Republic*, in which the author insisted that China, "by virtue of her dogged struggle for independence" could help the United States "immeasurably in winning the war quickly."[24] Meanwhile Paul G. Hoffman, national chairman of United China Relief, called for the American public to give more aid to China. "This country needs China as much as China needs us in the conflict with Japan," he asserted, "investment in Chinese morale as a vital move will help us to win this war and win it quickly."[25] Thus, the heroic and continuous Chinese struggle against Japanese aggression won high praise from the American public. The American press and other media fostered the impression that the Chinese under the leadership of Chiang Kai-shek and his American-educated wife Soong Mayling were fighting valiantly against Japanese aggression. Subsequently U.S. pro-China sentiment culminated in a powerful wartime wave stimulated by Mme. Chiang's visit to the United States in 1943.

Mme. Chiang arrived in the United States on November 27, 1942, supposedly for medical treatment, but stayed on until May 1943. To represent her husband and Nationalist China, she made her visit into a national campaign tour. Early in February 1943, Mme. Chiang visited the White House as the guest of Eleanor and Franklin D. Roosevelt and was invited to address both houses of Congress on February 18, 1943. During her address, she affirmed Chinese-American solidarity and pleaded for increased military aid from the United States. The speech was a triumph. The senators and representatives were "captivated and amazed" by this "graceful, charming and intelligent" Chinese First Lady. Mme. Chiang's address was rated as "one of the most impressive and effective speeches" ever made in Congress.[26] While showing China's strong desire for justice and freedom in her address, Mme. Chiang expressed Chinese determination to cooperate with the United States to construct a peaceful and democratic world, which "must be based on justice, coexistence, cooperation, and mutual respect."[27]

Figure 4 — American Image of Chinese in wartime. This poster was published by the U.S. Office of War Information in 1942 (Franklin D. Roosevelt Library).

Throughout the spring of 1943, Mme. Chiang traveled around the United States, from Washington D.C. to New York to Boston to Chicago to San Francisco to Los Angeles, pumping up American concerns for Nationalist China at every stop and arousing American enthusiasm for China. Wherever she traveled, Mme. Chiang tried every effort to arouse the American public for more military aid to

China. In the American press and media, for example, Henry Luce's *Time* and *Life*, Mme. Chiang was regarded as not only "the voice of Free China," but also as "the voice of Asia." Meanwhile, her husband, Chiang Kai-shek, was depicted as a symbol of building a "strong" and "democratic" China, which would remain America's closest Asian ally. Luce personally figured Chiang Kai-shek as "the greatest soldier in Asia, the greatest statement in Asia, America's best friend."[28] As an editorial in the *Washington Post* pointed out, "in American eyes Free China has become a great power with the title to determine the next world polity gained from its outstanding services in the extinction of world tyranny."[29] However, how could China become a "Great Power" while Chinese immigrants were still excluded by American legislation?

After·the United States entered the war, legal discrimination against the Chinese was brought to the forefront of American public awareness. In February 1942, Charles N. Spinks, a specialist on East Asian relations, published an article, "Repeal Chinese Exclusion" in *Asia and the Americas*. He pointed out that the United States was now fighting side by side with China, one of its most important allies, to destroy fascism and to build a new world order based on the fundamental principles of freedom, justice and equality for mankind. Nevertheless, he argued the United States was not treating "the Chinese people, our allies, with the justice and equality they deserve."[30]

The outbreak of the Pacific War altered America's attitudes towards the Chinese. Moreover, Mme. Chiang's national tour around America in early 1943 demonstrated that China shared the principles of democracy with the United States. Roosevelt himself considered China as "one of the great democracies of the world."[31] In the meantime, equality for all, which was one of the oldest American ideals, now became a new symbol of American democracy and freedom, brought forth again in the process of fighting against fascist aggression and winning the war. Pearl S. Buck, America's first woman Nobel-Prize winner, who spent half of her life in China and was known as the most influential Westerner to write about China since Marco Polo, quickly emerged as one of the most tenacious wartime opponents of racial discrimination. She used every occasion to press her demands for racial equality.

In February 1942, for example, speaking at a literary luncheon, Buck surprised the 1,700 people gathered at the Astor Hotel in New York. "The Japanese weapon of racial propaganda in Asia is begin-

ning to show signs of effectiveness," she told her audience, "prejudice is the most vulnerable term in our American democracy."[32] She
indicated in her address that victory in the war demanded the cooperation of peoples regardless of race, color or nation. If Americans
did not abandon "white supremacy," the United States would lose
the war. "We cannot win this war, " she asserted, "without convincing our colored allies – who are most of our allies – that we are not
fighting for ourselves as continuing superior over colored peoples."[33]

Figure 5 — Poster used for American China Aid Campaign in 1942
(Franklin D. Roosevelt Library).

In sum, in a variety of ways, in books, in magazines, in speeches and on the radio, Buck concluded bluntly that discrimination against the Chinese in the United States must "come to an end," because so long as it endured, "we are fighting on the wrong side on the war. We belong with Hitler."[34] Pearl Buck continued her crusade for total freedom and equality for all peoples throughout the war. She and her second husband, Richard J. Walsh, who was her publisher and editor of *Asia and the Americas*, became leading figures in the movement to abolish Chinese exclusion. On November 10, 1942, Richard Walsh made a speech at the Town Hall Round Table of New York City, urging that the United States repeal the Chinese Exclusion Acts, place Chinese immigration on a quota basis, and makes them eligible for American citizenship.[35] Under their leadership, a national campaign to repeal the Chinese Exclusion Acts was begun.

Meanwhile, the national tour of Mme. Chiang had aroused a wave of enthusiasm and reinforced American good feeling toward China. On February 17, 1943, when Mme. Chiang visited Capital Hill, Congressman Martin J. Kennedy (Democrat, New York) seized "the auspicious occasion" to introduce a bill to grant the Chinese rights to entry into the United States and rights of citizenship.[36] Kennedy's was the first bill calling for a repeal of the Chinese Exclusion Acts since they were enacted in Congress in 1882. Meanwhile, he sent a letter to Mme. Chiang on the same day. "A people who have shared with us the common danger, and will share with us the eventual victory," he wrote, "a people which have earned our friendship, our gratitude, and our respect, have by the same token surely earned our franchise."[37] Subsequently, several bills for repeal of the Chinese Exclusion Acts were introduced in Congress in addition to Kennedy's: Warren G. Magnuson's on March 26, and Samuel Dickstein's on April 4.

Under this circumstance, "The Citizens Committee to Repeal Chinese Exclusion and Place Immigration on A Quota Basis" was formed in New York City on May 25, 1943 by a group of notable intellectuals, including Pearl Buck, Richard Walsh, socialist Bruno Lusker and Henry Luce, founder of *Time, Life* and *Fortune*. These pro-China intellectuals served as the chief spokespersons in the repeal campaign. Over 250 persons, representing more than 40 states, joined the Citizens Committee, and hundreds more worked in close cooperation with the members and other organizations. Richard

Walsh, chairman of the Citizens Committee, appealed to the members in May, "Last year we celebrated Double Ten [October 10] by announcing the end of extraterritoriality. This year let Double Ten resound the news that we have repealed the exclusion laws." In the meantime, the Citizens Committee published a pamphlet – *Our Chinese War* – to arouse public interest. Over 20,000 copies were distributed to libraries, universities, religious, social and labor organizations, clubs and individuals.[38] The strategy of the Citizens Committee was to emphasize the importance of America's good relations with China and to lobby Congress to repeal the Chinese Exclusion Acts on October 10, China's Independence Day.[39]

Under this strategy, the press, radio and other media channels for repeal were utilized throughout the whole country. Commentators, Round Tables in New York, convention addresses, and local and national radio stations carried many types of programs on behalf of repeal. Congressman Walter H. Judd, a former medical missionary in China for over 12 years, served as one of the most active and important spokespersons for the repeal campaign. On September 2, 1943, Judd appealed on Town Meeting of Air, "we must do two things," he said, "We must get more material help to China – more guns, planes, medicines, munitions – and we must get more political help, more to justify and strengthen China's confidence in us." He insisted "the most dramatic and helpful thing imaginable would be for us to put the Chinese on the same quota basis as our other Allies, and thereby begin treating them as equals now."[40] The pro-China intellectuals and missionaries began to put pressure on Congress for the repeal of the Chinese Exclusion Acts. Finally, in May 1943 the House Committee on Immigration and Naturalization decided to hold public hearings to debate the repeal of the Chinese Exclusion Acts.[41]

In May-June of 1943, the House Committee summoned fifty-one witnesses during six hearings. The repeal campaign provoked a strong demonstration of American nativism. The traditional opposition forces, primarily labor, veterans' organizations, West Coast interests, and "patriotic" societies, took a vigorous stand against Chinese immigration. For example, representatives of the American Coalition, an association representing approximately one hundred "patriotic" societies, expressed a strong, racially motivated, dislike of the Chinese, calling them, for example, "morally the most debased people on the face of the earth."[42] In addition, representatives of the American Federation of Labor and the Veterans of Foreign Wars strongly opposed a "radical change of immigration laws" and affirmed their "support of rigidly restricted immigration" from "an economical standpoint."[43] However, influential groups such as the Citizens Committee and missionary organizations promoted the pro-repeal force. Pearl Buck and Richard Walsh testified before the House Committee on May 20, and insisted that the exclusion acts against the Chinese must be repealed "as a war measure," and that "China must be put on a quota basis, on an equality with other nations."[44] Mansfield Freeman, president of United States Life Insurance Company, who had lived in China for over twenty years, favored repeal, for "trade with China and cooperation with her four hundred million people are going to be very important factors in America's post-war prosperity." He also stressed that "there is no nation which has such potential opportunities in the Far East for the United States."[45] Congressman Judd testified before the House Committee, and asserted that "the Pacific would be pacific if America has on that side a strong, independent, democratic, friendly China." While showing Chinese strong faith to the United States, he concluded that "there never will be a war between the white and colored races, if only we keep the largest and strongest of them, the Chinese, with us."[46]

In all, forty-two witnesses testified before the Immigration and Naturalization Committee in favor of repealing the Chinese Exclusion Acts. They advocated a three-point program: the repeal of the Chinese Exclusion Acts, the establishment of a quota for Chinese immigrants, and the eligibility of Chinese immigrants for American citizenship. The argument with the widest appeal and greatest weight was that the repeal would help the United States to win the war, and win it quickly. Admiral H. E. Yarnell, speaking from the perspective of America's military strategy, claimed that it would be "the most effective method…in the conduct of the war and in the post-war settlement" to "put China as an equal in every respect with the other three Allied Nations."[47] Thus, the repeal of the Chinese Exclusion Acts became a new means for the United States to reform its East Asian policy, towards China in particular.

America's China's policy revealed this impulse in two ways. First, it reflected wartime necessities. Second, it acknowledged the need to address postwar possibilities. When Congressman Warren Magnuson introduced the bill to repeal the Chinese Exclusion Acts in Congress in October 1943, he stressed that the repeal of the anti-Chinese discriminatory laws went far beyond America's wartime needs:

> This bill goes far above and beyond its present war necessity. If any one position of our foreign policy should be clear in the post-war world it should be this, that we need in the Orient, democracy needs in the Orient, a strong Allied nation, practicing the same principles of democracy that we intend to keep. Without such a strong nation it does not take much intelligence to visualize what might come out of the great cauldron mass of millions of Asiatic peoples. Without the clear leadership of such a democratic Asiatic nation as China, with our help, alliances could form and other Japanese types of destructive empire could arise that would make the present island empire look like a dwarf.[48]

Under-Secretary of State Edward R. Stettinius held the same opinion and stressed that the repeal of the anti-Chinese laws should be undertaken "in recognition of China's place among the United Nations fighting for democracy and her great future in a democratic world."[49]

What was China's "great future in a democratic world"? For the United States, the most important question had to do with postwar politics. The stabilization of East Asia would require a strong counterweight to the Soviet Union. President Roosevelt outlined this position during British Foreign Minister Anthony Eden's visit to the White House in the fall of 1942. Talking about the role China would play in international politics after the war, Roosevelt told Eden that he believed that "in any serious conflict of policy with Russia, [China] would undoubtedly line up on our side."[50] Therefore, in order to be able to take up this position, China must not only emerge from the war as a "strong" nation with "Great Power" status, but also must also be oriented toward the Western powers and encouraged to practice "the same principles of democracy" as the United States.

On the other hand, China's cooperation was indispensable for the United States in helping to weaken British forces in postwar Asia. This strategy was expressed clearly in a conversation between U.S. General Joseph Stilwell, the Allied Military Commander in China, and Chiang Kai-shek in the winter of 1943. General Stilwell told Chiang that "the United States was against any form of imperialism, including British," and believed in "a free, strong, democratic China predominant in Asia" after the war.[51] As the following table indicates, public polls carried out by the Office of War Information in 1942 showed that the American public considered the British and Russians, and to a lesser degree the Chinese, as important allies. This means that cooperation with China was regarded as essential for the prosecution of the war and desirable for the solution of postwar problems. Thus, to the United States, if Japan were demilitarized, the emergence of a new China with "Great Power" status would be a prerequisite for the stable and peaceful Asia needed in America's global strategy.

Table Which country can be depended upon to cooperate with the US after the war?

1942	Russia	England	China
February	38%	76%	80%
May	45%	77%	83%
July	43%	68%	85%
August	51%	72%	86%

Office of War Information, "Report from the Nation, December 7, 1941-December 7, 1942," President Secretary's File, Box 156, Franklin D. Roosevelt Papers, Franklin D. Roosevelt Library.

What was China's response to the American vision of this world order in East Asia? During his visit to Chongqing in October 1942, Wendell L. Willkie, Roosevelt's Special Envoy, told Chiang Kai-shek that postwar cooperation between the two nations was indispensable to weaken the domination of British imperialism.[52] In response, Chiang explicitly declared China's commitment to cooperation with the United States in the postwar world.[53] Furthermore, in her visit to the United States in early 1943, Mme. Chiang declared unequivocally in conversations with President Roosevelt's Special Advisor, Harry Hopkins, that China would give strong backing to the United

States in international affairs.[54] Later, this commitment to "support America's proposals once a divergence of views among the United States, Britain, and the Soviet Union occurs," became one of the most important principles for Nationalist China's role in postwar international politics.[55] Thus, "practicing the same principles of democracy" and maintaining "pro-Americanism" in post war China was certainly an indispensable American diplomatic and political objective.

Undoubtedly, the support of President Franklin D. Roosevelt was a decisive element in the success of the repeal movement. When general debate about repeal opened in the House on October 11, some Congressmen expressed strong opposition to repealing the Chinese Exclusion Acts. For example, William P. Elmer from Missouri urged Congress to "tighten instead of loosening our immigration laws" in order to "keep America for Americans."[56] Edward O. McCowen of Ohio insisted that "the immigration laws should be amended to further restrict all present quotas and not to increase them."[57] However, Samuel Dickstein, Chairman of the House Committee of Immigration and Naturalization, favored repeal, for he thought that the repeal would be "not only as a simple matter of justice, but as a recognition of the heroic resistance of China against our common enemy."[58] In the midst of this heated debate, President Roosevelt immediately sent a special message in support of repeal. He appealed to Congress to "take the offensive in this propaganda war and repeal the laws that insult our only ally on the mainland of Asia."[59] Ten days later the House passed the Magnuson Bill. A month later the Senate gave its approval. On December 17, President Roosevelt signed the bill repealing the Chinese Exclusion, which had played an influential role in American history for more than sixty years.

Conclusion

The outbreak of the Pacific War threw the spotlight on the Chinese Exclusion Acts and cleared the path for a new direction in Asian American history. To some extent, the repeal of the Chinese Exclusion Acts did give the Chinese technical equality, in granting them a symbolic quota per annum and allowing Chinese immigrants to acquire American citizenship. From this point of view, the repeal of the anti-Chinese immigration laws marked a turning point in American history, since they codified, for the first time, the idea that Chinese immigrants were "assimilable" into American society, despite the fact that the quota granted to them was at first only symbolic. This means that World War II marked a decisive turning point in the Asian American experiences and represented a beginning and crossing in the making of multicultural America.

Even more important than the changes in law were the changes of American ideology. The United States was still patently a white man's country in wartime; however, the notion was beginning to prevail that equal opportunity ought to be given at least lip service. Japanese wartime racial propaganda, which denounced American racism, forced Americans to look critically at the racism within their own society. In fighting a "propaganda war," Americans realized that they must stand before the whole world in support of racial tolerance and equality.

On the other hand, before the war, as we have seen, the Chinese American community was largely shut out of the mainstream of American life because of the discriminatory laws. Changes in wartime attitudes towards the Chinese, however, accompanied a steady improvement of the image and reputation of Chinese Americans. During World War II, the changes of the American image of Chinese Americans had been almost all positive. Also Chinese Americans had contributed significantly to the war effort. According to service data, almost 16,000 Chinese Americans served in the U.S. military between 1940 and 1946. About 1,600 even served in the U.S. Navy, some in commission ranks.[60] The Chinese American "success" in the war fighting for democracy and freedom won high praise from the American society and enabled them to be "the Model Minority" in postwar era. Thus, the war all combined to transform American attitudes from what Harold R. Isaacs has called the "Age of Contempt" into the "Age of Admiration."[61]

Nevertheless, the repeal itself did not place Chinese on full quota parity with European countries eligible for immigration and citizenship. In fact, traditional nativism endured and played a significant role in the repeal debate. According to a Gallup Poll carried out in November 1943, the month after the House passed the repealing bill, the approval/disapproval rate was quite close, forty-two to forty.[62] Undoubtedly, the continuance of strong nativist sentiment during wartime impeded the development of the repeal campaign.

American Studies International. June 2000. Vol. XXXVIII. No. 2

219

The strategic significance of the repeal, however, went far beyond the repeal itself. In 1943, China's precarious military and political situation was reinforced, while the political and military necessities made psychological gestures appear more significant than ever before. Meantime, the wartime enthusiasm for China, dramatized by Mme. Chiang's national tour, made it difficult to resist efforts to aid China. Furthermore, China's postwar cooperation with the United States in America's global strategy became increasingly indispensable. Thus, the repeal itself became an essential prerequisite for America's policy of establishing China as a "Great Power," for the United States sought to keep an "equal" partner in postwar Asia so that the American vision of a "strong," "democratic" and American-oriented China could emerge in the postwar world. This implies that the abolition of the Chinese Exclusion Acts was not only the result of America's wartime strategy, but also a reflection of its long-term goals for East Asian policy in the postwar era.

Furthermore, it was on the basis of these same political and military goals that other anti-Asian discriminatory acts, such as those targeting Indians and Filipinos, were subsequently renounced. Finally, the U.S. Congress enacted the McCarran-Walter Immigration Act in 1952, which made other Asians including the Japanese eligible for immigration and citizenship. However, as was the case in the repeal of Chinese exclusion, these repeals did not alter the racially discriminatory treatment of Asian people. It would take another decade before they would achieve full equality in American legislation. After World War II, especially as a result of the emergence of the Civil Rights Movement in the 1960s, another campaign to repeal the nativist Immigration Law of 1924 was launched. This movement not only led to the enactment of a new immigration law in 1965, which placed Asian peoples on a full quota parity with European peoples eligible for immigration and citizenship, but also became a milestone in American history. It marked the beginning of a new era of racial tolerance and coming of a new century of coexistence of multiculturalism.

Chinese American experience in 1943 is merely one example of how World War II influenced almost every aspect of American foreign policy. During this period American relations with China, which had enjoyed a kind of "honeymoon," later became terribly complicated. The news was filled with the ignominious defeats of Chiang Kai-shek's Nationalist armies, the developments of "two Chinas," and the "Who lost China?" debate in American politics in the 1950s. There were now, in American eyes at least, two Chinas: Mao Tse-tung's Communist China, pagan and threatening; and Chiang Kai-shek's capitalist China (Taiwan), free and democratic. America's special relations with Taiwan have continuously been a main barrier between the two countries. Even today periodic improvements in overall Sino-American relations continued to be overshadowed by America's imaginations and experiences during World War II. Despite these problems, the Clinton Administration has continued to pursue a policy of engagement with China. As a U.S. State Department spokesman reiterated in a May 1999 press statement, apologizing for the NATO bombing of the Chinese Embassy in Belgrade, the United States continues to strive to "build a constructive strategic partnership for the 21st century" with China. To be sure, how to build this "constructive strategic partnership" between China and the United States for the 21st century will not only be an important issue between the two countries, but also will arouse great concern for the whole world.

---

*   *The paper on which this article is based is the result of the encouragement and help of Dr. Wong Sin Kiong of the Department of Chinese at the National University of Singapore. The author is also grateful for the help of the staff and financial support from the Franklin D. Roosevelt Library.*

1 "The American Century." *Life*, February 17, 1941.

2 Mary R. Coolidge. *Chinese Immigration* (New York, 1909), p. 498.

3 For the formation of the Chinese Exclusion Acts, see Elmer C. Sandmeyer, *The Anti-Chinese . Movement in California* (University of Illinois Press, 1973), and Alexander Saxton, *The Indispensable Enemy: Labor and the Anti-Chinese Movement in California* (University of California Press, 1971).

4 U.S. Congress renewed the Chinese Exclusion Act of 1882 in 1892 and enacted some new anti-Chinese immigration laws later. There had been fourteen discriminatory laws against the Chinese in American immigration legislation until 1904. Generally they were called the Chinese Exclusion Acts.

5 Zhang Yu-fa, ed., *Zhongguo xiandaishi lunji* [Selected Works on Modern Chinese History] vol.9, (Taibei, 1982), p. 383.

6 U.S. Department of State, *Papers Relating to the Foreign Relations of the United States*, 1942 (Britain), p.1. (Hereafter cited as *FRUS*).

7 U.S. Department of State, *Bulletin*, vol.6, January 3, 1942.

8 *FRUS*, 1942 (China), p. 443.

9 U.S. Department of State, *Bulletin*, May 2, 1942, p. 381.

10 Iriye Akira, *Power and Culture: The Japanese-American War, 1941-1945* (Harvard University

Press. 1981), pp. 53-54.

11 *FRUS*, 1942 (China), p. 186.

12 *Asahi Shimbun*, December 13, 1941.

13 *Toa Kaihou* [Emancipation of East Asia]. February 1942, p. 62.

14 *FRONT*, vol.5-6, 1943.

15 "Open Letters to Asian Peoples." *Asahi Shimbun*, June 24-30, 1942.

16 *FRONT*, vol.5-6, 1943.

17 "The War." Memorial Day Address by the Under Secretary of State (Sumner Welles, addressed at the Arlington National Amphitheater, May 30, 1942. State Department. *Bulletin*, May 30, 1942, p. 488.

18 Committee on Immigration and Naturalization. House of Representatives, 78th Congress, *Samples of Japanese-Controlled Radio Comments on America's Exclusion Act* (confidential print), 1943, p. 2. National Archives, Washington D.C.

19 *Zhonghua Ribao* [China Daily], June 24, 1943.

20 *Asahi Shimbun*, January 28, 1941.

21 Foreign Ministry of Japan, ed., *Nippon gaiko bunsho narabini shuyo bunsho* [Main Documents on the Foreign Relations of Japan] (Tokyo, 1969), pp. 576-578.

22 Harold R. Isaacs, *Images of Asia: American Views of China and India* (New York, 1962), p. 173.

23 *The New York Times*, December 9, 1941.

24 *The New Republic*, April 40, 1942, p. 544.

25 *The New York Times*, April 23, 1942

26 U.S. Congress, *Congressional Record*, 78th Congress, 1st Session, vol. 89, part 9, p. 2124.

27 *Ibid*.

28 T. Christopher Jeperson, *American Image of China, 1931-1949* (Stanford University Press, 1996), p. 37.

29 *Washington Post*, February 18, 1943.

30 Charles Nelson Spinks, "Repeal Chinese Exclusion." *Asia and the Americas*, February 1942, p. 92.

31 U.S. Department of State. *Bulletin*, February 18, 1943, p. 163.

32 Pearl S. Buck, "Tinder for Tomorrow," delivered at the Book & Author Luncheon, Astor Hotel. New York, February 10, 1942, reprinted in *Asia*, March 1942, pp. 153-155.

33 *Ibid*.

34 Pearl S. Buck, "Freedom For All." *Asia*, May 1942, p.324-326. For detail of Pearl S. Buck's crusade in wartime for freedom and equality, see Pearl S. Buck, *American Unity and Asia* (New York, 1942.) and *What America Means to Me* (New York, 1943).

35 Richard J. Walsh, "Our Great Wall against the Chinese." *The New Republic*, November 23, 1942, pp. 671-672.

36 U.S. Congress, *Congressional Record*, 78th Congress, 1st Session, vol.89, part 9, p. 634.

37 *Ibid*., p. 1136.

38 Report to Members, September 20, 1943. File of the Citizens Committee to Repeal Chinese Exclusion and Place Immigration on A Quota Basis. Tamiment Institute Library, New York University.

39 Report to Members, August 15, 1943, *ibid*.

40 Walter H. Judd, "Should we repeal the Chinese Exclusion laws now?" addressed at Town Meeting of the Air, September 2, 1943. Papers of Walter H. Judd, Hoover Institution. Stanford University.

41 Memorandum, May 18, 1943. Papers of Minutes Committee on Immigration and Naturalization. House of Representatives, U.S. Congress, National Archives, Washington, D.C.

42 U.S. House of Representatives. *Hearings before the Committee on Immigration and Naturalization, Repeal of the Chinese Exclusion Acts*, 78th Congress, 1st Session, May and June, 1943, p. 109.

43 *Ibid*., pp. 177-178.

44 *Ibid*., pp. 68-86.

45 *Ibid*., pp. 227-233.

46 *Ibid*., pp. 143-167.

47 *Ibid*., pp. 248-249.

48 U.S. Congress, *Congressional Record*, 78th Congress, 1st Session, vol.89, part 9, p. 4427.

49 The Under Secretary (Edward R. Stettinius) to the Speaker of the House of Representatives (Sam Rayburn), October 27, 1943, *FRUS,* 1943 (China), pp. 783-784.

50 Robert Dallek, *Franklin D. Roosevelt and American Foreign Policy, 1932-1945* (New York, 1979), p. 390.

51 Joseph W. Stilwell, *The Stilwell Papers* (New York, 1948), p. 240.

52 Memorandum of Conversation between Chiang Kai-shek and Wendell L. Willkie, October 5, 1942, Qing Xiao-yi, ed., *Zhonghuaminguo zhongyao shiliao chubian: Duiri kanzhan shiqi* [The Important Historical Documents of the Republic of China: During the Period of the Anti-Japanese War] part 3, vol.1 (Taiwan, 1981), p. 762. (Hereafter cited as *ZZSC*).

53 *Ibid.*

54 Robert E. Sherwood, *Roosevelt and Hopkins: An Intimate History* (New York, 1948), p. 706.

55 Qing Xiao-yi, ed., *ZZSC*, part 3, vol.3, p. 832.

56 U.S. Congress, *Congressional Record,* 78th Congress, 1st session, vol.89, part 6, p. 8595.

57 *Ibid.,* p. 8601.

58 *Ibid.,* vol.89, part 11, p. 3410.

59 Franklin D. Roosevelt, Message to Congress, October 11, 1943, National Archives, Washington, D.C.

60 Roger Daniels, *Asian America: Chinese and Japanese in the United States since 1850* (University of Washington Press, 1988), pp. 299-300.

61 Harold R. Isaacs, *Scratches on Our Minds: American Images of China and India* (New York, 1958), p. 71.

62 *The New York Times,* November 21, 1943.

America, Britain, and Palestine:
The Anglo-American Committee of Inquiry
and the Displaced Persons, 1945–46

LEONARD DINNERSTEIN

The Anglo-American Committee of Inquiry proved the last major attempt by the British government to keep its mandate in Palestine and satisfy both Arabs and Jews in the Holy Land. It was also the first time that the British managed to involve the American government in a formal examination of how many Jews should be allowed into Palestine. The establishment of the committee by both countries emerged as an immediate victory for British diplomacy. However, because the Americans involved themselves, the British ultimately would have to contend with a committee report somewhat responsive to the demands of the American Jewish population. And once the report became public, both governments would have to agree to implement, or ignore, the recommendations in order to avoid international repercussions. The final report of the Anglo-American Committee of Inquiry, however, proved impossible for the British government to accept, and for the Americans to reject, as written. As a result, the American government steadily withdrew support for the British position in Palestine, and less than a year after the committee completed its work the British government went to the United Nations and announced it could no longer attempt to find a solution to the Palestinian quagmire.

The Anglo-American Committee of Inquiry originated as a result of Earl G. Harrison's devastating report[1] on the conditions in the European displaced persons (DPs) camps. Harrison, dean of the University of Pennsylvania Law School and former U.S. Commissioner of Immigration, had been dispatched by President Harry S Truman in June 1945 to investigate the treatment of the DPs, especially the Jews. His three-week tour resulted in a shocking document. Harrison found the DPs ill-fed, ill-housed, ill-clad, idle, spiritless, dejected, and kept in camps surrounded by armed guards and barbed wire. He noted as well, in his report to the president, that as

matters now stand, we appear to be treating the Jews as the Nazis

---

[1] *New York Times,* 30 September 1945, pp. 1, 38.

treated them except that we do not exterminate them. They are in concentration camps in large numbers under our military guard instead of S.S. troops. One is led to wonder whether the German people, seeing this, are not supposing that we are following or at least condoning Nazi policy.[2]

That the Americans and British, who supposedly fought the war against Germany to exterminate Naziism, should perpetuate it in the displaced persons camps that housed the survivors, seemed shocking. Truman, beset with more problems than he knew how to handle, immediately ordered his commanding general in Europe, Dwight D. Eisenhower, to eradicate the most inhumane aspects of camp life, and then wrote to Prime Minister Clement Attlee on 31 August 1945, urging the British to open the gates of Palestine for Jewish entry.[3]

Both the Americans and the British had failed to exert themselves on behalf of the Jewish refugees from German-dominated Europe before and during the war, and Harrison's findings confirmed the fact that neither nation intended to do much to help the survivors. Antisemitism in the United States peaked during the thirties and forties, and rigid immigration restrictions, combined with prejudicial interpretations of the existing laws by State Department officials, ensured that even those quotas that did exist went unfilled before and during World War II. President Franklin D. Roosevelt had consulted with congressional leaders in 1942 about the possibilities of bringing more refugees to the United States. House Speaker Sam Rayburn had assured him that there would be strong opposition to that idea. The British government also could have helped save Jewish lives during World War II, but as Bernard Wasserstein has revealed in *Britain and the Jews of Europe, 1939–1945*, they preferred them dead in Europe to alive in Palestine.[4]

The complexities involved in opening the doors of Palestine to the Jewish DPs escaped Truman, but not Attlee. Therefore, when Truman's 31 August letter reached the prime minister, he did not respond immediately. Aside from the numerous domestic dilemmas that had to be handled more quickly, foreign policy concerns and the unexpected end of the war with Japan also made demands upon his time. The Labour party had not anticipated such a smashing victory as it had won in the polls in July 1945, and its leaders assumed responsibility for government without much thought having been given to major areas of British concern, including the

---

[2] Ibid., p. 38.

[3] Ibid.; Harry S Truman to Clement Attlee, 31 August 1945, Public Record Office, Prime Minister's Office Records 8/89, Kew, England (hereafter cited as PRO, PREM, followed by file number).

[4] Philip J. Baram, *The Department of State in the Middle East, 1919–1945* (Philadelphia, 1978), p. 54; Robert Dallek, *Franklin D. Roosevelt and American Foreign Policy, 1932–1942* (New York, 1979), p. 446; Bernard Wasserstein, *Britain and the Jews of Europe, 1939–1945* (New York, 1979).

Middle East. Palestine would prove almost immediately to be one of the thorniest issues of contention.

Between 1917, when British Foreign Secretary Arthur Balfour issued his famous declaration indicating that "His Majesty's Government [HMG] view[s] with favor the establishment of Palestine of a national home for the Jewish people, until May 1945, the Labour party had reaffirmed its support for a Jewish national home eleven times.[5] In September 1945, however, HMG stood by the White Paper edict of 1939 that limited Jewish land purchases in, and entry into, the Holy Land. The British government had issued the document in the hope of buying Arab goodwill, stopping pro-Axis sympathy in the Middle East, and maintaining its pipeline to Arabian oil and imperial possessions.[6] Unfortunately for the Jews, the issuance of the White Paper coincided with the outbreak of World War II and Hitler's policy of Jewish extermination. Despite many pleas during World War II, made by those anxious to save Jewish lives, the British War Cabinet made no effort to allow more Jews into Palestine. In May 1945, at the Labour party conference, Hugh Dalton reaffirmed the party's strong opposition to the existing policy: "It is morally wrong and politically indefensible to impose obstacles to the entry into Palestine now of any Jews who desire to go there."[7] No Labour party spokesman challenged Dalton's remarks.

The Labour victory in July raised Zionist hopes and President Truman's letter to Attlee, a few weeks later, forced the new cabinet to make some response. Attlee and his foreign minister, Ernest Bevin, retained most of the senior civil servants in the Foreign Office who had advised Churchill's war government and conservative cabinets before that. These men were pro-Arab and advised against altering established policies because of Britain's dependence upon Middle Eastern oil, its need to control the Suez Canal as a route to far-flung imperial possessions in Asia, and fear of Russian encroachment into the area should HMG falter or arouse Arab animosities.[8] Attlee had been prime minister for less than a week, in fact, when he received a memorandum from the Foreign Office advising him that "the existence of the Jewish State [in Palestine] would provide a source of conflict which would inevitably continue to have a deplorable effect on Anglo-Arab relations." The note concluded with three points: (1) that there was "general agreement that His Majesty's Government have vital strategic interests in the Near and Middle East," (2) "that the preservation of these interests depends largely on the good will of Arab peoples . . . ," and (3) "there is general agreement that it is

---

[5] Richard Crossman, *Palestine Mission* (New York, 1947), pp. 52–53.

[6] Nadav Safran, *The United States and Israel* (Cambridge, MA, 1963), p. 31.

[7] Crossman, *Palestine Mission,* p. 1186.

[8] Safran, *United States and Israel,* p. 31; Crossman, *Palestine Mission,* pp. 50, 54–55, 113; John Snetsinger, *Truman, The Jewish Vote and the Creation of Israel* (Stanford, 1974), p. 45.

desirable to maintain the closest possible cooperation with the United States in the Near and Middle East."[9]

This last statement was particularly significant. When Truman's 31 August letter arrived, Attlee saw it as an opportunity to involve the American government in British strategy without, at first, altering any of HMG's positions. On 16 September 1945 the prime minister responded to Truman cautiously, suggesting two North African camps as places that might be used to alleviate the overcrowding in the European DP centers and then advised the president that "we have the matter under urgent examination. . . . I shall be very happy to let you know as soon as I can what our intentions are in this matter."[10]

The British Cabinet discussed the Palestine issue at three or four meetings in the late summer and fall and the members agreed on several issues. "The admission of 100,000 Jews to Palestine," everyone seemed to feel, "while it would lead to an explosion in the Middle East, would not solve the problems of the Jews of Europe." Nevertheless since so many Jews were still living "in conditions of great hardship," no announcement of HMG could afford to ignore that fact. The foreign secretary stressed, however, that "it was essential to broaden the basis of British influence in the Middle East by developing an economic and social policy which would make for prosperity and contentment in the area as a whole."[11]

For several reasons it seemed unlikely that the British would alter their policies significantly. They feared that if they antagonized the Arabs these people might seek alliances with the Russians, who coveted a greater influence in world politics, Middle Eastern oil, and a Mediterranean warm water port. Bevin saw no reason for the Jews to have a "homeland" aside from their country of birth. He also showed a limited amount of sympathy with the survivors of the Holocaust. At the time when the displaced persons were clamoring for admission to Palestine he cautioned, "if the Jews, with all their suffering, want to get too much at the head of the queue, you have the danger of another anti-Semitic reaction through it all." But Bevin did want American support for British policies and hence suggested a fresh inquiry into the whole Middle East question. He thought Britain and the United States might investigate the problems of the Jews in Europe, see how many immigrants Palestine might be able to absorb, and "examine the possibility of relieving the position in Europe by immigration into other countries, including the United States and the Dominions."[12]

[9]PRO, Foreign Office, 371/45378/5539, July 1945 (hereafter references to the Foreign Office Papers at PRO will be cited by file number and FO volume).

[10]Attlee to Truman, 16 September 1945, National Archives, Washington, General Records of the State Department Office of Near Eastern Affairs, Record Group 59, General Records, Box 1.

[11]PRO, Minutes of the Cabinet Meetings, 128 #38, 4 October 1945 (hereafter cited as PRO, CAB, followed by appropriate volume/file number).

[12]Interviews with Bernard Wasserstein, London, 6 April 1978, and Simon Rifkind, New York, 24 July 1978; Chaim Weizman, *Trial and Error* (London, 1949), p. 541; PRO,

The Cabinet liked the foreign minister's idea because the United States would "thus be placed in a position of sharing the responsibility for the policy which she advocates. She will no longer be able to play the part of irresponsible critic."[13] And to get American support it was agreed "we should not resist their seeking further expansion of their oil concessions. . . ." For those and other reasons the Cabinet encouraged Bevin and Attlee to propose a joint Anglo-American Commission of Inquiry into the problems of the DPs and Palestine's capacity to absorb them. While the proposed committee conducted its investigation and until its report was received, the British government would not have to dwell on that particular problem.[14]

On 19 October 1945, Lord Halifax, the British ambassador to the United States, brought Bevin's proposal for a joint Anglo-American Committee of Inquiry to Secretary of State James F. Byrnes, who promptly discussed the matter with Truman. Lord Halifax had informed Byrnes that HMG regarded the Palestine problem as a "terrible legacy," and could not accept "the view that all of the Jews or the bulk of them must necessarily leave Germany, and still less Europe. That would be to accept Hitler's thesis." The president ignored the commentary but seemed eager to accept the proposal with modifications. The British wanted 14 members on the committee, the president wanted 10; they compromised at 12. The British wanted an indefinite inquiry with no cut-off dates; the president insisted and got a provision requiring a report in 120 days. As Truman later wrote: "I did not want the United States to become a party to any dilatory tactics."[15]

Truman welcomed the opportunity for the inquiry. Both the Republican and Democratic platforms in 1944 had promised to seek unlimited Jewish immigration to Palestine and a national home for the Jews there. In April 1945, however, shortly after Truman succeeded FDR in the White House, the State Department informed him of Roosevelt's dual commitments to Arabs and Jews. His predecessor, Truman discovered, had promised King Ibn Saud of Saudi Arabia that the United States would not act in Palestine without prior consultation with the Arabs.[16]

CAB 128 #40, 11 October 1945; PRO, British Cabinet Papers, 129, 10 October 1945 (hereafter cited as PRO, CP).

[13]Ibid.

[14]PRO, CAB, 128 #26, 30 August 1945, #38, 4 October 1945, and #40, 11 October 1945.

[15]Harry S Truman Library, Independence, MO, President's Secretary's Files, Subject File, Box 184, folder on Palestine-Jewish Immigration (hereafter cited as PSF); Herbert Parzen, "President Truman and the Palestine Quandary: His Initial Experience, April–December, 1945," *Jewish Social Studies* 35 (January 1973): 63, 68–69; Richard D. McKenzie, "Oral Interview with Loy W. Henderson," in Truman Library, p. 160; Harry S Truman, *Years of Trial and Hope* (New York, 1946), p. 142.

[16]Bartley C. Crum, *Behind the Silken Curtain* (New York, 1947), pp. 36–38; Esco Foundation for Palestine Inc., *Palestine: A Study of Jewish, Arab, and British Policies,*

American Jews, unaware of the dual commitments, had been pressing Truman from almost the end of the war in May 1945 to do what he could to fulfill Democratic campaign promises about a homeland for the Jews in Palestine. Both houses of Congress and the governors of thirty-seven states also favored this idea. According to analyses in the *American Jewish Yearbook* and competent pollsters, antisemitism in the United States continued unabated during the war, and most American Jews realized that Congress would not help bring their coreligionists to the country. Moreover, many of the more assimilated American Jews also feared that increased antisemitism would occur if too many foreign Jews were brought over. No doubt some congressmen and governors also wanted to keep Jews out of the United States. But many politicians also depended upon Jewish financial support, and in some states votes as well, and hence had no objection to supporting the Zionist* demands for a Jewish homeland in Palestine. Most Americans who thought at all about the question of immigration perceived of themselves as basically humanitarian and warmhearted, but could think of several "justifiable" reasons, such as tight housing conditions and the possibilities of increased unemployment, for not wanting more immigrants in the United States. Most of these people, though, wholeheartedly endorsed the idea of displaced European Jews going to Palestine. They were not zealots, however, like the American Zionists who were demanding the admission of one million Jews to the Holy Land "as rapidly as possible." Loy Henderson, head of the State Department's Near East Desk, later indicated that their pressure "was terrific, and my office unfortunately was one of the centers of the storm." However, the White House made the basic decisions about Palestine.[17]

The Department of State provided counterpressure to what Henderson referred to as "the Zionist juggernaut." The department, like its counterpart in Britain, housed contingents of pro-Arab staff members at its

---

2 vols. (New Haven, CT, 1947), p. 1188; Crossman, *Palestine Mission*, p. 44; James G. McDonald Papers, Herbert H. Lehman Papers, Columbia University, New York City, "Anglo-American Committee of Inquiry on Palestine: European Diary," p. 12 (hereafter cited as McDonald Diary).

*The Zionists were those Jews who dedicated themselves to establishing a Jewish homeland in Palestine. In the United States about 80 to 85 percent of the Jews supported Zionist goals, but the others were either opposed, like the members of the American Council for Judaism, or indifferent. The American Jewish Committee neither opposed nor supported Zionist goals until 1946, when it finally came around to supporting the idea of a Jewish home in Palestine. However, that organization could not be characterized as "Zionist."

[17]Joseph P. Lash, *Eleanor: The Years Alone* (New York, 1972), p. 144; Safran, *United States and Israel*, p. 39; *New York Times*, 5 July 1945, p. 14; *The Jewish Chronicle* (London; hereafter cited as *JC*), 13 July 1945, p. 1; Crossman, *Palestine Mission*, p. 43; Truman, *Years of Trial and Hope*, p. 137; Samuel H. Flowerman and Marie Jahoda, "Polls on Anti-Semitism," *Commentary* 1 (April 1946): 83; "Oral History Interview with Loy W. Henderson," pp. 104–5; "Memo of July 8, 1946," PSF, Box 184, folder on Palestine-Jewish Immigration.

Near East Desk. Both Roosevelt and Truman knew about their anti-semitic proclivities and always expected pro-Arab responses to any questions asked. The Jews in Palestine, in fact, had such a low priority in the State Department that although many officials spoke fluent Arabic no one claimed a working knowledge of Hebrew. State Department officials, however, were particularly concerned about American oil and aviation interests, and about the possibility of increasing Russian influence in the Middle East should the Western Powers force Jews into the Holy Land against Arab wishes. Thus with conflicting pressures from a major voting bloc—the Jews—and the State Department officials who favored the Arabs and feared Russian encroachment, Truman was probably just as glad as the British to buy time with the appointment of the Anglo-American Committee of Inquiry.[18]

But choosing members of the commission proved difficult for the president. Secretary of State Byrnes and White House Counsel Rosenman both submitted lists for consideration, but the former advised against the inclusion of elected officials.[19] "It really is not a friendly service to a Senator or Congressman to appoint him to this Commission," Byrnes wrote. "It may embarrass him." The president weighed the recommendations and then decided that he would like these men, "in the order listed":

1. John W. Davis	6. Learned Hand
2. Charles E. Hughes, Jr.	7. Frank W. Buxton
3. Frank Aydelotte	8. Walter Loudermilk
4. Mark Ethridge	9. James G. McDonald
5. Bartley C. Crum	10. Archibald MacLeish

But the president could get only four of his first ten choices. Byrnes declined to ask Hand because of illness, he eliminated Crum the first time around because of his supposedly "leftist" leanings, and dropped Loudermilk because he had just written a book about Palestinian agriculture

---

[18]"Oral History Interview with Loy W. Henderson," pp. 104–5; Snetsinger, *Truman, The Jewish Vote*, pp. 16, 55; Samuel Rosenman Oral History Memoir, American Jewish Committee, New York City; *Department of State in the Middle East*, pp. 72, 260–61; Crum, *Behind the Silken Curtain*, pp. 7–8; John A. DeNovo, "The Culbertson Economic Mission and Anglo-American Tensions in the Middle East, 1944-1945," *Journal of American History* 63 (March 1977): 924–25; Crossman, *Palestine Mission*, p. 46; McDonald Diary, p. 12; Kermit Roosevelt, "The Partition of Palestine: A Lession in Pressure Politics," *Middle East Journal* 2 (January 1948): 2.

[19]Rosenman's list included Sumner Welles, Archibald MacLeish, R. L. Buell, Reinhold Niebuhr, Bartley C. Crum, Mrs. Franklin D. Roosevelt, Fiorello LaGuardia, James McDonald, Walter Laudermilk, Senators Wayne Morse (R, Oregon), Robert A. Taft (R, Ohio), Robert F. Wagner (D, New York), and James Mead (D, New York). Papers of Samuel Rosenman, Truman Library, Box 3, Palestine file (1945), memorandum, 19 November 1945. Byrnes proposed John W. Davis, Learned Hand, Frank Aydelotte, Charles E. Hughes, Jr., Mark Ethridge, Frank Buxton, Harold W. Dodds, James P. Baxter, 3d, Judge Charles E. Clark, Judge Joseph C. Hutcheson, O. Max Gardner, and William Thomas Laprade. James F. Byrnes, "Memo for the President," 21 November 1945, PSF, Box 184, folder on Palestine 1945-47.

highly favorable to the Zionists. Ultimately a delegation was composed, but "it was no secret," Richard Crossman wrote, "that President Truman had found it difficult to collect six men willing to accept all the risks of serving on this committee."[20]

The joint announcement of the investigation ocurred simultaneously in Washington and London on 13 November 1945, but the names of the twelve-member committee were not announced until 10 December. The Americans included Joseph C. Hutcheson, Frank Buxton, James McDonald, Frank Aydelotte, William Phillips, and O. Max Gardner. Gardner, the former governor of North Carolina, accepted but suffered a gallstone attack during his first week on the committee and had to resign. Bartley C. Crum replaced him. Crum, a San Francisco attorney and a former campaign manager for Wendell Wilkie, hoped for a future political career and made no bones about where his sympathies lay. During the course of the investigation, he established close personal relations with the accompanying Jewish correspondents. The chairman of the American delegation, Judge Hutcheson of the 5th Circuit Court in Houston, Texas, started out with "strong feelings against any form of Jewish state and [was] quite unsympathetic to anything which smack[ed] of Jewish nationalism." McDonald, from New York, had been a League of Nations high commissioner for refugees in the early 1930s and had devoted himself ever since to finding a place where Europe's Jewish refugees could feel secure. The British regarded him "as hopelessly pro-Zionist." One of the British members also thought Frank W. Buxton, editor of the Boston *Herald*, was as close to the Zionist position as McDonald. Aydelotte, formerly president of Swarthmore College, and, at the time of his appointment, director of Princeton's Institute for Advanced Study, started out as he candidly admitted, "strongly anti-Zionist" and along with William Phillips, former undersecretary of state and ambassador to Italy, often appeared sympathetic to, and understanding of, British affection for the Arabs. Both Crum and McDonald were friends of David Niles, Truman's adviser for minority affairs in the White House, and all three were strong allies of several important Jewish organizations in the United States. Niles favored the Zionist cause and both his friends and concerned members of the State Department knew it. Aydelotte and Phillips were both Anglophiles. The former, in fact, served as American secretary of the Rhodes scholarship fund. Hutcheson started out with an almost blank mind about Arab-Jewish problems but ultimately came to favor dual development of both cultures in Palestine. Frank Buxton, Hutcheson's most devoted supporter on the committee, would later express strong Zionist sympathies. The views of the two American secretaries to the delegation, Leslie

---

[20]Truman, "Memo for Secretary of State," 27 November 1945, ibid.; Frank Aydelotte Manuscript, Friends Historical Library, Swarthmore College, Swarthmore, PA, ser. 6, Anglo-American Commission, "Palestine Diary," 5 December 1945; "Oral Interview with Loy W. Henderson," pp. 104–5; Crossman, *Palestine Mission*, p. 50.

L. Reed and Evan M. Wilson, are not known, but I have found no indication that they contributed significantly to the positions eventually taken by the six-member delegation.[21]

If the American contingent had some representatives who favored the Zionist point of view, the British contingent did not. Attlee had let it be known that "Zionist pressure was very irritating," while his foreign secretary perhaps tipped his hand when he asked Richard Crossman, one of his appointees to the Inquiry Commission, a rather strange question. Taken aback, Crossman later noted in his dairy: "Ernest Bevin in a three minute conversation confined himself to asking me whether I had been circumsized."

Other British appointees included Sir John Singleton, chairman of the delegation and judge of the king's bench Division of the High Court of Justice, London. This "John Bull in our midst," William Phillips noted, possessed a "touch of pomposity which was not altogether appreciated even by his own colleagues." James McDonald evaluated another member of the committee, Labour MP Lord Morrison (Robert Creigmyle, Baron Morrison) as "the most British of the group; even more sensitive than Sir John about any possible questioning of 'the infallibility' of British officialdom." Then there was Sir Frederick Leggett, former deputy secretary of the Ministry of Labour and National Service, who Crossman and McDonald predicted would be a conciliator. Wilfred Crick, economic adviser to the Midland Bank of London, proved Leggett's opposite in temperament. His colleagues on the committee found him "unnecessarily obstinate." The sixth member, Major Reginald E. Manningham Buller, a barrister and conservative MP, also appeared "stubborn as a mule," pro-Arab, and anti-Jew. Crossman, generally considered the most brilliant individual in the group, served as an editor of *The New Statesman and the Nation,* had taught at Oxford University, and in the summer of 1945 had won election to Parliament on the Labour ticket. He later declared that all of the British members "had been chosen either because of their strict impartiality—possible only if they were totally ignorant of the problem— or because they were anti-Zionist, which was also regarded as impartiality. . . ."[22] The British delegation included two staff members, H. G.

[21]"President Truman and the Palestine Quandary," pp. 68–69; O. M. Gardner to Truman, 14 December 1945, Truman Manuscript, Official File, 204b, Box 775, Truman Library (hereafter cited as OF); Aydelotte, "Palestine Diary," 14 December 1945, 11 April 1946; William Phillips, *Ventures in Diplomacy* (Boston, 1952), p. 448; McDonald Diary, pp. 12–13; Papers of Richard Crossman, Oxford University, St. Anthony's College, Middle East Library, Diary, January 1946, pp. 6–7, 8 April 1946 (hereafter cited as Crossman Diary); Crum, *Behind the Silken Curtain,* pp. 34–35.

[22]Crossman Diary, January 1946, pp. 7–8; Phillips, *Ventures in Diplomacy,* p. 448; McDonald Diary, p. 12, and entry for 8 April 1946; William Phillips Manuscript, Houghton Library, Harvard University, 9, Palestine 1945–46, Diary of William G. Phillips, entry for 14 April–18 April 1946 (hereafter cited as Phillips Diary); Crossman speech quoted in *JC,* 2 May 1947, p. 17; U.S., Congress, Senate, *Admission of Jews Into Palestine,* 79th Cong. 2d sess., 1946, p. 47.

Vincent and Harold Beeley, who represented the defenders of the British
pro-Arab policy in the Middle East, and whose views coincided with those
of the chairman, Sir John Singleton.

The British members journeyed to Washington, DC, to meet their
American counterparts and to open formal hearings. What they heard
struck them, for the most part, as Zionist propaganda. Richard Crossman
later wrote: "As an Englishman I was surprised and irritated during the
Washington hearings by the almost complete disregard of the Arab case."
In essence, several spokesmen for Jewish organizations recalled the
history of the Balfour delegation, the promise of a national home for the
Jews, the despicable introduction of the White Paper curtailing Jewish
immigration to the Holy Land at the very moment Hitler began preparing
his ovens, the millions killed by the Nazis during World War II, and the
world's obligation to provide a homeland for the war's survivors. At the
very least, they pleaded, consider why Jews had just suffered and died.
The British simply had to open the gates to Palestine! Not all of the Jews
reiterated these same points, but most did. Albert Einstein testified that
the committee was merely a "smoke screen" and that, in the end, the
British Colonial Office would impose whatever policies it chose in Palestine. Dr. Philip Hitti, a Christian Arab, spoke for the Institute of Arab-
American Affairs. The Arabs opposed Jewish immigration into Palestine,
he said, because it struck them as "an attenuated form of conquest." Hitti
also opined that the Arabs might be more open to accepting some Jewish
DPs in their midst if the Western Powers made some efforts to do
likewise. Although Richard Crossman met "no one in Washington [who]
denied that one of the main obstacles in the way of Arab acceptance of a
measure of Jewish immigration into Palestine was the refusal of the
Western democracies to open their doors to the refugees," he also found
"hardly anyone" who thought that the restrictive United States immigration laws would be modified.[23]

After concluding its hearings in Washington, the twelve men moved
to London for more of the same. In London, where the Jews were fewer
and therefore more restrained, the Arab case received a more forceful
presentation, and Foreign Secretary Ernest Bevin pledged that he would
follow the advice of a unanimous committee recommendation. By the end
of the London hearings one journalist commented: "In its hearings in
Washington and London, the Anglo-American Committee of Inquiry
turned up little that it could not have found in a public library."[24]

After London the delegation split up and ventured to different parts

---

[23]Crossman, *Palestine Mission,* pp. 24–28, 33, 37, 45, 46; Crum, *Behind the Silken
Curtain,* pp. 12–23, 26.
[24]Crossman, *Palestine Mission,* pp. 52, 180; David Horowitz, *State in the Making*
(New York, 1953), p. 62; Crum, *Behind the Silken Curtain,* p. 61; Phillips Diary, 30 Janu-
ary 1946; Crossman to Attlee, 7 May 1946, PRO, PREM 8/302/XM 03323; James G.
McDonald, *My Mission in Israel* (New York, 1951), pp. 23–24; Sidney Hertzberg, "The
Month in History," *Commentary* 1 (March 1946): 69.

of the continent to gather first-hand impressions of DPs and then regrouped in Vienna to exchange information. Almost all of them had similar experiences. They learned that Zionism for Jewish DPs was "the expression of the most primitive urge, the urge for survival." The vast majority of the DPs would have to "emigrate or perish." Every official with whom they spoke agreed that the Jews could not return to their homelands in Eastern Europe because they had no homes in which to go. Antisemitism pervaded all of Europe. Poland was a Jewish graveyard. A renewed Jewish community in Germany seemed out of the question. The Bishop of Vienna's solution for the Jewish problem "was the conversion of the Jews to the true faith." An officer in charge of the DPs and POWs in the British zone of Vienna thought that "it's too bad the war didn't last another two or three months. They'd [the Jews] all have been done away with by then. We'd have had no problem." Their experiences moved all of the members of the committee. Sir Frederick Leggett, previously hostile to the Jews, became "emotionally exhausted" by this trip and wanted to do something to help the surviving remnant. Not only did he start greeting everyone with the term, "Shalom," but he told his colleagues: "Unless we can do something and do it soon, we shall be guilty of having finished the job Hitler started: the spiritual and moral destruction of the tiny remnant of European Jewry." It seemed obvious to everyone that only Palestine would accept these people, but the committee would not go along with Crum's demand for an interim report urging the immediate admission of 100,000 Jews. As Crossman wrote, in Vienna: "We were still seeing everything from one single point of view, and inclined to regard Palestine, as the Jews in Europe regarded it, as a solution rather than a problem." The men argued that the mission should be completed before they issued any report.[25]

After Vienna there were stops in Cairo and Jerusalem for further investigations. Once again hearings were held but in Palestine members of the committee journeyed to different parts of the land. They agreed that Arabs lived as they had for centuries at a low standard, and Jews brought Western concepts of development, thus modernizing a traditional society. Nevertheless, they were looked upon as vanguards of Western imperialism who would eventually encroach on Arab territories and force them out. The Arab leaders feared Jewish immigration because it meant, ultimately, an upheaval in the way of life they had pursued for generations. The Jews did not dispute this point. "Our aim," David Ben-Gurion, head of the Jewish Agency in Palestine, told the Anglo-American Committee, "is a Jewish state."[26]

---

[25]Yehuda Bauer, *Flight and Rescue: BRICHAH* (New York, 1970), p. 202; Joseph C. Hutcheson, Jr., "Memorandum," February 1946, McDonald Papers; Crossman, *Palestine Mission,* pp. 81–82, 87, 90, 93, 96–97, 166, 176; Crum, *Behind the Silken Curtain,* pp. 117, 130, 137; George Vida, *From Doom to Dawn* (New York, 1977), p. 67.

[26]William R. Polk, *The U.S. and the Arab World,* 3d ed. (Cambridge, MA, 1975), p. 187; Papers of Sir Alan Cunningham, Oxford University, St. Anthony's College, Middle

British officialdom in Palestine favored the Arabs and disliked the Jews for several reasons. For one, the former accepted while the latter rebelled against the status quo. For another, the British felt superior to the Arabs but recognized the Jews as "a great deal abler than we are. And the Jews don't often permit us to forget it." Third, the Arab intelligentsia and upper class, a small minority of the population, exhibited a sophisticated, amusing, and "civilized" manner that British leaders found beguiling. The Jews, on the other hand, struck Palestinian officials as too intense, too enthusiastic about socialism, and devoid of either charm or breeding. Crossman found these sentiments of his countrymen, as well as their responses and attitudes that were the classic stereotypes held by anti-semites, "utterly nauseating." To his wife, he castigated the British officials as "snobbish, cliquy, second rate and reactionary. They like the Arabs because they are illiterate, inefficient, and easy to govern. They dislike the Jews because the Jewish leaders are ten times as able as they are."[27]

Jerusalem marked the last stop of the formal hearings. When the committee finished its work there, the members flew to Lausanne, Switzerland, for a few days of rest and then the arduous task of preparing their report. When they resumed working, Judge Hutcheson, the American chairman, suggested a framework that James McDonald considered "a masterly statement which I can confess amazed me because it was so out of keeping with many of his private comments and his questions during the public hearings. In his analysis he showed no influence of prejudice or dislikes." Arguing for unity, Hutcheson outlined his program somewhat as follows:

> Neither an Arab nor a Jewish state should be organized because neither people can justly claim the whole country. Moreover, there is a large Christian interest. The very great achievements of the Jews must be admitted and nothing done to check the normal development of the Jewish homeland. Immigration should be renewed on a substantial emergency scale and then to be continued on a regular basis but not with a view to "political conquest of the country." The [Jewish] Agency is not to be weakened. No reference was made to the Haggana [sic]. The political organization suggested was that of a binational state. J. H. indicated, however, that he was not finally wedded to any of his ideas and was open to argument and would change his conclusions if the reasons on which they were based were successfully challenged.[28]

East Library, Box 5, File 2, "Memorandum on the Administration of Palestine Under the Mandate," prepared for the Anglo-American Committee of Inquiry, February 1946, p. 6; Crossman, *Palestine Mission,* p. 144; *Commentary* 1 (January): 68.

[27] Phillips Diary, 11 March 1946; McDonald Diary, 2 March 1946; Crossman, "Chatham House Speech," 13 June 1946, Crossman Papers; Crossman, *Palestine Mission,* pp. 102, 123; Crossman to wife, Zita [n.d.] Crossman Papers.

[28] McDonald Diary, 1 April 1946.

Sir John countered with a proposal strikingly reminiscent of the White Paper. Then each of the others spoke in turn. By the end of the first day "it was clear that there were basic differences . . . on almost everything."[29]

As time passed several things jelled. The Americans unanimously supported entry of 100,000 Jews to Palestine. The British, with the exception of Crossman, favored either lowering the number and/or attaching untenable clauses, which would have made such entry impossible. Everyone agreed that Palestine should be dominated by neither Arabs nor Jews. Crossman, Crum, and McDonald opted for partition. The British believed that their country should be freed from the obligations of the Balfour declaration and the League of Nations mandate that reinforced it. They wanted the opportunity to start again with a clean slate. The result would have meant an Arab Palestine with no hope for further Jewish immigration. Moreover, Sir John and Manningham Buller, especially, demanded that the local, unauthorized Jewish army, the *Haganah,* be condemned and disbanded. The committee members knew, however, that this was impossible. The *Haganah* had, in the words of a British Cabinet member, "in some part originated as a protection against Arab violence," and at the time "was the most formidable fighting force in the Middle East because it was not a private army but simply the whole Jewish community organized" to defend itself. Neither the Jewish Agency in Palestine nor American politicians dependent politically on Jewish support would accept a provision requiring its abolition. Certainly, Crossman later wrote to Attlee, "such a recommendation, if made against the unanimous view of six Americans, would range all American public opinion against us and force the president to back the Zionists against the British government." Members of the British team also thought that the American government should help enforce the policies adopted. None of the Americans envisaged sending troops to Palestine and rejected that recommendation.[30]

Sympathy for the Jewish victims, which all the British members of the committee seemed to have had in Vienna, dissipated somewhat by the time they reached Lausanne. The opinions of the British colonialists in Palestine; the recognition of the fact that despite the desperate needs of the Jews, Arabs had inhabited the Holy Land for more than a millenium; and Foreign Office policy placating Arabs and guarding Middle East possessions tempered the urgency that the committee felt earlier. Committee members still believed that something had to be done to help remove the Jews from the DP assembly centers but were not convinced that unlimited immigration to Palestine was the answer.

Resentment, bitterness, and acrimony handicapped working relationships among committee members and aggravated the taxing nature of

---

[29]Ibid; Phillips Diary, 1 April 1946.

[30]Ibid., 31 March 1946; Crossman Diary, 8 April 1946; Phillips, *Ventures in Diplomacy,* p. 445; PRO, CAB 128 #51, 20 June 1946; Crossman, *Palestine Mission,* p. 168; Crossman to Attlee, 22 April 1946, with "Notes on Palestine Report of Anglo-American Committee," appended PRO, PREM 8 302/XM 03323.

their responsibilities. Crossman found himself getting "sick to death being told how Texan Judges prepare their judgments. . . ." He disagreed with Hutcheson who proclaimed "that you had to reach your conclusions first and then choose the facts which supported them: this was judicial procedure." Sir John also disturbed his junior colleague because he consorted only with Manningham Buller, and staff member H. G. Vincent. The three of them "work[,] eat, drink and for all I know sleep in the same bed," Crossman complained to his wife. Buxton disliked Manningham Buller, who along with Crick, disparaged Crossman, who, in turn, found Bartley Crum "a great disappointment. He reads nothing, drinks too much and changes his mind according to the last newspaper he receives from the States." Aydelotte agreed that Crum "did not read much" and thought that the San Franciscan "formed his opinions on pretty slender evidence." But Aydelotte found only William Phillips, among the Americans, a congenial colleague. He labeled Sir John "in some respects a perfectly impossible person," and regarded Hutcheson as "hopeless," Buxton as "the most maladroit of our members," and McDonald as "not any too useful." Neither Sir John, Manningham Buller, nor Vincent got along with any of the Americans, who always opposed the British chairman's suggestions, and the three of them disliked "their British compatriots even more than the Americans."[31]

By the end of the first week, it seemed to Crossman that the other five Englishmen would make one report, the Americans another, and himself a third. "But Morrison, Leggett and I were convinced that it would be disastrous if conflicting reports were issued," Crossman wrote. So he "talked to Phillips, Phillips talked to Aydelotte, Aydelotte talked to Morrison, and finally Aydelotte and Leggett played golf on Sunday. Result—a nucleus of a middle group which will try to mediate between the obstinate intransigeance of the two judges." Although Crossman credited Phillips, Aydelotte, Morrison, and Leggett for providing the nucleus of the middle ground and showed less appreciation for the American chairman, three of the American members seemed to think that "it was the leadership of Judge Hutcheson which kept us all together. He would not permit our initial differences to result in a breakup of a committee into American and British groups. It is not an oversimplification to say that had it not been for him, the final report would not have been unanimous."[32]

The final recommendation of the Anglo-American Committee, in a lengthy document that ran over 40,000 words, tried to placate Arabs, Americans, Jews, and Englishmen. None of these groups, however, embraced the report in its entirety; most rejected a substantial amount, if not

[31]Crossman to wife, 4, 8 April 1946, W. F. Crick to Crossman, 4 July 1946, Crossman Papers; Aydelotte, "Palestine Diary," 6, 7, 19, 20 April 1946.
[32]Crossman to Attlee, 22 April 1946, PRO. PREM 8 302/XM 03323; Crossman Diary, 8 April 1946; Phillips Diary, 14 April–18 April 1946; McDonald Papers, General Correspondence, Folder 187; Crum, *Behind the Silken Curtain*, p. 265.

all, of the report which suggested that the whole world, not just Palestine, open its doors for Jewish DPs; that 100,000 Jews be allowed into Palestine, and that that country should be dominated by neither group; that the British maintain the mandate until the United Nations executed a trusteeship agreement; that Arab economic, educational, and political advancement was necessary and measures should be taken to these ends; that Jews be allowed to purchase lands proscribed in the White Paper; that Jews and Arabs should cooperate with one another for economic development; that compulsory education be introduced; and that violence and terrorism by both sides be suppressed.[33]

Although each of the twelve men signed the report, the British members were less happy with their recommendations than the Americans. McDonald and Phillips speculated about why all the British had signed. Perhaps they felt unanimity with the Americans to be of great significance, or perhaps they believed that their privately held reservations might be independently communicated to members of the Cabinet. They may have also thought that modifications would certainly be made by the British government in any case. In fact, Crum recalled British staff member Harold Beeley saying to him in Lausanne: "Well, after all, we certainly won't implement any such program as this," and Sir John pontificating: "You know, Crum, these are only recommendations." To Manningham Buller, Sir John "revealed considerable bitterness" over the final product more openly, and voiced his concern that the British had "given way to American pressure." At a farewell dinner, which he hosted, Sir John "launched into a bitter attack on Hutcheson," and McDonald added: "I am afraid that what [he] said at this dinner represented what he really felt, nor am I surprised because the resolutions were clearly a defeat of his policies."[34]

If the British delegation faltered under American pressure, the British government certainly had no intention of doing so. While Hutcheson flew to Washington to present a copy of the report to President Truman, Sir John immediately returned to London to inform the prime minister of the commission's conclusions. Neither a unanimous verdict nor one recommending admission of 100,000 Jews to Palestine had been anticipated. Most British officials regarded the report "as a sellout to the Americans." Prime Minister Attlee made no effort to hide his displeasure. He had expected support for existing British policies and labeled the document that he received "grossly unfair to Great Britain." Furthermore, he wanted a recommendation that would have included the American government in any actions taken. Crossman was aghast. He had not known that Attlee wanted "to push responsibility on to America. If I had been told that that was your wish," he commented, "I would of course

[33]Crossman, *Palestine Mission*, pp. 1221–34.
[34]Crum, *Behind the Silken Curtain*, pp. 282–83; McDonald Diary, 19, 20 April 1946; Phillips Diary, 20 April 1946.

have declined to serve. . . ." "You've let us down," Attlee replied, "by giving way to the Jews and Americans."[35]

The British Cabinet discussed the report at length. According to Crossman, "a flow of fantastic misinformation" from the Chiefs of Staff and Foreign Office officials convinced Bevin that "a general Arab rising in Palestine would follow" its implementation. In actual fact, the commission had been informed, and so related to both Bevin and the prime minister, that the reverse was true. Except for a few scattered outbursts, the Arabs would have accepted the new policy and no additional troops would have been required in the Holy Land. Failure to follow through on the recommendations, however, would lead to a Jewish uprising. Crossman made several unsuccessful attempts to convince members of the Cabinet that their beliefs had no basis in fact but his words made no impact. The Cabinet stuck to its guns, agreeing that to allow 100,000 Jews into Palestine in 1946 would incur Arab wrath, imperil the British position in the Middle East, and therefore allow the Russians greater influence in the area. "The essence" of British policy, Cabinet members believed, "should be to retain the interest and participation of the United States government in this position." Attlee's announcement that the report would not be put into effect without American support, and until the "illegal armies" in Palestine had been disbanded, disturbed many officials in the United States.[36]

While the English took a position that made implementation impossible, Truman publicly committed himself to only one of the recommendations: the immediate admission of 100,000 Jews into Palestine. To this end he ordered the secretary of state to begin consultation with both Arabs and Jews, since he had pledged to consult with the Arabs before any change occurred in Palestinian policy, and then to speak with British representatives about emptying the Jewish DPs camps. The American government did not object to assuming financial and technical responsibility for getting the Jews to Palestine, but it had no intention of sending troops there.[37]

Talks on putting the plan into action resumed between the two governments in June. President Truman appointed a cabinet committee composed of the secretaries of State, War, and the Treasury, who immediately

---

[35]Crossman, *Palestine Mission,* pp. 188, 192; Washington embassy to FO, 23 April 1946, PRO, FO 371/52516/3634; Bauer, *Flight and Rescue,* p. 203; Noah Lucas, *The Modern History of Israel* (London, 1974), p. 225; Crossman to Attlee, 7 May 1946, PRO, PREM 8 302/XM 03323; Richard Crossman, *A Nation Reborn* (New York, 1960), p. 79.

[36]Ibid., pp. 81–83; PRO, CP (46), 27 April 1946; Crossman to Attlee, 7 May 1946, PRO, PREM 8 302/XM 03323; Crum, *Behind the Silken Curtain,* pp. 219–20; CAB 129 CP #258, 8 July 1946, p. 6; PRO, CAB 128 #38, 29 April 1946: *New York Times,* 2 May 1946; p. 1; telegram, Earl of Halifax to FO, 3 May 1946, FO 371/52520/4051.

[37]Chaim Weizmann to Attlee, 13 May 1946, PRO, PREM 8/304; FO 371/51609/A2155; General Records of the State Department, National Archives, Record Group 59, Box 1, memorandum, 21 June 1946.

appointed alternates in their stead, to meet with officials in London. The alternates "knew virtually nothing of Palestine and were singularly ill-equipped to face the real experts of the British Colonial Office on the other side of the table." The British delegation recommended a federal plan for Palestine that had been prepared in the Colonial Office even before the Labour government had come to power, and the Americans accepted it. The same plan had been submitted to, and rejected by, the twelve-member Anglo-American Committee of Inquiry.[38]

The new proposal divided Palestine into two federalized zones. The Arabs would receive approximately three times as much land as the Jews. The British Cabinet seemed pleased with this division and congratulated the negotiators for bringing "to so successful a conclusion their negotiations with the United States Delegation." Even President Truman seemed pleased and ready to accept the new proposal. But the "almost pathological frenzy" with which the Zionists and their allies opposed this solution forced the president to abandon the idea.[39]

By August 1946 more than a year had elapsed since Harrison had gone to Europe and examined the conditions in the DP camps. Since then the arrival of hundreds of thousands more east Europeans had swollen the camp populations and taxed the capacities of the military to provide necessary services. Therefore, on 16 August 1946, exactly one year after he announced that he favored entry of the Jews into Palestine, Truman, for the first time, publicly stated that he would recommend to the Congress that legislation be passed for the United States to accept a "substantial" number of DPs.[40] Two years later, after considerable activity on the part of the newly formed domestic lobby, the Citizens Committee on Displaced Persons, Congress passed the Displaced Persons Act of 1948 that allowed 205,000 European refugees into this country. Had the Anglo-American Committee of Inquiry's recommendations been accepted by the British, it is extremely unlikely that Truman or the Congress would have made any such efforts despite the fact that 80 percent of the DPs in Europe were Christian.

In retrospect, it is significant that neither Britain nor the United States showed any willingness to assume responsibility for aiding the victims of the Holocaust. Each nation expected the other to shoulder the burden, while conflicting domestic pressures resulted in inaction. Although Truman was bombarded by the Jews in the United States to insist that the British open Palestine, neither he nor the Zionists wanted to bring

[38]Crossman, *Palestine Mission*, p. 196.

[39]PRO, CAB 128 #73, 25 July 1946; FO 371/57756/WR2066; Richard P. Stevens, *American Zionism and U.S. Foreign Policy, 1942–1947* (New York, 1962), p. 152; Bauer, *Flight and Rescue*, pp. 203–4; John Morton Blum, *The Price of Vision: The Diary of Henry A. Wallace, 1942–1946* (Boston, 1973), p. 607; Cyril H. Cane to John Balfour, 7 September 1946, FO 371/52558/9379; FO 371/51671/Political Report from Washington, 3 August 1946.

[40]*JC*, 23 August 1946, p. 6.

any more Jews to the United States. Truman knew of Congress's reluctance to change the immigration statutes and the intensity of American antisemitism. The president also had to grapple with countervailing forces in the oil industry and the State Department that wanted to maintain harmonious relations with the Arabs. The British government, on the other hand, thought "no solution should be proposed which would alienate the Arab States" or fail to "have the backing of the United States government,"[41] two seemingly contradictory goals. It also feared possible Russian inroads in the Middle East and wanted to avoid any policy that might allow Stalin greater influence in the Mediterranean. As a result of these conflicting requirements in both Britain and the United States, the Jewish DP problem lingered, and the Zionists in Palestine and the United States became more aggressive in their demands for a national state. Ironically, one British historian speculated that "if the London government had with American help brought the hundred thousand to Palestine (against Arab opposition) the Jewish state might never have come into being. The militancy of the Jewish Agency and the appeal of the terrorist movement would undoubtedly have dwindled, and Zionism would have lost much of its emotional force if the survivors of the holocaust in direct need had been given shelter."[42]

Occasionally such speculation is fruitless. The fact remains that the British government did not accept the recommendations and the American government had neither the authority nor the will to execute them on her own. Moreover, the goals of the British and American governments differed widely. Officials in London and Washington did not perceive this dichotomy as acutely as did the members of the Anglo-American Committee of Inquiry. The British government really wanted support for a pro-Arab, anti-Russian policy in Palestine. Truman, more sympathetic than the British to aspirations of the Zionists and the plight of DPs in Europe, hoped to alleviate the sufferings of the European Jews while not alienating Palestinian Arabs. This, ultimately, could not be done. American politicians had to listen carefully to the representatives of the articulate, well-financed, and well-organized Zionists. The British did not. But the British government had to grapple with the problems of a disintegrating Empire, of which Palestine was only a part. And as a result of the conflicting national demands the Anglo-American Committee of Inquiry's report could not be accepted as written.

Perhaps the main reasons that the recommendations of the committee were never implemented were that the American government never had anticipated that it would be asked to send troops to back up British policies in the Middle East, or turn its back on the *Haganah*, or alter its rigid immigration policies at home to alleviate the sufferings of the

---

[41] PRO, CAB 128 #71, 22 July 1946.
[42] Lucas, *Modern History of Israel*, p. 225.

survivors of the Holocaust. Truman simply had not foreseen the conse-quences when he agreed to participate in the joint inquiry.

Although the Cold War was heating up by the spring of 1946, the Americans had not yet embarked upon any significantly new policies to fight the expansion of Communism. The idea of sending troops to the Middle East, therefore, did not appear among the more realistic American options. Fear of Russian expansion into the Middle East had concerned the British members of the committee much more than it affected the stand of the American members. To be sure, the State Department's Loy Henderson had briefed the Americans before they left for London, and the British secretaries continually interjected their apprehensions, but in reading the diaries and memoirs of Aydelotte, Crum, McDonald, and Phillips, I discerned no concern for this issue. What does occur frequently, and this fact seems to have motivated them, is the suffering of the European Jews and the need to find a place for them. Only Palestine would accept the vast majority of the Jews and therefore, by a process of elimination, the only viable solution seemed to allow the DPs into the Holy Land. No other aspect of international affairs seems to have affected American positions, and it therefore would be unwarranted to make too much of the influence of other contemporary concerns upon this issue.

A Peripheral View of the Origins of the Cold War: The Crises in Iran, 1941–47

STEPHEN L. McFARLAND*

In late 1945 columnist Walter Lippmann tried to come to grips with rapidly changing world events. The wartime alliance was in shambles, and the peace most Americans expected was being pushed beyond reach. Lippmann determined that: "American foreign policy is drifting. The United States is being sucked into conflict with the Soviet Union. Whose fault is it? No honest man can say. The United States is drifting toward catastrophe."[1] Although Lippmann was not referring to the Iranian situation, his analysis described the process by which the United States, during and after World War II, was "sucked" into an involvement in Iran that resulted from problems only remotely connected to the Soviet-American dispute over Eastern Europe. The reactions of the United States and the Soviet Union to events in Iran were due to the initiatives of the Iranians as well as to any preconceived policy of great power confrontation or global expansion. Domestic crises within Iran attracted great power intervention and anticipated the ensuing Cold War struggle.

This intervention, however, did not occur in a vacuum. The United States and the Soviet Union, pursuing their own interests, became conscious of Iran's economic and strategic importance at an early date and their policies evolved accordingly. The Soviets endeavored to preserve their sphere of influence in Iran and invited American intervention by

---

*The author wishes to thank Professors Robert Divine and Hafez Farmayan for their helpful suggestions in completing this article.

Official Iranian records for the World War II period either do not exist or are not accessible. This article therefore relies on other sources, including newspapers, foreign diplomatic records, and memoirs, to fill the gaps remaining in the general literature.

This article is not intended to condemn, excuse, or apologize for the actions of Iran, the United States, or the Soviet Union in the Iranian crises. I have not listed the many Soviet and American violations of Iranian sovereignty because they have been dealt with in depth elsewhere. The purpose of this effort is to demonstrate the complexity of the issue and reveal how foreign policymakers were forced to react to events beyond their ability to either control or understand.

[1] *Washington Post,* 1 November 1945, p. 11.

333

breaking their treaty obligations in Iran. American oil companies, advisers, and officials took up Iranian causes too readily and committed many anti-Soviet acts in Iran. In almost every case, Iranian statesmen, employing the century-old strategy of *movazaneh* (equilibrium), labored to intensify differences between their two traditional enemies, the British and the Soviets, in order to forestall any effort by either to make further inroads into Iranian independence and ultimately to regain complete independence.[2] They endeavored to attract the United States to act as a buffer and counterbalance to the Anglo-Soviet threat. Domestically, the government and various interest groups within Iran used the Allies as protectors and promoters in internal power struggles. In this manner, internal and external events were linked so that the Iranian monarchy was able to regain its supremacy and Iran its independence and territorial integrity, both of which had been lost in 1941. Iranians exploited the budding Soviet-American rivalry to their advantage. The main result of this Iranian manipulation was a series of crises that exacerbated great power differences and eventually helped to nudge the superpowers to the brink of war.[3]

The story of Allied interests and actions in Iran has been told in sufficient detail elsewhere.[4] The existing literature has recognized the importance of the 1946 Iranian crisis, labeling it the "turning point" in postwar relations, a "landmark," and the "point of departure."[5] The

---

[2]For a brief essay on the *movazaneh* strategy, see Rouhollah Ramazani, *Iran's Foreign Policy 1941–1973* (Charlottesville, 1975), pp. 70–72.

[3]For a brief examination of the role of small nations in big power diplomacy, see Annette Fox, *The Power of Small States: Diplomacy in World War II* (Chicago, 1959).

[4]In English, for example, see Peter Avery, *Modern Iran* (New York, 1965); George Lenczowski, *Russia and the West in Iran, 1918–1948* (Ithaca, 1949); Ramazani, *Iran's Foreign Policy;* and Bruce Kuniholm, *The Origins of the Cold War in the Near East* (Princeton, 1980). In Persian, among others, see Seyyed Hossein Amuzgar, *Naft va havades-e Azarbaijan* [Oil and the Events of Azerbaijan] (Tehran, 1947/48); Mohammad Khan Malek Yazdi, *Arzesh-e masa'i-ye Iran dar jang* [The Value of Iran's Efforts in the War] (Tehran, 1950/51); and Hossein Kuhi Kermani, *Az Shahrivar-e 1320 ta faji'eh-ye Azarbaijan va Zanjan* [From August 1941 to the Fall of Azerbaijan and Zanjan], 2 vols. (Tehran, 1946/47, 1950/51). In Russian, among others, see A. V. Bashkirov, *Ekspansia Angliiskikh i Amerikanskikh imperialistov v Irane (1941–1953 gg)* [The Expansion of English and American Imperialists in Iran (1941–53)] (Moscow, 1954); M. V. Popov, *Amerikanskii imperialism v Irane v gody vtoroi voiny* [American Imperialism in Iran in the Years of the Second War] (Moscow, 1956); E. A. Orlov, *Vneshniaia politika Irana posle vtoroi mirovoi voiny* [The Foreign Policy of Iran After the Second World War] (Moscow, 1975); and A. I. Demin and V. V. Trubetskoi, "Iran nakanune vtoroi mirovoi voiny" [Iran at the Beginning of the Second World War] in *Iran: ocherki noveishei istorii,* ed. A. Z. Arabadzhian (Moscow, 1976), pp. 120–66.

[5]Walter LaFeber, "American Policy-Makers, Public Opinion, and the Outbreak of the Cold War, 1945–50," in *The Origins of the Cold War in Asia,* eds. Yonosuke Nagai and Akira Iriye (New York, 1977), p. 50; Daniel Yergin, *Shattered Peace* (Boston, 1977), p. 179; and Harry S Truman, *Memoirs,* vol. 1: *Year of Decisions* (Garden City, 1955), pp. 551–52.

following conclusions are culled from the literature: the Allies "collided" in Iran; the crisis was due to Soviet-American competition over oil; the crisis was a "classic Great Power scramble"; the crisis was an American reaction to clear Soviet aggression; Iran was "impotent" during the war; the crisis was only a "rather macabre demonstration" by the Soviet Union to divert attention from Eastern Europe; Iran was a successful testing ground for a new active American policy of containment; the crisis was the result of Allied "wartime interaction"; the crisis was a "confluence" of both American national security and American domestic considerations; American policy in Iran was shaped by memories of Munich; and the crisis was a "testing ground for the principles of Dumbarton Oaks."[6] All of these interpretations focus on American, European, or Soviet policies or concerns; they assume that the Cold War stemmed from a confrontation over Europe and from domestic American politics. All ignore the impact of peripheral events outside of Europe on Soviet-American relations.[7]

The crises in Iran began in August 1941. The need for a supply route to the Soviet Union and Iran's pro-German policies necessitated the Allied occupation of Iran. The country was divided into three zones: Soviet in the north, British in the south, and nominally Iranian in the center. American forces entered Iran in 1942 to assist in the movement of war supplies to the Soviet Union. The 1942 Treaty of Alliance (the United States was not a signatory) governed the occupation and was designed to limit Allied interference in Iran's internal affairs and guarantee its postwar sovereignty.

Iran collapsed into confusion and disorder following the invasion. The rigidly controlled prewar society came apart at the seams: the army disintegrated, the old shah was forced to abdicate, government officials were imprisoned, political prisoners were freed, a Shi'i Islamic revival weakened reforms and advances in female emancipation, renascent tribes seized control of large areas, rural brigandage returned, and a plethora of diverse political groups were formed.

Before the occupation Iran began efforts to balance its foreign relations between British and Soviet interests and to attract American involvement. In 1940 Iran signed a trade agreement with the Soviet Union

---

[6]Thomas Paterson, *Soviet-American Confrontation* (Baltimore, 1973), p. 177; Stephen Ambrose, *Rise to Globalism* (Middlesex, 1971), p. 131; Yergin, *Shattered Peace,* p. 179; Richard Cottam, "The United States, Iran and the Cold War," *Iranian Studies* 3 (Winter 1970): 4–5; Lenczowski, *Russia and the West in Iran,* p. 176; Avery, *Modern Iran,* p. 390; Richard Pfau, "Containment in Iran, 1946: The Shift to an Active Policy," *Diplomatic History* 1 (Fall 1977): 359, 372; Eduard Mark, "Allied Relations in Iran, 1941–1947: The Origins of a Cold War Crisis," *Wisconsin Magazine of History* 59 (Autumn 1975): 51; G. R. Hess, "The Iranian Crisis of 1945–1946 and the Cold War," *Political Science Quarterly* 89 (March 1974): 119, 146; and Kuniholm, *The Origins of the Cold War in the Near East,* p. 304.

[7]Kuniholm, in *Origins of the Cold War,* attempts to examine the "regional perspective," but is unable to break free from the belief that events in Iran were controlled ultimately from Washington, New York, London, and Moscow.

that reportedly gave the Soviets the use of airfields in Iran and released imprisoned Iranian Communists. An agreement with the British-owned Anglo-Iranian Oil Company ended a dispute over wartime oil production. American claims against Iran for the seizure of missionary school property were settled. The problem facing Iran after the occupation was to reduce the threat to its independence created by its traditional enemies.[8]

Direct appeals for American intervention on the day of the invasion went unrewarded. Iran then took steps to come to terms with the occupiers, placating them with concessions, but it gave up most of those efforts in order to entice America into intervening. Iranians hated the British and feared the Soviets, making it more necessary to employ a third-power *movazaneh* strategy; to create a buffer between Iran and the occupiers. Trust in the United States developed from a history of detached interest and in no small part from the principles announced in the Atlantic Charter. Unable to attract official American government support at first, Iran initiated efforts to attract private American concerns and companies, hoping that the U.S. government could be drawn into intervention when private interests were threatened.

The Iranian government did not attempt to hide its strategy. One prime minister asked for American advisers to reform the army and national police and to run the government's economic administration (the Millspaugh Mission). Another expressed his desire to have additional advisers operate all government industrial and mining enterprises. A third told a personal representative of President Roosevelt that he wanted American business concerns to enter all fields of enterprise in Iran. When the United States notified Iran that it would be operating the British portion of the Trans-Iranian Railway (the supply route to the Soviet Union), Iran urged the United States to take over the entire system, replacing the British and the Soviets. Iran offered its opium crop for medicinal use as its contribution to the American war effort. The Iranian press backed the United States against Japan even before Pearl Harbor. *Ettela'at,* the semiofficial national newspaper, called the United States Iran's only hope for freedom and independence and pleaded for American intervention to end British and Soviet interference in Iran's internal affairs. The head of the Iranian Boy Scouts asked for State Department assistance in finding an American citizen to assume the position of head scoutmaster.[9]

---

[8]U.S., Department of State, *Foreign Relations of the United States: Diplomatic Papers, 1940,* 3:629–30 (hereafter cited as *FRUS,* followed by appropriate year); Nasrollah S. Fatemi, *Oil Diplomacy: Powderkeg in Iran* (New York, 1954), p. 186; and *FRUS, 1941,* 3:355–73, 388–99.

[9]*FRUS, 1941,* 3:418–19; Ramazani, *Iran's Foreign Policy,* pp. 70–72; *FRUS, 1942,* 4:238–39; *FRUS, 1943,* 4:417–19; U.S., Department of State, Decimal File, Record Group 59, National Archives, Washington, 891.114/344, 6 November 1941 (hereafter cited by decimal file number); *FRUS, 1942,* 4:316; *Ettela'at,* 17 Azar 1320, p. 1; 891.9111/436, 23 April 1941; 891.9111/437, 3 May 1941; *Ettela'at,* 30 Mordad 1321, p. 1; and 891.4081/6, 23 January 1942.

One of the chiefs of staff of the Iranian army during the war succinctly summarized this policy of courting American interest: "Our policy was to bring as many Americans as possible to Iran to be witnesses of the Soviet political encroachment and by their presence act as a deterrent for the more open violations of our independence and interference in our internal affairs." A member of the wartime Iranian Parliament similarly wrote:

> After the occupation . . . Iranians began looking for a new friend who would protect them against their two neighbors . . . the choice fell on the United States. . . . As already pointed out the project for the employment of the American missions and the plan for encouraging American capital in Iran had been outlined very carefully as early as the beginning of 1943.

Another member of Parliament, Mohammad Mosaddeq, attacked the policy of attracting American support, calling for an equilibrium based on the rejection of all foreign powers. An Iranian prime minister straightforwardly told American diplomats that the American advisers were invited to Iran not for their technical skills but to act as cushions between conflicting British and Soviet interests. An independent observer and the advisers themselves supported this assertion.[10]

The Big Three meeting at Tehran in November and December 1943 provided Iran with an opportunity to confront the Allies with its *movazaneh* strategy. The British and Soviets had signed the Treaty of Alliance containing guarantees of territorial integrity and independence for Iran. For various reasons, including a British request that it not, the United States never became a signatory—a glaring weakness in the Iranian campaign to ensure its postwar independence. Adding pro-American ministers to the Iranian government in early 1942 failed to win American support for the treaty. When Roosevelt and his entourage arrived in Tehran in November 1943, the Iranian government, on its own initiative, suggested a declaration, considered earlier by the United States, of the appropriate guarantees for independence, to be signed by the three Allied leaders. Because of greater problems facing them and in the interests of Allied unity, the American team was reluctant to introduce the proposal during the Big Three meetings. Iran gained American backing for the declaration, however, by falsely informing the U.S. delegation that Stalin and Molotov already had agreed to the Iranian proposal.[11]

---

[10]Hassan Arfa, *Under Five Shahs* (New York, 1965), p. 325; Fatemi, *Oil Diplomacy,* pp. 219, 234; Hossein Kay'Ustavan, *Siyasat-e movazaneh-ye manfi dar Majles-e Chahardahom* [The Policy of Negative Equilibrium in the Fourteenth Parliament], 2 vols. (Tehran, 1949–50), 1:193–94; *FRUS, 1944,* 5:390–92; James Thorpe, "The Mission of Arthur C. Millspaugh to Iran, 1943–1945" (Ph.D. diss., University of Wisconsin, 1973), p. 385; and Lenczowski, *Russia and the West in Iran,* p. 271.

[11]*FRUS, 1942,* 4:264–65; 891.00/1829, 2 March 1942; and *FRUS, 1943: The Conferences at Cairo and Tehran,* pp. 619–20, 648–49.

Iran kept the United States informed of all Soviet transgressions during the war, helping to convince American officials of the Soviet danger.[12] In 1941 the Iranian ambassador to Vichy France warned President Roosevelt's aide Admiral Leahy that the Soviets would pillage and destroy Iran. The Iranian government made repeated complaints to the American minister in Tehran regarding Soviet interference. On at least one occasion, when Soviet interference was neither clear-cut nor of a severe nature, Iran exacerbated the situation, enhancing the appearance of the Soviet violation. In 1942 Iranian officials informed the United States of Soviet actions that hindered the movement of Iranian troop reinforcements into Soviet-occupied Kurdistan for the purpose of preventing an uprising. Iran blamed the Soviets for the unrest despite the earlier Soviet permission Iran had received to attack the Kurds and despite several attempts by a Soviet consul general to urge the Kurds to disband. When the situation deteriorated, the Soviets permitted the Iranian army to send five hundred reinforcements against the Kurds. The Iranian minister of war delayed, insisting he would need fifteen hundred reinforcements to put down the rebellion. Once again the Soviets agreed to the demands only to have the war minister raise his demands to five thousand additional troops. The Soviets again gave their permission for the full-scale military invasion of Kurdistan. The American minister at Tehran earlier had warned the State Department that Iran was exaggerating its reports of Soviet interference in order to gain American sympathy and support. Consular intelligence reports indicated no signs of covert Soviet activities or serious interference in local affairs, concluding, to the contrary, that Soviet occupation forces were better behaved than the troops of the other three Allied nations in Iran—Britain, the United States, and Poland.[13]

The struggle of domestic political forces in Iran for supremacy was linked to these efforts to attract American support. Diverse power centers formed mercurial coalitions to fight in the social, economic, and political conflicts. The shah and the army he controlled formed one power center, relying on the United States for military advisers and aid. The government and the gendarmerie it controlled also sought American advisers and American intervention but often opposed the shah. The Parliament was a hodgepodge of eight factions: royalists, conservatives, bureaucrats (all three largely pro-American and somewhat pro-British), northern

[12]See, for example, Cordell Hull, *The Memoirs of Cordell Hull*, 2 vols. (New York, 1948), 2:1253; and *FRUS, 1944*, 5:442–43, wherein Secretary of State Hull and Secretary of War Stimson clearly expressed their fears of a Soviet campaign to absorb Iran into the USSR after the war.

[13]William D. Leahy, *I Was There* (New York, 1950), p. 49; *FRUS, 1941*, 3:383–477; *FRUS, 1942*, 4:318–25; *FRUS, 1943*, 4:319–427; *FRUS, 1944*, 5:445–86; *FRUS, 1945*, 8:359–522; 891.00/1827, 2 February 1942; 891.00/1866, 3 May 1942; 891.00/1874, 15 May 1942; 891.00/1875, 16 May 1942; *FRUS, 1941*, 3:463–64; 891.43/9–2244, No. 38; 891.00/3012, 3 February 1944; and *FRUS, 1943*, 4:338–42.

liberals, Tudeh Communist party (both pro-Soviet), southern liberals, southern tribal leaders (both pro-British), and independents (xenophobic).[14] The Tudeh Communist party gained its support from the industrial cities and the Soviet Union. Merchants and clerics in the traditional cities attracted British support. Other political factions organized more than two dozen political parties with various degrees of foreign support and backing by more than one hundred newspapers. Tribal and ethnic minority factions formed autonomous enclaves when the central government lost its power to control rural areas. Many of these enclaves existed within the Allied occupation zones.

These disparate elements pursued great power sponsorship for the special advantages it could provide in the competition for domestic supremacy. Reaction against the monarchy after the invasion left the shah with only the army for support, and he turned to the United States to strengthen it. The efforts of three prime ministers to attract American support through economic concessions and advisory programs already have been related. In September 1941 another prime minister called for Allied support, warning that the shah would have to be deposed if basic reforms were to be accomplished. The shah promised to return previously confiscated properties to certain large southern pro-British landlords in order to gain British support in the power struggle. The Tudeh Communist party served Soviet interests in Iran and flourished in areas under Soviet control. Several government members tried to balance their allegiances. One prime minister, for example, attempted to win an oil concession for American oil firms and was a member of the Iran-America Relations Society. He was also a member of the Irano-Soviet Cultural Relations Society and a large contributor to a relief agency for Soviet war victims. Pro-British and pro-Soviet groups used their connections to the Great Powers to force the recall of a governor general of Esfahan in 1944 because he had been suppressing their activities. This pattern of factionalism continued until 1944, when crises over labor unrest in Esfahan and over the issuance of an oil concession crystallized the domestic forces into those that supported the shah and the Western Allies and those that supported unrest, northern separatists, and the Soviet Union (though friction continued within the broad coalitions).[15]

Shah Mohammad Reza Pahlavi proved most adept at playing this game for supremacy, establishing ties with America lasting more than three decades. He convinced American diplomats of his progressive views and of his value in solving Iran's problems. His radio broadcast early in

---

[14]Ervand Abrahamian, "Factionalism in Iran: Political Groups in the 14th Parliament (1944–46)," *Middle Eastern Studies* 14 (January 1978): 32–35.

[15]891.00/1771, 12 September 1941; *FRUS, 1941,* 3:461; Office of Strategic Services, Numerical File, 115902, Record Group 226, National Archives, Washington (hereafter cited as OSS, followed by numerical file number), 13 February 1945; 891:43/5, 6 April 1943; and OSS, 84161, 8 July 1944.

the war, for example, identified democracy as Iran's best hope for the future. In December 1942 the shah used a serious food shortage, blamed on the British, to incite food riots, hoping to force the legal government to resign and open the way for a martial law administration under his control. In 1944 he tried to subvert the Parliament in order to establish a martial law administration. Soon after his arrival in Iran in 1942, American military adviser General Clarence Ridley became the object of a governmental disagreement. The shah wanted Ridley to serve as his aide in reorganizing the army, thereby maintaining court control over the military. The prime minister, on the other hand, wanted to make Ridley the assistant minister of war, under the authority of the minister of war, who also happened to be the prime minister. The effect would have been to interrupt the chain of command between the shah and the army. Ridley eventually became inspector general—a victory for the shah. Negotiations in 1943 for an early Allied withdrawal from Iran indicated the extent to which the shah was willing to go in order to achieve supremacy. The Iranian government was pushing hard for the proposal, intent on restoring order and internal security. The shah, in a confidential discussion with the American minister, implied he would prefer that Allied forces remain in Iran to prevent a revolution against the monarchy, at least until he could rebuild his army and gain an upper hand in the domestic power struggle. The Allies denied Iran's requests for an early withdrawal.[16]

By late 1943 Iran had succeeded in gaining at least a measure of American involvement. American advisers were helping to run the country, the United States had issued the Tehran Declaration, and Roosevelt had stated his desire to make Iran an "example of what we could do by an unselfish American policy." Just two years earlier the United States had refused to intervene in Iran, leaving it to the British.[17]

Actual Soviet aggression and interference in Iranian affairs was limited until October 1944, when Iran announced its decision to postpone all negotiations for an oil concession until after the war. The oil crisis of that month became a catalyst for the Soviet-American confrontation over Iran. The apparent anti-Soviet nature of the postponement encouraged the Soviet Union to see an American attempt to seize Iranian oil for itself.[18]

Iran had tried as early as the 1920s to attract American oil companies to balance the British-owned Anglo-Iranian Oil Company.

---

[16]*FRUS, 1945*, 8:384–86; *Ettela'at,* 4 Aban 1320, p. 1; 891.00/2042–7/8, 4 November 1943; *FRUS, 1942*, 4:219–20; 891.00/3005, 22 January 1944; Department of the Army, *United States Army in World War II: The Middle East Theater; The Persian Corridor and Aid to Russia,* ed. T. H. Vail Motter (Washington, DC, 1952; rep. ed., 1969), p. 172; and *FRUS, 1943*, 4:405–6, 408–10.
[17]*FRUS, 1942*, 4:242; and Hull, *The Memoirs of Cordell Hull*, 2:1507.
[18]891.00/3012, 3 February 1944; 891.00/7–1944; 891.00/9–2544; 891.00/10–944; Bashkirov, *Ekspansia Angliiskikh i Amerikanskikh imperialistov v Irane,* pp. 99–107; and Popov, *Amerikanskii imperialism v Irane v gody vtoroi voiny,* pp. 209–35.

Standard Oil of New Jersey and Sinclair received invitations for possible concessions but nothing came of them. In the 1930s Iran pursued six American oil companies, succeeding in 1937, over Soviet objection, with Seaboard Oil (a subsidiary of the Texas Company). This Amiranian concession was canceled in 1938 on Seaboard's initiative. In 1940 Standard Oil of New Jersey approached Iran for a concession and Iran responded positively. However, after the Soviet Union informed Iran that any new oil concession granted to a foreign power would be a threat to Soviet security, Iran advised Standard Oil that the concession would be held in abeyance because of the deteriorating world situation. The American minister in Tehran identified this episode as an Iranian attempt to attract American support against a perceived Soviet threat.[19]

In early 1943 the Iranian commercial attaché in Washington approached Standard Vacuum to seek an agreement for an oil concession. The American government and firms jumped on the invitation once it was made, in spite of warnings from the U.S. minister in Tehran and from the head of the American economic advisory mission that oil negotiations in Iran might jeopardize Allied unity. In December the Iranian government sent official invitations to Standard Vacuum and Standard Oil of New Jersey. Constant delays in the negotiations over the next year caused the Iranian prime minister to encourage American companies to forestall any Soviet or British interference. In February 1944 the Soviets reminded Iran of their "prior rights" to northern oil. Disregarding the warning, the Iranian government in April included the northern provinces in the prospective American concession. British oil interests joined the competition in late 1943, but the Soviets did not join until September 1944. On 2 October 1944 the Soviets made an official offer, followed shortly by the demand for an oil concession. Iran's *movazaneh* strategy had backfired. Instead of attracting the United States as a buffer against Anglo-Soviet participation in oil matters, Iran was left with all three countries simultaneously demanding concessions. The only way out was to deny concessions to all, which Iran did on 8 October. After more than a year of visible efforts to win a concession for American oil interests, Iran decided, only six days after the arrival of a Soviet offer, to postpone negotiations until after the war. The employment of two American petroleum geologists as advisers on oil matters made the postponement seem more sinister, raising the specter of American involvement in denying the Soviets a concession. In 1941 the Soviets had attempted to resurrect a defunct oil agreement with Iran, but they were told new negotiations would have to be held. In 1944 the Soviets attempted new negotiations but again were denied.[20]

---

[19]*FRUS, 1940*, 3:659–63; and 891.6363 STANDARD OIL/430, 7 May 1940.
[20]891.6363/12–1144, No. 148; 891.6363/808, 20 October 1943; *FRUS, 1943*, 4:625; *FRUS, 1944*, 5:343–45; 891.6363/802, 22 June 1943; *FRUS, 1943*, 4:627–28;

The Soviet reaction was severe. For the first time in the war, Moscow openly employed the Tudeh Communist party to organize demonstrations against the Iranian government. Traffic heading north into the Soviet zone was halted and food shipments south out of Soviet-occupied Azerbaijan were temporarily stopped. Soviet representatives threatened Iranian officials with dire consequences for the affront. The disruptive acts ended only after the resignation of the prime minister and the cabinet, who were responsible for the postponement, and after announcements of American support for the Iranian decision. This ultimate American backing proved the advisability of the *movazaneh* strategy.[21]

Soviet scholars and American revisionist historians have blamed the United States, specifically the oil companies, for the 1944 crisis, although the evidence indicates they did not create the problem. Iran instigated the affair as another attempt to gain American involvement in Iran. Still, all concerned parties should have anticipated the Soviet response. Throughout the twentieth century Russia continually had indicated its objections to any other foreign powers establishing a presence in northern Iran. In 1921 a Soviet-Iranian treaty canceled a Tsarist concession in northern Iran with the understanding that the concession area would never be ceded to a third power. In 1940 the Soviets clearly stated their objection to an American concession anywhere in Iran. In 1941 the Soviets expressed their continuing desire for an oil concession, and by 1944 they claimed "prior rights" to northern oil. Despite these actions, Iran pursued a concession with American companies. Iran's decision canceling negotiations was aimed clearly at the Soviet Union. The United States, by announcing support for Iran in the crisis, by permitting two American oil experts to advise Iran on oil matters, and by ignoring the warnings of its own officials, came out in strong support of Iran and its anti-Soviet stand. Soviet Ambassador Andrei Gromyko in Washington cited "hidden influences" behind Iran's actions. The lines of confrontation had been drawn, with the United States and Iran opposing the Soviet Union, but the Soviets postponed the battle over Iran until after the war with Germany.[22]

891.6363/826, 28 February 1944; 891.6363/836, 3 April 1944; *FRUS, 1944,* 5:445–46; and 891.6363/12–1144, No. 148.

[21]*FRUS, 1944,* 5:456–57, 462–63; 891.6363/12–1144, No. 148; OSS, L49460, 16 November 1944; and *FRUS, 1944,* 5:457–61.

[22]Popov, *Amerikanskii imperialism v Irane v gody vtoroi voiny,* pp. 218–19; Paterson, *Soviet-American Confrontation,* p. 177; Gabriel Kolko, *The Politics of War* (New York, 1968), pp. 300–1; Lloyd C. Gardner, *Economic Aspects of New Deal Diplomacy* (Madison, 1964), p. 229; L. P. Elwell-Sutton, *Persian Oil: A Study in Power Politics* (London, 1955; rep. ed., 1975), pp. 11, 14, 18, 21, 33, 36–42; *FRUS, 1943,* 4:626; Fatemi, *Oil Diplomacy,* pp. 244–45; Bashkirov, *Ekspansia Angliiskikh i Amerikanskikh imperialistov v Irane,* pp. 56–57; *FRUS, 1943,* 4:625; and 891.6363/12–2844, No. 7288.

On 2 December 1944, under the sponsorship of Mohammad Mosaddeq, the Iranian Parliament passed a law outlawing any discussions with foreigners on the subject of an oil concession. In Iranian historiography this Mosaddeq law has received special emphasis and

Actions taken by the Iranian government after the oil crisis indicated additional efforts to attract American involvement in Iranian affairs, especially since Iran had goaded its northern neighbor into an aggressive stance. In late 1944 Iran notified the Allies that its internal air routes would be closed to all foreign air carriers after the war, but it privately told the United States that the prohibition was aimed at the USSR and not the United States. In early 1945 Iran dropped all pretense and appealed to the United States for direct military intervention to stop Soviet aggression and to support Iran in its efforts to send forces into the northern areas to quelch unrest. It also attempted to negotiate an early Allied withdrawal, although the Treaty of Alliance clearly gave the Allies the right to remain in Iran until six months after the war with "Germany and her associates." At the same time, the Iranian government was secretly advising the American government that the withdrawal demands applied only to British and Soviet and not American forces. Ironically, despite Iran's efforts, the Americans were the first to withdraw in December 1945, followed two months later by the British and five months later by the Soviets (the latter in clear violation of treaty requirements).[23]

Beginning in the summer of 1945, local unrest in Soviet-occupied Azerbaijan and Kurdistan, encouraged but not created by the Soviets, led the central authorities in Tehran to initiate military measures to restore order and control. Iran retained the right to maintain internal security, according to Article 3 of the Treaty of Alliance, although that right was subordinate to Iran's responsibility under Article 4 to safeguard the security of Allied forces. Iran exacerbated an already tense situation by moving into direct confrontation with Soviet forces still occupying the northern provinces. The Soviets claimed this threatened the security of their forces in Iran.[24]

On 19 November 1945 Soviet forces at Qazvin, ninety miles northwest of Tehran, halted an Iranian army column ordered into Azerbaijan. The Iranian government assumed a three-sided response to the issue. First, it doubled its efforts to keep the United States constantly informed of all Soviet actions and especially misdeeds. Second, it labored to preserve the crisis atmosphere until the Soviets withdrew from Iran and until the control of the central authorities could be restored in the northern

---

has been glorified as one of the first examples of nationalist reaction against foreign imperialists in modern Iranian history. The law also forms part of the mystique surrounding Mosaddeq. The Mosaddeq law was largely bravado, designed for internal consumption, because the 8 October government announcement postponing discussions was the coup de grâce of the wartime oil question. For the text of the law, see *FRUS, 1944*, 5:479. For the Iranian view, see Amuzgar, *Naft va havades-e Azarbaijan*, pp. 45–74; and Kay'Ustavan, *Siyasat-e movazaneh-ye manfi dar Majles-e Chahardahom*, 1:184–87.

[23]*FRUS, 1944*, 5:492–93; and *FRUS, 1945*, 8:360–62, 373–74, 383.
[24]"Treaty of Alliance Between the United Kingdom and the Soviet Union, and Iran," *Department of State Bulletin* 6 (21 March 1942) : 249–52; and *FRUS, 1945*, 8:470–71.

areas. And third, it sent a trusted representative, well known as a friend of America, to Washington, an ambassador capable of working on public opinion and able to pressure government officials.

The greatest immediate problem confronting the United States was the acquisition of accurate intelligence on the incident. With Iran controlling the initial sources of information, reports were forwarded of six thousand Soviet troops manning the roadblock at Qazvin and of widespread Soviet efforts to encourage revolts against the Iranian government. The American ambassador was careful to warn the State Department that: "Communications difficulties plus the unreliability of even official Iranians as factual reporters make it impossible . . . to vouch for the absolute accuracy of reports forwarded." He described reports of the Soviets arming civilians in the North and reports of six thousand Soviet troops in civilian clothing pouring over the border as mere "fabrications." After American diplomatic personnel visited the area of the disturbances and observed events firsthand, a different situation was revealed. The American military attaché traveled to Qazvin and Karaj, scenes of the purported obstructions, and called Iranian reports "alarmist." The Soviets had created roadblocks, but at Qazvin the blocking force was composed of two armored cars and a small infantry detachment, not six thousand armored troops. He found no Soviet troops at Karaj. The ambassador repeated his warning to Washington on the unreliability of information given by Iranian sources. Traveling on into Azerbaijan by car, the military attaché found no evidence of open Soviet intervention, although he felt the Soviets in spirit backed northern insurrectionists. The Soviets had interfered in Iranian domestic affairs but no attempt was made at the time to construct satellite regimes in northern Iran.[25]

The Iranian army chief of staff asked the government for permission to withdraw the column from Qazvin and return to Tehran several days after it was forced to halt. He saw no military reason for encamping there unable to advance. The government denied his request outright and ordered him to keep the troops at Qazvin, because a withdrawal in the face of the enemy would be politically impossible. The case claiming Soviet interference would dissolve unless the evidence was preserved. The American ambassador cited this incident as more evidence of Iran's efforts to exacerbate the crisis and to keep it alive. The troops were not withdrawn from Qazvin until 18 December 1945.[26]

In Washington, Hossein 'Ala, the new Iranian ambassador, arrived in time to further exaggerate the reports. 'Ala was a former court minister, right-hand man of the shah, and a public figure well known for his pro-American leanings. Stepping off the plane from Iran at New York's La

---

[25]*FRUS, 1945*, 8:436–37, 442–43, 433, 440–41, 447–48; 891.00/11–2845, No. 1009; and *FRUS, 1945*, 8:470, 472, 477.
[26]*FRUS, 1945*, 8:491, 501–2.

Guardia Airport, he assailed Soviet policy before American newspaper-men. In Washington, he insisted on presenting his credentials directly to President Truman, but his petitions were initially rejected. He persevered and on 29 November appeared before Truman. 'Ala told him that the United States alone could save Iran and asked for immediate intervention by American military forces and for an American promise to get a seat on the UN Security Council for Iran. 'Ala's major themes, presented to government officials and to the press, were that the crisis would destroy the United Nations if not met head-on by direct American action and would become the "first shot fired in a third world war." He found a receptive audience among some State Department officials, who seemed willing to ignore the warnings of Iranian exaggerations and manipulations. High-level officials and a majority of the American people, as demonstrated by public opinion polls, remained cautious and perhaps unconvinced of the critical nature of the crisis until early 1946.[27]

The crisis over troop obstructions never was resolved but rather was preempted by a new crisis. On 12 and 15 December 1945 separatist forces in the North established the Autonomous Republic of Azerbaijan and the Kurdish People's Republic. The declarations of autonomy were the results of domestic issues, though the Soviets certainly had encouraged them, and came only after four years of demands for basic rights by the northern minorities. The central government continually failed to respond to the demands. In 1945 the Tehran government appointed a reactionary as governor general of Azerbaijan and used the army to suppress leftist forces all over Iran, especially Tudeh offices. Mohammad Mosaddeq accused the government of driving Azerbaijan toward rebellion. Separatist sentiments existed apart from the Soviet occupation and were either supported by or used by the Soviets. The Iranian government used the Soviet presence as an excuse for an age-old internal problem. Under Iranian tutelage, this attempt to dismember the Iranian state intensified the drive toward a direct Soviet-American confrontation. The existence of Soviet troops in the area, the Iranian accusations of Soviet involvement, and the expanding Cold War atmosphere in the United States and

---

[27]*New York Times,* 11 November 1945, p. 19; Matthew Connelly (secretary to the president) to Stanley Woodword (acting state department chief of protocol), 26 January 1946, Box 569, Official File, Papers of Harry S Truman, Harry S Truman Library, Independence, MO; and *FRUS, 1945,* 8:461–62, 500–1, 508.

The idea of Iran as a spark for a third world war was a popular theme among Iranian writers during the period. See, for example, Mohammad Khan Malek Yazdi, *Jang-e jahangir-e sevom dar Iran* [The Third World War in Iran] (Tehran, 1952).

Loy Henderson, director of the Office of Near East and African Affairs, and Harold Minor, chief of the Division of Middle East Affairs, were two of the most visible advocates of pursuing a hard line. Henderson, for example, accepted and repeated Iran's claim that the United States was Iran's only hope for freedom. See *FRUS, 1945,* 8:501.

elsewhere magnified this largely internal concern into what has been commonly declared the first battle of the Cold War.[28]

The crisis developed rapidly. 'Ala, always the agent provocateur, identified this crisis as one of Soviet initiative because the northern peoples were true patriots incapable of rebellion. His analysis of events negated the domestic issues and concentrated on what he declared was open and vicious Soviet aggression. He asked for an American military demonstration in Tehran and insisted that the United States confront the Iranian issue at the Moscow Conference of Foreign Ministers. He also pressed for an early hearing of Iran's case at the United Nations. The shah had tried as early as November 1945 to obtain American support for an appeal to the UN but instead was told to try bilateral negotiations. By 19 January 1946, under the impetus of events both inside and outside Iran, American policy had changed. Iran presented its complaints to the Security Council, thus succeeding in expanding the fledgling Soviet-American confrontation over Iran into an international concern more than a month prior to the 2 March 1946 deadline for the Soviet withdrawal from Iran. Over the following months the initiative behind the crisis shifted from Iran to the United States and the Soviet Union. Soviet troop movements into Iran caused the American consul in Azerbaijan to report a Soviet armored thrust to seize Iran, Turkey, and the entire Middle East. Stalin reasserted the struggle against capitalism; President Truman became tired of "babying" the Soviets; Secretary of State James Byrnes decided to give the Soviets "both barrels"; Charge George Kennan from Moscow sent his famous "long telegram"; Winston Churchill identified Soviet "expansive and proselytizing tendencies" and popularized the term "iron curtain"; and the American public turned rapidly against the Soviet Union.[29]

---

[28]Arfa, *Under Five Shahs*, p. 346; and Mohammad Mosaddeq, speech before Parliament, *Mozakerat-e majles* [Parliamentary Debates], sess. 171, 14th Majles, 23 Azar 1324.

Ja'far Pishevari, head of the Azerbaijani movement, was born in Iran but moved to Russia where he participated in the Bolshevik Revolution. He returned to Iran after World War I to aid the short-lived uprising in Gilan. In the 1920s and 1930s he vacillated between exile in the Soviet Union and Communist activities in Iran. He was the Iranian delegate in the Communist International for a time and in 1945 became the head of the Democratic party of Azerbaijan. His record reveals the extent of Soviet involvement in the events of 1945–46.

Qazi Mohammad, head of the Kurdish movement, was a religious figure and leading citizen of Mahabad, the capital of the Kurdish People's Republic. He had few, if any, ties to the Soviet Union, though he visited Baku in 1945. For him the Soviets were a means to achieve Kurdish autonomy or independence. His record reveals the nationalist impetus behind the events of 1945–46.

[29]Hussein Ala, "Iran's Dilemma: Promises of Allies Not Kept," *Vital Speeches of the Day* 12 (1 March 1946) : 305; *FRUS, 1945*, 8:487–88, 500–1, 508; *FRUS, 1946*, 7:292–94, 309, 340–45; Joseph Stalin, "New Five-Year Plan for Russia," *Vital Speeches of*

'Ala continued making bellicose speeches to the American public, appealing to America's sense of justice and fair play. He described the Soviets as "contagious bacilli." He disobeyed orders and retained the Iranian complaint before the United Nations at a time when his prime minister was attempting to defuse an issue becoming too hot to handle. The shah dramatically informed the American ambassador in Tehran that the United States should pursue Iran's appeal to the United Nations in case the Soviets captured Iran. The government of Iran continued the pressure on Washington by passing reports of large Soviet troop movements all over northern Iran. The American consul at Tabriz, capital of Azerbaijan, reported similar movements, although some of his reports were based on sightings passed to him by Iranian sources. The New York *Times*'s reporter in Iran wrote that he saw no sign of Soviet troop concentrations or movements at Qazvin, based on a reconnaissance flight over Azerbaijan, but he found fourteen tanks and other vehicles at Karaj. The revelation several years later that the shah had ordered the minister of war to announce a Soviet drive on Tehran, in order to inhibit a prime minister's efforts to reach a compromise with the Soviet Union, further challenged the accuracy of the accounts. The Soviet advances certainly occurred, but the reports of them probably were exaggerated.[30]

Public exposure at the United Nations, strong statements of American support, and a Soviet-Iranian oil agreement of 4 April 1946 ended the crisis over Moscow's refusal to withdraw from Iran. The oil agreement, the result of purely bilateral negotiations outside the Soviet-American confrontation, gave the Soviets a face-saving excuse to leave Iran and also repaired damaged relations caused by the Iranian decision in 1944 to deny a Soviet request for an oil concession. The Soviet evacuation was completed by 9 May 1946. An agreement in June temporarily reconciled the Iranian government and the northern separatist regimes. The situation was defused for the moment. The *movazaneh* policy had paid off once again. Iran's independence was secured and American support against Iran's foreign enemies had been essential in obtaining it. According to the American ambassador, Iran had invited the United States to interfere in Iranian affairs in order to eject the powerful northern

---

the Day 12 (1 March 1946) : 300–4; Truman, *Memoirs*, 1:552; *FRUS, 1946*, 7:346–48; *FRUS, 1946*, 6:696–709; and Winston Churchill, "Alliance of English-Speaking People," *Vital Speeches of the Day* 12 (15 March 1946) : 329–32.

　　In September 1945 the Gallup Poll indicated 54 percent of the American people still trusted the Soviets. By March 1946, 77 percent decried Soviet policies in Iran. *Washington Post,* 24 March 1946, p. 5B.

　　[30]Hussein Ala, "Iran's Dilemma," p. 305; Hussein Ala, "Power Politics in the Near East: Crossroads of Russia," *Vital Speeches of the Day* 12 (15 August 1946) : 662; *FRUS, 1946,* 7:350–54, 340, 342–43, 344–45; *New York Times,* 14 March 1946, p. 1; and Mehdi Davudi, *Qavam al-Saltaneh* (Tehran, 1948), pp. 115–16.

intruder. The American involvement with Iran was firm and growing.[31]

The 4 April 1946 agreement also had its domestic aspects. Prime Minister Ahmad Qavam, responsible for the agreement, had received parliamentary approval for his premiership by a one-vote margin provided by the Tudeh Communist party. To strengthen his position, Qavam first solidified his ties to leftists and to the Soviet Union. He lifted a ban on Tudeh activities, dismissed a reactionary chief of staff, journeyed to Moscow, arrested the strongly anti-Communist Seyyed Zia Tabataba'i, completed the oil agreement, and arrested a major, politically active cleric. He created his own power base, the Democratic party of Iran, and brought three members of the Tudeh party into his government in August 1946, placing them in an embarrassing position for opponents of the constitutional monarchy. According to the shah and the American ambassador in Iran, these steps indicated Qavam's weakness, leftist tendencies, and desire to overthrow the shah. Ambassador George Allen then schemed with the shah and several of his supporters to force Qavam to eject the Tudeh cabinet ministers, or, failing that, to overthrow him by means of a military coup.[32]

Qavam's actions prior to these plans indicated, however, that he was following a logical plan to reunite the country and reduce Soviet influence. In the weeks after the admission of the Tudeh ministers, Qavam cracked down on Tudeh demonstrations, arrested several prominent pro-Soviet activists and Tudeh labor leaders, launched raids on a number of Tudeh offices, completed an agreement with Azerbaijan to occupy Zanjan, announced new parliamentary elections, and curtailed the activities of the leftist press. He told the American ambassador he was looking for a safe way to remove the Tudeh ministers and other government officials with Tudeh connections before the shah and Ambassador Allen planned their moves. Then, under the impetus of a southern tribal uprising against Tudeh and Soviet influences in the government and under pressure from Ambassador Allen and the shah, Qavam tipped his hand and ejected the Tudeh ministers from his government, replaced several Tudeh governors, and announced his decision to use security forces to supervise the upcoming parliamentary elections throughout Iran. The immediate result was a standoff between Qavam and the shah. Qavam received the official support of the United States as the legal head of the government, which helped him to victory over various domestic foes. The American ambassador, however, established a close personal relationship with the shah, used his influence to get involved in a proposed coup against the

---

[31]*FRUS, 1946,* 7:495–96. For a treatment of Iran's case before the United Nations and of American support for Iran, see Richard W. Van Wagenen, *The Iranian Case, 1946* (New York, 1952).

[32]Kay'Ustavan, *Siyasat-e movazaneh-ye manfi dar Majles-e Chahardahom,* 2:245; Fatemi, *Oil Diplomacy,* p. 320; 891.00/6–146, No. 792; 891.00/10–2446, No. 231; and George V. Allen, "Mission to Iran," pp. 111–21, unpublished manuscript, Box 1, Papers of George V. Allen, Harry S Truman Library, Independence, MO.

legal government, and labored to undermine the coalition cabinet of Ahmad Qavam.[33]

Iran's ruling elite next used the American connection to restore their authority throughout the country and secure their own positions against domestic foes. Reports of Communist activities and the continued presence of the regimes in northern Iran maintained America's interest. The United States, under an increasingly activist foreign policy, promised arms for the Iranian army and announced its readiness to support, with words and actions, Iran's efforts to consolidate the rebellious provinces. In early December Iranian troops recaptured the northern areas and restored government control throughout Iran. The Iranian government credited the United States with preventing Soviet interference on behalf of the separatist regimes.[34]

The shah, Prime Minister Qavam, the Parliament, and other forces on the domestic political scene continued their struggle for supremacy after the national consolidation. In February 1947 the shah again planned a coup against Qavam. The shah expanded his cultivation of the United States by entertaining the American ambassador and promising strong anti-Soviet policies and a powerful Iran in return for American support. He claimed responsibility for Iran's successes over the Soviet Union: the denial of an oil concession in 1944 and the decision to invade Azerbaijan and Kurdistan. For the United States, the shah was important because of his control over the army. Qavam also claimed responsibility for the victories over the Soviet Union, and American diplomats in Iran supported his claim. To gain American support and domestic backing to enable him to weaken the shah's control over the armed forces, Qavam continued to publicize the Soviet threat. The American ambassador expressed his frustration over Qavam's constant efforts to make the still pending oil agreement with the Soviet Union into a Soviet-American issue instead of a strictly Soviet-Iranian concern. Qavam again offered American oil companies a concession, in part to balance the anticipated Soviet concession. Qavam's power base in the struggle was his Democratic party of Iran, created with the temporary and superficial support of a number of delegates to the Parliament, a majority of the civil servants, and a handful of anticourt aristocrats.[35]

---

[33]891.00/10–1446, No. 1359; 891.00/9–846, No. 1199; and *FRUS, 1946,* 7:512–13, 533, 537–39, 545–48.

[34]891.00/8–2246, memorandum; and *FRUS, 1946,* 7:515–16, 529–36, 544–47, 560–61. A recent article in *Diplomatic History* traces the development of this activist foreign policy in Iran. See Pfau, "Containment in Iran, 1946: The Shift to an Active Policy," pp. 359–72.

[35]891.00/2–2647, No. 138; *FRUS, 1944,* 5:455; 891.00/11–2446, No. 1517; 891.6363/8–2947, No. 816; Hassan Arfa, *The Kurds* (London, 1966), p. 97; Allen, "Mission to Iran," p. 59; *FRUS, 1947,* 5:912–13, 965–66; and *FRUS, 1946,* 7:34, 373.

The victory over Azerbaijan and Kurdistan should be attributed to Qavam and the shah. The shah all along had wanted to use the army to reunite the nation. Qavam

On the eve of the parliamentary debate over the proposed Soviet oil concession, Prime Minister Qavam informed the United States of intense Soviet military activities along the Soviet-Iranian border—a clear and present danger to Iran's security. The immediate response was a change in American policy. Initially in favor of oil concessions for all interested parties, the United States by mid-1947 opposed the establishment of any Soviet presence in Iran. Still, Iran received a strong public statement of American support to decide the fate of the oil issue free from outside pressure. Qavam temporized, trying to avoid any overt, provocative anti-Soviet moves. He had been the architect of the strategy to achieve a Soviet withdrawal by completing the 4 April 1946 agreement, and his political reputation rested with his success in balancing the Soviets, the shah, the United States, and liberals within his country, while dealing with the oil agreement. The shah strongly urged immediate action to deny the concession in order to attract American support, embarrass Qavam, and rid Iran of Soviet influence. On 22 October 1947 the Iranian Parliament voted 102 to 2 (both abstentions) to cancel the oil agreement with the Soviet Union. Iranian cold warriors were in control. The shah secured his supremacy over Qavam, who went into exile, and over his other opponents, though several of the forces released during the anarchy and freedom of wartime Iran continued to threaten the monarchy until 1953.[36]

In 1947 in a document handed to the Iranian government, the Soviets listed their grievances concerning the events of the previous seven years. They accused Iran of favoring American oil and aviation companies; of inviting American experts to run the army, police, and economy; and of creating international incidents by dragging the Soviets before the United Nations and then crushing the progressive democratic movements in northern Iran—all without consulting the Soviet government. The dialectics of the Cold War normally mandated blaming the United States for all such actions. The interesting point here is that the

restrained him, aware of the army's weakness and the probability of Soviet intervention to rescue the northern separatists. Qavam skillfully waited until strong statements of American support were forthcoming, announced the need to supervise elections in the North, correctly determined that Soviet interest in having a new Parliament approve the 4 April 1946 agreement would keep them from intervening, negotiated a joint occupation of Zanjan to act as a launching point for the eventual invasion of Kurdistan and Azerbaijan, and broke the power of the pro-Soviet Tudeh by coopting its leaders into his cabinet. Once these steps were taken, the shah then could order the army to press forward. This researcher has been unable to find any supporting evidence to indicate whether this process was accidental or part of a strategy. See *FRUS, 1946*, 7:511–12, 545–48; 891.00/9–846, No. 1199; and Fatemi, *Oil Diplomacy*, pp. 320–21.

[36]*FRUS, 1947*, 5:463-65; *FRUS, 1946*, 7:34–35; *FRUS, 1947*, 5:904–5, 909–10, 934–36; the public statement of support came in a speech before the Iran-America Cultural Society in Tehran by Ambassador Allen, 11 September 1947; 891.6363/10–2347, No. 1031; 891.6363/10–2347, No. 1035; *FRUS, 1947*, 5:929–30; Fatemi, *Oil Diplomacy*, p. 325; 891.00/8–3047, No. 3049; and *FRUS, 1947*, 5:948–50, 969–70.

Soviets correctly identified the root of the problem: all of these major conflicts between the involved parties occurred from Iranian initiative and not from a preconceived Soviet-American policy of confrontation.[37]

The Iranian Cold War crisis evolved from the interaction of two forces. First, Iranians laid the foundation for the confrontation and worked to enlarge it for Iran's advantage. Second, international representatives entered Iran for their own purposes, reacted to domestic events, became entangled in the maelstrom of Iranian politics, and ultimately assumed the initiative in intensifying the confrontation. They then used Iran as a stage for acting out international disputes arising from additional points of contention outside of Iran. The United States reacted to apparent anarchy in Iran in order to protect Middle Eastern oil and to help Iran by aiding the Iranian government and by intervening in Iranian affairs. American diplomats failed to heed signs of Iranian complicity in creating the perception of a Soviet threat and to recognize the continuity of Iranian politics. Although more than thirty cabinets served between 1941 and 1947, they were formed from a close clique of seventy to eighty politicians.[38] All of the prime ministers during these years were members of the old Qajar (the dynasty ruling Iran from 1794 to 1925), elite, trained in Iranian statecraft, in dealing with the Russians, and in using the *movazaneh* strategy to attract the support of a counterbalancing great power. The only newcomer on whom the United States placed its hopes for a stable Iran was the shah. Over the next three decades, America's ties to the shah and the shah's ties to America were solidified, and the interests and perceptions of the United States merged with those of the shah of Iran.

The Soviet Union searched for oil in Iran during 1945 and 1946, despite the lack of an agreement. Perhaps the reason they did not insist more forcibly on the approval of the 4 April 1946 agreement was their inability to find oil in the concession area. George Kennan, writing from Moscow in 1944 in response to the oil crisis of that year, determined that the Soviets were pushing the concession issue in late 1944 to ensure no other great power established a presence in northern Iran and therefore had no real interest in Iranian oil. See *FRUS, 1944,* 5:470–71. Intensive Soviet drilling in northern Iran after the war would, at least in part, refute his analysis. For a record on the Soviet oil search, see 891.6363/11–2645, No. 163; 891.6363/1–846, No. 35; and 891.6363/12–2446, No. 28. See also OSS files: XL22220, 9 October 1945; XL26453, 16 October 1945; XL26521, 22 October 1945; XL27875, 29 October 1945; XL30644, 15 November 1945; XL30645, 26 November 1945; XL44109, 29 January 1946; and XL47939, 4 March 1946.

[37]*FRUS, 1947,* 5:906–7.

[38]L. P. Elwell-Sutton, "Political Parties in Iran, 1941–1948," *Middle East Journal* 3 (Winter 1949) : 46.

Indochina and Anglo-American Relations, 1942-1945

Christopher Thorne

The author is reader in international relations in the University of Sussex.

W ITHIN THE SPACE of a single article, it is impossible to do justice to all the factors which, at various times during the Second World War, affected the particular issue of Indochina between Britain and the United States. At the outset, therefore, the most one can do is to recall some of the main contextual elements which were involved, and which, it is hoped, eventually will be treated in the book form which they require. There was, for example, the shifting overall relationship between Britain and the U.S.A., in which, from a position of morally, if not materially, equal partnership around 1941-1942, Britain declined to junior status from about the time of the Cairo Conference onwards. Thus, for example, soon after that conference, Secretary of the Treasury Henry Morgenthau, Jr. could observe (and President Franklin D. Roosevelt, who read what

This article is based on a paper read to the Southern California Japan Society. My thanks are due to the British Social Science Research Council for supporting my wider studies of the Second World War in the Far East, of which this is only one aspect.

Since this paper went to press, Walter LaFeber has published one on a similar subject entitled "Roosevelt, Churchill, and Indochina: 1942-45," *American Historical Review*, LXXX (1975), 1277-1295. It will be seen that, while agreeing with LaFeber in several respects, the present article (making use of papers of Foreign Office departments other than the Far Eastern one, and, for example, of the SEAC War Diary) offers a differing emphasis on such matters as the setting up of Southeast Asia Command and the complexity of Churchill's policies in 1945. I also disagree with LaFeber's interpretation of British policy toward China, though that is a matter for a subsequent book and not the present article.

he had written, did not contradict him) that "the Roosevelt-Stalin axis is gaining strength and the Roosevelt-Churchill axis is losing strength in about equal ratio";[1] thus a State Department bureau-crat like Stanley Hornbeck could see his country as being "in a po-sition to get from the British agreement to and cooperation in any reasonable course of action upon which we may choose to insist";[2] thus, by the end of 1944, the head of the Foreign Office's North American Department would even feel bound to acknowledge that in order to secure essential postwar financial aid from the United States, "we may well find ourselves forced to follow [her] in a line of policy with which we do not fundamentally agree."[3]

The position of France and of Charles de Gaulle between both Britain and the United States is another obviously relevant factor, with various local episodes not only sharpening the hostility ex-pressed towards the General in Washington, but also making Winston Churchill—as opposed to the Foreign Office—far more in-clined to adopt the stance of Cordell Hull, William Leahy, and Roosevelt. As one example, trouble over the Levant and the Val d'Aosta in 1945 diminished the likelihood that the Prime Minister would enter the fray there and then on behalf of France over Indo-china.[4] At the same time, two developments were taking place which also affected that issue, although they are too well-known to require further elaboration: the mounting evidence of ineptitude and declining authority on the part of the Chiang Kai-shek regime in China, and the growing stresses in Soviet-American relations, as perceived in Washington. Both these last-named factors, of course, worked to the benefit of France where Indochina was concerned.

Other international issues becoming entwined in our subject in-cluded designs for the postwar political and security system in the Far East, trusteeships, access to markets and raw materials, and the fear, especially among certain American officials, that, even whilst losing the war, Japan might successfully create a fundamental divi-

1 Morgenthau, Presidential Diaries, vol. 5, Morgenthau Papers, Franklin D. Roose-velt Library, Hyde Park.
2 Hornbeck to Cordell Hull, Jan. 3, 1944, box 180, Hornbeck Papers, Hoover In-stitution, Stanford University.
3 UE 615/169/53, F.O.371 (all Foreign Office, Cabinet and Premier papers, Public Record Office, London).
4 For example, UE 2711/2/G, F.O.371.

sion along racial and color lines between Asia and the West.[5] For the moment, however, this sketch of the background requires a concluding emphasis upon certain aspects of the Anglo-American relationship as it evolved in Southeast Asia and the Far East. First, there is the fact that nowhere was American preponderance more evident than in the war against Japan: most surveys in official circles in Washington took the line that the United States was conducting that particular conflict virtually single-handedly, and the British effort within the Southeast Asia Command ("Save England's Asiatic Colonies," as it was known by Americans on the spot[6]) was regarded as not only small, but too often fainthearted. "The British," wrote George C. Marshall in a draft note to the President in October 1944, "have never been in accord with [Joseph Stilwell's] aggressive policy."[7] Moreover, within SEAC and neighboring areas, the prevailing view in Washington was that American and British policies were very far apart. It was wrongly assumed (and trumpeted from the spot by that buffoon among ambassadors, Patrick Hurley[8]) that Britain was working for a divided China; in late 1944 it was passed on to the President by the Office of Strategic Services, the State Department, and again Hurley, that Britain, France, and the Netherlands had closely coordinated their policies in Southeast Asia in the interest of rampant imperialism;[9] and while there was no foundation for this belief, there was more reason for American watchfulness over Siam, where Britain was rightly suspected ("Churchill" would be more accurate than "Britain") of wanting some special arrangement by which the Kra Isthmus could be fortified to help prevent a repetition of the 1941–1942 attack on Singapore.[10]

---

[5] See, for example, U.S. Dept. of State, *Foreign Relations of the United States, 1942: China* (Washington, D.C., 1956), 71.

[6] See, for example, E. Taylor, *Richer by Asia* (London, 1948), and *Awakening from History* (London, 1971).

[7] Draft of Oct. 4, 1944, Exec. file 10, item 60, Army Operational Plans Division files, (hereafter cited as Army OPD files), National Archives.

[8] See Hurley's messages to Roosevelt, Map Room, box 11, Roosevelt Papers, Franklin D. Roosevelt Presidential Library, Hyde Park, N.Y.

[9] See, for example, Hull to Roosevelt, Sept. 8, 1944, Map Room, box 166; and Edward Stettinius to Roosevelt, Nov. 2, 1944, President's Secretary's file, box 53, Roosevelt Papers.

[10] See, for example, material marked 1–945 and 1–1045 in file 892.01, Dept. of State Papers, National Archives.

Thus, in Washington, it was believed, in the words of Assistant Secretary of State Adolf Berle, that Britain and the United States were "miles apart in Asia."[11] And on the spot, whilst Stilwell's Ledo Road strategy and personal bitterness toward the British ("pig-fuckers," he called them in his diary[12]) helped to sour relations between the China-Burma-India command and SEAC, the general's political adviser, John Davies, warned of wider dangers:

In so far as we participate in SEAC operations, we become involved in the politically explosive colonial problems of the British, Dutch and possibly French. In doing so, we compromise ourselves not only with the colonial peoples of Asia but also the free peoples of Asia, including the Chinese. Domestically, our Government lays itself open to public criticisms—"Why should American boys die to recreate the colonial empires of the British and their Dutch and French satellites?" Finally, more Anglo-American misunderstanding and friction is likely to arise out of our participation in SEAC than out of any other theatre. There-fore we should concentrate our Asiatic efforts on operations in and from China. . . .[13]

Within SEAC, then, it seemed in General R. A. Wheeler's words that "American interest points north to [China and] Japan, British interest south to Singapore."[14] And two other features concerning this theater were to become important as far as Indochina was con-cerned: its command structure and its boundaries. Before the Que-bec conference in August 1943 at which SEAC was set up, Churchill and the British chiefs of staff had wanted to secure a Douglas MacArthur-like status for a British supreme commander, answer-able to them alone;[15] however, although General Marshall privately acknowledged that the British had not been kept adequately in-formed of developments within MacArthur's South West Pacific Area, the importance of SEAC for supply routes to China led the American side to insist upon and obtain a Dwight Eisenhower-type command.[16] This meant that while immediate operational matters

11 Berle to Roosevelt, Oct. 2, 1943, file 740.001 P.W./3499a, *ibid.*

12 Stilwell Diary, Aug. 8, 1944, Hoover Institution.

13 U.S. Dept. of State, *Foreign Relations of the United States, 1943: China* (Wash-ington, D.C., 1957), 188.

14 Wheeler to George C. Marshall, March 24, 1945, Army OPD files, Exec. file 17, item 26.

15 Material in PREM 3,147/2,4; Chiefs of Staff minutes, Nov. 22, 1943, CAB 99/25.

16 Joint Chiefs of Staff minutes, Aug. 16, 1943, Record Group 218, National Archives.

were dealt with by London, the Joint Chiefs in Washington, through the Combined Chiefs of Staff, were equally responsible for overall strategy.

As for the boundaries of SEAC, as initially drafted on the American as well as on the British side they included not only Burma and Malaya but also Siam and Indochina. Belatedly, however, it was realized that for reasons of "face" Chiang Kai-shek, within whose China theater these two last named territories had been placed in 1941–1942, would be unlikely to welcome such an arrangement. There seems little reason to believe that at this stage long-term political considerations predominated in this matter; what was to prove unfortunate, however, was the blurred nature of the arrangements which were arrived at thereafter.[17] (On into 1945, for example, one can find much confusion within both Whitehall and official Washington as to whether Siam was or was not in SEAC.) Briefly, what happened was that when the new supreme commander of SEAC, Admiral Lord Louis Mountbatten, visited Chunking with the American General Brehon Somervell in October 1943, the Generalissimo, according to Somervell's notes, confirmed that he

felt that the inclusion of Thailand and Indochina in the Southeast Asia theatre would not be practicable . . . [because] of the effect which a change of boundary would have on the Chinese people, on Chinese troops, on the people of Thailand and Indochina, and on the Japanese . . . [but] as the war develops, the scope of operations of the . . . Southeast Asia theater . . . may involve Thailand and Indochina, . . . [when] the boundaries between the two theaters are to be decided at the time in accordance with the progress of advances the respective [Chinese and SEAC] forces make.

This so-called "Gentleman's Agreement" was accepted by the President and Joint Chiefs of Staff. It was not, however, formalized

---

[17] See, for example, the draft of June 22, 1943, by Marshall that proposed "unity of command for Southeast Asia, that is, for operations against Burma, Indochina, Thailand, Malaya and Sumatra" (Map Room, box 3, Roosevelt Papers). See also Leahy's observations at Quadrant, Aug. 23, 1943, CAB 99/23; Joint Chiefs of Staff minutes, Aug. 29, 1944; Churchill directive for Louis Mountbatten, Oct. 21, 1943, PREM 3,147/4; U.S. Dept. of State, *Foreign Relations of the United States, 1943: Cairo and Tehran* (Washington, D.C., 1961), 391; U.S. Dept. of War to Dept. of State, Nov. 1, 1943, file 740.001 P.W./3575, Dept. of State Papers; Churchill to Roosevelt, June 28, 1943, and Roosevelt to Churchill, June 30, 1943, PREM 3,471, in which the President originally accepted Indochina as within SEAC.

by the Combined Chiefs of Staff. Nor did it spell out that Chiang Kai-shek had also assured Mountbatten that, in the latter's words, "I should have the right to send in any agents or carry out any subversive activities that are required for a campaign in Siam or Indochina." Somervell's record did not contain this last point, which, as we shall see, was to be the focus of much controversy between Mountbatten and General Albert Wedemeyer in China in 1945. It is worth noting, therefore, that this point was recorded by Mountbatten at the time; moreover, despite later American denials of any knowledge of the agreement, evidence of its existence can be found in the files of the War Department's Operational Plans Division in Washington.[18] Meanwhile, in the rearrangement of the purely American military commands which took place in October 1944, following the recall of Stilwell from China, Siam was placed by the Joint Chiefs of Staff in General Daniel Sultan's India-Burma sphere, while Indochina remained in the China sphere under Wedemeyer.

If this background of command arrangements and boundaries was confused, so, too, was the development of political policies over Indochina within both United States and British official circles, and between the two. The principal agitator among those concerned was, of course, Roosevelt. From May 1942 onwards, he let it be known to representatives of other Allied nations, mainly through the medium of the Pacific War Council in Washington, that he did not consider France worthy, in the light of her colonial record, of receiving back Indochina after the war.[19] To Chiang Kai-shek at Cairo and to Stalin at Tehran and Yalta he expressed the same thought, obtaining in return a broad assent; to De Gaulle himself, in January 1943, he developed the accompanying idea, that France in her present state was like a "child" in need of trustees— not that assent was forthcoming on this occasion. As for his own

---

18 Somervell memoranda, Exec. file 1, item 23, Army OPD files; Mountbatten to Chiefs of Staff, Nov. 9, 1943, Exec. file 10, item 66, *ibid.*; Mountbatten to Churchill, Nov. 26, 1943, Exec. file 5, item 15, *ibid.*; Mountbatten memo, Nov. 25, 1943, and Chiefs of Staff to Mountbatten, Nov. 29, 1943, CAB 99/25; SEAC War Diary, Nov. 8, 1943, Jan. 4, April 19, Sept. 9 and 14, 1944, Jan. 18, 1945, Federal Archives, Suitland, Md.; material in file 35968, F.O. 371.

19 See, for example, Lord Halifax to Anthony Eden, May 20, 1942, F 3825/1417/61, F.O. 371; Halifax to Eden, Dec. 17, 1942, F 6656/1422/61, *ibid.*; Halifax to Eden, Jan. 14, 1944, F 285/285/61 and F 360/66/61, *ibid.*; U.S. Dept. of State, *Foreign Relations, 1943: Cairo and Tehran*, 322, 482; U.S. Dept. of State, *Foreign Relations of the United States, 1945: Malta and Yalta* (Washington, D.C., 1955), 766.

officials, the President was likewise giving them, on into the beginning of 1945, a strong, if somewhat confused, negative line. To the Joint Chiefs of Staff, for example, he emphasized that no binding promises had been or could be made over Indochina, while to the State Department he chose to assert, in November 1943, for example, that Indochina posed "entirely a military problem," and then, in January 1945, that the Indochina question should not be touched until after the war.[20]

For all the subsequent modifying which Roosevelt's line was to undergo (as we shall see later), there can be little doubt that he did seriously hope to see France deprived of her main Far Eastern colony. His broad anti-imperialism had attached itself to this particular issue as to no other (except, perhaps, to the cause of greater self-rule for India in 1942). His disappointment with the French showing during the early stages of the war may well have been partly responsible—the Vichy government, in return, listed all its fruitless appeals for United States assistance in resisting Japanese pressure in Indochina[21]—while his antipathy towards De Gaulle, encouraged by Hull, Leahy, and others, certainly made it easier to think in these terms. It is also worth noting that Roosevelt was by no means alone in adopting such a stance in 1942. Within the State Department's Advisory Committee on Post-War Foreign Policy, for example, there was a widespread feeling that French surrenders to Japanese demands in the Far East justified an overriding of French wishes as to the future. "It was not felt," recorded the subcommittee on political problems in August 1942, "that France had any claim to regain Indochina."[22] Stanley Hornbeck was to supply similar arguments.[23]

Moreover, the President's own wishes were made sufficiently known to affect American wartime policies in various respects. The

---

[20] See, for example, Joint Chiefs of Staff minutes, Jan. 7, 1943; U.S. Dept. of State, *Foreign Relations, 1943: China*, 886; Roosevelt to Hull, Oct. 16, 1944, file 851G.00/10–1644, Dept. of State Papers; Roosevelt to Hull, Nov. 3, 1944, and Roosevelt to Stettinius, Jan. 1, 1945, President's Secretary's file, box 53, Roosevelt Papers; U.S. Dept. of State, *Foreign Relations of the United States: Conferences at Washington and Casablanca* (Washington, D.C., 1968), 694; Charles de Gaulle, *War Memoirs, 1942–1944* (London, 1960), 83.

[21] Henry-Haye to Hull, March 5, 1942, file D2 E118 (18), Netherlands Foreign Ministry Archives.

[22] See Harley Notter files, box 55, Dept. of State Papers.

[23] For example, Hornbeck to Hull, April 3, 1944, box 173, Hornbeck Papers.

French Committee of National Liberation was denied the place it sought on the Washington Pacific War Council;[24] the assumption put to Roosevelt by Edward Stettinius in February 1944, that French troops would be used in the liberation of Indochina and French officials employed there in an interim military administration, was drastically revised;[25] approval for a French military mission to go to SEAC in the summer of 1944 was vetoed by the President;[26] a French request for a civil affairs agreement over Indochina was turned down by the State Department in April 1945;[27] the Office of War Information received "quite rigid" orders from the highest quarters that it was to play down French resistance to the Japanese in Indochina when it finally emerged in March 1945;[28] and in Chunking, General Wedemeyer felt obliged at first not to allow supplies to be flown in by American planes to aid that resistance.[29]

Yet the President's anti-French observations and occasional instructions did not amount to a clear and coherent policy, and both civil and military branches of the government were often moved to bemoan their lack of a comprehensive directive on the subject. In October 1943, for example, Assistant Secretary of State Adolph Berle was emphasizing the need for a presidential policy decision on the entire question of Western colonial empires.[30] Hornbeck, as political adviser, was asking in December of the same year what was going on (the State Department did not receive minutes of the Pacific War Council);[31] and Robert Stewart, responsible for relations with British Commonwealth countries, was trying in vain to get an answer to the same question in the following year when the Australian Minister for External Affairs, Herbert Evatt, referring to Roosevelt's musings at the council table, took up the cause of France in a sharp exchange with Hull.[32] In September 1944 John

24 Dept. of State to Roosevelt, Oct. 29, 1943, file 740.0011. P.W./3648, Dept. of State Papers.

25 See file 851G.01/46, ibid.

26 Joint Chiefs of Staff minutes, Aug. 29, 1944; Henry Stimson to Roosevelt, Nov. 24, 1944, and Roosevelt to Stettinius, Nov. 24, 1944, President's Secretary's file, box 53, Roosevelt Papers.

27 See file 740.0011. P.W./3-2645, Dept. of State Papers.

28 File 851G.00/3-2145, ibid.

29 File 740.0011, P.W./3-1245, ibid.; SEAC War Diary, March 11, 1945.

30 U.S. Dept. of State, Foreign Relations, 1943: China, 883.

31 Hornbeck to James Dunn, Dec. 18, 1943, box 172, Hornbeck Papers.

32 Stewart to Hornbeck, April 3, 1944, box 262, ibid.

Paton Davies, back from China, asked Harry Hopkins about Indo-china, but was told that the President was more interested in European matters at the time.[33] The U.S. Army's representative on the State-War-Navy Coordinating Committee was still observing in April 1945 that "the lack of a policy is a source of serious embarrassment to the military,"[34] whilst on the spot the OSS were eventually ordered by Wedemeyer to give arms both to the French and to Annamite resistance groups, with instructions to the latter not to use them against the former. (As is well known, some OSS members did in fact aid the rebels.)[35] It was not, in all, a helpful picture, and in a way it anticipated the situation in postwar years when Sir Robert Thompson, British special adviser on counterinsurgency in Vietnam, found no two Americans in Washington agreed on what their country was seeking to do in that part of the world.[36]

Meanwhile, estimates of the Indochinese situation and proposals as to its future varied considerably among American officials between 1941 and 1945. There was at least general agreement in 1942, when the question first arose, and afterward that if strategic needs were met, there was no objection to the Chinese invading Indochina.[37] (Both Vichy and Gaullist French regimes were loud in their warnings against such a move.) From 1942 onwards it was also generally accepted that the "politically conscious" Annamites were anti-French,[38] and indeed Joseph Ballantine, who became chief of the Far Eastern Division of the State Department, had in the 1930s gone to Indochina and studied the history of the Vietnamese people and their enduring sense of national identity.[39] But judgments as to the current strength and capabilities of the nationalist movements were usually extremely tentative: in October 1945, a survey by the Research and Analysis branch of the OSS would still find it impossible to give a firm opinion.[40] True, an earlier OSS

---

[33] Davies memo, Sept. 4, 1944, box 15, Stilwell Papers.

[34] State-War-Navy Coordinating Committee minutes, April 13, 1945, National Archives.

[35] China Command, Wedemeyer files, box 1, Federal Archives, Suitland, Md.; see also file 851G.00/6–445, Dept. of State Papers; P. Kemp, *Alms for Oblivion* (London, 1961), 46; R. H. Smith, *O.S.S.* (Berkeley, 1972), 330.

[36] Robert Thompson, *No Exit from Vietnam* (London, 1969), 112.

[37] See, for example, files 740.0011. P.W./1956, 1957, and 1877, Dept. of State Papers.

[38] See, for example, file 851G.00/75 and 76, *ibid.*

[39] Ballantine, Diary, chap. VII, Ballantine Papers, Hoover Institution.

[40] O.S.S. Research and Analysis Study No. 3336 (Oct. 1945), National Archives.

survey, in March 1942, had gone so far as to pronounce that "the Annamites have proven themselves capable of self-government,"[41] and a Far Eastern Division memorandum supplied similar testimony in July of the same year. Yet the advice received from American diplomats in China was mainly to the effect that the Indochinese nationalists who had found shelter in that country were being used by Chiang Kai-shek's regime for its own opportunist ends. The consul general in Kunming, who fiercely criticized the French colonial record, nevertheless judged in August 1944 in a highly-praised despatch that

the Annamites are not yet materially or politically prepared for independence or capable of resisting aggression from neighbours. Nor would they be able alone to hold back the peaceful but nonetheless racially annihilating, smothering penetration of Chinese immigration. Therefore . . . independence at this time would be doing the Annamite people no real kindness . . . [and] a further period of dependence and protection seems to be the only logical proposition. . . . As to which power should exercise this temporary dominion, obviously [it] must be France for practical reasons.[42]

The American ambassador to China, Clarence Gauss, took a similar line in September 1944: "It appears to this Embassy that the Indochina Independence League is of Chinese origin, has little or no basis of support in Indochina, and is unlikely to influence further developments in Indochina."[43] Within the State Department itself, meanwhile, no agreement could be reached on whether France should be allowed to return. The Inter-Divisional Area Committee on the Far East confessed itself in February 1944 "perplexed" over the matter: "about half the Committee favored international trusteeship as the best preparation for self-government or independence, and half favored a continuation of French administration under some form of international accountability."[44] In particular, there was a considerable difference of opinion between the European and Far Eastern offices. In April 1945, when a reexamination of policy was being prepared for presentation to the

---

41 O.S.S. Research and Analysis Study No. 719 (March 1942), *ibid*.

42 William Langdon to Dept. of State, Aug. 3, 1944, file 851G.00/8–344, Dept. of State Papers.

43 Gauss to Dept. of State, Sept. 30, 1944, file 851G.00/9–944 and 9–3044, *ibid*.

44 Box 118, Notter files.

new President, this disagreement would still be in evidence, this time over how specific should be the pledges and reforms obtained from France before she was allowed to resume control of Indochina.[45]

One aspect of the situation which troubled the State Department during these debates was the number of clear assurances which had been given to the French by American officials during the early stages of the war, stating, as Sumner Welles put it to the French ambassador in April 1942, that "the government of the United States recognizes the sovereign jurisdiction of the people of France over the territory of France and over French possessions overseas." Such pledges did not appear to trouble Roosevelt, but they helped to increase the bewilderment and exasperation over American policy which was felt in London. Within the Foreign Office it was even suggested that the President was beginning to show signs of that megalomania which had marked Woodrow Wilson in 1919.[46] "I find it very difficult," wrote the head of the Far Eastern Department in January 1944, "to comment seriously on this flow of eloquence which from anyone but the President of the U.S.A. would not command the attention of anyone."[47] Reasons were sought which went beyond simple anticolonialism. Perhaps it was part of a plan to keep SEAC out of Indochina and Siam, and to minimize the British role generally against Japan, a tendency for which there was sufficient evidence for a new head of the Far Eastern Department to write in May 1945: "The Americans are virtually conducting political warfare against us in the Far East."[48]

The Foreign Office's own interpretation of the French record in Indochina was that on the whole it was a good one, holding together an area which otherwise would be fragmented and chaotic.[49] In contrast to the Washington scene, there was little disagreement in the Foreign Office over either the present or the future: the Annamite revolutionaries had been stirred up by the Chinese for their own ends, and this should not prevent a continuation of French sovereignty. (Only Sir Maurice Peterson, an assistant under secre-

---

[45] See file 851G.00/4–2045, 4–2145, and 4–2345, Dept. of State Papers.
[46] F 6656/1422/61, F.O. 371.
[47] F 285/285/61, *ibid.*
[48] See, for example, F 184/52/61 and F 2873/69/23, *ibid.*
[49] See, for example, F 6656/1422/61 and F 6582/6582/61, *ibid.;* and PREM 3, 180/7..

tary of state, disagreed over this last point, and then because he thought France would be too weak to undertake all her former commitments, and had best concentrate on her recovery in Europe and the Mediterranean.)[50] It was believed that Britain and France had common interests in Southeast Asia: a desire to resist Chinese territorial ambitions, to prevent trouble from expatriate Chinese communities,[51] and to re-establish prewar sovereignties. (The communique originally proposed by the Americans for the Cairo Conference was disliked because it made no mention of this restoration of European-owned territories.) "In view of the well-known American attitude towards the restoration of colonies generally," wrote Sir Alexander Cadogan, permanent under secretary at the Foreign Office, to Churchill in November 1944, "there is much to be said for the colonial powers sticking together in the Far East."[52] A common interest was also discerned in their being producers of such raw materials as rubber, a commodity which had long been a source of tension with the United States, a major consumer. (London sought in vain to obtain Washington's consent to French representation on the newly formed International Rubber Committee.)[53] On the spot in SEAC, Mountbatten from early 1944 onwards strongly expressed the view "that French help was essential in the reconquest of Indochina."[54] And although one general in the War Office did foresee "that the inhabitants . . . will be more than anxious to throw off French rule,"[55] care was taken that in conducting political warfare in the region, Britain "refrained from taking a line with the native population which could undermine French sovereignty."[56] In addition, both the Australian government, as has been mentioned, and the government of India—for obvious reasons—supported the sustaining of that same sovereignty.[57]

---

[50] See F 1784/779/61; F 4646/1422/61; F 6441 and 6808/4023/61; F 3812/58/61, all in F.O. 371.

[51] F 242/71/61 and F 5964/74/10, *ibid.*

[52] See PREM 3,180/7; and F 6583/6583/61 and F 4028/9/61, F.O. 371.

[53] See, for example, UE 2435/2/53 and F 5868/168/61, F.O. 371.

[54] SEAC War Diary, Feb. 3, 1944.

[55] SEAC War Diary, April 19, 1944.

[56] F 242/71/61, F.O. 371.

[57] U.S. Dept. of State, *Foreign Relations of the United States, 1944* (Washington, D.C., 1965), III, 185; Australian Dept. of External Affairs Papers, files A 981, War/France/13; A981/New Caledonia/7; A989/43/735/310/2; A989/43/735/302, Commonwealth Archives, Canberra; and F 6353/11/61 and F 4220/4220/10, F.O. 371.

Leaving aside the vicissitudes of Anglo-Gaullist relations, therefore, the only reason for hesitation on the British side was the desire to avoid a confrontation over this issue with one's dominant partner, the United States. It was for this reason, no doubt, that Eden, visiting Washington in the spring of 1943, did not speak out bluntly when the President aired his ideas once more. (Some American officials, indeed, read the record as indicating that the Foreign Secretary had expressed his agreement on the matter; but as others pointed out, the wording was ambiguous, and it seems likely that the agreement referred to another matter covered in the same paragraph.)[58] But although, in August 1943, a Foreign Office minute concluded that Britain could not afford to break with the U.S. over Indochina,[59] even this was eventually to change, so that the briefing prepared for the delegation to the United Nations Conference at San Francisco warned: "We might find ourselves forced to side against the United States" if the question should come to a head.[60]

In short, as far as the Foreign Office was concerned, Britain urgently needed a strong, friendly France after the war, both for reasons of European defense and as a counterweight to the growing predominance in world affairs of the United States and the Soviet Union. And a strong and friendly France meant supporting the continuation of her rule in Indochina.[61] As expressed in a Post Hostilities Planning Committee/Foreign Office paper, approved by the Cabinet in February 1944:

The menace of a rearmed Germany being greater than the menace of a rearmed Japan, a friendly and prosperous France is a strategic necessity to the Empire and Commonwealth as a whole. . . . To deprive her of her economic stake in French Indochina would weaken her seriously . . . and would be passionately resented.[62]

At the same time, a stable Indochina was also seen by the committee as a vital "anchor" for the defensive chain of bases (stretching through Formosa, the Philippines, Marshalls, and Carolines) which

---

[58] U.S. Dept. of State, *Foreign Relations of the United States, 1943* (Washington, D.C., 1963), III, 36; Hornbeck to Dunn, Dec. 18, 1943, box 172, Hornbeck Papers.

[59] F 4646/1422/61, F.O. 371.

[60] F 2431/11/61, *ibid.*

[61] See, for example, Z 605/60/17, Z 4105/77/17, F 1269/11/6, and F 2010/2/61, all in F.O. 371.

[62] W.P. (44) 111, CAB 66/47; Cabinet Minutes, Feb. 24, 1944, CAB 65/41.

would be needed after the war. (Needed against whom was another matter. For the Foreign Office, a resurgent Japan was the only likely threat; in the British armed services in 1944–1945, there was a tendency to see the Soviet Union as the greater menace. Happily, the services were able to argue that a defense line ostensibly drawn up against Japan would also serve against the Soviet Union.)[63] Yet France alone might not be strong enough to make Indochina fully secure. It was held, therefore, in the words of the paper endorsed by the Cabinet, that "it is important to the future security of India, Burma, Malaya and the British Commonwealth and Empire in the South Pacific that the United States should be directly involved in the event of an attack on Indochina." France should agree to include the territory, as Britain would agree to include her territories, within an international security system, and to accept in those areas the establishment of international bases "under U.S. control or otherwise."

If this policy position seemed clear enough, however, there was much frustration in London, as in Washington, over a lack of leadership and clarity at the top. For Churchill, like Roosevelt, declined to bring the matter of Indochina to a head. The reason was not that he doubted the wisdom of the conclusions reached by the Foreign Office and Cabinet; indeed, he regarded the President's notions as almost too absurd to be worthy of discussion between the two of them.[64] But the Prime Minister was always inclined to put consideration of postwar issues well below immediate business, and took little sustained interest in Southeast Asia generally. (In March 1945, when the French troops in Indochina clashed with the Japanese, he had to ask his aide, General "Pug" Ismay, how the French had got there in the first place.)[65] Moreover, he was too often angered by De Gaulle and, above all, too anxious to preserve his relationship with the President—"My whole system," he wrote, "is based on partnership with Roosevelt"—to take up the French cause when so many other and bigger issues were pending.

Thus, in November 1943, Churchill merely observed that the whole matter could "certainly wait."[66] In the following January he

63 See, for example, U 36/36/G, U 3390/36/G, U 4024/36/G, and U 4757/36/G, all in F.O. 371.
64 F 6808/4023/61, ibid.
65 F 1648/11/81, ibid.
66 F 5608/1422/61, ibid.

told the Foreign Office to take up the subject with the State Department, but in March and May 1944, he found various reasons why things should be left for the time being: the election was pending in America; the French would only make trouble within SEAC to ease their pride; it was only a bee in the President's bonnet.[67] Although a brief on Indochina was prepared for the Prime Minister to use in talks at Hyde Park after the second Quebec conference, he chose not to raise the subject, and again in November 1944 observed: "This can certainly wait," and "Nothing doing while de Gaulle is master."[68] He again avoided the issue at Yalta, and it was only on April 11, 1945, the day before Roosevelt's death, that he finally sent a message to the White House, urging that every assistance be given to the French forces which were now fighting the Japanese in Indochina.[69] Even then, this soon became a small matter by comparison with, for example, worsening relations with the Soviet Union and the uncertainty over lend-lease supplies to Britain during Phase Two (the war against Japan alone).[70] When the ambassador in Paris, Duff Cooper, remonstrated in June over Britain's failure to support the French on Indochina, Churchill—already angered by De Gaulle over Syria and the Val d'Aosta—snapped back: "We have reached a point where any decisive taking up of position by the United States should, in nearly all cases, be supported by us, and we should not drag our feet in matters of passing importance."[71]

The key to the mounting impatience of both the Foreign Office and Service Chiefs in the matter in 1944–1945, and to the eventual British proposal that Indochina should come within the area of SEAC, lay in the tangled history of command boundaries which, for this reason, was sketched earlier in this essay. During 1944, the idea of ultimately increasing SEAC's territory was always in Mountbatten's mind. "If SEAC was to play a part in the final thrust against Japan," he told his staff in January, "it was essential that the boundary should be extended further eastwards to cover part of the South China Sea, and if possible ports on the China coast. He felt that Hong Kong should be included."[72] Siam and Indochina were

---

[67] PREM 3, 178/2, 180/7.
[68] PREM 3, 180/7.
[69] F 986/11/61 and F 1829/11/61, F.O. 371; cf. PREM 3, 178/3.
[70] See, for example, the messages in PREM 3,473.
[71] UE 2583/2/53, F.O. 371.
[72] SEAC War Diary, Jan. 4, 1944.

a matter of particular concern to SEAC because, in the words of Mountbatten's political adviser, "through them lies the enemy land and air reinforcement route to Burma and Malaya."[73] By the late summer of 1944 it was considered a matter of urgency to clarify the question of boundaries and jurisdiction, not in order to undertake a full-scale attack in the near future, but to build up clandestine operations which could provide intelligence on the situation in Indochina and Siam and make it possible to cut vital communications to assist major SEAC thrusts elsewhere.[74]

Meanwhile, the French were themselves urging that a mission under General R. C. Blaizot be allowed to go to SEAC, that there should follow a body of troops ready to go into Indochina (the Corps Léger d'Intervention), and that they should have a share in the planning of operations.[75] Their case was strengthened in that their battleship *Richelieu* had already been working for some time in the area, as part of the Eastern Fleet. Mountbatten, too, supported them, warning London that if the French were rebuffed, they might seek entry into Indochina via China and in collaboration with the Americans there (there was already a Gaullist mission in Chungking). He also urged that the French staff and troops be allowed quietly to filter into his command, thus eventually presenting Washington with a *fait accompli*.[76] Such tactics seemed necessary because of the attitude of the President. The Chiefs of Staff in London had, in August 1944, supported the proposal for the Blaizot mission and the Corps Léger; the joint Chiefs in Washington had agreed, but Roosevelt had thereupon revoked that agreement. London, therefore, allowed Blaizot to proceed "temporarily" to Mountbatten's headquarters—a move which provoked loud warnings to the State Department from the American consul general in Colombo, Max Bishop, who was keeping an eye on SEAC affairs.[77]

It was an unsatisfactory situation all round, and was worsened

---

[73] SEAC War Diary, Sept. 9, 1944.

[74] See, for example, SEAC War Diary, Sept. 14, 1944.

[75] See, for example, F 4870/1422/61; F 3017/100/23; F 9/9/61; and F 4028/9/61, all in F.O. 371.

[76] See F 19111/9/61; F 2703/9/61; F 3948/9/61; F 4495/9/61; and F 3404/69/23, *ibid.*

[77] F 4930/9/61, *ibid.*; files 740.0011. P.W./10-2444 and 10-2844, Dept. of State Papers.

by three new developments. First, there was the sudden increase in the pace of SEAC's advance towards Rangoon, which brought nearer the possibility of action in Indochina and Siam. Second, there arose between Mountbatten and his former deputy, Wedemeyer, now commander of U.S. forces in China and chief of staff to Chiang Kai-shek, a major dispute over the control of clandestine operations in those two territories. The details need not concern us, but, briefly, Mountbatten stood upon his 1943 "Gentleman's Agreement" with the Generalissimo, while Wedemeyer insisted that the latter's approval must be obtained for any activities which SEAC wished to carry on in Indochina. Eventually, in the Spring of 1945, the Chiefs of Staff in London got Churchill to raise the matter, first with Roosevelt and then with Harry Truman. A solution based on an exchange of information was patched up, and there was agreement on the spot when Wedemeyer visited Mountbatten's headquarters in April; it broke down, however, because, in Mountbatten's words, Wedemeyer continued "to take unto himself the right to evaluate my operations and oppose them as he wishes even though they do not conflict in any way with his own operations in French Indochina."[78]

It was this continuing friction which prompted the Chiefs of Staff in London to proffer a still more drastic solution. In April, as the American attack upon Japan drew nearer to her home islands, the American Joint Chiefs had proposed that, in order to relieve MacArthur of some of his responsibilities, the British and Australians should take over his South West Pacific Area, excluding the Philippines and Hainan.[79] Now, in June, the British Chiefs of Staff suggested in turn that Indochina, too, should go to SEAC, a change which was finally agreed to in July at Potsdam, although, with the Generalissimo's *amour propre* in mind, the area north of the 16th parallel was left in the China theater.[80] Meanwhile, in March 1945, there had occurred the third development which heightened the whole problem: the outbreak of fighting between the Japanese and

---

[78] See the material in files 46305, 46306, and 46307, F.O. 371; PREM 3, 178/3 and 473; SEAC War Diary, Feb.–May 1945, *passim*.

[79] PREM 3, 159/7.

[80] Chiefs of Staff minutes, April 26, 1945, CAB 79/32; May 30 and June 11, 1945, CAB 79/34; June 21 and 26, 1945, CAB 79/35; July 17 and 20, 1945, CAB 99/39; Combined Chiefs of Staff minutes, July 24, 1945, CAB 88/4.

the French forces within Indochina, resulting in insistent calls for help from the Provisional Government in Paris to London and Washington. Mountbatten, with the limited resources at his disposal, sent in what aid he could to the beleaguered French troops. The dilemma, however, was above all an American one. What now of Roosevelt's anti-French line? Should Claire Chennault's 14th Air Force be allowed to fly in supplies from China?[81]

In fact, unknown to his civil and military officials, the President had already begun to shift his ground. In January, told by Halifax that Mountbatten considered the need to employ Frenchmen for clandestine operations in Indochina to be urgent, he had replied, in the ambassador's words, "that if we felt it was important we had better tell Mountbatten to do it and ask no questions."[82] (When Mountbatten did go ahead, he was formally opposed by his American deputy, General Wheeler, and by General Sultan of the Burma-India theater, whom London felt unable to tell of the President's strictly confidential approval. This was a typically Rooseveltian episode.[83]) In March, the President went further. To his adviser, Charles Taussig, on the 15th he conceded that France could, after all, have Indochina back following the war, provided that she accepted the obligations of a trustee, including the eventual granting of independence.[84] And on the 19th, he authorized Chennault's planes to fly in aid to the French in Indochina itself, so long as this did not interfere with other operations already planned.[85] The limitations on what he could do were closing in upon the ailing President. As he had wearily written in January to his friend Harold Laski, who had urged on him the necessity for creating a revolutionary peace: "Our goal is, as you say, identical for the long range objectives, but there are so many new problems arising that I still must remember that the war is yet to be won."[86]

---

[81] See, for example, file 740.0011. P.W./3–1245, Dept. of State Papers; SEAC War Diary, March 20, 1945.

[82] F 190/11/61, F.O. 371.

[83] Wheeler to Marshall, March 22, 1945, Exec. file 17, item 26, Army OPD files; file F 163/11/61, F.O. 371; B. Sweet-Escott, *Baker Street Irregular* (London, 1965), 238.

[84] Taussig memo, March 15, 1945, box 49, Taussig Papers, Roosevelt Library; U.S. Dept. of State, *Foreign Relations of the United States, 1945* (Washington, D.C., 1967), I, 121.

[85] Files 740.0011. P.W./3–1945; 851G.00/3–1945, Dept. of State Papers.

[86] Roosevelt to Laski, Jan. 16, 1945, box 75, Felix Frankfurter Papers, Library of Congress.

Yet Roosevelt's own shift was only part of a series of developments within Washington official circles which, in the latter part of 1944 and in early 1945, made it increasingly unlikely that a radical American line on Indochina would be forthcoming. For one thing, there was an admission on the part of the United States of the increasing status of France and of the Gaullist movement. In October 1944, after much delay and sourness, the French Committee of National Liberation was given official recognition as the provisional government of the country; thereafter, the briefing papers prepared by the State Department for the conferences at Yalta and Potsdam emphasized the rapid strides France had taken toward regaining her position as an ally of substance—a status eventually recognized by the award of her own occupation zone in Germany.[87] On his visit to Paris in January 1945, Harry Hopkins was accommodating and friendly in a manner very different from the American approach to De Gaulle in earlier years.[88] The General himself, despite his continuing prickliness, had for some time been ready to flatter American susceptibilities. (To James Forrestal, in August 1944, he even observed that "the United States and France are the only two major powers with no imperialist ambitions."[89]) For good measure, the Gaullists were emphasising their reformist —though in fact by no means radical—colonial policies at the Brazzaville Conference of January–February 1944. Their views about Indochina in particular were proclaimed in a declaration in March 1945, in which an Indochinese Federation was promised a degree of administrative autonomy within a French Union.[90]

At the same time, the emphasis of American policies over colonial and trusteeship issues was moving away from the brave days of 1942–1943, when Washington's insistence on the word "independence" and on specific dates being given for the achievement of that status had prevented agreement being reached with London on a

---

[87] See, for example, U.S. Dept. of State, *Foreign Relations, 1945: Malta and Yalta*, 300; U.S. Dept. of State, *Foreign Relations of the United States; Conference of Berlin* (Washington, D.C., 1960), 1, 251.

[88] Caffery to State Dept., Jan. 28 and 30, 1945, box 337, Harry Hopkins Papers, Roosevelt Library.

[89] James V. Forrestal, Diary, Aug. 18, 1944, Princeton University Library.

[90] See D. B. Marshall, *The French Colonial Myth and Constitution-Making in the Fourth Republic* (New Haven, Conn., 1973), 102 ff., 133 ff; U.S. Dept. of State, *Foreign Relations of the United States, 1945* (Washington, D.C., 1969), VI, 295.

joint declaration of colonial principles.[91] The shift can be traced, for example, in the discussions of the State Department's Advisory Committee on Post-War Foreign Policy. In 1942, there had been a strong feeling in that body that all colonies, and not simply former League of Nations mandates, should become trusteeships under an international organization: "the United States must take a stand on its principles at the end of the war, since the imperial powers might desire to return to the status quo ante." By March 1943, however, the changed mood was reflected in Sumner Welles's remark that "perhaps the most that can be hoped for is that the administration of colonies [belonging to the United Nations] will be kept in harmony with the principles of trusteeship by the pressure of international public opinion."[92] By the summer of 1944, when Isaiah Bowman of Johns Hopkins University visited London as part of the Stettinius mission, he confided that the American approach to these matters would be "entirely realistic,"[93] and at Yalta Washington's proposal was indeed a modest one: that trusteeship status should be given only to ex-League mandates, ex-enemy territories, and any colonies voluntarily placed in that category by the sovereign power concerned. This line was further pursued at the San Francisco Conference, where Harold Stassen, speaking for the United States, joined Britain and France in opposing the wishes of the Soviet Union and China to enshrine in the U.N. Charter a universal obligation for colonies to be led towards "independence."[94]

Britain's own stubborn refusal to consider surrendering supreme administrative powers over her colonies had contributed to the change in the American position after 1942. So, too, had the embarrassing question of United States possessions in the Western Hemisphere.[95] Another major factor, of course, was the well-known desire of the U.S. Navy and War departments to lay their hands for all time on the Japanese mandated islands in the Pacific, and the com-

---

[91] See, for example, files 31526 and 35311, F.O. 371; box 120, Notter files, Dept. of State Papers.

[92] Minutes of Subcommittee on Political Problems, March 13, 1943, box 55, Notter files, Dept. of State Papers.

[93] Record of Bowman talks with Foreign Office officials, April 14, 1944, U 3386/3386/74, F.O. 371.

[94] See, for example, U.S. Dept. of State, *Foreign Relations, 1945*, I, 790 ff., 954.

[95] See, for example, the minutes of the Committee on Political Problems of the Post War Advisory Committee, April 10, 1943, box 55, Notter files, Dept. of State Papers.

promise which was reached with the State Department before the San Francisco conference whereby their wishes could be fulfilled without going so far as to proclaim American sovereignty over the islands in question.[96]

Meanwhile, similar changes of emphasis had been taking place over the specific colony of Indochina. Since at least late 1943, Isaiah Bowman, as special adviser on such matters, had been advocating leaving France in control there (although with the understanding that she would be obliged to permit international inspection), lest independence should lead to "division within the country and social and political disintegration." Sumner Welles had put the same line to Halifax and Eden even earlier, in March 1943.[97] In September 1944, two of the more powerful men within the State Department, Joseph Grew and James Dunn, drew up for the President their own suggested solution for the whole Southeast Asian region. They stressed that American interests there might best be served by limited, rather than total, forms of independence:

These areas are sources of products essential to both our wartime and peacetime economy. They are potentially important markets for American exports. They lie athwart the Southwestern approaches to the Pacific Ocean and have an important bearing on our security and the security of the Philippines. Their economy and political stability will be an important factor in the maintenance of peace in Asia. Emergence of these regions as self-governing countries would appear desirable as soon as they are capable of self-rule, either as independent nations or in close voluntary association with Western powers, for example as dominions. Such association might indeed lend them political and economic strength (the weakness of Asiatic powers has long been a cause of war) and help prevent further cleavage along regional or racial lines.[98]

A need for an even more drastic revision of the President's ideas was put forward by Harry Hopkins at a meeting on January 3, 1945,

---

[96] Edward Stettinius, Diary, April 1945, Dept. of State Papers; James Forrestal, Diary, March–April 1945; Henry Stimson, Diary, Jan.–April 1945, Sterling Memorial Library, Yale University; box 49, Taussig Papers; U.S. Navy, General Board Studies No. 450, U.S.N. Operational Archives.

[97] Bowman memorandum, Oct. 24, 1943, box 70, Notter files, Dept. of State Papers; Halifax memorandum, March 25, 1943, F 1851/877/61, F.O. 371.

[98] Grew and Dunn to Roosevelt, Sept. 8, 1944, file 851G.01/9–844, Dept. of State Papers.

with Secretary of War Stimson, Secretary of the Navy Forrestal, and Secretary of State Stettinius. As Stettinius recorded it,

Mr. Hopkins suggested that there was need for a complete review not only of the Indochina situation but of our entire French approach. In this connection he referred to instances in the past where we had held back on certain French matters, but on which we had finally, because of British pressure and other reasons, changed our position. He expressed the opinion that this had resulted in the French feeling that we were opposed to their regrowth.

The feeling seemed to be that with the British position what it is our policy of deferring a decision on Indochina until some general peace settlement would probably be doomed to failure.[91]

Allied diplomats were also hearing similar opinions expressed to them privately by American officials. Grew observed in January to the Australian minister, Sir Frederick Eggleston, that he believed Indochina would stay French, and Dr. George Blakeslee, special assistant to the chief of the Far Eastern Division, voiced the same opinion a month later.[100] Back in 1944, the French ambassador to China, General Ziaovi Pechkoff, had told a British official that while he was in Washington both General Marshall and Assistant Secretary of War John J. McCloy had spoken to him in favor of a restoration of the French empire.[101] Now in March 1945, following a highly confidential conversation with Admiral Ernest J. King, the head of the British naval mission in Washington, Admiral Sir James Somerville, wrote to Mountbatten: "It seems quite clear to me that the U.S. Chiefs of Staff are by no means in favour of the President's policy of keeping the French out of Indochina."[102]

Within the State Department, the difference of opinion between Far Eastern and European officials clearly inclined in favor of the latter. "We have no right to dictate to France," wrote Assistant Secretary Dunn, "nor to take away her territory."[103] For President Truman, a list of reforms which the United States would like to see undertaken in Indochina was drawn up for use in discussions

---

[99] Stettinius memorandum, Jan. 4, 1945, file 851G.00/1–445, *ibid.*

[100] File A1066/P45/153/2, Australian Dept. of External Affairs Papers, Canberra.

[101] John Keswick memo, March 20, 1944, F 1450/100/23, F.O. 371.

[102] Somerville to Mountbatten, March 27, 1945, file 9/2, Somerville Papers, Churchill College, Cambridge University.

[103] Dunn to Grew, April 23, 1945, file 851G.00/4–2345, Dept. of State Papers.

with General de Gaulle.[104] But the fundamental issue of sovereignty was no longer in doubt. At the San Francisco Conference, indeed, Stettinius assured the French foreign minister, Georges Bidault, that there had been no official U.S. statement which "even by implication" called for the removal of that territory. When Madame Chiang Kai-shek visited Truman in August, he swept aside all notion of a trusteeship.[105] Everywhere—with the exception of a few anticolonial stalwarts like Charles Taussig—there had been a retreat from Roosevelt's more extreme utterances, a retreat in which the late President himself had taken part. As John Hickerson of the State Department's European Office put it to a British colleague,

the American proposal at Yalta in connection with trusteeship had been partly phrased by the State Department in order to permit a climbdown from the position that President Roosevelt had taken in conversation as regards Indochina. . . . He made it clear that the State Department felt that President Roosevelt had gone too far and that Category C [the voluntary placement of colonies under trusteeship] was a useful face-saver.[106]

These changes of emphasis arose partly from the recovery of France and from the increasing likelihood that confusion and weakness, rather than great-power stability, would characterize China's contributions to East and Southeast Asia immediately after the war. There was also the significant fact that major military operations against the Japanese were passing Indochina by. In addition, however, increasing tension between the United States and the Soviet Union was making its influence felt. De Gaulle himself stressed the Soviet threat to Europe and asked whether the United States, in antagonizing France, wanted to play into the hands of the Communists.[107] The State Department, for its part, was drawing up briefing papers which emphasized that the process of moving towards colonial self-government should not "undermine the influence of the West,"[108] while a memorandum from the OSS, pre-

---

104 Grew to Hurley, June 7, 1945, file 851G.00/6–745, *ibid.*

105 U.S. Dept. of State, *Foreign Relations, 1945*, VI, 312, VII, 540; cf. Truman-Grew conversation, May 19, 1945, Joseph C. Grew Papers, vol. 7, Houghton Library, Harvard University.

106 Neville Butler memo, July 10, 1945, F 4240/11/61, F.O. 371.

107 U.S. Dept. of State, *Foreign Relations, 1945*, VI, 300.

108 *Ibid.*, 556 ff.

pared just before Roosevelt's death, went farther still: "The United States should realize its interest in the maintenance of the British, French and Dutch colonial empires. We should encourage liberalization of the colonial regimes in order the better to maintain them, and to check Soviet influence in the stimulation of colonial revolt."[109] The same thought was expressed during the private discussions of the American delegation to the San Francisco conference —discussions which frequently took on an aggressively nationalistic tone. "When perhaps the inevitable struggle came between Russia and ourselves," observed Isaiah Bowman, "the question would be, who are our friends . . . [?] Would we have the support of Great Britain if we had undermined her [colonial] position?" As Representative Charles Eaton put it: "The basic problem was who was going to be masters of the world."[110]

As they had for Britain throughout the period, European questions thus came back to affect American policy on Indochina. Even without the Cold War aspect, however, it is unlikely that Roosevelt's early desires would have been fulfilled. It was one of a good many foreign policy issues for which, at his death, he had provided little solution beyond brave talk and bonhommie. In the meantime, the question had remained in a curiously suspended and inarticulated state between the United States and Britain. Churchill was ready at times to have it discussed at a Foreign Office-State Department level, but would not talk it through with the President; the latter was ready to air his personal views, but not to allow officials to negotiate on the matter. The result was virtual noncommunication, coupled with a certain amount of bewilderment and suspicion. For this, Roosevelt may have been the chief culprit. But at least he had divined and supported more than most the direction of the nationalist tide which was beginning to flow strongly in Southeast Asia. And had his early wishes been fulfilled, France herself—perhaps the United States as well—would have been spared much agony.

---

109 OSS memo, April 2, 1945, Harry S. Truman Papers, Harry S. Truman Presidential Library, Independence, Mo.

110 U.S. Dept. of State, *Foreign Relations, 1945*, I, 790 ff.

The Other China Hands: U.S. Army Officers and America's Failure in China, 1941–1950

Marc Gallicchio
Villanova University

In the early summer of 1941, after nearly four years of isolated struggle against superior Japanese forces, officials of the beleaguered Chinese Nationalist government received from Washington assurances of increased support against the invaders. The passage of the Lend Lease Act the previous March and President Franklin D. Roosevelt's decision to make China eligible for such assistance seemed to signal the beginning of a new phase in American-Chinese relations. In anticipation of a closer relationship between Washington and Chungking, members of the Army general staff recommended sending a military aid mission to China.[1] The distribution of Lend Lease supplies necessitated the creation of an Army team in Chungking to coordinate orders, determine priorities, and evaluate the performance of Chinese forces and American materials. As they prepared for their new role in China, Army officers had occasion to commend their own foresight in planning for just such a moment. "For many years," wrote Edwin Clark, a liaison officer for the Chinese Mission in Washington, "the United States has detailed officers to China to learn the language, study the country and its people, which knowledge presumably was for use when an emergency confronted the United States with which China might have some connection. It is submitted that such an emergency has now arrived."[2]

As Major Clark noted, the United States Army seemed surprisingly well prepared for the new role it was about to play in China. Officers

The Journal of American–East Asian Relations, Vol. 4, No. 1 (Spring 1995)
© Copyright 1995 by Imprint Publications, Inc. All rights reserved.

The author wishes to thank Warren I. Cohen, Sally Griffith, Waldo Heinrichs, Seth Koven, Adele Lindemeyr, Richard Manser, and Michael Sherry for their comments on various drafts of this essay. This article is part of a larger project that has been generously supported by the American Philosophical Society, the Military History Institute, the National Endowment for the Humanities, and Villanova University.

1. For editorial purposes, "Army" is capitalized throughout this essay when specifically referring to the United States Army.
2. MacMorland to assistant chief of staff, War Plans Division, 20 June 1941, transmitting Clark to MacMorland, 16 June 1941, no. 4389, General Correspondence, War Plans Division, RG 165, Records of the War Department Army General and Special Staffs, Modern Military Branch, National Archives (hereafter cited as NA), Washington, D.C.

for the new military aid mission could be drawn from the Army's Chinese language training program, begun in 1919 by the Military Intelligence Division. Most of the Army's language officers had served as military attachés in the American embassy in Peking and accumulated valuable experience reporting on military activities, politics, and economic and social conditions during the rise of revolutionary nationalism in interwar China. At the same time, an even larger number of officers had received at least some exposure to Chinese life while serving with the 15th Infantry regiment stationed at Tientsin until 1938.[3]

During the 1920s and 1930s Army officers were among a host of Americans who ventured to China. But unlike the numerous missionaries, educators, technical advisers, and journalists who hoped to remake China in the American image, Army officers in Peking or Tientsin observed but did not participate in the Western reform effort. By 1941, however, rapidly changing international conditions prodded the Army toward active involvement in China. Following the attack on Pearl Harbor, the initial aid mission evolved into a larger task force with the goal of training and advising a more effective Chinese army. As China's resistance against Japan became more important to U.S. global strategy the Army's secular missionaries crossed the Pacific to help save China for the Nationalists.

To fully appreciate the part Army officers played in the larger American-Chinese relationship it is helpful to reconceptualize their role in broader terms. The Army's China Hands shared many of the basic values and assumptions of their civilian counterparts, but they also represented a separate and distinctive group within American society with its own customs and institutions. And unlike their civilian brethren, U.S. Army officers proffered the tools and techniques of modern military power, commodities in great demand in an embattled China. In their capacity as facilitators of Sino-American cooperation the Army's China Hands became interpreters of Chinese military and civil society for the less experienced American officers and enlisted men who came to the China theater.[4] This study offers a different perspec-

---

3. For the history of the Army in China before Pearl Harbor see Louis Morton, "Army and Marines on the China Station: A Study in Military and Political Rivalry," *Pacific Historical Review* 29 (February 1960); Charles G. Finney, *The Old China Hands* (Westport, Conn., 1973); John N. Hart, *The Making of an Army "Old China Hand": A Memoir of Colonel David D. Barrett* (Berkeley, Calif., 1985); Dennis Laviere Noble, "China Hands: The United States Military in China, 1901–1937" (Ph.D. diss., Purdue University, 1988); Edward M. Coffman, "The American 15th Infantry Regiment in China, 1912–1938: A Vignette in Social History," *Journal of Military History* 58 (January 1994).

4. I have chosen the term "cultural interpreters" rather than the more familiar "cultural intermediaries" because, although this study discusses Chinese perceptions of and interaction with American officers, it is mainly concerned with how Army officers ex-

tive on the Sino-American relationship by identifying the ways in which the Army's China Hands explained China to their colleagues and by analyzing the strategies they developed for completing their mission. In particular, it calls attention to how the they came to represent the Chinese in terms that encouraged American officers to perceive important similarities between their own professional values and the culture of their hosts. As U.S. Army officers adapted to their new role in China, they would begin to gain confidence in their ability to formulate solutions to China's most pressing problems. By the war's end, these Army officers, the other China Hands, would rely on their own experience to justify an expanded role for the Army in the development of postwar policy toward China.

Although the Army made its first steps toward direct involvement in China with the creation of a Lend Lease mission in the summer of 1941, it did not cross the threshold of intervention until after Japan's attack on Pearl Harbor. In February 1942, as Japanese forces threatened to rout British and Chinese troops in Burma, the Army sent a task force under Lieutenant General Joseph Stilwell to China. Stilwell's directive made him the senior American commander in the newly formed China-Burma-India theater and chief of staff to Generalissimo Chiang Kai-shek, the theater commander, and charged him with the task of improving the fighting efficiency of the Chinese army. Army Chief of Staff General George C. Marshall, himself a veteran of the 15th Infantry, chose his friend for this daunting task because of Stilwell's lengthy experience in China. Stilwell's China service included tours with the 15th Infantry and as an attaché, during which time he became fluent in Chinese.[5]

Marshall hoped that Stilwell would be able to regroup Allied forces in Burma in time to halt the Japanese offensive, but the Americans arrived just in time to lead the retreating Allies into India. In the weeks

---

plained and responded to the customs and behavior of their hosts. It should also be noted that American officers rarely referred to Chinese "culture" and that they were far more likely to comment on Chinese "character" and "customs" when describing the complex system of values anthropologists currently define as "culture." For discussions of other Americans in China as cultural intermediaries see Akira Iriye, "The China Hands in History: American Diplomacy in Asia," in Paul Gordon Lauren, ed., *The China Hand's Legacy: Ethics and Diplomacy* (Boulder, Colo., 1987), and James Huskey, "The Cosmopolitan Connection: Americans and Chinese in Shanghai during the Interwar Years," *Diplomatic History* 11 (Summer 1987).

5. Forrest Pogue, *George C. Marshall: Education of a General* (New York, 1963), and Larry I. Bland, ed., *The Papers of George Catlett Marshall*, vol. 1, *"The Soldierly Spirit," December 1880–1939* (Baltimore, 1981); Charles Romanus and Riley Sunderland, *Stilwell's Mission to China* (Washington, D.C., 1953), 70–76; Barbara Tuchman, *Stilwell and the American Experience in China* (New York, 1971), 311–18.

after the fall of Burma, Stilwell moved between India and Chungking in an effort to create the basic organizations for rebuilding the Chinese army. The first of these, the Chinese Army in India (CAI), was supervised by Brigadier General Haydon Boatner and located in Ramgarh, India. Boatner was a forty-year-old China Hand who had moved from the 15th infantry to the language school as an assistant attaché in the late 1920s and early 1930s. During his six-year tour in China Boatner had also found time to earn an M.A. in Chinese history.[6]

The second training center, under Brigadier General Frank Dorn, was located in Yunnan Province in China. Like Boatner, Dorn was also a language student in China, having served as assistant attaché to Stilwell in the late 1930s. A soldier-scholar, during the course of his military career Dorn produced the first syllabary of the Negritos dialect in the Philippines, wrote a monograph on the Negritos' life and customs, was offered a post as assistant professor of anthropology at the University of the Philippines, and published a novel based on his experiences with the tribe. Dorn's appreciation of other cultures continued during his tour in China, where he developed an interest in Chinese art.[7]

In selecting Boatner and Dorn, Stilwell chose two officers who could be counted on to listen to the Chinese point of view and avoid bruising Chinese sensibilities while they undertook the task of constructing a Westernized Chinese army. As Stilwell later explained to Chiang, "I know that he [Boatner] is intensely interested in the Chinese troops and that he would do anything in his power for them. He is a very capable officer and was chosen for this position on this account and because of his sympathetic attitude towards the Chinese."[8]

From the outset, Boatner sought to build Chinese confidence and foster harmony between Americans and Chinese. As chief of staff to the CAI, he immediately decided to work with the existing Chinese staff system rather than adopt the standard American Army organization. To facilitate this process, Boatner enlisted his American subordinates in a crash course in Chinese. Several months later, in February 1943, Boatner could report, "We have completely broken the ice in reference to the distinction of two staffs. . . . We have a joint mess in

---

6. Boatner was in the same langugue class with the historian John King Fairbank. For Fairbank's favorable assessment of Boatner see John King Fairbank, *China Bound: A Fifty-Year Memoir* (New York, 1982), 95, 179; "Biographical Resume of Haydon L. Boatner," Haydon L. Boatner Papers, Hoover Institution on War, Revolution, and Peace (hereafter cited as HI), Stanford, Calif.

7. "Brief Biography of General Frank Dorn," Frank Dorn Papers, HI.

8. Stilwell to Chiang, 27 Sept. 1943, Personnel File, box 4, Boatner Papers, HI.

operation, and all the American officers are assigned to specific Chinese staff branches." According to Boatner, the joint mess was "a tremendous success and influence in welding a joint staff."[9]

Aware of the potential for conflict between American advisers and Chinese officers, Boatner emphasized the importance of tact in resolving disputes. In notes made after the war, Boatner gave two examples of how he dealt with recalcitrant Chinese officers. In one case, he privately informed a Nationalist colonel in Chinese that his medical officers were obstructing an American medical team's treatment of Chinese patients and that such conduct would have to stop. Boatner recorded that this effort succeeded because his discretion prevented the Chinese officer from losing "face." "By that time," he wrote, "I had a year's experience with the Chinese and had had some experience with them and the 'face' of the senior Chinese with whom I dealt." In a second incident, Boatner clashed with a Chinese transportation officer who twice ignored written orders to send two truck companies by rail, which would have minimized the opportunities for graft. After the second set of orders failed to get the train rolling, Boatner summoned the Chinese officer and relieved him of his command in front of two other Nationalist officers. "It was his face or mine," he explained.[10]

As Boatner's anecdotes suggest, Americans viewed the concept of "face" as a key to understanding Chinese behavior. Most Americans, however, construed "face" almost solely in terms of preserving appearances and avoiding embarrassment. This emphasis on the superficial aspects of human interaction tended to minimize the deeper cultural reasons for the Chinese concern with "face." For traditional Chinese elites, "face" involved what one anthropologist has described as "the most profound ideas of right and wrong in handling human relations." In a society based on social inequality, what was right was what sustained "the graded ranks of status difference," which is to say that one kept one's "face" by dutifully showing ritual obedience

9. Boatner to Siebert, 5 Feb. 1943, folder: Troops, box 4; "Notes on Ramgarh" for Office of Military History, folder: Campaigns and Strategy, Subject File, box 2; Memorandum for Maj. Gen. Liao, 4 Nov. 1942, Personnel File, box 4, Boatner Papers, HI.

10. "Chinese Liaison Detail," Boatner's comments on James H. Stone's "Crisis Fleeting," ibid. In 1943, Boatner was surprised when a group of high-ranking Chinese officers reacted favorably to the news that one of their comrades, an officer named Woon, had been replaced. Boatner was surprised because earlier the same group had sought Boatner's intercession to prevent Woon's removal. When Boatner asked them about their previous support for Woon, one of the officers replied, "Oh that didn't mean a thing, we were only trying to save Woon's face." Boatner concluded that this episode offered "Another example of the Oriental's mind." Boatner to Stilwell, 7 Oct. 1943, Stilwell File, box 1, Boatner Papers, HI.

to one's superiors and thus contributing to the preservation of the existing social hierarchy.[11]

U.S. Army officers also existed in a hierarchical society and thus they readily understood the importance of public displays of respect to superiors. Officers in the regular Army in the interwar period also cultivated their own etiquette and ceremonies.[12] In the long run, however, such surface similarities made it harder for Americans to see how traditions such as "face" supported a social order that hindered Western-directed efforts to transform Chinese institutions. Chiang and his supporters were not simply concerned with avoiding public embarrassment, they sought to reinvigorate the whole system of Confucian ethics. Significantly, Chiang rated ethical regeneration and a revival of Confucian values as more important than economic and political reform.[13]

With some practice, most American officers would learn to treat their Chinese colleagues with ritual politeness and courtesy by placing themselves in the other soldier's boots. The conformist nature of military service with its emphasis on measurable goal-oriented activities also encouraged a sense of shared purpose and perspective on the part of liaison officers and their counterparts. Boatner seemed to reflect this belief that the nature of military service reduced the cultural differences between the two peoples. "Be American," he told his officers "but not too American, let the Chinese be Chinese, but not too Chinese."[14] As Chinese officers and enlisted men donned American uniforms and adopted American military doctrine they would begin to seem less foreign and China's problems would begin to appear more tractable.

Learning to interact with Chinese officers, even at the professional level, was, however, a significant challenge in itself. Some American officers learned the nuances of command relationships in the Chinese army only through trial and error. According to the unofficial history

11. This interpretation of the meaning of "face" is taken from Leon E. Stover, *The Ecology of Chinese Civilization: Peasants and Elites in the Last of Agrarian States* (New York, 1974), 242–63; See also H. G. Creel, *Chinese Thought from Confucius to Mao Tse-tung* (Chicago, 1953), 130–31, 260–62.

12. For a discussion of the importance of these values to American officers see Samuel P. Huntington, *The Soldier and the State: The Theory of Civil-Military Relations* (Cambridge, Mass., 1957), 303–5; and Morris Janowitz, *The Professional Soldier: A Social and Political Portrait* (New York, 1960), 196–211.

13. Kenneth Shewmaker, *Americans and Chinese Communists, 1927–1945: A Persuading Encounter* (Ithaca, N.Y., 1971), 299–301, 323–24; John King Fairbank, *The United States and China*, 3rd ed. (Cambridge, Mass., 1971), 119, 244–46.

14. Boatner's notes, n.d. (ca. 1973), Supplementary Documents File, box 2, Haydon L. Boatner Papers, Military History Institute (hereafter cited as MHI), Carlisle, Pa.

of the CAI, the American instructors committed several errors that created problems once the army took to the field. The first of these was "the very great mistake of having American officers and enlisted men attempt to train Chinese enlisted men direct and not under the surveillance of their unit commanders. This was a tremendous loss of face to the Chinese officers and non-commissioned officers, and they did everything possible to block instruction." The unit history concluded that if the Americans involved the officers and passed information through them "much better instruction would have resulted, better feeling, and a better army."[15]

Although Boatner did not have direct control over training, he did exert greater influence over American-Chinese relations once the CAI began to move back into Burma in the fall of 1943. As chief of staff, Boatner oversaw the creation of special American liaison teams attached to Chinese units. These teams acted as advisers on tactical matters and provided special expertise on communications, supply, and medical problems. They also gave Boatner a reliable source of information on Chinese performance and overall compliance with orders. Before going into the field, however, the liaison officers received special training and instructions prepared by Boatner. As part of this "indoctrination" the liaison officers were constantly reminded that their duty was "liaison not command." Officers were told to "Place yourself in the Chinese officer's situation—think how you would feel as a company or battalion commander, loyal and responsible to your own superior officer throughout many years of service, if a foreign officer assumed the right to give you direct orders." "The most important feature of that training," Boatner recalled, was to "scrupulously respect the command authority, prestige, and dignity of the Chinese officer." Leaving nothing to chance, Boatner also made it clear that matters of face dictated that Americans were "never to get mad at Chinese officers in the presence of others." Eventually, as the teams gained field experience, Boatner assigned newer officers to the most successful teams to learn how to achieve their goals.[16]

In May 1944, several months after the CAI reentered Burma, a second, larger army—the Chinese Expeditionary Force (CEF)—also

---

15. "Chinese Army in India" (Unofficial History), pp. 17–18, box 1, Richard D. Weigle Papers, HI; Charles Romanus and Riley Sunderland, *Stilwell's Command Problems* (Washington, D.C., 1956), 306–12, 346.

16. "Instruction for Liaison Officers," n.d., Supplementary Documents File, box 2, Boatner Papers, MHI; "Chinese Army In India," p. 7, box 1, Weigle Papers, HI; "Command of Chinese Troops in WWII" (ca. 1975), Troops File, box 4, Boatner Papers, HI. For an account by one of the liaison officers see Breidster to whom it may concern, 3 Oct. 1944, Troops File, box 5, ibid.

known as the Y-Force, moved southwestward from Yunnan across the Salween River into Burma. Based in Kunming, the Y-Force began receiving American instruction in April of the previous year. Like Boatner, Dorn supervised the Americans assigned to the Y-Force and made sure they understood the implications of their mission. To foster harmony, Dorn's staff prepared several memoranda on how to function smoothly with Chinese officers and enlisted men.

To officers reading these guidelines, the Chinese must have seemed a curious blend of the exotic and the familiar. As at Ramgarh, the Americans were asked to put themselves in the place of the Chinese officers who would be placing their units under the guidance of outsiders. To avoid friction, the Americans were told to emulate the Chinese method of indirectness in communication and to avoid public displays of anger. Dorn also introduced American officers to the intricacies of Chinese etiquette on visits and other formal occasions, but on this point the instructions sounded a reassuring note. "The most important thing to remember," the Americans were told, "is that if you live up to the standards of gentlemanly conduct, which as an officer of the United States Army you are already familiar, you are certain to get along with your Chinese associates."[17]

Dorn's efforts to acquaint Americans with Chinese customs were designed to keep conflict to a minimum within Y-Force, but there was probably little that he could do to soften the shock that the Americans experienced when they saw the wretched condition of the Chinese army and the poor quality of its leadership.[18] Nevertheless, Dorn attempted to create a context for better understanding the deplorable condition of China's forces. Before anyone jumped to conclusions, they were asked to remember that the Chinese had been fighting against heavy odds for five and a half years. Some of their practices may have seemed odd to Americans, but it was necessary to bear in mind that Chinese methods were probably "developed through experience during the long war period and adapted to the means at hand." Although Dorn lauded the courage and ingenuity of the average Chinese soldier, he warned American officers that the venality and incompetence of most of the Nationalist senior officers posed the greatest obstacle to the completion of their mission. Even here, however, Dorn asked the

---

17. "Notes to Bear in Mind When Dealing or Working with the Chinese," "Notes for Officers Detailed to Serve with Units of the Chinese Army," and "Some Common Courtesies and Formalities," file 83, box 8, Joseph W. Stilwell Papers, HI.

18. On the glaring shortage of Chinese officers with adequate professional education and training see Hsi-Sheng Ch'i, "The Military Dimension, 1942-1945," in James C. Hsiung and Stevine I. Levine, eds., *China's Bitter Victory: The War With Japan, 1937–1945* (Armonk, N.Y., 1992), 135–56.

Americans to relate this information to their own experience. Most Chinese officers, he explained, held their posts through political influence, which was a practice not all that different from "our National Guard."[19]

As Dorn predicted, the plan to introduce American methods and instructors into the Y-Force met with more than a little resistance from the Chinese. Some Nationalist officers with other instructional backgrounds (Japanese, German, Russian, Chinese) opposed any innovations that devalued their professional education. Others disliked foreign interference of any kind. Still others feared that their corruption might be uncovered.[20] American conduct also contributed to a sense of resentment among some Chinese. According to Eugene Wu, a Chinese interpreter for the Y-Force, American officers ate in separate messes and interacted with the Chinese only on formal occasions. He also recalled how the Americans seemed unaware that differences in housing created ill feeling among Chinese officers. Fifty years later he still remembered how the American barracks were so well heated that the occupants wore undershirts and shorts to stay comfortable, whereas the Chinese coped with fuel shortages and drafty quarters by shivering under three suits of clothing.[21] Chinese resentment of the housing conditions in Kunming underscored how difficult it was even for Americans with the best intentions to bridge the cultural divide separating them from their allies. Even in China, America's abundance seemed capable of providing its citizens with a level of material comfort beyond the reach of most their hosts. The Americans, however, especially those who had lived the good life in Tientsin before the war, would have been surprised to learn that others envied them for the lavishness of their accommodations.

Army officers in Kunming encountered in microcosm some of the same structural problems the United States has faced in its relations with much of the Third World. The Americans took for granted their standard of living and seemed unaware of how it affected their behavior and their interaction with Chinese. Given the enduring nature of this problem in U.S. foreign relations, it seems doubtful that a brief orientation program could have sensitized liaison officers to the divisiveness produced by the great disparities of wealth between the United States and its ally. There is some evidence, however, that Dorn's counseling of Y-Force liaison officers influenced some aspects of their in-

19. Ibid.

20. "Yoke Force Training Effort with Chinese Expeditionary Force," n.d., file 183, box 15, Stilwell Papers, HI.

21. Eugene Wu (director, Harvard-Yenching Library), telephone conversation with author, 8 June 1994.

teractions with Chinese officers and enlisted men. When illiterate Chinese soldiers showed up for instruction as artillery officers, the Americans did not send them back to their units for fear that the students would "lose face" with their comrades. Instead, the Americans gave them basic instruction which often qualified the students as noncommissioned officers.[22] It is less clear how well Dorn's guidelines helped the Americans deal with Chinese efforts to thwart significant reforms, but the unofficial chronicler of the program indicated that the Americans pursued an indirect course toward their objective. According to the draft history of the unit, little could be accomplished "until the active control had quietly been 'absorbed' by the Americans." But to "achieve this absorbing of authority without incurring ill will took time and care."[23]

The process of waiting out the Chinese was not without consequences, however. In March 1944, before the CEF joined the Burma campaign, Dorn polled some of his experienced officers to obtain their opinions of the Chinese armed forces. The results consisted of ten single-spaced pages of almost unrelieved criticism of the Chinese army. Most of the seventeen respondents agreed with the officer who complained that "Many Chinese officers are absolutely incompetent to lead anything."[24] Even more appalling was the apparent absence of patriotism or loyalty among the senior officers. The notorious corruption among senior officers, the graft-ridden supply system, and the near-total indifference to the plight of enlisted men betokened an officer corps unqualified "either professionally or morally for the grave task of leading men in battle."[25]

None of this would have surprised Dorn and the men at his headquarters, but neither would the few positive themes sounded by the Americans have been unexpected. Most officers agreed with Dorn's earlier assessment of the abilities of the Chinese soldier. The Americans commented favorably on the enlisted man's responsiveness to training, and they noted his doggedness and determination. Soldiers returning to their units after American-supervised instruction showed "a great deal more enthusiasm and desire to fight." One American even declared that his division would be "well trained by November," but most seemed closer to the officer who predicted that "If prop-

22. "Historical Report of Y-Force Operations Staff," 25 Nov. 1944, folder 169, box 14, Stilwell Papers, HI.
23. Ibid.
24. "Personal Opinion of the Chinese Army," 21 Mar. 1944, file 31, box 1, Dorn Papers, HI.
25. Ibid.

erly supplied, equipped, trained and led, the Chinese Army could become a fairly effective fighting force in two years."[26]

The American officers' ability to see *any* possibility for real improvement testified to their self-confidence and to the high opinion most had of the junior officers in the Nationalist army. Indeed, American references to the enthusiasm and discipline of Chinese junior officers appeared throughout the papers and reports of the Americans who served with the CAI and the CEF. "These people (Junior Officers and non-commissioned officers)," read one survey, "are capable of training efficiently their units, *provided they are not hindered by higher headquarters.* Should these people be given a free rein, I feel confident that within six months the 53rd Army *under American supervision* can and will prove to be a very efficient combat unit."[27]

Although Dorn's men were appalled by the Chinese senior officers' apparent lack of martial virtues, in the Chinese junior officers they found a group that seemed to share their ideals of patriotism and professionalism. "The officer that [*sic*] some day may make the Chinese Army into a real force," wrote Colonel Reynolds Condon, "are those young officers who have been imbued with a sort of patriotism and who have not yet had all their initiative and desire to serve ground out of them by the deadening effect of example. We have found in the XX group Army there is a considerable percentage of such officers up to the grade of Brig. General."[28] For Stilwell, who spent much of his time wrangling with Chinese generals, "control of the young officers through officers schools for Artillery, Infantry, and Engineers" offered a means for transforming the entire Chinese army.[29]

As much as the Americans might have preferred to look ahead to better days, they faced a more immediate test of their efforts in the field against Japanese troops. Here, despite the obvious grounds for pessimism, the results were mixed. Boatner's two divisions bogged down at first, but after command problems were resolved, they began to push the Japanese back. In May, Dorn's expeditionary force initially ignored American advice at a great cost in lives, but eventually began to advance with surprising results. Frequently Boatner's force closed with smaller Japanese units but permitted the enemy to escape. Nevertheless, the Chinese were at last beginning to retake ground and gain confidence in themselves. As one officer with the Y-Force explained, the training periods were probably too short to be of much use, but the Americans did "gain valuable experience in dealing with

26. Ibid.
27. Ibid. (emphasis in original).
28. Dorn to commanding general, HQ, USAF in CBI, on Condon's observations, 31 Dec. 1943, box 1, Dorn Papers, HI.
29. "Notes," n.d. (ca. winter 1942–43), file 83, box 8, Stilwell Papers, HI.

the Chinese and made friends and acquaintances among them. This materially assisted the Americans when later they were sent on liaison detail."[30] By November, Dorn was able to send a self-congratulatory report to Washington proclaiming that "the Y-Force staff discovered this year what they had long contended to be true: that the Chinese with training and modern equipment, can press an offensive—and win."[31]

Dorn issued his report shortly after Stilwell's recall from China, and he probably intended it to be read as a vindication of his chief's efforts in the theater. Although he did not know it at the time, the report would also serve as an epitaph of sorts for his own work in China. The circumstances surrounding Stilwell's recall have been ably told elsewhere, for our purposes it is more important to assess the effects of this high-level political dispute on the American liaison officers and advisers in the field. Stilwell's replacement, Lieutenant General Albert C. Wedemeyer, arrived in China in October 1944. The general's experience in China consisted of an abbreviated tour with the 15th infantry in the 1920s, during which time he declined an appointment as a language officer for fear that it would hinder his career. He achieved distinction on the Army general staff at the beginning of the war and as a staff officer in Admiral Lord Louis Mountbatten's Southeast Asia Command. While serving in the latter capacity Wedemeyer encountered Stilwell at several Allied conferences. Stilwell regarded the younger officer as a "puffed up" paper pusher, while Wedemeyer rated "Vinegar Joe" passable as a regimental commander but unfit for the demanding staff work required by larger operations.[32]

Dorn, who was already suspect because of his membership in what Wedemeyer contemptuously called the "walking out of Burma crowd," sealed his own fate when he counseled his new commander against implementing a reform program that would separate the training and command organizations, reorganize the supply service, and reconstitute the staff system along American lines. After being asked for his advice, Dorn recommended more modest changes and suggested that the new leadership could learn from the successes on the Burma front.

30. "Yoke Force Training Effort With the Chinese Expeditionary Force," file 183, box 15, Stilwell Papers, HI; Jonathan Spence, *To Change China: Western Advisors in China, 1620–1960* (Boston, 1969), 257–58.

31. "Historical Report of Y-Force Operations Staff," 25 Nov. 1944, file 169, box 14, Stilwell Papers, HI.

32. Entries for 27, 30 Nov. and 15 Dec. 1943, Stilwell Diary, no. 9, ibid; Wedemeyer to George A. and Lawrence J. Lincoln, 26 Nov. 1944, Lincoln File, box 3-E; Wedemeyer to Handy, 7 Feb. 1945, Handy File, box 3-E; Wedemeyer to Hull, 25 Nov. 1945, box 3-E, all in Albert C. Wedemeyer Papers, HI.

Wedemeyer took this as a sign of disloyalty, gave Dorn a poor efficiency rating, and banished him from the theater.[33]

Despite Stilwell's and Dorn's removal, the system of liaison in the field remained relatively undisturbed. This continuity is most readily explained by Wedemeyer's decision to assign Haydon Boatner, who had recently fallen out with Stilwell, as chief of staff to the newly formed Chinese Combat Command. Moreover, Wedemeyer's programs tended to expand upon rather than depart from those of his predecessor. At the heart of Wedemeyer's plan was the creation of thirty-six fully equipped American-trained divisions. Assigned to these "Alpha" divisions were teams of American liaison officers from the Chinese Combat Command. Unlike the previous system of liaison, however, the Americans in the new teams carried specific instructions for dealing with Chinese officers who consistently rejected American advice. All complaints would be sent up the chain of command. If disagreement persisted the liaison teams would be withdrawn and American supplies withheld from the offending Chinese unit.[34] Wedemeyer's new instructions were appreciated by frustrated liaison officers, many of whom had come to believe that their Chinese counterparts looked upon them as supply officers rather than as advisers.[35]

For their part, Chinese officers often resented what they perceived as American efforts to take charge of operations. Boatner took pains to remind Army officers that their role was to advise, but American control over Lend Lease supplies blurred the lines of authority between the Americans and Chinese. Years later, General Li Tsung-jen complained that the Americans displayed an imperious disregard for Chinese sensibilities. General Ho Ying-ch'in, supreme commander of the Chinese Army, also called attention to this problem during an unprecedented press conference with foreign reporters. After Ho praised General Robert McClure, head of the Chinese Combat Command, by noting that the two men "had practically merged into one," he complained that "Some Americans have misunderstood that every Chinese army unit with American officers participating is under the

33. Dorn to Wedemeyer, 31 Dec. 1944, folder 8, box 2; and Dorn to adjutant general, 16 July 1945, folder 19, box 2, CBI Theater, Dorn Papers, HI.

34. "Operational Directive No. 5 to Commanding General, Chinese Combat Command," 15 Feb. 1945; and "Letter of Instruction to all U.S. Officers Serving with the Chinese Combat Command," n.d., both in file 1-A, Black Book-China, box 1548, RG 332, Records of the Commanding General, China-Burma-India Theater, Federal Archives and Records Center (hereafter cited as FARC), Suitland, Md.

35. Col. Trevor Dupuy, telephone conversation with author, 12 July 1944. Dupuy served as a liaison officer with the CAI.

command of Americans. This is inaccurate information. The actual fact is that no matter whether the Chinese army units are supplied or trained by the Americans, or whether they have American advisors they are under the command of Chinese generals."[36]

These tensions that arose over command and control of Chinese units would persist for the remainder of the war, but Wedemeyer was able to ameliorate them somewhat by establishing more cordial relations with Chiang. It also seems clear that the Generalissimo became more cooperative as a result of the meeting of Soviet, American, and British leaders at Yalta in February 1945. The likelihood that the United States would rely on Russian troops to pin down Japanese forces on the mainland worried Chiang, as did the shift in the internal balance of power toward his Communist enemies. Japan's offensive in 1944, code-named ICHIGO, severely weakened Nationalist forces, raised the specter of a Chinese collapse, and fueled skepticism about Chiang's ability to maintain power after the war. Thus, Wedemeyer's tenure in China was made somewhat smoother by Chiang's greater willingness to accept American advice once ICHIGO had run its course.[37]

In early 1945, while Wedemeyer was overhauling the Chinese army and reequipping the Nationalist divisions, combined Chinese and British forces were continuing the reconquest of Burma. The sight of Chinese forces chasing the Japanese out of the jungles proved an exhilarating experience even for the journalist Theodore White, who by now had completely soured on the Nationalist regime. "Stilwell's training effort was now paying off," White recalled, "the thousands of Americans posted as liaison and training officers with Chinese troops, sleeping in hammocks in the jungle, in mud huts, in old Chinese temples, were now proud of the force they had created."[38] In January, General Daniel I. Sultan, the new commander of the Chinese Army in India, reported that the Chinese divisions fighting in Burma were "now first class. . . . In recent operations they have killed many Japanese. The comparison with Chinese casualties is very favorable."[39] *Newsweek*

36. Li Tsung-jen and Te Kong Tong, *The Memoirs of Li Tsung-jen* (Boulder, Colo., 1979), 159; Langdon to secretary of state, enclosing translation from *The Morning Post*, 26 June 1945, file 800/891, China, Kunming consulate, RG 84, General Records of the Department of State, FARC.

37. John W. Garver, *Chinese-Soviet Relations, 1937–1945: The Diplomacy of Chinese Nationalism* (New York, 1988), 207–14. Tang Tsou has pointed out that Chiang became more cooperative because the Americans no longer asked him to make difficult choices. Tsou, *America's Failure in China, 1941–1950* (Chicago, 1963), 118.

38. Theodore H. White, *In Search of History: A Personal Adventure* (New York, 1978), 222–23.

39. Sultan to O'Laughlin, 25 Jan. 1945, General Correspondence, box 68, O'Laughlin Papers, Library of Congress, Washington, D.C.

reporter Harold Isaacs also found evidence of swelling pride on the part of the Americans. "You can say anything you want about these people," one American told him, "but give me the infantry and give Colonel W. here the artillery and give us six months and we'll make an army that goes through Germany."[40] General Tōjō Hideki, Japan's wartime premier agreed. "The Chinese Army in India" he observed, "is a highly trained crack army to which we should give our close attention." According to one assessment of the Burma campaign, by early spring, the Japanese had suffered 72,000 men killed out of a force of approximately 100,000.[41]

In July, Wedemeyer's forces began offensive operations in China. The Japanese were now withdrawing forces from south and central China in anticipation of American landings along the coast, and although the newly trained Chinese units could not turn this retreat into a rout, their performance impressed their American advisers. These were heady times. The Chinese "were fighting better each succeeding day," reported Deputy Chief of Staff Brigadier General Paul Caraway, and they were "really enthusiastic about this business of attacking Japanese."[42] Wedemeyer, however, was somewhat more restrained in his reports to Washington. He noted that the Japanese had been "cooperating" but he added that "There have been some improvements in combat effectiveness, principally in spirit," and he also reported greater cooperation between the different Chinese units and "also between the Americans and Chinese."[43]

In order to build on this momentum, Wedemeyer requested additional American personnel to act as advisers to the American-trained and also the Chinese-sponsored divisions. The general also envisioned the use of American specialists to assist in the reorganization of those agencies most concerned with military affairs.[44] Confident that they had begun to transform China's army, Wedemeyer's staff even produced a short-range plan for China's administrative and economic reorganization patterned after the liaison system. "Because the Government is more nearly a military dictatorship than a true democracy," read the report, "the same factors which have resulted in the strengthening of the Chinese Army will accomplish the strengthening

40. "Harold Isaacs, Notes," n.d., WWII Correspondent, box 21, Harold Isaacs Papers, Institute Archives, Massachusetts Institute of Technology, Cambridge.

41. Tōjō quoted in Dick Wilson, *When Tigers Fight: The Story of the Sino-Japanese War, 1937–1945* (New York, 1982), 224; Hsi-Sheng Ch'i, *Nationalist China at War: Military Defeats and Political Collapse, 1937–1945* (Ann Arbor, Mich., 1982), 81.

42. Caraway to Armstrong, 2 Sept. 1945, Paul Caraway Papers, MHI.

43. Wedemeyer to Handy, 13 July 1945, Handy File, box 3-E, Wedemeyer Papers, HI.

44. Ibid.

of the Chinese government. Organization and administration of supply, and advisors in all echelons will have to be provided if the Chinese government is to be strengthened in the next few months in the same way the Chinese army has been strengthened in the last few months."[45]

Wedemeyer's offensive never moved beyond its initial stages, however, for in less than a month the Japanese surrendered. The outbreak of peace in China presented Wedemeyer with a new set of problems. Instead of slowly extending control over Japanese occupied areas, the Nationalist army hurriedly redeployed to major urban centers to maintain order and to prevent the Communists from expanding their hold over north China. Training areas were also abruptly emptied as part of the postsurrender operations. Faced with these new circumstances, Wedemeyer nevertheless expected U.S. military assistance to China to continue into the postwar era. Asked by reporters if the Americans would stay on, Wedemeyer implied that they would. After referring to earlier Russian and German military missions in China, Wedemeyer announced that now the Chinese would "unlearn to goosestep."[46] Although Wedemeyer explained that he awaited instructions from the Pentagon, clearly he intended to play a more active role in developing policy for China. In early September, the general returned to Washington where he worked with his former subordinates on the general staff to overcome State Department opposition and create a military advisory group for China. Wedemeyer and his advisers hoped to create a postwar mission of four thousand officers and enlisted men modeled on the liaison and advisory system created during the war. State Department critics led by John Carter Vincent, the chief of the Office of Far Eastern Affairs, charged that the proposed advisory mission would create a "semi-colonial Chinese army." Vincent and others also feared that by providing assistance at the operational level the advisory mission would entangle the United States in the growing civil conflict in China. In the end, the State and War Departments compromised on a scaled-down mission of nine hundred officers and enlisted men who would be prohibited from offering operational advice or basic instruction to Nationalist forces.[47]

45. Olmsted to commanding general (Wedemeyer), 8 Aug. 1945, file: China, Misc. Information, China-Burma-India Theater, box 1555, RG 332, FARC.

46. It is ironic, given Wedemeyer's remark, that the general actually advised the Chinese government to adopt a military staff system more like the German staff than the American. "Transcript of Press Conference (16 Aug 45)," 17 Aug. 1945, box 1, Weigle Papers, HI; F. F. Liu, *A Military History of Modern China, 1924–1949* (Princeton, N.J., 1956), 234.

47. Minutes of the State-War-Navy Coordinating Committee (SWNCC)—Far Eastern Subcommittee, 11 Sept. 1945, SWNCC Papers, RG 353, Interdepartmental and

Vincent's fears that an expanded advisory mission might lead to direct U.S. intervention in China's internal conflicts were warranted. Although American officers hoped to foster in their Chinese colleagues the professional ideal of noninvolvement in political affairs, they nevertheless understood that they were preparing Nationalist forces for struggles beyond the immediate war with Japan. As Boatner recalled, "A great many U.S. officers told me that our lower level Chinese officials (in the regimental level and lower) would tell them frequently about the BIG war to come—i.e. their war against the Communists."[48] During the war the Americans could rationalize that all Chinese were united in the fight against Japan, but in the aftermath of Japan's surrender it became increasingly difficult for American officers to reconcile their image of themselves as politically neutral advisers with the reality of impending civil war in China.[49]

Although the scope of the American advisory mission was reduced significantly, in other ways the Army still exercised considerable influence over the implementation of U.S. policy in China. In November 1945, when American Ambassador Patrick Hurley unexpectedly resigned, President Harry S Truman appointed the recently retired George Marshall as special ambassador to China. In preparation for his mission, Marshall met with Wedemeyer's former associates in the Operations and Plans Division of the general staff, and with their help rewrote the State Department's draft of his instructions. He also met with Stilwell and officers who served in the theater and received correspondence from others, including Boatner and Colonel Morris DePass, the wartime attaché in Chungking. Although DePass's recommendations dealt with economic and political questions, his most useful advice concerned planning for the integration of Communist and Nationalist military forces.[50] When Marshall assembled his team

Intradepartmental Staffs, NA.; Hull to Patterson, 17 Jan. 1946, Radios-Eyes Alone Book VII, box 1541, RG 332, FARC; Liu, 236–40; Marc S. Gallicchio, *The Cold War Begins in Asia: American East Asian Policy and the Fall of the Japanese Empire* (New York, 1988), 100–102; James F. Schnabel, *The History of the Joint Chiefs of Staff: The JCS and National Policy, 1945–1947* (Wilmington, Del., 1979), 419; Forrest Pogue, *George C. Marshall: Statesman* (New York, 1987), 60–68.

48. Boatner's notes (ca. 1973), Supplementary Papers, box 2, Boatner Papers, MHI.

49. "As the internal war is developing, the Generalissimo and his main advisors are ... putting us squarely into the business of deploying their forces for operations against the Communists and not for the maintenance of order and the disarmament of the Japanese." Caraway to Maddocks, 5 Nov. 1945, Caraway Papers, MHI.

50. Memo for the record, 10 Dec. 1945, and Notes on a meeting of General Marshall, 11 Dec. 1945, both in file: ABC 336 China (26 Jan. 1942) sec 1-E, RG 165, NA; Dupuy, telephone conversation with author, 12 July 1994; Gallicchio, 131–32; Gary May, *China Scapegoat: The Diplomatic Ordeal of John Carter Vincent* (Washington, D.C., 1979), 140–42.

for the mission, he chose Army officers with China experience. In many other respects, the Marshall Mission was an Army undertaking. Marshall communicated through military channels, eventually set up truce teams staffed by Army officers, a system first proposed by Wedemeyer at the end of the war, and even made Wedemeyer his first choice to replace Hurley as ambassador.[51]

Immediately upon arriving in China in late December, the general entered into an exhausting round of talks with representatives of the Nationalists and Communists. By early February these efforts seemed to be producing results. On 5 February, Marshall notified Assistant Secretary of State Dean Acheson that "Things today, about an hour ago as a matter of fact, give some indication that the Nationalization of the army . . . will not be too difficult."[52] The talks dragged on longer than Marshall expected but the two sides appeared to be getting closer. During one of these meetings, however, Marshall grew concerned by the Communists' insistence on delaying the integration of their forces with the Nationalist army. Suddenly the efforts of the past several weeks seemed in jeopardy. Fearful of losing ground in the negotiations, Marshall approached Chinese Communist negotiater Chou En-lai privately after the meeting.[53] The ensuing exchange took place off the record and has thus gone unnoticed by historians.

In a subsequent memorandum to Chiang Kai-shek, however, Marshall revealed that, as a result of his private meeting with Chou, he believed that "one possible reason for the reluctance of the Communists to undertake integration earlier than twelve months was due to their appreciation of the difficulties and appearance [sic] that would not involve a serious loss of face."[54] Four days later, Marshall told General Douglas MacArthur that Chou was reluctant to merge his irregular forces with the American-trained Nationalists because the Communists would be embarrassed by comparison. In order to clear this last hurdle, Marshall hoped to borrow sixty junior officers and an equal number of noncommissioned officers from MacArthur's forces

---

A number of DePass's suggestions concerning the deactivization of troops, the creation of border guards (Peace Preservation Corps in Marshall's plan) as well as the pay, and supplying of troops found their way into Marshall's later proposals. DePass to Marshall, 25 Jan. 1946, folder 29, box 124, George C. Marshall Papers, George C. Marshall Library, Lexington, Va.

51. Wedemeyer to Marshall, 1 Aug. 1945, in Keith E. Eiler, ed. *Wedemeyer on War and Peace* (Stanford, Calif., 1987), 124–32; Pogue, *George C. Marshall: Statesman*, 54–73.

52. Marshall to Acheson, 5 Feb. 1946, folder 3, China Mission, 1945–47, box 122, Correspondence, Marshall Papers, Marshall Library.

53. Minutes of the Military Sub-Committee, 18 Feb. 1945, *Marshall's Mission to China, December 1945–January 1947: The Report and Appended Documents*, 2 vols. (Arlington, Va., 1976), 2:238–51.

54. Marshall to Chiang, 20 Apr. 1946, McNeil Folder, Alvin C. Gillem Papers, MHI.

so they could begin an "elementary school for infantry and artillery officers and for division and corps staff officers" in the Communist-held areas.[55] The idea, as Marshall later explained to an appalled Chiang, was "to prepare the communist officers concerned for the formal organization of their troops into divisions that could at least march and parade in an acceptable manner."[56]

Marshall's belief that Chou's reservations arose from a fear of losing "face" to the better equipped and formally trained Nationalists seems strikingly naive but altogether consistent with the attention that Americans gave to matters of "face" when dealing with Chinese. Marshall's concern for the "face" of the Chinese, in this case the Communists, even led him to recommend outfitting the designated Communist units in American uniforms so that they would wear the same khaki as the American-sponsored Nationalist troops. Thus, like his predecessors, Marshall sought to Americanize Chinese forces, quite literally it would seem, while simultaneously attempting to show some sensitivity to the sensibilities of his hosts.

On a return visit to the United States, Marshall recruited eighty-three American officers for the training program and stockpiled supplies at Peking. The Communists were spared the rigors of an American boot camp, however, by the resumption of skirmishing between Communist and Nationalist forces.[57] Much to the consternation of Chiang's American supporters, the general embargoed supplies to the Nationalists while trying to avert the final breakdown in negotiations. In early 1947 Marshall admitted defeat and returned home to become secretary of state. Later that year he dispatched Wedemeyer on a fact-finding mission to China and Korea. Although the former commander of U.S. forces in China recommended a program of supervised aid to the Nationalists, the Truman administration refused to make any large new committments to them.[58] The American advisory group operated in China until Chiang fled the mainland in 1949 and then folded its tents. It would not resume its mission until after the outbreak of the Korean War.

55. Marshall to MacArthur, 22 Feb. 1946, folder: Communist Training, box 33, Marshall Mission Files, RG 59, Records of the Department of State, NA.

56. Chiang already feared that Marshall did not share his views on the Communists. Chiang's diary entry for 19 Jan. and 2 Feb. 1946 cited in Keiji Furuya, *Chiang Kai-Shek: His Life and Times*, tr. Chun-ming Chang (New York, 1981), 863–65; Marshall to Chiang, 20 Apr. 1946, McNeil Folder, Gillem Papers, MHI.

57. Abbey to Lucas, submitting report on the Army Advisory Group, China, 5 Nov. 1946, file: 091 China, box 61, Plans and Operations Division of the Army General Staff, RG 319, FARC.

58. William Stueck, *The Wedemeyer Mission: American Politics and Foreign Policy during the Cold War* (Athens, Ga., 1984), passim.

The interlude between the defeat of the Nationalists and the creation of an American military mission on Taiwan provides a convenient point at which to stop and assess the Army's early efforts to improve the combat efficiency of Nationalist forces. In 1941, after nearly two decades in which they studied and commented on a host of developments related to the growth of Chinese nationalism, U.S. Army officers abandoned their positions as aloof observers in favor of direct participation in the defense of China. In their role as advisers to the Chinese army, American officers needed to exercise considerable finesse if they were to succeed in their mission. The Americans could not command the Chinese as if they were a colonial army, nor could they brush their allies aside and wage the war with U.S. forces as was later done in Vietnam.[59] Americans controlled the distribution of Lend Lease aid, an important means of leverage to be sure, nevertheless, the officers sent to China could only advise and train their allies. For this they needed the cooperation of their Chinese counterparts. Faced with a frustrating distribution of power between host and outsider, Americans needed to make at least some effort to understand and cooperate with their allies.

Within this context, educated and sympathetic China Hands like Dorn and Boatner actively and sincerely tried to reduce cultural conflicts and facilitate cooperation. In preparing their subordinates for the job of liaison officer, Dorn and Boatner acted as cultural interpreters, drawing on their personal experience to explain China and the Chinese to the American newcomers. These officers made it abundantly clear to their subordinates that they were expected to observe a respectful relationship with their Chinese counterparts. Prejudice and feelings of superiority cannot be eradicated on command and it is clear that tensions remained within the Chinese Combat Command up to the end of the war. In mandating specific behavior from their subordinates, however, Dorn and Boatner took the first step in developing American attitudes. As one liaison officer who served for two years in China explained, "My association with Chinese commanders in this capacity was pleasant. I learned that if I couldn't say 'yes,' I could say 'no' nicely."[60] Whatever their private views, American officers knew they had to behave in ways that took Chinese sensibilities into account.

Significantly, U.S. Army officers returned from China with a mildly optimistic view of what was possible in China, a point frequently over-

59. George C. Herring, "'Peoples Quite Apart': Americans, South Vietnamese, and the War in Vietnam," *Diplomatic History* 14 (Winter 1990).

60. Mitchell to Boatner, 7 May 1945, box 1, Boatner Papers, HI.

looked by historians.[61] Few other Americans who served in China during the war shared the Army's interpretation of events. By the end of the war, most American foreign service officers were arguing that an alternative had to be found to Chiang's misrule of China. For China specialists like John Carter Vincent and John Stewart Service, the Western-educated liberals of China appeared to be a third force for positive change in that troubled country. As Kenneth Shewmaker has shown in his study of Westerners who visited the Communist base at Yenan, journalists also believed that Chiang's corrupt regime would have to make way for a modern progressive government like the one they thought that they found in the Communist base camp. Reporters, who admired the Communists' informality and their apparent egalitarian values, saw the traditionalism and formality of Chungking as the outward symbols of a reactionary and corrupt society.[62] Western journalists also had difficulty accepting Chinese ideas about rectitude in public discourse. Progressives intent on exposing the Nationalists to the world believed the Chinese used traditional etiquette and concern about "face" to hide the rot in Chungking.[63]

American military officers also identified a third force for modernizing China. For American advisers, the junior officers in the Chinese army constituted a solid foundation on which to build a modern military establishment.[64] Like American journalists and foreign service officers, American military officers identified with a group in China that appeared to share their own values. As Dorn and Boatner reminded them, Chinese formality and customs were not so different from those followed in an American army that observed its own ceremonies, practiced its own etiquette, honored its ancestors, and esteemed personal loyalty to one's superiors. It is not surprising therefore that American officers were so receptive to the importance the Chinese placed on "face." Indeed, as they employed the idea, this concept of "face" seemed to provide the key to understanding the Chinese by placing them in a familiar context.

61. See, for example, Spence, 278; Tuchman, *Stilwell;* Charles Romanus and Riley Sunderland, *Time Runs Out in CBI* (Washington, D.C., 1959).

62. Shewmaker, 335–46.

63. Ibid., 341; Harold Isaacs "Dorn of the Salween," *Newsweek,* 1 Jan. 1945; idem, *No Peace for Asia* (Cambridge, Mass., 1967), 29.

64. Although Americans praised the young officers they encountered, the actual overall quality of junior officers in the Nationalist army probably declined during the war. During the war the percentage of officers who graduated from the military academy or received levels of training and education on a par with other modern armies steadily declined. In the last years of the war many junior officers were promoted from the ranks of enlisted men. Lloyd E. Eastman, *Seeds of Destruction: Nationalist China in War and Revolution, 1937–1949* (Stanford, Calif., 1984), 144–45.

Although most Americans in China often reduced every issue in China to a matter of "face," they sometimes used the concept in ways that contributed to better relations with their allies. At times, as when Army officers improvised a training program for illiterate artillery recruits, this attention to "face" helped Americans develop thoughtful approaches to problems. In other instances, "face" helped the Americans understand the source of the resistance they encountered in reforming the Chinese army. This was the case at Ramgarh when American officers realized, belatedly, that they had paid insufficient attention to the "face" of their Chinese counterparts. When Japan capitulated, Wedemeyer "cognizant of the importance of 'face,'" urged the Generalissimo to personally accept the surrender of the Japanese commander in China. Wedemeyer might have added that attentiveness to the symbolic importance of such events came naturally to military men, as was evidenced by the battle being waged at that moment by U.S. Army and Navy commanders over who would have the honor of taking the surrender in Japan.[65]

"Face," as the Americans defined the term, could, however, become a way of patronizing the Chinese and trivializing serious conflicts by reducing Chinese problems to matters of symbols and appearances. General Marshall slighted the bitter antagonism that divided the Communists and Nationalists when he attributed Chou's resistance to military unification to a fear of losing "face." As Marshall's offer to the Communists demonstrates, an apparent sensitivity to Chinese feelings did not necessarily lead to a better understanding of China's problems.[66] Despite the sincerity of their efforts, most Americans remained too strongly wedded to their own institutions and values to see China's turmoil from the perspective of the Chinese. In the end, this reliance on American points of reference made the process of understanding China's problems seem deceptively easy.

If Army officers misjudged conditions in China, it is nevertheless important to understand how their sense of achievement during the last fleeting weeks before Japan's surrender shaped the Army's perception of U.S. China policy for years to come. Emboldened by their experience, General Wedemeyer and his supporters regularly advocated more military aid to the Nationalists during the civil war.[67] State

65. Albert C. Wedemeyer, *Wedemeyer Reports!* (New York, 1958), 350.

66. Given that the Communists specifically denounced the whole system of ritualized conduct in traditional China, one can only wonder at Chiang's reaction when Marshall informed him that he wished to help the Communists save face. Shewmaker, 300.

67. For examples of the U.S. Army and Navy's effort to maintain aid for the Nationalists, see Ernest R. May, *The Truman Administration and China* (Philadelphia, Pa., 1976); Dorothy Borg and Waldo Heinrichs, eds., *Uncertain Years: Chinese-American Relations,*

Department efforts to withhold or place limits on such aid drew sharp criticism from veterans of the China-Burma-India theater. Such interference, they argued, amounted to a breach of America's "moral committments" to China. Army officers charged that "whatever tangible and measurable benefits might have accrued from U.S. aid have been lost in the adherence to a confused neutrality."[68] Institutionally, Army China Hands sought to promote their interpretation of Sino-American relations within the Army by revising course materials on China at West Point and the National War College.[69] As the civil war intensified, how one interpreted the recent history of American-Chinese relations had become a central issue in the debate over policy.

In 1949, as the Nationalists seemed headed for oblivion, the Army attempted to stop the publication of the State Department's White Paper on China "Since the paper shows the Communists in a far better light than the Nationalists."[70] Failing that, the Army prepared an unpublished rebuttal to the State Department's White Paper on China. The Army's critique of the White Paper contested the secretary of state's view that the United States had been unstinting in its support of Chiang's government and catalogued numerous instances, beginning with the advisory group, in which recommendations by the Joint Chiefs of Staff were opposed or weakened by the State Department.[71] Although less strident than other prominent friends of Chiang Kai-shek, such as Claire Chennault and Admiral Charles Cooke, the Army's China Hands actively participated in the campaign to keep aid flowing to the Nationalists after 1945.

1947–1950 (New York, 1979); Michael Lewis Baron, "Tug of War: The Battle Over American Policy Toward China, 1946–1949" (Ph.D. diss., Columbia University, 1980); William Whitney Stueck, *The Road to Confrontation* (Chapel Hill, N.C., 1982); idem, *Wedemeyer Mission*, 86–102; and Michael Schaller, *The Origins of the Cold War In Asia: The American Occupation of Japan* (New York, 1985).

68. Seedlock to Wedemeyer, 19 Dec. 1947, P&O 091 China Top Secret, Records of the Planning and Operations Section, 1946–1948, RG 319, FARC. Col. Robert F. Seedlock served in Burma during the war on the construction of the Stilwell Road. He returned from the theater with a strong admiration for the abilities of the Chinese engineeers with whom he worked. Papers of Maj. Gen. (ret.) Robert F. Seedlock, in possession of the author.

69. Colonel M. B. Raymond, "Lessons of the China-Burma-India Theater," Appendix F, 21 June 1946, U.S. Command and General Staff College, Command Class, 196, George A. Lincoln Papers, U.S. Military Academy, West Point, N.Y.; Lawrence Lincoln, "Comments on 'China in War and Victory,'" n.d., Lawrence Lincoln Papers, MHI; Wedemeyer to Caraway, 24 Oct. 1946, and Caraway to Gruenther, 15 Apr. 1947, Caraway papers, MHI.

70. Memorandum for General Bolte, 21 July 1949, RG 319, Records of Planning and Operations, 1949–1950, P&O 091 China Section 1-A, FARC.

71. Memorandum for the chief of staff, 10 Aug. 1949, 091 China Section 1, Plans and Operations, box 152, RG 319, Army General and Special Staffs, NA.

The outbreak of the Korean War settled the question of aid but it also sharpened the sense of frustration felt by many of Chiang's supporters in the Army. Perhaps if someone other than Stilwell had been in China during the war Chiang would have been in a better position to defeat the Communists. Or perhaps if Marshall had not adopted Stilwell's policy of pressuring Chiang and advocating a coalition government China could have been saved. For Wedemeyer and his supporters, Marshall's friendship with Stilwell seemed to explain much about the failure of American policy. Thus, even the Army's official history of the China theater was viewed as putting Stilwell "in the best light possible, [because] the War Department backed him up for so long."[72] Although Stilwell died in 1947, his bitter feud with Wedemeyer had taken on a life of its own. In 1958, General Wedemeyer published his memoir criticizing Stilwell and Marshall for their confrontational approach to the Nationalists. Wedemeyer also blamed the Truman administration for not following through on "the success which even our limited effort had achieved during the war" in building up Nationalist forces. The general maintained that the State Department's restrictions on the size of the postwar advisory group and the prohibition against American officers accompanying Nationalist troops into the field deprived Chiang's men of vital support against the Communists.[73]

In retrospect, it seems clear that Army officers had produced an alternative history of the American experience in China that emphasized, indeed exaggerated, their successes at the end of the war and minimized the imposing problems that still awaited them after Japan's surrender.[74] In their historical interpretation, America's supposed failure in China was recast as a failure to continue the Army's program to improve the combat efficiency of Nationalist forces. Today, few historians would accept this view of American-Chinese relations. Nevertheless, during the Chinese civil war, this dissenting view of the recent past became a rallying point for Chiang's American supporters. In asserting their newfound authority to speak on China policy, Army officers, the other China Hands, came to the aid of their former comrades, but they also helped to initiate the noxious public debate over who lost China.

72. Roberts to Sunderland, 4 Apr. 1950, Papers of Frank Roberts, Harry S. Truman Library, Independence, Mo.

73. Wedemeyer, 400–401; Wedemeyer to Eng, 10 July 1946, Horace Eng File, box 3-E, Wedemeyer Papers, HI.

74. For a detailed analysis of the internal weaknesses of the Nationalist army during the civil war see Eastman, 158–71.

The U.S. Army, Unconditional Surrender, and the Potsdam Proclamation

BRIAN L. VILLA

O N August 10, 1945, the Japanese government finally announced its willingness to surrender on the sole condition that the imperial institution not be prejudiced. In roundabout ways, the American government met the request, one which virtually everyone had anticipated and which many in Washington had long been prepared to make. Still, for both governments these gestures represented an abandonment of intransigent postures adopted in wartime propaganda.

The postwar world might have been very different if the timing had been other than what it was. If the surrender had occurred later, the Russian military position in China, Korea, and Japan would have been much stronger. Conversely, if Tokyo and Washington had reached an agreement earlier, the atomic bomb would not have been used, Russia would not have entered the war in the Pacific, the Yalta agreement on the Far East would have remained a dead letter, and the American military position in Europe would have been much stronger. The many possibilities revealed by an awareness of this contingency and the importance of timing have stimulated an enormous amount of speculation by historians and the public at large.

Two broad trends can be recognized in this speculative enterprise. At the height of the Cold War many Americans felt that the bomb alone had ended the war, that Soviet entry in the Far East should not have been encouraged, and that Russia had reaped the Yalta rewards without any sacrifice. Presumably communist sympathizers within the state department had "duped" the government into prolonging the war to make Soviet entry possible. Historians have recently turned this interpretation on its head. Agreeing that the war had been unnecessarily prolonged, they contend that the purpose was to terrorize the Soviets by demonstrating

Brian L. Villa is assistant professor of history in the University of Ottawa.

the bomb on a prostrate Japan, something which could not be arranged before August 1945.[1]

There may well be an answer to both interpretations: the reorientation of policy required to make peace took more time than seemed necessary simply because there were deep divisions in government, divisions which in any complicated distribution of power could not be decisively resolved without struggle and, ultimately, a redistribution of power through the formation of new decision-making bodies. In this perspective all speculation about what decision makers could do quickly should be tempered by some appreciation of the channels through which they had to work. This essay seeks to explain not so much the particular positions taken by individuals in the internal debates as the process by which they interacted. No attempt is made here to study the decision-making process in Japan.[2] Nor is any attempt made here to study all aspects of decision making in Washington, though some effort is made to complete what is known about the position taken by the state department. This essay does attempt to describe how the army's position on unconditional surrender came to be formulated and to assess, from this perspective, whether the final peace terms might have been reached earlier.[3] For these purposes some understanding of army administrative structures is necessary. Equally necessary is an appreciation of the theory and practice of unconditional surrender in the years before the fateful decision on Japanese surrender was reached.

The war department, a huge structure for conducting the war, had been given a tiered structure of small, manageable, and well-organized policy-making bodies. Army records for 1944 and 1945, incomparably better organized and maintained than state department records, reflect the clarity and thoroughness with which army administrative structures had been established during the war and the importance of the Operations

---

[1] Athan G. Theoharis, *The Yalta Myths: an issue in U.S. politics, 1945-1955* (Columbia, Mo., 1970), 105-29, 154-79; Gar Alperovitz, *Atomic Diplomacy: Hiroshima and Potsdam: The Use of the Atomic Bomb and the American Confrontation with Soviet Power* (New York, 1965), 14, 237, 239, 241. For a recent reworking of Gar Alperovitz's theme with some added twists, see Charles L. Mee, Jr., *Meeting at Potsdam* (New York, 1975), 205, 238-39, 288-89.

[2] For Japanese peace-making, see Robert J. C. Butow, *Japan's Decision to Surrender* (Stanford, 1954).

[3] The principal unpublished sources for this study are Joint Chiefs of Staff (JCS) and JCS Committee files relating to the end of the Pacific war; state department files on the Potsdam Conference; Secretary's Staff Committee Minutes and documents; the Joseph Grew Papers (Harvard University), and interviews with Gen. George A. Lincoln, Nov. 1967, and Oct. 1968.

Division (OPD) advising the chief of staff, General George C. Marshall.[4] With fewer than 200 officers, OPD was the coordinating agency, responsible for all aspects of future military strategy and policy, issuing all military orders emanating from Washington, monitoring the results obtained in each theater, and coordinating army strategy with other departments of the government and with the Allied (United) Nations. OPD attracted and produced some very distinguished American officers, including Dwight D. Eisenhower, Albert C. Wedemeyer, and John Hull.

OPD itself had a small manageable center of gravity—the Strategy and Policy Section (S&P)—which clearly overshadowed the other five major divisions within OPD. The particular responsibility of S&P was army strategic planning at its highest level and its integration with civilian objectives for the war. Headed by a junior brigadier general, S&P carried enormous responsibilities during the war. Between February 1942 and September 1945, four generals successively directed S&P: Thomas T. Handy, Wedemeyer, Frank N. Roberts, and George A. Lincoln. S&P's chief was "the Army Planner" and directly advised General Marshall and the chief and deputy chief of OPD. This remarkable organization placed a junior one star general on top of so important a structure as S&P and beside the chief of staff. There had to be, of course, a substantial measure of confidence between the chief of S&P and his superiors, which was usually the case.[5] Clearly, the position taken by the chief of S&P would be of crucial importance in determining the army's position on unconditional surrender.

The army, however, did not run the war. Above OPD, and the chief of staff—General Marshall—were the Joint Chiefs of Staff (JCS), headed by Admiral William D. Leahy, the latter handpicked by Marshall and Franklin D. Roosevelt to be the remote and distant arbitrator over interservice rivalry.[6] JCS submitted military policy to the President. In practice army policy worked out in S&P was presented to at least two subcommittees of JCS before being formally considered by the chiefs. Less frequently

[4] For an example of state department files at their worst, see 740.00119 [Potsdam] 7-2345, General Records of the Department of State, RG 59 (National Archives), a loose unbound file containing over 100 documents from sundry and miscellaneous sources, currently (1973) in no particular order. See also Ray S. Cline, *United States Army in World War II: The War Department: Washington Command Post: The Operations Division* (Washington, 1951), 195, 108-09.

[5] Cline, *Washington Command Post*, 103, 121, 166, 363 (organizational tables); "General George A. Lincoln on W.W. II," transcript of television program, Department of Social Science, United States Military Academy (West Point).

[6] Forrest C. Pogue, *George C. Marshall: Organizer of Victory, 1943-1945* (New York, 1973), 7, 8, 70.

the chief of staff would present ideas through JCS to these subcommittees, when he was not pleased with the alternatives being presented at JCS levels.

The most important of these subcommittees was the Joint Staff Planners, comprised of the principal planning staff in the services. The head of S&P represented the army there. Helping the Joint Planning Staff and responsible to it was the Joint War Plans Committee. Important proposals touching on grand strategy might also go through the Joint Strategic Survey Committee, a high level "blue ribbon" review board of senior officers, at times equal in influence to the joint chiefs themselves. From there papers went to JCS and the President.[7]

Policy initiatives did not just rise from below; they also came from the President, from the joint chiefs, and from principal cabinet officers. As far as the army was concerned the unconditional surrender doctrine was just such a gift from on high. Though the state department Committee on Post War Planning had considered forms of surrender and expressed a marked preference for unconditional surrender, the army had not taken part in these deliberations. It is true that Roosevelt had notified the chiefs of staff before the Casablanca Conference that he would announce unconditional surrender as the objective of the United Nations, but the reference to it had been so brief that after the war Marshall could not recall hearing of the formula until it was publicly announced by the President at Casablanca. There certainly was not thorough consultation.[8]

That doctrine was not generally understood at the time, nor have subsequent scholars grasped its full implications, though one has come quite close.[9] The doctrine was, of course, intended to strike awe in the enemy as it helped develop confidence and a sense of solidarity among the United Nations. But its central purpose was juridical. Roosevelt was aware of the debate over the legality of the Versailles settlement. The Germans

[7] Cline, *Washington Command Post*, 107-42, 188-212, 234-68. Unfortunately, the volumes of the official history of the joint chiefs have not been published. But copies of Vernon E. Davis, "Origin of the Joint and Combined Chiefs of Staff in WW II" (1972) and Grace P. Hayes, "History of the Joint Chiefs of Staff in WW II, The War against Japan" (2 vols., 1953) are available in the Records of the United States Joint Chiefs of Staff, RG 48 (National Archives).

[8] [Harley A. Notter] *Postwar Foreign Policy Preparation, 1939-1945* (Washington, 1949), 126-27; Department of State, *Foreign Relations of the United States: The Conferences at Washington, 1941-1942, and Casablanca, 1943* (Washington, 1968), 506, 506n. JCS formal participation in the subcommittee did not occur until after March 1943. [Notter] *Postwar Foreign Policy Preparation*, 125.

[9] Paul Kecskemeti, *Strategic Surrender: The Politics of Victory and Defeat* (Stanford, 1958). For the literature on unconditional surrender, see Raymond G. O'Connor, *Diplomacy for Victory: FDR and Unconditional Surrender* (New York, 1971).

argued, with some support in the United States, that they had surrendered their arms on the basis of the Fourteen Points and had then been forced to sign something entirely different. The solution was fairly obvious: next time no political promises would be made prior to an unconditional military surrender. The only guarantees that the defeated would have against abuse by the victor would be those recognized by international law, particularly the Geneva conventions.

Roosevelt would accept no restrictions whatsoever on the victor, from Geneva or elsewhere. "Please note," he once angrily stated, "that I am not willing at this time to say that we do not intend to destroy the German nation."[10] His motivation was clearly announced at Casablanca: "Unconditional surrender . . . does mean the destruction of a philosophy in Germany, Italy and Japan which is based on the conquest and subjugation of other peoples."[11] Rooting out a philosophy, Roosevelt recognized, was difficult business. In his mind the process might well have to include such things as war trials, elimination of dangerous parties, prolonged occupation, careful control of all levels of education, de-industrialization, and territorial dismemberment. To achieve these goals it was necessary that a people, a nation, as well as a government be entirely at the mercy of the conqueror. The right even to abuse the defeated was to be claimed. As Winston Churchill expressed it: "If we are bound, we are bound by our own consciences to civilization."[12] Accordingly, in discussing the surrender documents that were to implement this philosophy there was a marked preference for Hobbesian language. Instruments of surrender were to be framed to allow the United States to assume "supreme" or "absolute" power.[13]

There was widespread skepticism among the military toward Roosevelt's unconditional surrender policy based on three important considerations. First, the military questioned the need for a legally perfect carte blanche to justify occupation policies. The officers felt that all the legal documents in the world would not add anything to a sound occupation policy, and, similarly, no amount of legal documents could justify an unnecessarily brutal occupation. Second, even if some benefit could be gained from a legally more correct position, the price paid for it would be too high.

[10] Department of State, *Foreign Relations of the United States: Diplomatic Papers 1944.* Vol. I: *General* (Washington, 1966), 501-02.

[11] *Foreign Relations of the United States . . . Casablanca*, 837.

[12] Winston S. Churchill, *The Second World War: The Hinge of Fate* (Boston, 1950), 690-91.

[13] For example, see Department of State, *Foreign Relations of the United States: Diplomatic Papers 1945.* Vol. III: *European Advisory Commission; Austria; Germany* (Washington, 1968), 169, 378-81.

The very nature of the unconditional surrender formula caused too much uncertainty for the enemy as to what surrender and occupation might mean, and this uncertainty would be converted into desperate, last ditch fighting. Third, if the officers saw the formula as a legal nicety with a very high price, this was because, for a variety of reasons, they tended not to share Roosevelt's primary objective—the rooting out of evil philosophies. Few shared his belief that international conflicts were basically caused by pernicious philosophies. Even if Roosevelt's analysis proved correct, there was much skepticism that his corrective could be administered by an occupation army. In any case the attempt to uproot a philosophy and instill a new one would take a long time. Roosevelt spoke of an educational process of forty years for Germany.[14] While he never seems to have defined how long the military occupation proper would last, the army was disinclined to think in terms of more than a few years. Nor was the sharing of occupation responsibilities with civilian experts in the restructuring of societies looked on with much enthusiasm. But the most serious consideration from the military point of view was the drain on military resources implied in a prolonged occupation and the risk of retaining troops in one theater for an indefinite period. The prevalent view was summarized by one officer directly involved: the doctrine ". . . was open to serious doubts as to its practical horse sense."[15]

Important civilians within the government supported the military in their doubts about restructuring foreign societies. Their motives for supporting the military were less practical and more ideological. Everyone agreed vaguely that the Axis nations had to be restructured. But when it came to specific planning there was disagreement on how far this social engineering should go, divisions which reflected America's own post-Depression politics. The left wanted to go beyond fostering political change to produce profound, even revolutionary, economic and social changes. The right feared the precedent such massive intervention overseas might have on America. Accordingly, the right tended to be lukewarm in its support of unconditional surrender and the extraordinary measures it implied. There were important exceptions to this division—Cordell Hull, most noticeably—but if one pictures Henry L. Stimson, Joseph Grew, James Forrestal, and William Phillips on the right, resisting unconditional

[14] Department of State, *Foreign Relations of the United States: The Conference at Quebec 1944* (Washington, 1972), 144.
[15] Interview with Lincoln, Nov. 1967, Oct. 1968; Lincoln to author, Nov. 12, 1970; Charles H. Bonesteel to author, May 28, 1974. See also, *Foreign Relations of the United States . . . Germany*, 380, 419, 509.

surrender, and Harry Hopkins, Dean Acheson, Archibald MacLeish on the left, insisting on unconditional surrender, one can arrive at an idea of the division among American policy makers by 1945.[16]

By the end of the war this division over unconditional surrender and the associated occupation policies had produced a certain amount of name-calling. Stimson and Grew were labeled reactionaries. Their opponents came to be dubbed communist sympathizers. The division would have momentous consequences for postwar America. For better or worse, the right, which opposed revolutionary uses of unconditional surrender, came to support the military in their practical objections to unconditional surrender. That alliance would also have important implications for postwar America.

The divisions over unconditional surrender began to manifest themselves with the army's reluctance to insist on unconditional surrender for Italy in 1943. This dissent was blurred by the fact that Roosevelt and many of his advisers were themselves not convinced that unconditional surrender was required of Italy. Roosevelt, in fact, had not intended to include Italy among the powers required to surrender unconditionally. Only at British insistence, partly motivated by colonial and naval considerations, was Italy included.[17] But since neither Churchill nor Roosevelt believed that dictatorship and militarism were anything but superficial grafts on the Italian nation, there was little incentive to insist on unconditional surrender when the Italian government asked for generous peace terms.[18] All the more so, since the Italian request came just as the Allies were about to launch an extremely hazardous invasion of the Italian mainland with insufficient troops. Little wonder that Eisenhower, Roosevelt, and Churchill tried to meet the Italians, compromising here and there until the legal status of the Italian surrender could no longer be sorted out. At the same time, there was just enough insistence on unconditional surrender in the form of refusing Italian requests for immediate co-belligerency status to take away the incentive for a major Italian military effort. The end result was what Eisenhower called "a crooked deal," a failure to exploit the Italian surrender, a particularly cruel extension of the war for Italy, and at

[16] For Franklin Roosevelt's perception of this issue, see Department of State, *Foreign Relations of the United States: The Conferences at Washington and Quebec 1943* (Washington, 1970), 521.

[17] *Foreign Relations of the United States . . . Casablanca*, 506n., 635n.; *Foreign Relations of the United States . . . Quebec*, 496; Cordell Hull, *The Memoirs of Cordell Hull* (2 vols., New York, 1948), II, 1548; Department of State, *Foreign Relations of the United States: Diplomatic Papers, 1943*. Vol. II: *Europe* (Washington, 1964), 330-31.

[18] *Times of London*, Dec. 24, 1940; also *Foreign Relations of the United States . . . Washington and Quebec*, 328.

home the feeling that someone had betrayed the unconditional surrender formula as the United States was still doing business with fascists.[19]

The experience with the Italian surrender was not likely to resolve the unconditional surrender debate. On the contrary, it encouraged both sides to prepare themselves for the next test of strength. By the Second Quebec Conference these divisions had clearly emerged as disagreements over the occupation policies for Germany proposed by Henry Morgenthau. The army officers, trying to remain aloof, reluctantly allowed themselves to be talked into at least four major revisions of military directives for German occupation. But quietly and decisively the army chief of staff threw his weight against any implementation of the Morgenthau plan, as did Secretary of War Stimson.[20]

When the time came to present Germany with the actual surrender documents, the military's resistance to the unconditional surrender doctrine became even more apparent. After the experience in Italy, extensive preparations had been made to draft legally flawless surrender instruments for Germany, embodying at least in theory Roosevelt's doctrine in its full rigor. Though the military tried to take some of the harshness out of these, drafts embodying the unconditional surrender doctrine in its most rigorous form were virtually ready for use in May 1945. And still, Eisenhower, thoroughly disgusted with the Italian surrender and convinced that Germany's defeat was clear enough, took the advantage of technical imperfections to shelve the approved drafts and substitute a simple instrument of military surrender for Germany. The Allied Powers found this entirely unsatisfactory and issued instead a proclamation of unconditional surrender for Germany as the legal basis for the occupation.[21]

[19] See Kecskemeti, *Strategic Surrender*; Albert N. Garland and Howard McGaw Smyth, *United States Army in World War II: The Mediterranean Theater of Operations: Sicily and the Surrender of Italy* (Washington, 1965); Robert J. Quinlan, "The Italian Armistice," Harold Stein, ed., *American Civil-Military Decisions: A Book of Case Studies* (Birmingham, Ala., 1963), 203-310; Harry C. Butcher, *My Three Years with Eisenhower* (New York, 1966), 405; Kenneth Strong, *Intelligence at the Top: Recollections of an Intelligence Officer* (London, 1968), 104, 113; *Foreign Relations of the United States . . . Washington and Quebec*, 209, 326, 414, 521, 567, 576, 1261-62; Raffaele Guariglia, *Ricordi: 1922-1946* (Napoli, 1949); *Foreign Relations of the United States . . . Europe*, 332. Harold Nicolson, *The War Years 1939-1945* (New York, 1967), 318.

[20] *Foreign Relations of the United States . . . Germany*, 378, 434, 484; Pogue, *George C. Marshall*, 466-69; Walter L. Dorn, "The Debate over American Occupation Policy in Germany in 1944-1945," *Political Science Quarterly*, LXXII (Dec. 1957), 481-501.

[21] For questioning of unconditional surrender for Germany, see John P. Glennon. "This Time Germany is a Defeated Nation: The Doctrine of Unconditional Surrender and Some Unsuccessful Attempts To Alter It," Gerald N. Grob, ed., *Statesmen and Statecraft of the Modern West: Essays in Honor of Dwight E. Lee and H. Donaldson Jordan* (Barre, Mass., 1967), 109-51. Maurice Matloff, *United States Army in World War II: The War Depart-*

Even before the final outcome of the German surrender was known advocates and opponents of unconditional surrender began to take positions for the final test of strength, the Japanese surrender. Among civilian supporters of unconditional surrender there was already much displeasure over military "obstructionism" and a firm resolve not to be outmaneuvered. Military leaders sensing this had reservations about the wisdom of a direct clash over surrender terms for Japan. If there existed a surplus of force to throw against Japan, if the cost in lives for insisting on unconditional surrender were not too high, then the military might well retreat and allow the Casablanca formula to be implemented. Anything else would defy the tradition requiring subordination of the army to civilian war objectives. But if the military cost of insisting on unconditional surrender should be high then some challenge on practical military grounds could be expected. Thus, military planning for the final defeat of Japan would be crucial to the development of the army's position on surrender for Japan.

Prior to February 1945, planning for the defeat of Japan had not progressed sufficiently to affect decisively the unconditional surrender debate. Until well into May 1944 details of the Normandy invasion absorbed most to the planners' attention. By that time it was evident the break-out in Europe and the gathering momentum of war in the Pacific would absorb more men and materials than had been predicted in the first years of the war. Fearing that manpower resources were limited and that civilian and military morale would be strained in the process, army planners followed civilian leadership in hoping for the speediest possible defeat of Japan. The goal was to achieve victory within twelve months after victory in Europe. Such a rapid conclusion, it was felt, could only be brought about by a direct invasion of the Japanese homeland.[22]

But if the desire for a quick conclusion to the war implied invasion, the invasion itself implied delays. It would not only require long logistic

ment: Strategic Planning for Coalition Warfare 1943-1944 (Washington, 1959), 430. Foreign Relations of the United States . . . General, 517. On drafting the surrender instruments, see [Notter] Postwar Foreign Policy Preparation, 125; Foreign Relations of the United States . . . General, 100, 256; Foreign Relations of the United States . . . Germany, 162, 216, 447. For Dwight D. Eisenhower's evasion, see John Wheeler-Bennett and Anthony Nicholls, The Semblance of Peace: The Political Settlement After The Second World War (London, 1972), 204-65; Herbert Feis, Between War and Peace: The Potsdam Conference (Princeton, 1960), 327-28. For documentation, see Foreign Relations of the United States . . . Germany, 259. Robert Murphy's admission that Eisenhower's headquarters had "made up its mind" to control the surrender and exclude diplomatic interference is correct. Ibid., 294.
[22] Foreign Relations of the United States . . . Washington and Quebec, 975-80. See also Cline, Washington Command Post, 334-46.

preparations but also provoke a Japanese defense of the homeland. If the Japanese had fought stubbornly to defend their recent acquisitions, how hard would they fight for sacred soil?

The more closely the planners looked at the military situation the more difficult it appeared. In September 1944 a study noting that the Sea of Japan was much wider than the English Channel concluded that an invasion of Japan would be a more difficult and hazardous operation than had been the Normandy invasion.[23] Clearly, the army was just beginning to fathom the magnitude of the problem. The topography of the home islands provided the Japanese with opportunities for resistance much superior to those that had existed in Germany. Even after a successful Allied invasion, the Japanese would have the option of continuing resistance from elsewhere in their still vast empire, notably from China. In preparation for the Malta-Yalta conversations the planners thus began to express some doubts about the twelve-month deadline for defeating Japan.[24]

There was, then, just enough concern about the problems of defeating Japan to make military leaders worry about the cost of insisting on any surrender formula likely to prolong Japanese resistance. Against this view was balanced the known insistence by Roosevelt and Hopkins on unconditional surrender. The army sought a compromise. In December 1944 one of the army members of the Joint Post War Committee, General George Strong, presented Undersecretary of State Grew with two unsolicited drafts for surrender instruments. Strong made it clear that he preferred a short, more conventional surrender instrument, but his second draft, much longer, attempted to embody most of the unconditional surrender doctrine. Neither of his drafts called for the emperor to resign; both drafts implicitly allowed for the continuation of a Japanese government, even if entirely under the control of the occupiers. The two leading state department experts on Japan, Eugene Dooman and Joseph Ballantine, were shocked because these drafts still departed from unconditional surrender and suggested a softer peace than anything they had dared to suggest.[25]

The divergence of civilian and military perspectives on the future of Japan had, however, been clearly anticipated. In November 1944 Secretary of State Edward Stettinius had taken the initiative in proposing a "co-

[23] Cline, *Washington Command Post*, 339-40.
[24] *Ibid.*, 340; Department of State, *Foreign Relations of the United States: Diplomatic Papers: The Conferences at Malta and Yalta, 1945* (Washington, 1955), 827-33, especially 830.
[25] Department of State, *Foreign Relations of the United States: Diplomatic Papers 1945*. Vol. VI: *The British Commonwealth, the Far East* (Washington, 1969), 497-515, 517.

ordinating" committee which was finally established in February 1945 as
the State, War, Navy Coordinating Committee (SWNCC). In theory it
was a committee of equals, and the actions of any single department were
to be subjected to the common purpose. But the state department was to
preside, and since military policy was to serve national policy, the state department would have an effective veto. In effect the committee was designed
to prevent the sort of initiatives in policy matters which the army had shown
in Italy and was evidencing on Germany.[26]

SWNCC's ability to restrain army initiatives on surrender policy for
Japan was soon demonstrated. As soon as it was organized General Strong's
drafts were forwarded for SWNCC's consideration, where they were
promptly handed over to its far eastern subcommittee, chaired by Dooman,
representing the state department. Not surprisingly, the drafts were substantially modified to comply with the doctrine of unconditional surrender.
An additional proclamation was also drafted by which the emperor would
announce to the Japanese people his own personal "unconditional surrender," and which would conclude: "I am relinquishing all my powers and
authority this day to the Commander in Chief, United National Armed
Forces."[27]

SWNCC's insistence on strict unconditional surrender would appear to
be rather incomprehensible if one follows Grew's memoirs or Dooman's
later recollections. From those sources one gets the impression that
Grew, Dooman, and Ballantine all agreed on modifying unconditional
surrender to allow for retention of the emperor and some continued use
of a Japanese government during the occupation. In SWNCC and elsewhere their full energies were thrown against those very positions.[28]

In retrospect it is easy to see why Grew and his staff were circumspect in
expressing his views on how Japan ought to be treated in the postwar world.
Grew, after all, had been the last American ambassador in Tokyo, and
the public tended to assume that if he had "talked straight" to the Japanese the war might have been avoided.[29] But Grew had other reasons for

[26] See Annex to State, War, Navy Coordinating Committee (SWNCC), 16/2, Feb. 19,
1945, in Combined Chiefs of Staff (CCS) 092 Pacific Ocean Area (POA) (1-31-45),
Records of the United States Joint Chiefs of Staff, RG 218 (National Archives). For the
formation of SWNCC, see [Notter] *Postwar Foreign Policy Preparation*, 347-48; Cline,
Washington Command Post, 326; *Foreign Relations of the United States . . . General*,
1466-70.
[27] *Foreign Relations of the United States . . . British Commonwealth, the Far East*, 517-
29, 522.
[28] Joseph C. Grew, *Turbulent Era: A Diplomatic Record of Forty Years 1904-1945* (2
vols., Boston, 1952), II, 1421-22. See also Len Giovannitti and Fred Freed, *The Decision to Drop the Bomb* (New York, 1965).
[29] Waldo H. Heinrichs, Jr., *American Ambassador: Joseph C. Grew and the Development of the United States Diplomatic Tradition* (Boston, 1966), 364-86. Joseph Grew's

being reserved. He was, after all, undersecretary, not secretary. The fact that he was often acting secretary during 1945 really changed little in the equation. His decisions could be appealed to Stettinius or James F. Byrnes. More important, Grew had qualms of conscience about exercising his authority arbitrarily in the presence of the new consultative structures established in the state department reorganization of December 1944. Central to the new organization was the secretary's staff committee, which was to assist and advise the secretary. It was composed of the undersecretary, all the assistant secretaries, the legal adviser, and the special assistant for international organization, and it was gradually expanded by such other high officials as the secretary invited.[30] Grew religiously met this committee every day and almost always deferred to the majority view.

On the issue of unconditional surrender this committee reflected deep ideological divisions. Conservative views where represented by Grew along with veteran diplomat Phillips and administrative chief, General Julius C. Holmes, all favoring concessions on the emperor issue. Ranged on the other side were MacLeish and Acheson, supported by Nelson Rockefeller and legal adviser Green Hackworth. Assistant Secretary James C. Dunn was the obvious exception of someone relatively conservative—he was once sympathetic to Franco's Spain—who nevertheless sided with the majority against Grew.[31] Grew fought hard for his views. But clearly he did not have the votes in this division, and to his credit he refused to represent the department's policy other than what it was—opposed to any dilution of unconditional surrender.

The state department thus spoke with one voice, that representing the secretary's staff committee. This effectively muzzled Grew and gave the military officers, in their search for modification of surrender terms, a very

sensitivity to charges of "appeasement" and "pampering the Emperor" were reflected in meetings of the secretary's staff committee. For example, see 27 meeting, Feb. 19, 1945, State Department Staff Committee Files, General Records of the Department of State, RG 59 (National Archives). See also *Foreign Relations of the United States . . . The British Commonwealth, the Far East*, 515-16.

[30] [Notter] *Postwar Foreign Policy Preparation*, 349; Grew, *Turbulent Era*, II, 1494.

[31] For Nelson Rockefeller, Archibald MacLeish, Dean Acheson, and Julius C. Holmes, see minutes of Secretary's Staff Committee, meetings of May 28, June 19, 26, July 19, 1945, in State Department Staff Committee Files. On Dunn, see SWNCC minutes of Feb. 7, 1945, Records of Interdepartmental and Intradepartmental Committees, RG 353 (National Archives). See also JCS 1275/2, in CCS 387 Japan (2-7-45), section 1, Records of the United States Joint Chiefs of Staff. For Green Hackworth, see *Foreign Relations of the United States . . . British Commonwealth, the Far East*, 905. There is no record of Will L. Clayton's position, but a remarkably well-informed columnist, Drew Pearson, identified Clayton with Acheson on this issue. Drew Pearson in the Washington *Post*, July 21, 1945. The ideological nature of the dispute is reflected in the tendency to use the anti-militarist 1945 leftist position as a model in the Vietnam debate. Ralph Stavins, Richard J. Barnet, and Marcus G. Raskin, *Washington Plans An Aggressive War* (New York, 1971), 300.

formidable opponent. Systematically the military spokesmen were obliged to retreat so that in fairly short order the revised drafts of the surrender instruments sponsored by the state department were approved by SWNCC and sent to the joint chiefs for their views. Thereupon the joint chiefs sent the drafts, now designated as JCS 1275 through the various joint commit- tees.[32] The drafts were in an advanced stage by the time of the Malta-Yalta discussions; only final approval at the highest levels was wanting.

The purpose of the Malta-Yalta discussions was to provide a high level review of military planning for the defeat of Japan and to determine Russia's role in that campaign, but inevitably these discussions had an impact on the unconditional surrender question. All the problems involved in invading Japan, vaguely perceived in the fall of 1944, now loomed threateningly on the horizon. Understandably at Malta the military chiefs began to place more emphasis on weakening Japan before invasion. But such strategy, involving more reliance on bombardment and blockade, would tend to prolong the war. Soviet assistance would be important, but there was still some feeling that there was a gap between military re- sources and the objective of imposing unconditional surrender on Japan within twelve months of victory in Europe.[33] Churchill was the first to confront the problem directly and propose a new course. He suggested some "mitigation" of unconditional surrender would be desirable if it led to the saving of a year or a year and a half of a war in which "so much blood and treasure" had been poured out. The prime minister thought such mitigation could be presented in conjunction with a four power ultimatum calling on Japan to surrender at a given moment.[34]

Churchill's idea, and not the subsequent work of Grew and Stimson, was the true origin of the Potsdam proclamation. The proposal reflected the prime minister's growing concern over long-term European problems and his unwillingness to see any major diversion of American energies to Asia after V-E Day. He attached little importance to America's hopes for China or the democratization of Japan.[35] Churchill was aware that his suggestion would not be well received by Hopkins and the other civilian advisers, and thus he made it directly to the military chief. Shortly there- after army planners began to weigh Churchill's suggestion against the costs

[32] SWNCC Minutes, 9 and 11 meetings, Feb. 7, 16, 1945, Records of Interdepartmental and Intradepartmental Committees. For routing, see tally sheet and documentation in CCS 387 Japan (2-7-45), section 1, Records of the United States Joint Chiefs of Staff.
[33] *Foreign Relations of the United States . . . Malta and Yalta*, 395-400, 388.
[34] *Ibid.*, 825-26.
[35] [Charles Wilson] *Churchill: Taken from the Diaries of Lord Moran: The Struggle for Survival 1940-1965* (Boston, 1966), 140, 207.

of the invasion strategy. Among these planners was General Lincoln, chief of S&P, who would have primary responsibility for the actual formulation of the invasion plans.

General Marshall's feeling that the options had to be completely re-examined was reflected in his decision to send Lincoln directly from Yalta to the Pacific to confer with Asian theater commanders on future strategy. Lincoln returned to Washington at the beginning of March with a still more sober view of the difficulties of defeating Japan and obtaining unconditional surrender.[36] After consultation with the planners, Marshall abruptly rejected the draft surrender instruments prepared by SWNCC, which had been circulated as JCS 1275. His secretary, Colonel Florence T. Newsome wrote:

> The Chief of Staff is not satisfied that all of the military implications in JCS 1275 have been thoroughly considered and assessed in JCS 1275/1. For example it appears that the study has not taken into account the views of qualified Far Eastern specialists in the War Department with respect to various matters, including the advisability of requiring the Emperor of Japan personally to sign the surrender documents. . . .[37]

Marshall thus took direct responsibility for challenging the surrender policy. Hurriedly an ad hoc meeting of the authorities Marshall had mentioned was convened. There army and navy representatives expressed their opposition to provisions for the emperor's unconditional surrender. But the army spokesmen had not thought through the relationship between unconditional surrender and a prolongation of the war. Army representatives were unable to present convincing "military" reasons against the draft surrender instruments. State department spokesmen argued that such a surrender was a political objective of the war and that it was the military's job to fight until that objective was reached. In the absence of any compelling military arguments to attenuate the surrender policy JCS 1275 would have to stand unaltered.[38]

Marshall duly noted these conclusions without taking issue; but he suggested that the views of field commanders would have to be obtained before he or the other chiefs of staff could formally consider JCS 1275.[39]

[36] Cline, *Washington Command Post*, 307-08; U.S. Department of Defense, *The Entry of the Soviet Union into the War Against Japan: Military Plans, 1941-1945* (Washington, 1955), 50.

[37] Memorandum from Lt. Col. Florence T. Newsome for Gen. Andrew J. McFarland, March 5, 1945, in CCS 377 Japan (2-7-45), section 1, Records of the United States Joint Chiefs of Staff.

[38] JCS 1275/2 March 17, 1945, *ibid.*

[39] Memorandum from Newsome for MacFarland, March 23, 1945, transmitted by JCS-SM929 of March 23, 1945, to the other chiefs, *ibid.*

Patently, General Marshall was procrastinating. In this he was aided by Admiral Leahy, who concurred with Marshall's suggestion and added that he did not want to hear any more on the subject until the field commanders' reports had been received.[40] These reports were not complete until April 21. Marshall's action had resulted therefore in a full month's delay.[41] The reprieve would mean nothing unless military reasons could be produced to support modification of unconditional surrender. In delaying final approval, Marshall knew that the entire Pacific strategy was about to come under final review.

By April 12, Marshall in a cable to General Douglas MacArthur was forced to admit that the review had produced some division over strategy for the Pacific. One school of thought still held to "driving straight into Japan," but another school had emerged calling for blockade and bombardment as necessary preliminaries to, perhaps even substitutes for, invasion.[42] Churchill's suggestion of mitigating surrender terms was not directly mentioned, but it was implicit that bombardment and blockade without invasion would only produce a limited pressure for surrender.

In weighing the options of direct assault or siege warfare the essential problem was the nature of Japanese political and military resistance, and how that resistance might be affected by insistence on unconditional surrender. This continued to be a worrisome imponderable in the debate over unconditional surrender. The relative absence of Japanese surrenders in the Pacific campaigns, the fanatical resistance appearing with every approach to the home islands, and the increasing use of suicide forces, all these factors suggested that Japanese resistance might be longer than that of Germany. Perhaps the Japanese would never surrender.

The planners had requested, therefore, on April 7 that the Joint Intelligence Staff (JIS) make an estimate of the resistance that could be expected from Japan to an invasion of Honshu or any of the home islands before unconditional surrender had been obtained. Because it was feared that some Japanese might never surrender, JIS was also asked to evaluate possible resistance after a formal unconditional surrender. These questions led directly to the political aspects of the problem; Japanese appreciation of the unconditional surrender formula. The planners completed their request to JIS by asking:

[40] Memorandum of conversation, G. G. Epley with Newsome, March 27, 1945, *ibid.*
[41] CCS 377 Japan (2-7-45), section 1, *ibid.* See also Annex to JCS 1275/3 of May 5, 1945, *ibid.*
[42] Department of Defense, *Entry of the Soviet Union into the War Against Japan*, 54-55.

a) At what stage of the war will the Japanese realize the inevitability of absolute defeat?

b) Will such realization result in their unconditional surrender, passive submission without surrender or continuing resistance until subdued by force?[43]

Three days later JIS replied expressing confidence that the Japanese would recognize defeat by autumn. But the report carefully distinguished between recognition of defeat and unconditional surrender. The literal meaning of unconditional surrender, JIS noted, "is unknown to the Japanese. . . . Our meaning of the term cannot be comprehended by the vast majority of Japanese." The report forecast little resistance from the Japanese once a legitimate Japanese government had accepted surrender terms, unconditional or not. But in the more likely possibility that there would be no unconditional surrender, JIS predicted long and determined Japanese military resistance even after invasion. The conclusion of this study was to argue that unconditional surrender ought to be attenuated so that it would resemble what the Japanese could recognize as a simple admission of complete defeat. JIS went on to note: "If without compromising Allied objectives the Japanese can be made to understand that unconditional surrender does not imply annihilation or national suicide, we believe it quite possible that unconditional surrender would follow fairly quickly the Japanese realization of the inevitability of absolute defeat."[44]

JIS further attacked the concept of unconditional surrender by suggesting that a surrender would be accepted by the Japanese people only if they thought the government signing it was acting with the authority and sanction of the emperor. On the occupation problems after surrender, the study concluded: "the resulting political situation in Japan proper would remain fairly stable for as long as this Japanese government . . . remained in power and was supported by the Emperor as well as by Allied authority." Here was a clear implication that the supreme authority during the occupation would be shared, at least nominally, between the emperor and the Allied authority. Here was another blow to the doctrine of unconditional surrender. It gave a military reason for a concession Japan was certain to request, the right to retain the emperor.[45]

The members of JIS and particularly the area teams that prepared this general study on Japanese resistance had considerable freedom in making recommendations. They acted within the staff as experts, not as representatives of their departments. It was otherwise in the Joint Intelligence Committee which reviewed their work. There departmental positions were

[43] Joint Intelligence Staff (JIS) 143/M, April 7, 1945, in CCS 387 Japan (4-6-45), Records of the United States Joint Chiefs of Staff.
[44] JIS 143/1, April 10, 1945, *ibid.*
[45] *Ibid.*

represented. Predictably state department representatives found the study unacceptable. Erle Dickover attacked the implied continuation of a Japa- nese government after surrender, since "State Department considered that legally no Japanese Government would exist." As for the whole problem of Japanese resistance he thought it was more a function of the force allocated to the occupation and its extent than of the circumstances sur- rounding surrender and defeat. He thus neatly shifted responsibility for the presence or absence of occupation problems to the military and their relative efficiency or lack of it. The military reasons for modifying sur- render were put down to a loss of nerve and energy. He rejected out of hand the possibility of ending the war by autumn with some change in the surrender formula. The question of whether the Japanese ever could accept unconditional surrender without clarification, he similarly dismissed as "pure speculation."[46]

In the presence of this determined protest by state department spokes- men JIS entirely recast the paper, eliminating practically all of the attacks on the unconditional surrender policy. Only an echo of these remained in the redrafted report. It still stressed that, if the Japanese equated un- conditional surrender with national annihilation, they would resist until fully subdued by force. Even this substantially revised version was not satisfactory to the state department, which prepared its own separate reply to the original set of questions the planners had asked. This draft entirely glossed over the problems which might occur if there were no surrender prior to invasion. It characterized these as largely "administrative." Fanati- cal resistance was nowhere suggested.[47]

Concurrent with discussions over the general JIS study of Japanese resistance (JIS 143) a second effort was made to develop military reasons for questioning unconditional surrender. On April 6 the planners had asked JIS for an estimate of the possibility of producing a Japanese surrender by bombardment and blockade.[48] This time, however, the reply was drafted by the service members of the Far East team, without the explicit concurrence of state department members. Significantly, their ap- proval was neither sought nor obtained. The service members expressed the view that a program of intensive bombardment coupled with a stringent blockade might produce a surrender but only after unacceptable delay, perhaps "a great many years." The service members took the opportunity,

---

[46] Minutes, Joint Intelligence Committee (JIC) 125 meeting, April 20, 1945, in CCS 334 Joint Intelligence Committee (10-13-44), *ibid.* (Note that JIS 143/1 was discussed at this meeting under its JIC designation 268.)
[47] JIS 143/3, April 24, 1945, and appendix, in CCS 387 Japan (4-6-45), *ibid.*
[48] JIS 141/M, April 6, 1945, in CCS 381 Japan (4-6-45), *ibid.*

however, to express the belief that a "clarification of Allied intentions with regard to the Japanese nation might bring nearer the possibility of unconditional surrender." They further ventured that if such a statement could be made "which would be acceptable to the Allies" the war could be concluded before the end of 1945 or early in 1946. These conclusions echoed and reinforced those made in the other JIS study of the same period. This second study—on resistance to bombardment and blockade—had been prepared by only a portion of JIS and had no formal status unless approved by the full Joint Intelligence Committee. An attempt to secure such approval was certain to draw a state department veto. Accordingly, formal approval was not requested, and the paper was circulated only for purposes "of information."[49] This was the price that had to be paid for bringing these issues to the attention of the joint chiefs.

By mid-April a formal division of opinion between the military spokesmen, particularly the planners, and state department representatives over unconditional surrender had emerged into the open. With the state department exercising a de facto veto over joint policy, the military spokesmen had no choice but carry forward the plans for the invasion of Japan. But General Lincoln and the staff planners saw to it that the final planning report expressly called for a definition of unconditional surrender for the Japanese and implied that only the refusal to make such a clarification made an invasion absolutely necessary. As the planners expressed it:

Unless a definition of unconditional surrender can be given which is acceptable to the Japanese, there is no alternative to annihilation and no prospect that the threat of absolute defeat will bring about capitulation. The accomplishment of the unconditional surrender objectives then must be entirely brought about by force of arms.[50]

Not surprisingly the joint chiefs decided to advance slowly and give only tentative approval to the invasion plans. Indeed, by August 1945 only the invasion of Kyushu had actually been set in motion and subsequent operations were approved only for preliminary preparations and planning purposes. But even approval for planning purposes meant extensive preparations. As the army moved millions of men into these preparations,

[49] JIS 141/1, 141/2, 141/3, JIC 266/1, *ibid.*; Cline, *Washington Command Post*, 343.
[50] JCS 924/15, April 25, 1945, in CCS 381 POA (6-10-43), section 12, Records of the United States Joint Chiefs of Staff. See also Department of Defense, *Entry of the Soviet Union into the War Rgainst Japan*, 61. See JPS minutes, meetings, April 25, Aug. 3, 1945, pp. 199, 212, in CCS 334 JPS Minutes, Records of the United States Joint Chiefs of Staff. Hayes, *History of the Joint Chiefs*, 374; Cline, *Washington Command Post*, 340-45.
[51] Bonesteel to author, May 28, 1974.

opinion samples were quietly taken on whether the Japanese should be allowed to keep the emperor. The ordinary soldier thought the question was irrelevant as long as surrender could be brought about quickly.[51] Few wanted to carry on the struggle simply to dethrone the emperor or give Admiral William F. "Bull" Halsey his vaunted ride through Tokyo on the emperor's white horse. The inevitable conclusion was that army morale during the invasion might be low, unless some better rationale for the invasion were presented.

At the beginning of May, while the invasion preparations were taking shape, General Marshall intervened directly if discreetly in matters affecting unconditional surrender. Using a channel to the President free from state department vetoes, the joint chiefs structure, Marshall reactivated a languishing psychological warfare project to wear down Japanese resistance. On May 9, he asked through JCS structure that the Joint Staff Planners and the Joint Intelligence Committee study one of these projects. It called for the government to demand the unconditional surrender of Japan at a time when Japanese morale was at a low point and before the determination to resist had hardened under the pressure of Allied bombings. Formally the memorandum forwarded by Marshall seemed to be solidly grounded on the unconditional surrender formula. It argued that if the initiative were not seized the Japanese would propose a negotiated peace under circumstances which would undermine American determination to secure unconditional surrender: "War weariness in the United States may demand the return home of those who have already fought long and well in the European war regardless of the effect of such return on the prosecution of the Japanese war."[52]

The doctrine of unconditional surrender seemed to be in danger, and the draft memorandum proposed saving it by a timely demand to Japan that, at the very least, would have the advantage of recalling to the American people the goal of the war. There was only one hint in the draft of an attenuation of unconditional surrender where it was noted that any surrender would be "essentially military in character" and would "not affect the peaceful pursuits of the Japanese people." But President Harry S. Truman, after consulting the military, had just made this concession in his V-E speech of May 8. In that speech he not only repeated Roosevelt's assurance that unconditional surrender did not mean extermination or enslavement but also emphasized that such a surrender

[52] JCS 1340, May 9, 1945, in CCS 387 Japan (5-9-45), Records of the United States Joint Chiefs of Staff.

would be effected by the "armed forces of Japan" and not, as Roosevelt had insisted, by the Japanese nation.[53]

After such review Marshall could duly approve the study (now identified as JCS 1340) after striking out the apparently excessive references to American war weariness. The other chiefs concurred.[54] An interdepartmental paper for presentation to the cabinet secretaries destined eventually for the President on the subject of unconditional surrender had been approved! Japan would be asked to surrender on the basis of a new statement. Thus Churchill's idea of encouraging Japanese surrender was given new life. The paper did not develop the possibility of reformulating unconditional surrender any more precisely than Truman had, but it certainly opened the door to high level review.

Given the state department's resistance to changing unconditional surrender, it is not surprising that Marshall had chosen this route, relying on extensive staff work and avoiding a frontal confrontation on what was essentially a political question. But by this particular approach he put the question of surrender terms on the treacherous ground of psychological warfare. Concessions to the enemy are notoriously difficult to achieve if approached from the viewpoint of psychological warfare. If the enemy appears strong, a concession is feared as an admission of weakness. If the enemy appears weak, no reason for concession is seen. Even though a strategy of concession might be approved, the correct moment might be hard to find.

In point of fact the problem of timing would be greatly complicated by the Okinawa campaign just then beginning. The campaign would produce the highest army casualty rates of the war. The navy's losses in ships were among the greatest in its history. As a navy spokesman pointed out, this was no time for a surrender demand.

The Japanese military leaders may be able to make us look ridiculous before the Japanese people by pointing out our naval losses at Okinawa. Furthermore they would probably contend that a small number of Japanese were holding off large U.S. forces in the island itself.[55]

This problem had been on the mind of the Joint Intelligence Committee in considering JCS 1340. It had agreed, with the concurrence of the

---

[53] Harry S. Truman, *Memoirs by Harry S. Truman: Year of Decisions* (Garden City, N. Y., 1955), 207; Herbert Feis, *The Atomic Bomb and the End of World War II* (Princeton, 1966), 16.

[54] Memorandum, Newsome for Secretariat JCS June 4, 1945, in CCS 387 Japan (2-7-45), section 1, Records of the United States Joint Chiefs of Staff; JCS 1340/2, June 9, 1945, *ibid*. JCS 1340 became SWNCC 149 on June 9, 1945.

[55] JCS 1340/1, May 19, 1945, in CCS 387 Japan (5-9-45), *ibid*.

Joint Planning Staff, to recommend waiting until the operation had progressed sufficiently "to insure success" before issuing the surrender demand.[56] When JCS 1340 came before the joint chiefs for final approval, Admiral Leahy, while accepting the report, added a personal note that he preferred action a little later, "after the capture of Okinawa."[57] Chiefs of staff carefully respected each other's personal preferences. The surrender demand would wait. At the end of April, this seemed like a small concession. But the Okinawa campaign turned out to be a difficult test of strength between two exceptionally competent commanders, neither of whom survived their contest. Japanese resistance was fierce and superbly directed. The campaign begun on April 1 dragged on week after week. It was not until June 21 that Okinawa was declared "secure." The losses were incredibly high, nearly 50,000 American casualties and over 350 ships damaged of which thirty-six were sunk.[58] Even then, with Okinawa seized, concessions to Japan still seemed unwise. The victory seemed very much of the Pyrrhic variety. The Americans had paid a nearly intolerable price for Okinawa. The Japanese could claim that insistence on unconditional surrender or anything like it would cost the Americans many more Okinawas. As a platform to demand unconditional surrender, Okinawa was less than effective.

By placing the question of concessions in the context of war morale and psychological war, Marshall made it necessary to accompany concessions with some more decisive blow than the Okinawa campaign. Inevitably this meant a further delay until the additional shock could be prepared. The shock could take any one of three forms: Russian intervention, invasion of one of the home islands, or, a new possibility, the use of an atomic weapon. Russian intervention still seemed uncertain. The invasion was what everyone wanted to avoid. Understandably, there was a fever of

[56] See memorandum from secretary JIC for secretary JPS of May 14, 1945, *ibid.* The wording quoted was retained in the SWNCC version (SWNCC 149), June 9, 1945.

[57] SM 2013, June 4, 1945, *ibid.*

[58] Roy E. Appleman, James M. Burns, Russell A. Gugeler, and John Stevens, *United States Army in World War II: The War in the Pacific: Okinawa: The Last Battle* (Washington, 1948). Implicitly the present author supports Stimson's assertion that the Okinawa campaign was the reason why a·surrender demand was not made earlier. Henry L. Stimson, "The Decision to Use the Atomic Bomb," *Harper's Magazine*, 194 (Feb. 1947), 97-107. Grew noted this explanation, but was very skeptical. Grew, *Turbulent Era*, II, 1424. Privately Grew was even angry saying, in 1947, that Stimson's explanation reiterated in a letter was "no less disingenuous than his article," adding "the fighting in Okinawa was practically over, or at least the issue was no longer in doubt." Grew to Eugene Dooman, June 30, 1947, Joseph Grew Papers (Harvard University). Of course the issue had never been in doubt. What was very much in doubt in May and June was whether Japan could convert defeat into a psychological victory. On the whole Japan succeeded, with tragic consequences.

interest in the third possibility. All three possibilities implied some delay. Russian intervention, if it came, was not expected before the second week of August. The invasion of Kyushu was not to come before November. An atomic weapon would not be ready until the end of July. The schedule seemed almost to impose itself: a demand for surrender late in July, an atomic attack in early August, and finally Soviet entry. The invasion could be kept as a last resort. Between June and the end of July no crushing blow was expected to offset the psychological advantage Japan had gained by her resistance in Okinawa. A surrender demand would have to wait until then.

Grew did not want to wait. He saw the issue of concessions on the emperor as a matter of statesmanship, altogether too important to be jeopardized by the vagaries of public opinion and the need to save face. Thus he took the issue of the surrender demand directly to the President. In doing so Grew made a very substantial contribution to the resolution of surrender terms, for the result of his action was the creation, at Truman's suggestion, of a new committee to study the surrender. This committee, loosely based on the informal Committee of Three, would consist of Grew, Stimson, and Forrestal, two secretaries, one acting secretary drawn from the identical departments represented in SWNCC. But now they were to meet as individuals, not as representatives of departments. It was a situation tailored for Grew, who could now express his personal views. Unlike SWNCC, this committee could be enlarged to include the military chiefs directly. Indeed, Truman suggested that Marshall and Admiral Ernest J. King be brought directly into the discussions.[59]

The President's new, high level committee made possible the creation of ad hoc working committees at a lower level. The most important of these was headed by Assistant Secretary of War John J. McCloy and was to draft the actual surrender demand. The committee included many of the same people who had written SWNCC papers for their respective departments, but the chairmanship went not to a state department representative but to McCloy. Army planner, General Lincoln, who had sought to keep open the possibility of inducing a Japanese surrender, was represented by his very able policy section chief, Colonel Charles H. Bonesteel. With strong support from Marshall, careful guidance from Lincoln, and hard work from Bonesteel, S&P's staff took the initiative in producing the basic draft.[60] Dooman was present but not as a state department

---

[59] Grew, *Turbulent Era*, II, 1423; Truman, *Year of Decisions*, 417.
[60] The basic reports of this committee are in ABC 387 Japan (15-2-45), section 1B, Records of the War Department General and Special Staffs, RG 165 (National Archives);

representative. Presumably, he could speak much more freely in his capacity as an expert.

Nevertheless, Dooman and Ballantine came very close to wrecking the efforts of McCloy's subcommittee. Still apparently very conscious of the feeling in the state department against any "soft policy" toward Japan, they leaned noticeably in the opposite direction. At the first meeting of McCloy's subcommittee, Ballantine produced a draft surrender demand to Japan heavy with ridicule of Japanese leaders, specific on threats, and extremely vague about any inducement to surrender. It unfavorably impressed the others present in McCloy's office, who found it quite unconstructive.[61]

Dooman's interventions in the discussion were even more negative. He seemed to Lincoln to be set against the Stimson-Grew concept of concessions on the emperor. Voicing his concern to General John Hull, Lincoln noted that "Mr. Dooman apparently has so little hope of Japanese acceptance that he is trying really only to insure that the terms will cause no criticism in the U.S." Consistent with the impression of firmness he was displaying, Dooman seemed to emphasize the need for threats, ready to be implemented on short notice. On the central issue of the emperor he wanted to avoid all commitment. As Lincoln rightly noted it was not possible to follow Dooman's advice and still induce surrender. Everyone knew that Japan would insist on keeping the emperor. Dooman and Ballantine were overruled, and a surrender demand allowing the retention of the emperor was drafted. But Dooman and Ballantine dutifully noted that their concurrence was only provisory and that the decisions reached would have to be reviewed in the state department.[62]

Dooman and Ballantine were right, of course, in predicting a negative reaction by state department officials to the new draft. The President's special committee's recommendation to allow the Japanese to retain the imperial institution if dissociated from militarism challenged the views of the advocates of more extensive social engineering for Japan. In the view of

Cline, *Washington Command Post*, 345-49; Bonesteel to author, May 28, 1975; Lincoln to author, May 12, 1970.

[61] Joseph Ballantine's draft attached to Bonesteel to Lincoln, June 27, 1945, in ABC 387 Japan (15-2-45), section 1B, Records of the War Department General and Special Staffs; Lincoln for John Hull, June 28, 1945, *ibid*. There is reason to take issue here, on the basis of OPD files, with Heinrich and Lisle A. Rose on the drafting of the surrender demand. See Heinrich, *American Ambassador*, 376; Lisle A. Rose, *After Yalta* (New York, 1973), 67-71.

[62] Memorandum Brig. Gen. Lincoln for Lt. Gen. Hull, June 29, 1945, subject: "Demand for Japanese Surrender," in ABC 387 Japan (15-2-45), Records of the War Department General and Special Staffs; memorandum Brig. Gen. Lincoln for Lt. Gen. Hull, June 29, 1945, no subject, *ibid*.

Acheson and MacLeish such a separation could not be made; the institution of emperor was intimately tied to the Gumbatsu—"the current coalition of militarists, industrialists, large land owners and office holders," the true source of militarism and the principal obstacle to social changes.[63]

These objections should not have had much impact on the surrender terms since Acheson had never been to the Far East and MacLeish hardly qualified as an authority on that area. Moreover the committee that drafted the new surrender terms had been selected by the President. And yet, though the draft was ready on July 2, the surrender demand was not issued until July 26, and then only with the clause allowing the retention of the emperor deleted.

Once again the shifting nature of decision-making structures came into play in a decisive way. The crucial event was the Potsdam Conference. Some of the President's advisers, most noticeably Grew, would be left behind while others traveled to Potsdam. In such circumstances, the President would inevitably rely on his closest personal adviser, Byrnes, recently named as secretary of state. Not only did this mean that Grew's influence would be eclipsed but also that the President's committee would be virtually disbanded.

What Byrnes thought became crucial. Politically sensitive, Byrnes was very troubled by the discrepancy between the draft Potsdam proclamation and the previously announced positions of Roosevelt and Truman. It took little, principally a call from Cordell Hull, to persuade Byrnes that the recommendations of the President's special Committee of Three were political dynamite. Byrnes' decision against concessions would be final unless challenged directly by the military.[64]

The effectiveness of the army's organization was also reduced by the Potsdam Conference. The departure for Potsdam of Marshall and his key advisers, including Lincoln, served to leave the Washington command post without effective spokesmen for the new surrender policy. Unfortunately, the draft surrender demand had been circulated in the war department only after Marshall's departure, and it had drawn some fire.

On July 14 the "blue ribbon" high level review panel, the Joint Strategic Survey Committee, submitted its comments, which curiously reflected the political objection of Acheson and others in the state de-

[63] Department of State, *Foreign Relations of the United States: Diplomatic Papers: The Conference of Berlin (The Potsdam Conference) 1945* (2 vols., Washington, 1960), I, 896.
[64] Henry L. Stimson Diary, July 24, 1945, Henry L. Stimson Papers (Yale University); James F. Byrnes, *Speaking Frankly* (New York, 1947), 209. Hull, *Memoirs*, II, 1594-95.

partment. JSSC specifically recommended deleting the paragraph allowing for the retention of the emperor because it would be objectionable to the "radical elements in Japan who might assume major importance at a later stage." This report came rather close to agreeing with Acheson that the radical group should be favored in the occupation.[65]

The prestige of JSSC was such that this report could not be overlooked. OPD staff in Washington was understandably aghast at the development. They noted that everyone in McCloy's committee had agreed that the emperor issue was vital and that there should be "no beating around the bush." They further pointed out the fallacy of deciding so important an issue on the basis of the opposition of a small group within Japan that could neither help nor hinder the projected invasion.[66] But the staff in Washington could do little to counter the new opposition. The officers most experienced in political and diplomatic matters were in Potsdam.

Marshall's presence in Potsdam offered, however, an opportunity to influence events down to the last minute. With the help of his staff, principally Lincoln, Marshall arrived at a subtle solution to the problem. Cordell Hull's advice and the JSSC report would be accepted, of course. But Marshall would insist that "nothing should be done prior to the termination of hostilities that would indicate the removal of the Emperor of Japan since his continuation in office might influence the cessation of hostilities in areas outside Japan proper."[67] Marshall's military view expressed so clearly was not one which the chiefs could dispute or the President ignore.

Marshall's success seemed slight. No explicit offer on the emperor would be made from the Allied side. But his recommendation, which became the official JCS policy for the guidance of the President, was that the emperor must remain to help effect orderly surrender throughout the empire. If the emperor survived with some authority through the surrender period and the start of the occupation, he was likely to survive much longer. The Japanese of course asked, and Byrnes, much against his

[65] The Joint Strategic Survey Committee (JSSC) report, JCS 1275/5, in CCS 387 Japan (2-7-45), Records of the United States Joint Chiefs of Staff.

[66] Foreign Relations of the United States . . . Berlin, 1267-68; Hull, Memoirs, II, 1594; memorandum, Maj. Gen. Howard Craig for Lt. Gen. Hull, July 14, 1945, in OPD 387.475, section I, case 1015, Records of the War Department General and Special Staff.

[67] Foreign Relations of the United States . . . Berlin, 39-40, 64; drafts attached to SM-2611, Secretary to JCS, July 17, 1945, in CCS 387 Japan (2-7-45), section 1, Records of the War Department General and Special Staff; interviews with Lincoln, 1966, 1969, 1970. Marshall thus seemed to be opening the door for secret, as opposed to public, assurances to Japan. There is some evidence that a secret approach to Japan was contemplated, but the evidence of an actual attempt appears inconclusive. A secret approach was fraught with danger in terms of inter-allied relations and American public opinion.

will, had to say that the authority of the emperor would be subject to the supreme commander of the Allied powers.[68] It was a perfect restatement of Marshall's position that the emperor's retention was required by the military. Byrnes could not have made any other response without overruling Marshall and the joint chiefs.

The military officer's attack on the doctrine of unconditional surrender was neither frontal nor complete. Indeed, the joint chiefs insisted absolutely on the unconditional surrender of the enemy armed forces. The army shared with the state department the desire to have a free hand in the occupation. The military respected the psychological importance of the doctrine at home and dutifully reported each surrender as being unconditional. But the army clearly did not like the long range political objectives of the doctrine and in the end refused to prolong the war to secure the carte blanche necessary to those ends. The army's requirements were simple: the enemy must recognize total defeat, must surrender militarily and accept occupation. On this basis the army assumed the defeated countries could be easily redirected so that they would not threaten the United Nations in the foreseeable future. Further than this the army would not go, and this reluctance would mean that, for better or worse, Italy, Germany, and Japan would be spared the extremes of American reforming zeal.

Unconditional surrender, though partially or totally circumvented in the Italian, German, and Japanese surrenders, had shown itself to be a tenaciously defended doctrine. No doubt part of that tenacity resulted from the fact that it was presidential policy, which few dared to challenge directly. As MacLeish heatedly argued: "If what we propose is to replace the policy of unconditional surrender . . . we should say so and say so in words which no one in the United States will misunderstand."[69] Needless to say, no one took up the gauntlet. As a battle cry the doctrine had psychological importance at home, which was clearly reflected in concern over any attenuation of the formula. As the legal underpinning for all the planned political and social reform of the Axis countries, unconditional surrender seemed essential to Roosevelt and the state department. The doctrine crumbled only very slowly.

That the surrender policy for Japan could not have been modified sooner so as to avoid use of the bomb must remain something of a

---

[68] Byrnes, *Speaking Frankly*, 209; *Foreign Relations of the United States . . . British Commonwealth, the Far East*, 627.
[69] *Foreign Relations of the United States . . . Berlin*, 895-96.

tragedy. The reasons for that delay, at least on the American side, are clear; they had nothing to do with any scheme to prolong the war deliberately, either to allow a Soviet entry or to allow a combat demonstration of the bomb. Indeed the anti-Soviet Grew, the loyal and correct General Marshall, and the conservative practitioner of *Realpolitik*, Stimson, all worked to shorten the war by modifying the surrender terms. They shared that goal despite differences of temperament and ideology. If they did not shorten the war as much as they wanted it was for two main reasons: the doctrine of unconditional surrender was powerfully defended by the state department in interdepartmental agencies, and both Grew and Marshall had scruples about how to circumvent that opposition. Eventually they both found ways of dealing with the state department, Grew by approaching the President directly, Marshall by avoiding those interdepartmental agencies in which it was represented, but this took time. There was present the eternal dilemma of truce making, the endless truism, "If the enemy is weak, concessions are unnecessary, if he appears strong concessions look like a confession of weakness." In May, June, and July of 1945 the strength of Japan's defense of Okinawa seriously undermined efforts to attenuate the surrender formula. Japan's prostration in August made Byrnes more or less reluctant to make any concessions. In the heat of war statesmanship did not come easily.

Copyright Acknowledgments

Leonard Dinnerstein. "America, Britain, and Palestine: The Anglo-American Committee of Inquiry and the Displaced Persons, 1945–46." *Diplomatic History* (Summer 1980): 283–301. Reprinted with the permission of *Diplomatic History.*

Marc Gallicchio. "The Other China Hands: U.S. Army Officers and America's Failure in China, 1941–1950." *The Journal of American-East Asian Relations* (Spring 1995): 49–72. Reprinted with the permission of Imprint Publications.

Crister S. Garrett and Stephen A. Garrett. "Death and Politics: The Katyn Forest Massacre and American Foreign Policy." *East European Quarterly* (Winter 1986): 429–446. Reprinted with the permission of *East European Quarterly.*

William Roger Louis and Ronald Robinson. "The Imperialism of Decolonization." *The Journal of Imperial and Commonwealth History* (September 1994): 462–511. Reprinted with the permission of Frank Cass & Co. Ltd.

Xiaohua Ma. "The Sino-American Alliance During World War II and the Lifting of the Chinese Exclusion Acts." *American Studies International* (June 2000): 39–61. Reprinted with the permission of George Washington University.

Elizabeth Kimball Maclean. "Joseph E. Davies and Soviet-American Relations, 1941–1943." *Diplomatic History* (Winter 1980): 73–93. Reprinted with the permission of *Diplomatic History.*

Stephen L. McFarland. "A Peripheral View of the Origins of the Cold War: The Crises in Iran, 1941–47." *Diplomatic History* (Fall 1980): 333–351. Reprinted with the permission of *Diplomatic History.*

Hugh Phillips. "Mission to America: Maksim M. Litvinov in the United States, 1941–43." *Diplomatic History* (Summer 1988): 261–275. Reprinted with the permission of *Diplomatic History.*

Albert Resis. "Spheres of Influence in Soviet Wartime Diplomacy." *The Journal of Modern History* (September 1981): 417–439. Reprinted with the permission of the University of Chicago Press, publisher.

John J. Sbrega. "Determination versus Drift: The Anglo-American Debate over the Trusteeship Issue, 1941–1945." *Pacific Historical Review* (May 1986): 256–280. Reprinted with the permission of the

University of California Press. Copyright by the Pacific Coast Branch, American Historical Society.

G. D. Sheffield. "The Anglo-American Alliance, 1941–45." *The Journal of Mississippi History* (Winter 1995): 289–303. Reprinted with the permission of the State of Mississippi, Department of Archives and History.

Mark A. Stoler. "A Half Century of Conflict: Interpretations of U.S. World War II Diplomacy." *Diplomatic History* (Summer 1994): 375–403. Reprinted with the permission of *Diplomatic History*.

Christopher Thorne. "Indochina and Anglo-American Relations, 1942–1945." *Pacific Historical Review* (February 1976): 73–96. Reprinted with the permission of the University of California Press. Copyright by the Pacific Coast Branch, American Historical Society.

Brian L. Villa. "The U.S. Army, Unconditional Surrender, and the Potsdam Declaration." *The Journal of American History* (June 1976): 66–92. Reprinted with the permission of the Organization of American Historians.